Symbolic Logic

By

John Venn

Published by Forgotten Books 2012

Originally Published 1881

PIBN 1000107209

SYMBOLIC LOGIC.

SYMBOLIC LOGIC

.

BY

JOHN VENN, M.A.,

FELLOW, AND LECTURER IN THE MORAL SCIENCES,
GONVILLE AND CAIUS COLLEGE, CAMBRIDGE.

"Sunt qui mathematicum vigorem extra ipsas scientias, quas vulgo mathematicas appellamus, locum habere non putant. Sed illi ignorant, idem esse mathematice scribere quod in forma, ut logici vocant, ratiocinari."

LEIBNITZ, *De vera methodo Philosophiæ et Theologiæ* (about 1690).

"Cave ne tibi imponant mathematici logici, qui splendidas suas figuras et algebraicos mæandros universale inventionis veri medium crepant."

RÜDIGER, *De sensu veri et falsi*, Lib. II. Cap. IV. § xi. (1722).

London:

MACMILLAN AND CO.

1881

Cambridge:

PRINTED BY C. J. CLAY, M.A.

AT THE UNIVERSITY PRESS.

TABLE OF CONTENTS.

INTRODUCTION.

CHAPTER I.

CHAPTER II.

CHAPTER III.

CHAPTER IV.

CHAPTER V.

CHAPTER VI.

CHAPTER VII.

CHAPTER VIII.

CHAPTER IX.

CHAPTER X.

CHAPTER XI.

CHAPTER XII.

CHAPTER XIII.

CHAPTER XIV.

CHAPTER XV.

PREFACE.

I HAVE so fully explained the nature and aim of this system of Logic, in the Introduction, that nothing further need be said on this head. The substance of most of these chapters has been given in my college lectures, our present intercollegiate scheme of lecturing (now in operation for about twelve years) offering great facilities for the prosecution of any special studies which happen to suit the taste and capacity of some particular lecturer and a selection of the students. I mention this in order to explain what might seem a disproportionate devotion of time to one peculiar development of Logic.

Besides Mr C. J. Monro, who has repeated the kind help he gave on a former occasion, I have to thank several friends and fellow-lecturers (amongst whom I must mention Mr H. Sidgwick, Mr H. S. Foxwell, Mr J. Ward, and Mr J. N. Keynes, before whom several of these chapters were read and discussed) for many valuable suggestions and criticisms. I must also express my obligations to Prof. G. Croom Robertson, of University College, London, for his kindness in procuring me several rare works from the valuable library of his college.

I should add here that the substance of some of the following chapters has already appeared elsewhere : viz. Chap. I in *Mind* (July, 1880), Chap. v in the *Philosophical Magazine* (July, 1880), and Chap. xx in the *Proc. of the Cambridge Philosophical Society* (Dec., 1880), but all of these have been rewritten and enlarged. The general view adopted in this work was sketched out in an article in the *Princeton Review* of September, 1880.

CAMBRIDGE,
April 7, 1881.

INTRODUCTION.

THERE is so certain to be some prejudice on the part of those logicians who may without offence be designated as anti-mathematical, against any work professing to be a work on Logic, in which free use is made of the symbols $+$ and $-$, $\times$ and $\div$, (I might almost say, in which x and y occur in place of the customary X and Y,) that some words of preliminary explanation and justification seem fairly called for. Such persons will without much hesitation pronounce a work which makes large use of symbols of this description to be mathematical and not logical. Though such an objection betrays, as I shall hope to show, some ignorance as to the nature and functions of mathematics[1],—confounding the accident of expression with the substance of meaning and application,—yet there is certainly a fragment of truth suggested by it.

This truth consists in what may be described as being the present accidental dependence of the Symbolic Logic upon Mathematics. Those generalizations to which Boole

---

[1] I may remark that by 'mathematics' here I refer, broadly speaking, to questions of number, magnitude, shape and position. I am quite aware that some exponents of the higher branches would not admit the exhaustiveness of this description, but it will well include all that can be meant by those with whom I am arguing.

was the first to direct attention, and which (as will be fully
explained in due place) are purely and entirely logical in
their origin and nature, are yet of a character which it is
very difficult for any one to grasp who has not acquired
some familiarity with mathematical formulæ. It should
not be so, and I hope it will not always continue to be
so, but at present it can hardly be otherwise. This state of
things arises from the fact that we have to realise a certain
generalized use of symbols; that is, to take account of an exten
sion of their use to cases distinct from, but analogous to, that
with reference to which they first had their meanings assigned.
In such extension, it must be understood, we have to anticipate
not only a merely wider range of application, but also a con
siderable transfer of actual signification. This deliberate and
intentional transfer of signification to analogous cases, as
it happens, is perfectly familiar to the mathematician, but
very little recognized or understood in other departments of
thought. Hence it comes about that when people meet with
such an expression as $x + y$ in a work which is professedly
logical, they are apt to say to themselves, 'This is a mathe
matical symbol: the author is diverging into mathematics,
or at least borrowing something from that science.' If they
were to explain themselves they would probably maintain
that the sign (+) stands for addition in mathematics, and
therefore should not be resorted to when we have no idea of
adding things together[1].

[1] Presumably this is Prof. Spalding's feeling when he says: "All
attempts to incorporate into the universal theory of Thought a special
and systematic development of relations of number and quantity must
be protested against....No cumbrous
scheme of exponential notation is
needed, and none is sufficient, for
the actual guidance of thought when
its objects are not mathematical."
(*Logic*, 1857, p. 50.) He might have
set his mind quite at rest as regards
the relations of number and quantity.
We have no more intention than
himself of introducing these relations

What such objectors must be understood to mean, or rather what they ought to mean, is of course that (+) is the sign of addition in *Arithmetic*, and of nothing else there ; but they should not confound Arithmetic with the whole of mathematics. Even to go no further than Algebra, we find that (+) has already extended its signification, having come to include ordinary subtraction, in case the quantity to which it is prefixed has itself a negative value. Go a little further and we find that the same sign is used to indicate direction in space instead of merely ordinary addition. For instance, let any one take up some work imbued with the spirit of

into our treatment of propositions:— in fact decidedly less so, inasmuch as we do not quantify predicates. 'Exponential notation' is, I suppose, here employed as a vague epithet of dislike, but it is ill chosen ; for whilst the rejection of all exponential notation is the formal differentia of the true logical calculus as compared with the mathematical, Mr Spalding's own work happens to be the only one I have ever seen which *does* introduce exponents into Formal Logic. He writes A^2 and I^2 for ‘All X is all Y’, and ‘Some X is some Y’, giving as the merit of this notation that it “intimates a relation of the two forms to the received A and I ; and the character of this relation is faintly hinted at when the added forms are symbolized as higher powers of the old ones”!

It is curious at what an early date the pure logicians began to get into this scare at the threatened inroad of mathematical notation, as the reader will see by the extract which I have given from Rüdiger on the title page. Any modern protester against Boole might quote his very words. But who these mathematical logicians are I have not yet succeeded in determining. The two editions of the work published in the author's life time appeared in 1709 and 1723. I know of nothing answering to such a description, so early as this, except a few letters and other short papers by Leibnitz (most of which cannot be said to have been published), and one by James Bernoulli. The only authors whom he mentions in this context are, I think, Descartes, Spinoza and Tschirnhausen. The reference to the two former suggests that what he had in view was the employment of the so-called ‘mathematical method,’ *e.g.* starting with definitions and so on, rather than an actual employment of mathematical notation. Prof. Adamson confirms me in this opinion.

modern analysis (Clerk Maxwell's Elementary treatise on *Matter and Motion* will answer the purpose), and he will perceive that $A + B$ has come to indicate a certain change both of magnitude and direction. Similarly with other suc cessive transfers of signification. The full application of this principle to Logic must be reserved for discussion in future chapters. At present it will be enough to remark that before any one assumes what he considers to be a mathemati cal signification on the part of these symbols $(+, -, \times, \div)$ he should endeavour to ascertain with some degree of adequacy what range of interpretation they already possess within that science.

But it is here that the difficulty already alluded to makes itself felt, owing to which some acquaintance with mathematics becomes what I have called an accidental or practical neces sity. We propose to carry out, in Symbolic Logic, a precisely similar extension of signification of symbols to that just men tioned in mathematics. Such an extension as this might conceivably, no doubt, be thoroughly attained within the province of Logic alone, for none but logical conceptions and processes will need to be appealed to. And when these developments of the subject are more generally known, and more fully worked out, they probably will be so attained. There is indeed no reason, in the nature of things, why the logical calculus should not have been developed to its present extent before that of mathematics had made any start at all. The Greeks, for instance, had almost nothing which we should term symbolic language in use for their arithmetic or geometry, but there was no actual obstacle to their inventing for their own logical purposes all those symbols which Boole and others before him borrowed from the sister science. Had this been so there might in time have been corresponding protests, on the part of the mathematicians, against the extension of these symbols to do duty in the new department, on the ground that they were an introduction of 'relations which are *not* of number or quantity.'

At the present time discussions of this particular kind,—that is, having reference to symbolic language in general, or to that of Logic and not Mathematics,—are hardly to be found anywhere. Boole's work of course implies much thought in this direction, but there is very little in the way of direct explanation offered by him ; as is evidenced by the mere fact that he attempts no explanation whatever of his use of the sign of division in Logic. In fact the student must consult the works of some of the more philosophical mathematicians[1] in order to find what he wants; though naturally their discussions are so much confined to their own wants and aims, and often presuppose such an acquaintance with their own subject, that much of the value of what they say is lost to ordinary lay-readers.

This explanation of the principles of the logical calculus, in entire independence of those of the mathematical calculus, is one of the main objects which I have had before me in writing this book. Every criticism and explanation offered here is to be regarded as standing on a purely logical basis,

---

[1] There is probably no better book in English, for this purpose, than De Morgan's *Trigonometry and Double Algebra*, which is however unfortunately out of print. Useful suggestions will also be found in the easier introductory parts of such a work on *Quaternions* as that of Kelland and Tait. Of course both of these demand some familiarity with more than merely elementary mathematics. There are several valuable works in German : *e.g.* Schroder's *Arithmetik und Algebra*, Hankel's *Vorlesungen uber die Complexen Zahlen*, and Lipschitz's *Grundlagen der Analysis*.

The first of these discusses very fully the nature of the elementary direct and inverse operations of Arithmetic, the others (I speak from a very slight acquaintance) are of too advanced a character to be readily intelligible to those who do not bring some corresponding knowledge with them.

and therefore as being on all essential grounds well within
the judgment and appreciation of any ordinary logician.
I say 'essential grounds' in consequence of the accidental
impediments above mentioned. It is at the present time
almost impossible to find any good discussion of the nature
of symbolic language in general except in the works of a few
mathematicians, therefore there can be no disguising the
fact that those who come here without some acquaintance
with that science will stand at a certain disadvantage.

There can surely be no doubt as to the desirability of
thus opening out a second means of acquiring an intelligent
command of the principles of a really general symbolic
language. Taking the most earnest anti-mathematician's
own view as to the probable origin of the existent symbols
cannot they sympathise with Wesley's resolve that the good
tunes should not all remain in bad hands[1]? There is no
vested right in the use of $+$ and $-$, and it is therefore as
open to them as to any one else to express themselves by aid
of these symbols. So far as one can judge by the present
course of the more abstract sciences, whether physical or
mathematical, the value of symbolic language, in respect of
the possibility of eliciting new and unexpected meanings out of
old and familiar forms, is likely to be continually more appre
ciated. It will be a real gain to the cause of philosophy if some
alternative branch of knowledge can be found which will afford
a field for acquiring and realising such conceptions as this.

The relation of these languages of Logic and of Mathe
matics to one another as mere languages, signification apart;
the extent to which they can be considered to be one and the

---

[1] There are reasons for supposing,
according to De Morgan, that these
signs $+$ and $-$ were not invented by
the mathematicians, but borrowed
by them from the practice of the
counting house (*Camb. Phil. Tr.*
No. xi. "On the early history of the
signs $+$ and $-$ in mathematics").

same tongue; and the respects in which they differ from one another, may be familiarly illustrated as follows.

Suppose that any one came into a lecture room and saw the expression $A + B$ written on the board : Could he infer the subject of the lecture, or the meaning of the signs ? Certainly not : but of one thing he may feel confident, viz. that, whichever of the various admissible meanings it may have borne, he will not do any mischief by transposing A and B, because the commutative law is tolerably certain to be accepted by any person who wrote down such an expression. Now let him be told that the lecture was one on Logic, and the language therefore in which the symbols were written was logical. He may go a step further, by putting some significance into the signs. He knows that A and B stand respectively for classes, and that $+$ aggregates those classes. But here again he comes to a stop. Though he knows the *language* of the lecturer he does not know his *dialect,* so to say. Was it the exclusive or the non-exclusive dialect for alternatives[1]? If the former, he can infer that A and B have nothing in common ; as otherwise $A + B$ would have been bad grammar for 'A or B'; it ought then to have stood $A + AB$. The dialect settled, he is of course still in entire darkness as to what A and B may mean. He cannot even know that they are classes strictly so called, for they may equally stand for single events. For such detailed information, he must apply to the lecturer himself, or to one of his class ; for nothing but specific information can possibly enable him to infer such facts as these.

But suppose on the other hand, that he were told that the lecture had been on mathematics, would his uncertainty be more completely or immediately removed ? Certainly not. It is true that there are not here what I have just

---

[1] For explanation of this point, see Chap. XIX.

called dialectic varieties, because almost all who use the language of mathematics upon the same subject use it according to precisely the same laws; that is, the differences of usage depend here not upon the speaker but upon his subject. But the nature of that subject would make all the difference in the interpretation of the symbols. Had the lecture been on Arithmetic, he would know that A and B had stood generally for numbers, or specially for some number, and that + had stood for simple addition. Had it been on Statics, he would reasonably infer that A and B had stood for *forces*, and had indicated both their magnitude and their direction, and that + had stood for the *composition* of these forces, so that the whole expression represented the resultant force. But then again he would come to a stop. He could no more draw lines representing those forces, in the absence of information as to the scale and direction adopted by the lecturer, than he could say, without corresponding information from the logical lecturer, what sort of things *he* had in view with his A and his B.

We may therefore regard Symbolic Logic and Mathematics as being branches of one language of symbols, which possess some, though very few, laws of combination in common. This community of legislation or usage, so far as it exists, is our main justification for adopting one uniform system of symbols for both alike. The older branch,—that of mathematics,—may be divided, in reference to its mere form, into several different languages. The distinction between these depends almost entirely upon the nature of the subject matter. There is a language, for instance, of Algebra, and one of Quaternions, besides others which have been proposed or adopted. These differences are what may be called scientific, rather than dialectic. Of the latter there is not much trace in mathematics; in other words, there are few, if any, differences of symbolic usage depending not upon subject matter but upon the custom of individual writers, of schools, or of nations. The language of Logic on the other hand has hardly yet begun to show any subdivision according to the subject matter treated of, the present diversity of usage being one between different schools treating of one and the same subject. Where it shows signs of such differentiation is in respect of the Logic of Relatives. So far as this is cultivated we certainly demand some relaxa tion, if not entire rejection of, the law that $xx = x$, viz. that repetition of class attribution does not alter the result. Such a change as this, as will be pointed out in due place, is of a far more serious character, on any formal or systematic grounds, than the most extensive transfer of mere application of the rules of operation.

It ought to be pointed out here that some of those who maintain that this system of Logic is to be called 'mathematical' labour under no confusion whatever as to the real nature of each of these subjects. With them it is mainly a question of definition, since they understand by mathematics any such language of pure symbols as I have above described, and which I prefer to regard as a genus which includes mathematics as one of its species. There can be little doubt that this was Boole's own view, for I think that Mr Harley is right (*Report of British Association*, 1866; see also the Report for 1870) in thinking that the term mathematical was used by him "in an enlarged sense, as denoting the science of the laws and combinations of symbols, and in this view there is nothing unphilosophical in regarding Logic as a branch of Mathematics instead of regarding Mathematics as a branch of Logic[1]".

---

[1] Boole himself has said the same: "It is simply a fact that the ultimate laws of Logic,—those alone upon which it is possible to construct a

The extract from Leibnitz which I have placed on the title page is couched in a similar spirit. There is nothing erroneous in this interpretation, provided we clearly understand that the principles and procedure of the logical calculus must be justified in entire independence of any other science. When however we have, as here, two cognate branches of abstract science of almost equal antiquity, it seems to me to be likely to lead to misconception if we thus stretch the name of one of them so as to cover the other also. It is better to use some vaguer general name to include them both.

As regards the utility of the Symbolic Logic, the defence is sometimes rested almost entirely upon the great increase of power which it affords in the solution of complicated problems. I should be perfectly prepared to support its claims on this ground alone, even were there nothing else to be said in its favour. It is scarcely conceivable that any one who has been in the habit of using these symbolic methods should doubt that they enable us easily to thread our way through intricacies which would seriously tax, if they did not completely baffle, the resources of the syllogism. As well might one endeavour to discard the help of Algebra and persist in trying to work out our equations by the aid of Arithmetic only. But then it must be admitted that these really intricate problems are seldom forced upon us in any practical way. Regarded as means to an end, rather than as studies on their own account, Logic and Mathematics stand on a very different footing in this respect. We acquire skill with the weapons of the former rather with a view to our general culture, whereas in learning to use the latter we are

science of Logic,—are mathematical in their form and expression, though not belonging to the mathematics of quantity." (*Lecture delivered at Cork*, 1851.)

also training ourselves for perfectly serious intellectual war fare. Without consummate mathematical skill, on the part of some investigators at any rate, all the higher physical problems would be sealed to us; and without competent skill on the part of the ordinary student no idea can be formed of the nature and cogency of the evidence on which they rest. Mathematics are here not merely a gate through which we may approach if we please, but they are the only mode of approach to large and important districts of thought.

In Logic it is quite otherwise. It may almost be doubted whether any human being, provided he had received a good general education, was ever seriously baffled in any problem, either of conduct or of thought (examinations and the like of course excluded) by what could strictly be called a merely logical difficulty. It is not implied in saying this, that there are not myriads of fallacies abroad which the rules of Logic can detect and disperse, as well as abundance of fallacious principles and methods resorted to, which logical training can gradually counteract. The question is rather this:—Do we ever fail to get at a conclusion, when we have the data perfectly clearly before us, not from prejudice or oversight but from sheer inability to see our way through a train of merely logical reasoning? The mathematician is only too well acquainted with the state of things in which he has got all the requisite data clearly before him, (the problem being fully stated by means of equations), and yet he has to admit that the present resources of his science are quite inadequate to effect a solution. It is almost needless to say that there is nothing resembling this in Logic; the difficulties which persistently baffle us here, when we really take pains to understand the point in dispute, being philosophical rather than logical. The collection of our data may be tedious, but the steps of inference from them are mostly very simple.

When it is said that the main advantages to be derived from the study of these extensions of Logic are specu lative rather than practical, it may be well to spend a few pages in illustrating and expanding this statement. The general intellectual advantages of any serious mental exercise may, it is to be hoped, be taken for granted here. I will therefore start with the assumption that the ordinary Logic has some use in it, and will only direct attention to such special advantages as the logical student may derive from our subject, since these are more likely to be overlooked.

To begin with : the mere habit and capacity of *generali zation* is surely worth a great deal. As one entire chapter is devoted to pointing out the various directions in which Symbolic Logic is to be regarded as generalizing the pro cesses of the ordinary Logic, a few indications must suffice here. The common Syllogism may be described as being a solution of the following problem :—' Given the relations in respect of extension of each of two classes to a third, as conveyed by means of two propositions, find the relation of the two former to one another'. Of course it is not maintained that this is the only account to be given of the syllogistic process, or even, the most natural and fundamental one, but it is certainly *one* account. Well, the general problem of which this is a very special case, may be stated thus :—
'Given any number of propositions, of any kind, categorical disjunctive or otherwise, and involving any number of terms, find the mutual relation to one another, in respect of their extension, of any selection from amongst all these terms to any other such selection'. Again, the syllogism is a case of *Elimination* as well as of inference; that is, we know that we thus get rid, in our conclusion, of one term out of the three involved in our premises. Here the corresponding general problem would be to ascertain whether there is any

limit to the number of terms which can be thus eliminated from one proposition, or from any assigned group of pro positions; and to give general rules for such a process of elimination.

A thorough generalization assumes sometimes an entirely unfamiliar aspect to those who were previously acquainted only with some very specialized form of the generalized pro cess :—thus we all know what a step it is to most beginners to extend 'weight' into 'universal gravitation.' In such cases the realization of the generalization may amount almost to the acquisition of a new conception, rather than to the mere extension of one with which we were already intimate. For instance, there is an inverse process, as distinguished from a direct, of which we may get a rudimentary notion in what is called Accidental Conversion. Given that 'All X is Y', what is known about Y in relation to X? Logic, as we know, answers at once that 'Some Y is X', by which it may be seen to mean, interpreting the statement in terms of extension, that the class Y certainly includes all X and for aught we know may include anything besides. Now differently worded, this process may be generalized as follows :—Given the relation of one class to another, find the relation of the second to the first[1]. The relation here is of course to be confined to those of which our Logic takes cognisance, but

---

[1] That is, Given $x = f(y)$, we express the inverse in the form

$$y = f^{-1}(x).$$

This is, so far, a mere expression or definition of what we want, and not at all a solution nor even a declaration that there is a solution. What is necessary is to rationalize the latter expression. The wide range which f assumes in mathematics pre- cludes any general solution there. But, as will be found, there are such restrictions and simplifications upon all logical functions as to render a general solution perfectly feasible. It may be remarked, that the answer is an indefinite one, as is mostly the case with inverse solutions; that is, there is not one single answer, and only one, to the problem.

the classes themselves, it must be remembered, need not be of the simple X or Y type. On the contrary they may be composed of any number of terms, and these any how combined by aggregation, exception, restriction and so forth. When the process of Conversion is thus regarded, it is seen to be a restricted case of a much more general problem.

The generalizations here referred to are but one or two out of a number with which we shall have to occupy our selves. What reason can be urged why those who are able to understand Logic thoroughly in its common form, should not also go on to study it in this extended form? Whatever objections we may feel to doing so let us not rest them on the ground that these discussions are no part of Logic. Say, if we like, that such questions are so simple that the traditional methods can readily grapple with them; say, if we like, that they are logically insoluble; say, if we like, that they are frivolous or absurd, (we are all supposed to agree that the syllogism is useful), but do not let us maintain that they are not logical. They belong to that science by a double right, both positively and negatively. Positively they belong to Logic because they are simply generalizations of processes of which Logic is universally admitted to take cognisance. Negatively they belong to it because they certainly do not belong to Mathematics, which is presumably the only other abstract science to which they are likely to be relegated. There is no more of enumeration or valuation of any kind of *unit* in them, than there is in the syllogism. They can be so stated as to involve nothing whatever but the mutual relations of various classes or class terms to each other in the way of inclusion and exclusion, of existence and of non-existence. So far from being fairly open to the charge of being too numerical, we are really more open to that of being almost prudishly averse to being seen or thought to enumerate, as will be found when we discuss the treatment of 'particular' propositions.

One great advantage of this kind of study is to be sought even within the sphere of ordinary Logic, in the increased clearness of view and philosophic comprehension which results from carrying our speculations well outside that sphere. As De Morgan has said, " Every study of a generalization or extension gives additional power over the particular form by which the generalization is suggested. Nobody who has ever returned to quadratic equations after the study of equations of all degrees, or who has done the like, will deny my assertion that ου βλεπει βλεπων may be predicated of every one who studies a branch or a case, without afterwards making it part of a larger whole." (*Syllabus* p. 34.) So I should say here that the student will understand the nature of the simple logical processes in a better way when he has investigated the general processes of which they are particular cases. For instance, as I shall hope to show, one of the most essential characteristics of logical Elimination is loss of precision and determination ; but this is a characteristic which is by no means obvious in the ordinary treatment.

To this should be added another important consideration. There are several rather perplexing questions in Logic in regard to which it does not seem possible to appreciate fully the grounds of decision, if we confine ourselves to the narrow field afforded by the ordinary treatment. I may offer, as an instance in point, the explanation of the Import of Propositions proposed in Chap. VI. The view there propounded :— viz. that, for purely logical purposes, the only unconditional implication of even an Affirmative is to be found in what it *denies ;* what it asserts being only accepted on the hypothesis that there are things existent corresponding to the subject and predicate :—will probably, on the first enunciation, sound very far-fetched and needless. In this systematic form the interpretation is, I believe, novel; but a partial form of it, viz. the hypothetic interpretation of categoricals, has been frequently proposed and debated. Now I cannot but think that the very inadequate discussion of the subject, indeed its almost entire rejection from all English manuals, has arisen from the fact that the reasons for such a proposal cannot possibly be estimated within the boundaries of the common treatment. Within those boundaries the traditional explanation, or absence of one, will answer in a somewhat lame way; but when we seek for some account which shall be really general, adapted to any propositions or groups of propositions however complicated, we seem to be forced towards the explanation in question. The reader will find another analogous instance to this in our treatment of the word 'some', where the utter inadequacy of the Quantification of the Predicate will come out in the course of the discussion.

The solution of difficulties of the kind in question is often greatly aided by the careful examination of extreme or limiting values of our terms and operations. Popular feeling and popular thought, as a rule, object strongly to the recognition of cases of this description, and not without reason on the whole. Far the larger part of the meaning of our statements is made up of implications, sometimes remote and subtle, and these rest upon various tacit restrictions as to the range of application of the terms in question. Hence our meaning would often be seriously disturbed by pushing on to an extreme case [1]. But in any abstract science we are

---

[1] The mathematician of course is perfectly familiar with all this; but to the popular mind even extreme cases (*i.e.* such as fall distinctly within the given limits) would often seem to be nothing but rather feeble attempts at a joke. Thus the statement that St Helena contains a large salt lake or sea, studded with islands, might call for some explanation as to

bound not to neglect the examination of such cases, since many valuable hints may be gained by their discussion ; and under any circumstances every scientific statement is bound to be explicit and precise as to its limits. Hence I have made a point of going tolerably fully into enquiries of this nature wherever they have happened to lie near our path. I have been the more prompted to do so owing to the fact that most logicians have been far too ready to acquiesce in the popular prejudices on this point, instead of insisting that their own scientific language should be adapted to every scientific use.

Some of the remarks hitherto made will suggest the question whether it is proposed that the study of the Symbolic Logic should supersede that of the traditional Logic as a branch of education? By no means. No one can feel more strongly than I do the merits of the latter as an educational study. And this conviction is even enhanced by the fact that some of the most instructive portions of the common system are just those which Symbolic Logic finds it necessary to pass by almost without notice. Amongst these may be placed the distinction between Denotation and Connotation, the doctrine of Definition, and the rules for the Conversion and Opposition of propositions from the common point of view. Perfect clearness of apprehension on all these points seems essential to accuracy of thought, and it is difficult to find any better means of acquiring this clearness than the study of some of the ordinary logical manuals. Indeed one merit of the common system seems to me to lie in the comparative empiricism and restriction of its point of view ; for it

what was meant. And yet, unless we insist upon some limit as to the relative extent of the land or water assignable to compose an island, what definition could be laid down for either lake or island, on a closed surface like a sphere, which should not make such a statement strictly true?

is this which enhances its educational value by keeping its rules and forms of expression in tolerably close harmony with the language of ordinary life[1]. It is often, as we know, diffi cult to say what is a grammatical and what a logical question, owing to the fact that the forms of proposition in the ordi nary logic are just those of common life with the least degree of modification consistent with securing accuracy of meaning. Common Logic should in fact be no more regarded as super seded by the generalizations of the Symbolic System than is Euclid by those of Analytical Geometry. And the grounds for retaining in each case the more elementary study seem to be identical. The narrower system has its peculiar advantage, owing to the fact that. being by comparison more concrete, it is easier for a beginner to understand ; that there is thus less

---

[1] Some philologists have recently directed an attack against the whole science of Formal, viz. Aristotelian or Scholastic Logic, on the ground that it is so.largely made up of merely grammatical necessities or conven tions ; nearly all its rules being more or less determined by characteristics peculiar to the Aryan languages. Thus Mr Sweet (*Trans. of the Philo logical Society*, 1876: quoted and endorsed by Mr Sayce), says that as a consequence of philological an alysis "the conversion of propositions, the figures, and with them the whole fabric of Formal Logic fall to the ground". It is no business of mine here to defend the old-fashioned Logic, which has plenty of champions still, so I merely remark that I can not think its case so desperate as this. It is quite true (so far as I can judge) that its dependence upon the accidents of speech is much closer than logicians have generally admit ted. This would be a serious consi· deration if we maintained that the common schedule of propositions re presents the way in which men neces sarily assert and reason, instead of (as I have urged in the following chapter) merely one of several ways in which they may do so. For my self, I regard this close dependence up on popular speech as being rather a merit than otherwise for educational purposes. The Symbolic Logic is as nearly free from all such accidents of speech as anything dealing with hu man thought well can be. The fact that this is so, constitutes one great reason why I should be very sorry (as above remarked) to see the com mon Logic superseded by a more scientific rival.

danger of its failing to exercise the thinking faculty and merely leading to dexterity in the use of a formula; and that it is much more closely connected with the practical experiences and needs of ordinary life. The more general system, on the other hand, has vastly extended capacity, practises much more thoroughly the faculty of abstraction, and corrects and enlarges the scientific bases of the narrower system.

I think then that the Common Logic is best studied on the old lines, and that the Symbolic Logic should be regarded as a Development or Generalization of it. It is for this reason that I cannot regard the attempts made, in such very different directions, by Hamilton and Prof. Jevons, with any great satisfaction. The petty reforms represented by the Quantification of the Predicate and so forth, seem to me to secure the advantages of neither system. We cut ourselves loose from the familiar forms of speech, and yet we do not secure in return any of the advantages of wide generalization. Prof. Jevons' individual reforms seem to me to consist mainly in excising from Boole's procedure everything which he finds an "obscure form", "anomalous", "mysterious", or "dark and symbolic", (*Pure Logic*, pp. 74, 75, 86). This he has certainly done most effectually, the result being to my thinking that nearly everything which is most characteristic and attractive in the system is thrown away. Thus every fractional form disappears, so does the important indeterminate factor $\frac{0}{0}$, and all the general functional expressions such as $f(x)$ and its derivatives. That these are symbolic I freely admit, but that they are dark, mysterious, and obscure, in any other sense than can be predicated of all which is worth a serious effort in abstract speculation, or that they are anomalous in any sense whatever, I wholly deny. In particular, as will be presently pointed out, to reject fractional forms is not merely to maim our system by omitting the necessary inverse process to that of multiplication, but actually to fall back behind the stage reached by more than one logician in the last century.

As the references to Boole in this volume are frequently those of criticism on subordinate points, something ought to be said here as to the position which I conceive him to occupy as an exponent of this subject. His actual originality, as will presently be shown, was by no means so complete as is commonly supposed and asserted. But none the less I hold him to be the indisputable and sole originator of all the *higher* generalizations of the subject. Other writers have spoken of their "systems", and contrasted them with that of Boole[1]; but at present there is, I think, only one thing be-

[1] Prof. Jevons' logical works are so well known, and in several respects so deservedly popular, that I have done my best to make out in what relation he himself considers that his exposition of the subject stands to that of Boole; but so far without success. He says indeed (*Pure Logic*, p. 87), "The work I have attempted has been little more than to translate his forms into processes of self-evident meaning and force". Just so, but then (*ib.* p. 83), "My third objection to Prof. Boole's system is that it is inconsistent with the self-evident law of thought, the Law of Unity". (Is not the process of converting into self-evident truths that which is inconsistent with self-evident laws, more in the way of 'paraphrase' than of 'translation'?) Again (*Pr. of Science*, p. 113), "It is wonderful evidence of his [Boole's] mental power that by methods fundamentally false, he should have succeeded in reaching true conclusions"; but (*Pure Logic*, p. 3), "The forms of my system may in fact be reached by divesting his system of a mathematical dress which, to say the least, is not essential to it". So too (*Pr. of Science*, p. 71), "Boole...produced a system which, though wonderful in its results, was not a system of Logic at all"; but (*ib.* p. 113), "In spite of several serious errors into which he fell, it will probably be allowed that Boole discovered the true and general form of Logic, and put the science substantially into the form which it must hold for evermore".

The above criticisms are intelligible when kept well apart, but the following puzzle me even separately:—"Logic resembles Algebra as the mould resembles that which is cast in it. Boole mistook the cast for the mould" (*Pr. of Science*, p. 156). "Boole's system is like the shadow, the ghost, the reflected image of Logic, seen among the derivatives of Logic" (*Pure Logic*, p. 86).

fore the world which can without abuse of language be called a system, (unless the single methodical alteration of marking alternatives on the non-exclusive plan be allowed to rank as such), and this is exclusively due to Boole. Apart from this exception (discussed in Chap. XIX.) I have seen scarcely anything which deserves to be called an enlargement of Boole's system, scarcely anything indeed but reconstructions of portions of that system with some modifications of notation.

But though the system, as a system,—that is, in its purely formal shape,—seems to me for the present complete and almost perfect, it still lies open to a good deal of explanation and justification. There is very little indeed in Boole's work which is erroneous, but there are many and serious omissions. Thus for instance there is little or no interpretation offered by him for the inverse forms and functional expressions. There is no attempt to develop what may be called the genius of the system ; to compare it with the traditional system ; to examine where it is strong and where it is weak ; to revise the schedule of propositions, their import and so forth, in accord ance with this new theory. To supply these deficiencies has been one of my main objects, so that in point of fact the following pages are hardly ever occupied with going over exactly the same ground as he or others have tra versed.

To those who already know something of the subject the following brief indication will convey a sufficient account of what may be supposed to be characteristic and original here :—The thorough examination of the Symbolic Logic as a whole, that is, its relation to ordinary Logic and ordinary thought and language : the establishment and explanation of every general symbolic expression and rule on purely logical principles, instead of looking mainly to its formal justification;

and the invention and employment of a new[1] scheme of diagrammatic notation which shall be in true harmony with our generalizations. As this work is intended to be an independent study of the subject from its foundations, and in no sense a commentary or criticism upon Boole, I have never discussed his particular opinions except where this seemed likely to throw light upon my own treatment of the subject.

Such anticipations of Boole's principles and results as I have succeeded in discovering have, as a rule, been mentioned in notes at the appropriate places. I have been the more careful to do this owing to the remarkable absence of any such references in almost every recent treatise on Symbolic Logic ; on which subject indeed one may say, as Hamilton did on another branch of science, that "it seems to have been fated that every writer should either be ignorant of or should ignore his predecessors" (*Discussions*, p. 183). It would certainly seem that Boole had no suspicion that any one before himself had ever applied algebraic notation to Logic : (I am far from urging this as a reproach, for few men have had slighter opportunities for research than were open to him during the greater part of his life : moreover any anticipations which he could have found of his grander generalizations are indeed scanty and remote). Professor Jevons has roundly asserted, (*Principles of Science*, Ed. I. 1874, p. 39), that " Boole is the only logician in modern times

---

[1] I have only during the last few weeks seen H. Scheffler's *Naturgesetze*, Vol. III. The work is far too large for me to have had time to do more than glance at it, but I see that he has adopted a plan of diagrammatic notation which makes it doubtful whether the word 'new' ought to be left standing. Some of his illustrations are carried out on the old Eulerian plan, but he also adopts a plan of shading his diagrams, which seems in all essential points the same as mine. Which scheme was actually published first I do not know; his work is dated 1880, and my paper in the *Phil. Magazine* appeared in the July number of the same year.

who has drawn attention to" the logical law[1] that $A = AA$. Frege (*Begriffsschrift*, 1877), has no reference to any symbolic predecessor except a vague mention of Leibnitz. R. Grassmann's *Begriffslehre*, (1872), has, I think, no reference what ever to any predecessor in this line. Delboeuf wrote the original of his *Logique Algorithmique* (in the *Revue Philosophique*, 1876), without having heard of Boole, as Mr Maccoll tells us he wrote his papers without having read that work.

It is true that since Leslie Ellis and Mr Harley called attention to some of the pregnant hints given by Leibnitz [2], he at least has been occasionally referred to. But I hope that this volume will convince the reader that there are some more

---

[1] Three perfectly explicit antici pations may be mentioned here, be sides that of Leibnitz referred to in the next note. *First*, Lambert, as quoted below. *Secondly*, Ploucquet, who in discussing an example for mally stated as 'N is g, N is r, N is f', goes on to say, "Nun ware ungercimt zu setzen......$NNNgrf$, sondern es muss nur so ausgedrückt werden, $Ngrf$". (*Sammlung, &c.* p. 254 :—Some account of the notation will be found in Chap. xx.) *Thirdly*, Segner; "Subjecti enim idea cum se ipsa composita novam ideam producere nequit; pariterque; Linea est extensa, curvum est extensum, ergo linea curva est extensa, ubi prædicatum cum se ipso compositum non mutatur" (*Specimen Logicæ*, p. 148). I have little doubt that any one better acquainted than myself with the Leibnitzian and Wolfian logicians could add many more such notices.

[2] Ellis first called attention to

Leibnitz, in this connection, in a note to Vol. I. (p. 281) of the edition of Bacon's works by him and Mr Spedding (1858); but the reference there given to p. 130 of Erdmann's edition is clearly wrong. Mr Harley suggested (*Rep. of Brit. Ass.*, 1866) that Ellis probably meant to refer to p. 103, where Leibnitz represents the proposition 'All A is B' in a form equivalent to $A = AB$, for when $A = B$ we have $A = AA$. A more appropriate passage, I think, is to be found in the *Non inelegans specimen demonstrandi in abstractis*, (Erdmann, p. 95), where Leibnitz says "si idem secum ipso sumatur nihil constituitur novum, seu $A + A \infty A$ ", where ∞ is a sign of identity. At first sight this looks like a statement of Prof. Jevons' 'Law of Simplicity', viz. $A + A = A$. But we must remember that Leibnitz represented by his symbols *attributes* rather than *classes*, (this becomes evi dent when he gives a concrete in

serious and successful attempts at Symbolic Logic, which deserve notice at the hands of those who undertake to treat the subject. At least it would be well to consult some of these before laying down what has *not* been said or done by any who have gone before us. Of the labours of one of these writers, Lambert,—"der unvergleichliche Mann", as Kant himself termed him,—it will be best to give a very succinct account here, since the references afforded by occasional notes will not yield any adequate impression of the remarkable progress he had made. To my thinking, he and Boole stand quite supreme in this subject, in the way of originality; and if the latter had knowingly built upon the foundation laid by his predecessor, instead of beginning anew for himself, it would be hard to say which of the two had actually done the most.

Summarily stated, then, Lambert had got as far as this. He fully recognized that the four algebraic operations of addition, subtraction, multiplication, and division, have each an analogue in Logic; that they may there be respectively termed aggregation, separation, determination, and abstraction, and be symbolized[1] by $+, -, \times, \div$. He also perceived the

stance: Homo – rationalis ∞ brutum, where the subtraction is plainly intensive not extensive). 'Addition' of attributes, as explained below (p. 300), is almost equivalent to 'multiplication' of classes. Accordingly the formula in question becomes really equivalent to Boole's $AA = A$. Prof. Jevons has also pointed out (*Pr. of Sc.* Ed. ii. 1876, Pref. p. 13), a passage at p. 98, which is in closer literal accord: "ut b est aa, vel bb est a,... sufficit enim dici a est b".

Students of Leibnitz are well aware that several of his short logical essays were first published by Erdmann in 1840. All the principal logical extracts are also very conveniently brought together in a little volume by Kvet (*Leibnitzen's Logik*, 1857).

[1] One of the clearest statements to this effect is in the *Logische Abhandlungen*, i. 150: but it is too long to quote. (My readers will find several extracts of similar purport in various notes in Chh. ii. and iii.) The logical equivalents he actually uses are Zusammensetzung, Absonderung, Bestimmung, Abstraction.

inverse nature of the second and fourth as compared with the first and third [1]; and no one could state more clearly that we must not confound the mathematical with the logical signification [2]. He enunciates with perfect clearness the principal logical laws, such as the commutative, the distributive, and the associative [3], and (under restrictions to be presently noticed) the special law [4] $AA = A$. He develops simple logical expressions precisely as Boole does [5], though without assigning any generalized formulæ for the purpose. He fully understood that the distinctive merit of such a system was to be found in its capacity of grappling with highly complicated terms and propositions; and he accordingly applies it to examples which however simple they may seem to a modern symbolist represent a very great advance

---

[1] "Die Operationen + und − sind einander entgegengesetzt und sie leiden einerlei Verwechselungen wie in der Algeber" (*ib.* II. 62).

[2] "Wir haben die Beweise der Zeichnungsart kurz angezeigt, die Zeichen selbst aus der Algeber genommen, und nur ihre Bedeutung allgemeiner gemacht" (*Log. Ab.* I. 137).

[3] "Da man in vielen Sprachen das Adjectivum vor- und nach-setzen kann, so ist es auch einerlei ob man *nR* oder *Rn* setzt" (*ib.* I. p. 150).

" Da es in der Zeichenkunst einerlei ist ob man $a + b$ oder $b + a$ setzt" (*ib.* I. p. 33).

"Will man aber setzen $(m + n) A$, so ist dieses $= mA + nA$. Es sei

$$m = n + p + q$$
und $\qquad A = B + C + D + E,$
so hat man

$$mA = (n + p + q)(B + C + D + E)\ldots"$$

[4] "Man kann zu einem Begriffe nicht Merkmale hinzusetzen die er schon hat... weil man sonst sagen konnte ein *eisernes Eisen*", (*ib.* II. 133). The reason why he did not admit this law universally was (as presently noticed) that he endeavoured to make his formulæ cover *relations* as well as common logical predications. This comes out clearly in the following passage: "Wenn der Begriff = a ist, $a\gamma$ das Geschlecht, $a\gamma^n$ ein höheres Geschlecht, $a\delta$ der Unterschied, $a\delta^n$ ein höherer Unterschied, $a\gamma + a\delta = a$ die Erklärung, $(a\gamma + a\delta)^n$ oder $a(\gamma + \delta)^n$ eine höhere Erklärung" *i.e.* a being a true logical class term $a^n = a$; but γ, being a relative term, γ^n does not $= \gamma$, (*ib.* p. 133).

[5] His formula is $a = ax + a|x$ (where $a|x$ means a not-x, viz. our ax). He also has $x + y = 2xy + x|y + y|x$; just as Boole develops the expression. ·

beyond the syllogism [1]. Moreover, in this spirit of generali zation, he proposed an ingenious system of notation, of a 1 and 0 description, for the 2^n combinations which may be yielded by the introduction of n class terms or attributes [2]. Hypothetical propositions he interpreted and represented pre cisely as we should [3]. Still more noteworthy is the fact that in one passage at least he recognized that the inverse process, marked by division, is an *indeterminate* one [4].

These are the main truths of this kind which Lambert had seized. Whatever the defects and limitations in their expression they represent a very remarkable advance on any thing known to have been done before him. Where he mainly went astray was, I think, in the following respects.

---

[1] Take, for instance, the follow ing:—

$F :: H = S :: (P + G) :: V :: (A + C + Se)$

as expressive of "Die Glückseligkeit des Menschen besteht in der Empfin dung des Besitzes und Genusses der Vollkommenheiten des innerlic und ausserlichen Zustandes". The sign :: here denotes a relation (*ib.* I. 56).

[2] His scheme is this. Let 1 re present the presence, and 0 the ab sence of any attribute. Then, if we keep the order in which the terms stand in our expression unaltered, 10101 and 10111 will take the place of what we might indicate by $xyzwv$ and $xyzwv$. He then compares the extent to which various complex terms thus agree with each other or differ. He also employs the slightly more convenient notation of letters and their negation, thus: ABC, $AB0$, $A00$, and so on, to stand for our ABC, ABC, ABC, (*ib.* II. 134). Of

course there are great imperfections in such a scheme.

[3] "Die allgemeinste Formel der hypothetischen Sätze ist diese, Wenn A ein B ist, so ist es C. Diese For mel kann allezeit mit der folgenden verwechselt werden; Alles A so B ist, ist C. Nun ist, Alles A so B ist $= AB$. Folglich, Alles AB ist C. Daher die Zeichnung $AB > C$ oder $AB - mC$" (*ib.* I. 128).

[4] "Wenn $x\gamma = a\gamma$, so ist

$$x = a\gamma\gamma^{-1} = a\frac{\gamma}{\gamma}.$$

Aber deswegen nicht allezeit $x = a$; sondern nur in einem einzigen Falle, weil x und a zwei verschiedene Arten von dem Geschlecht $x\gamma$ oder $a\gamma$ sein können. Wenn aber $x\gamma = a\gamma$ nicht weiter bestimmt wird, so kann man unter andern auch $x = a$ setzen" (*ib.* I. 9), (as this expressly refers to rela tive terms only it is not at variance with the note below, at p. 40).

Though he realized very clearly that logical division is the inverse of multiplication, he failed to observe the indefinite character commonly assumed by inverse operations :—that is, he failed to observe it except in certain special cases, as just pointed out. He regarded the inverse as being merely the *putting back* a thing, so to say, where it was before[1], and accordingly omitted altogether that surplus indefinite term yielded by logical division, and which is so characteristic of Boole's treatment. Probably no logician before Boole (with the very doubtful exception of H. Grassmann, as mentioned in the note on p. 204) ever conceived a hint of this, as not many after him seem to have understood or appreciated it. As a consequence of this, Lambert too freely uses mathematical rules which are not justifiable in Logic. For instance, from $AB = CD$ he assumes that we may conclude $A : C = D : B$.

Another point that misled Lambert was the belief that his rules and definitions would cover the case of *relative* terms[2]. This will explain what might otherwise seem a complete misapprehension of the very first principles of the Symbols of Logic, viz. his admission of *powers,* e.g. of the difference between mA and m^2A. I think it a mistake to endeavour thus to introduce relative terms, but, if we do so, we must clearly reject the law that $x^2 = x$, in the case of such terms.

In thus realizing what Lambert had achieved (I have purposely brought a number of extracts together as the only

---

[1] "Auch ist klar dass man sich dabei Operationen muss gedenken können, wodurch die veränderte Sache in den vorigen Stand konnte hergestellt werden. Diese Wiederherstellung giebt demnach den Begriff der reciproken Operationen, dergleichen im Kalkul + und − , × und ÷ "(*ib.* II. 150).

[2] "Unter den Begriffen $M - A : B$ kommen einige vor, die sehr allgemein sind. Dahin rechnen wir die Begriffe; Ursache, Wirkung, Mittel, Absicht, Grund, Art und Gattung "(*Architectonic,* I. 82).

way of conveying a just idea of their combined effect, though several of them have been quoted elsewhere in this volume) the reader must remember that he by no means stood alone. Two of his friends or correspondents,— Ploucquet and Holland,—are worthy coadjutors; and such logical writings as they have left behind are full of interesting suggestions of a similar kind, as the reader will see by referring to their names under the references in the bibliographical index at the end. These men all took their impulse from Leibnitz and Wolf. During the 80 or 90 years which elapsed from their day to that of Boole there was almost a blank in the history of the subject, for we cannot put the efforts of Maimon and Darjes into the same category, ingenious as these were. One cannot but speculate upon the causes of this total disregard of these remarkable speculations[1]; a disregard which had already astonished J. Bernoulli, the editor of Lambert's posthumous works and

---

[1] Lambert's *Neues Organon* is frequently referred to, in connexion with his doctrine of the different principles which govern the four Syllogistic Figures; but none of his best Symbolic speculations are to be found there. These are given most fully in the *Logische Abhandlungen*; but several of the important principles are also to be found in the *Architectonic*; in his *Briefwechsel* (Vol. I.); in his correspondence with Ploucquet, in the collected logical works of the latter; and in a paper in the *Nova Acta Eruditorum* for 1765. The only work by Ploucquet which I have seen is the one just mentioned, and referred to throughout this volume as the "*Sammlung*". It contains, I believe, nearly all his logical treatises; also

several reviews of these, and some interesting letters by Lambert and Holland. I know of no independent logical treatises by Holland except a very small volume entitled "*Abhandlung über die Mathematik, die allgemeine Zeichenkunst und die Verschiedenheit der Rechnungsarten*, (1764). For procuring me access to Ploucquet's works and Lambert's *Log. Abhandlungen*, and others, I have to thank Prof. Croom Robertson of University College, London. (The library of this College deserves to be better known. Several of the works of most importance for my purpose were not, so far as I could ascertain, to be found in any other likely library in the kingdom.)

letters, and which has been so complete since then that I have never even seen these speculations of his referred to by any modern symbolic logician. For myself I confess to an uneasy suspicion that, great as may have been the in fluence for good of Kant in philosophy, he had a disastrous effect on logical speculation. In any case it is instructive to notice the vigour and originality with which the science was being treated whilst the great philosopher was still to be spoken of as "Herr Immanuel Kant, Professor der Philosophie zu Konigsberg in Preussen" (Lambert's *Brief-wechsel*), with the monotonous flood of logical treatises which spread over Germany for so long afterwards, and the wash of which reached us in the works of Hamilton and Mansel. I deeply admire the learning and acuteness of many of these works produced during the days of strictest preservation from mathematical encroachment, but confess that they seem to me rather narrow in comparison with what was produced when the spirit and the procedure of the sister science were more freely welcomed by the logician.

For the convenience of the reader a few brief biblio graphical notes are added in conclusion. Boole's logical publications, so far as I know, are the following :—

The Mathematical Analysis of Logic (1847).

The Calculus of Logic. (*Camb. Math. Journal*, 1848.)

Lecture delivered at Cork (1851—touches slightly on the subject).

The Laws of Thought (1854).

On Propositions numerically definite. (*Camb. Phil. Tr.* XI.) There does not seem to me to be anything much of value in the first three beyond what is given more fully in his mature work. There are also a variety of papers of a more mathematical kind, mostly on Probability, in the *Philoso phical Magazine,* and elsewhere.

As regards the incidents of his life, there is a good account in an article by Mr Harley in the *British Quarterly Review* for July 1866. The reader will also be interested by three papers of a more domestic character (by his widow) in the *University Magazine* for Jan. Feb. and March, 1878. They are entitled "The Home side of a scientific mind."

Though Boole's productions did not encounter the neg lect which befell those of Lambert[1], his admirers will mostly agree that they have not yet been appreciated and utilized as they deserve. I do not propose (as already remarked) that they should be incorporated into the common system, still less that they should supersede it; but one might well have expected some more serious attempts at criticism and exposition of their general spirit, purport, and place in the science of inference. There have been, it need not be said, many minor criticisms and references in Journals and inde pendent works, especially of recent years. All of these which I have seen, and which appeared deserving of notice, will be found referred to in the Index. Three notices of a more distinctly expository kind have been given respectively by Mr Harley, Prof. Bain, and Prof. Liard of Bordeaux.

[1] There is a curious correspond ence in the circumstances of the two men. Each was born in very humble circumstances; was almost entirely self-educated,—that is, was trained at no University or superior school;— and had to do much of the work of his earlier life against the disadvan tages of a pressure of routine and elementary educational work, and comparative absence of intercourse with scientific society. They were both first-rate mathematicians. They died at the same age, viz. forty-nine. Lambert was born at Mülhausen in Elsass,—the town was at that time connected with the Swiss Con federation,—in 1728. He lived for some years as tutor to the family of Count de Salis in Chür. He moved to Augsburg in the year 1759, where he was "agregé à l'Académie electo rale de Baviere, avec le titre de pro fesseur honoraire et un traitement", (*Biographie generale*, Didot), and to Berlin in 1763, where he was "aca demicien pensionnaire." He died there in 1777.

The two former (*Brit. Quarterly*, July, 1866; *Deductive Logic*, pp. 190—207) are very brief, but trustworthy. The latter is of a more ambitious kind, being an attempt to give a general account of the "Modern English Logic," i.e. of the works of Mr G. Bentham, Hamilton, De Morgan, Boole, and Prof. Jevons. He has evidently taken pains to study these authors, and the volume possesses the national merit of lively and transparently clear exposition of all that is under stood, but its critical value seems to me of a humble order. The portions treating respectively of the works of Boole and Prof. Jevons had already appeared in substance in the *Revue Philosophique* for March and Sep., 1877.

I take this opportunity of referring to two works which have only come under my notice since this volume was already under the printer's hands. The first of these is H. Scheffler's *Naturgesetze*, which, (having only quite recently seen it,) I have not had time to do more than glance at. As indicated in a note some pages back the author's scheme of diagrammatic notation seems nearly the same as mine. Of the general treatment of Logic adopted by him it would be presumptuous to form an opinion, seeing that the third volume (the one mostly dealing with this subject) contains 742 closely printed pages. The other work is Prof. Jevons' Studies in Deductive Logic. This seems to me decidedly the best collection of logical examples to be found,—indeed the only good one I have ever seen. Had it appeared earlier it might have saved me some trouble in the composition of my own work. As it was, not being able to find any good examples which were sufficiently complicated to illustrate the symbolic methods, except one or two well-worn ones first proposed by Boole, I had to work them all out for myself. Except therefore where otherwise stated the examples are my own composition.

CORRIGENDA ET ADDENDA.

p. 9. *Note.* The statement that Hamilton maintains that the scheme of eight propositions "is not connected with the quantification doctrine" is perhaps rather too strong ; but I find much difficulty in understanding his remark that his "doctrine has, and could have, no novelty from a mere recognition, as possible, of the eight propositional forms." (*Dis cussions*, p. 162).

p. 78. *Note* 1. The last reference should be to Günther (not Guhring) in the *Vierteljahrsschrift für wissenschaftliche Philosophie* for 1879.

p. 144. *For* A. T. Ellis *read* A. J. Ellis.

p. 158. *For* 1877 *read* 1876.

p. 174. *Note* 2. This note must be supplemented and corrected by that on p. 324.

SYMBOLIC LOGIC.

CHAPTER I.

ON THE FORMS OF LOGICAL PROPOSITION.

IT has been mentioned in the Introduction that the System of Logic which this work is intended to expound is not merely an extension of the ordinary methods—though this is perhaps its principal characteristic—but that it also involves a considerable change from the ordinary point of view. This latter characteristic is one which has not, I think, been sufficiently attended to in discussions upon the subject, and the neglect of it has blunted the point of much of the criticism on one side and the other. I propose therefore, before explaining the foundations on which the Symbolic Logic must be understood to rest, to give a brief discussion of the corresponding substructure in the case of some other systems with which the reader is likely to be more or less familiar. It will be readily understood that we shall not dig down any deeper than is absolutely necessary, and this is fortunately not far below the surface. Psychological questions need not concern us here; and still less those which are Meta physical. Differences of this kind have very little, if any, direct relation to one logical method rather than another.

If we were constructing a complete Theory of Logic we should have to attack the question as to what is the *true* account, by which we should understand the most fundamental account, of the nature and import of a proposition, and on this point different accounts would be to some extent in direct hostility to one another. But when we are discussing methods rather than theories this is not necessarily so. The question then becomes, which is the most convenient account rather than which is the most fundamental; and convenience is dependent upon circumstances, varying according to the particular purpose we have in view. So far as we are now concerned there seem to be three different accounts of the import of a proposition; the ordinary or *predication* view, the *class inclusion and exclusion* view, and that which may be called the *compartmental* view. It may perhaps be maintained that one of these views must be more fundamental than the others, or possess a better psychological warrant, but it cannot be denied that they are all three tenable views; that is, that we may, if we please, interpret a proposition in accordance with any one of the three. And this is sufficient for our present purpose.

The question to be here discussed is simply this. What are the prominent characteristics of each of these distinct, but not hostile, views? What are their relative advantages and disadvantages; to what arrangement and division of propositional forms do they respectively lead; and, in consequence, which of them must be adopted if we wish to carry out the design of securing the widest extension possible of our logical processes by the aid of symbols?

The neglect of some such enquiry as this seems to me to have led to error and confusion. Logicians have been too much in the habit of considering that there could be only one account given of the import of propositions. In consequence, instead of discussing the number of forms of pro position demanded by one or the other view, they have attempted to decide absolutely *the* number of forms. This has led, as every one acquainted with the subject is aware, to a most bewildering variety of treatment in many recent logical works. And the very useful question as to the fittest view for this or that purpose has been lost in the too summary decision that one view was right, and consequently the others wrong.

Let us first look at the traditional four forms, A, E, I, O, in reference to which a very few words will here suffice. The light in which a proposition has to be consistently interpreted on this view is that of *predication*. We distinguish between subject and attribute here, and we assert that a given subject does or does not possess certain attributes. These forms appear to be naturally determined by the ordinary needs of mankind, and the ordinary pre-logical modes of expressing those needs; all that Logic has done being to make them somewhat more precise in their signification than they conventionally are. They adopt, as just remarked, the natural and simple method of asserting or denying attributes of a subject, that is, of the whole or part of a subject; whence they naturally yield four forms,—the universal and particular, affirmative and negative. For all ordinary purposes they answer admirably as they are, and by a little management they can be made to express nearly all the simple forms of assertion or denial which the human mind can well want to express.

With regard to these forms it must be very decidedly maintained that as they generally and primarily regard the predicate in the light of an attribute, and the subject in that of a class (whole or part), they do not naturally quantify this predicate: that is, they do not tell us whether any other things besides the whole or partial class referred to in the

subject possess the assigned attribute. No doubt they some
times decide this point indirectly. Thus, in the case of a
universal negative proposition we can easily see that any
thing which possesses the attributes in the predicate cannot
possess the attributes distinctive of the subject; that is, that
the proposition can be simply converted. But this does not
seem to be any part of the primary meaning of the proposition,
which thinks of nothing but asserting or denying an attribute,
and does not directly enquire about the extent of that
attribute, or where else it is or is not to be found.

As just remarked, these forms of proposition certainly
seem to represent the most primitive and natural modes in
which thought begins to express itself with accuracy[1]. By
combining two or more of them together they can readily be
made equivalent to much more complicated forms. Thus,
by combining 'All X is Y' with 'All Y is X,' we obtain the
expression 'All X is all Y,' or 'X and Y are ooextensive,' and so
forth. As these familiar old forms have many centuries of
possession in their favour, and the various technical terms
and rules for Conversion and Opposition, and for the Syllo
gism, have been devised for them, there seem to be very
strong reasons for not disturbing them from the position they
have so long occupied. At least this should only be done if
it could be shewn either that they are actually insufficient
to express what we require to express, or that they rest upon
a wrong interpretation of the import of a proposition. The
former is clearly not the case, for as was just remarked (and
as no one would deny) a combination of two or more of these
forms will express almost anything in the way of a non-

[1] At least this seems so in all the languages with which we need consider ourselves concerned. What might be the most natural arrangement of the forms of propositions in non-inflectional languages must be left to philologists to determine.

numerical statement. And as regards the latter, the point of this chapter is to shew that we are not necessarily tied down to one exclusive view as to the import of a proposition; a point which must be left to justify itself in the sequel. I should say, therefore, that whatever other view we may find it convenient to adopt for special purposes, either of sensible illustration or with a view to solving intricate combinations of statements, there is no valid reason for not retaining the old forms as well. They may not be the most suitable materials for very complicated reasonings, but for the ex pression and improvement of ordinary thought and speech they are not likely to be surpassed.

So much for this view. Now suppose that, instead of regarding the proposition as made up of a subject determined by a predicate, we regard it as assigning the relations, in the way of mutual inclusion and exclusion, of two classes to one another. It will hardly be disputed that every proposition *can* be so interpreted. Of course, as already remarked, this interpretation may not be the most fundamental in a Psycho logical sense; but when, as here, we are concerned with logical methods merely, this does not matter. For the justification of a method it is clearly not necessary that it should spring directly from an ultimate analysis of the phenomena; it is sufficient that the analysis should be a correct one.

Now how many possible relations are there, in this respect of mutual inclusion and exclusion, of two classes to one another? Clearly only five. For the question here, as I apprehend it, is this:—Given one class as known and determined in respect of its extent, in how many various relations can another class also known and similarly deter mined, stand towards the first? Only in the following: It can coincide with the former, can include it, be included by it, partially include and partially exclude it, or entirely exclude it. In every recognized sense of the term these are distinct relations, and they seem to be the only such distinct relations which can possibly exist[1]. These five possible arrangements would be represented diagrammatically as follows :—

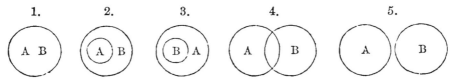

1.   2.   3.   4.   5.

Before comparing in detail the verbal statement of these five forms with that of the four old ones, it must be pointed out how entirely the distinction between subject and predicate is robbed of its significance on such a scheme as this. The terms of the proposition here stand for two classes of

[1] That these are the only really distinct forms of class relation has been repeatedly recognized by logical writers. The earliest explicit statement of the matter that I have seen is by Gergonne (*Annales de Mathematiques*, VII. 189). He has gone very fully into the comparison between the five diagrammatical forms, and the four common propositional ones, ascertaining in detail (with aid of a peculiar system of notation) how many of the one set can be considered to correspond collectively or individually to any single form of the other. He also notices the divergence of this scheme from the common one : "Il n'est aucune langue connue dans laquelle une proposition exprime précisement et exclusivement dans lequel de nos cinq cas se trouvent les deux termes qui la composent. Une telle langue si elle existait serait bien plus precise que les notres : elle aurait cinq sortes de propositions, et sa dialectique **serait toute différente de celle de nos** langues." F. A. Lange again (*Logische Studien*) has worked out the same view, emphasizing, even more strongly than I have done, the radically distinct theories as to the import of propositions involved in these two ways of stating or representing them. Other writers, for instance Twesten (*Logik*. p. 30) and the author of a little volume entitled *Thoughts on Logic, or the S. N. I. X. Propositional Theory*, reduce the five forms to four, by not distinguishing between (2) and (3) ; in other words by supposing that we have no means of distinguishing and recognizing one of the two classes from the other.

things possessing some mutual relation of extension, so that this distinction sinks down into one which is purely gramma tical. It is the merest accident which of the two classes oc cupies the first place in our verbal statement; whether, for instance, in (2) we say that B lies partly outside A or that A lies inside B. Certainly when the diagrammatic representation alone was shewn to us no one could give a guess as to which circle was intended to stand for a subject and which for a predicate. He could not, that is, read the diagram off in one way and one way only, with confidence.

A very little consideration will serve to convince us that this scheme of five forms, and the old one of four, will not by any means fit in accurately with one another. Con- sidering that they spring from different interpretations of the import of a proposition it could not be expected that they should do so. No. (5) is the one unambiguous exception, corresponding precisely to the universal negative 'No A is B.' That is, given 'No A is B,' we could only select this diagram; and conversely, given this diagram we could only describe it as 'No A is B.' But such correspondence does not exist in any other case. Given 'All A is B' we could not but hesitate between diagrams (1) and (2); and if diagram No. (4) were chosen we should not know whether to describe it as 'Some A is B' or 'Some A is not B,' for it would fit either equally well.

Is there then no precise and unambiguous way of de scribing these five forms in ordinary speech? There is such a way, and to carry it out demands almost no violence to the usage of ordinary language. It is merely necessary to employ the word 'some,' and to say definitely that it shall signify 'some, not all;' a signification which on the whole seems more in accordance with popular usage than to say with most logicians that it signifies 'some, it may be all.' If we adopt this definition of the word our five diagrams will be completely, accurately, and unambiguously expressed by the five following verbal statements :—

All A is all B,

All A is some B,

Some A is all B,

Some A is some B,

No A is any B.

That is : given one of these statements, only one diagram could be selected for it : and conversely, given any one diagram it could be matched with one only of these forms of words.

The tabular expression of these five forms will naturally recall to the reader's mind the well-known eight forms adopted by Hamilton[1], (*Logic* II. 27*l*) viz :—

---

[1] Hamilton's name is deservedly the best known in connection with this scheme, for the claim put forward in favour of Mr G. Bentham on the ground that he had (*Logic*, 1827) drawn up the same eightfold arrangement, seems to me quite untenable. For one thing, he had been anticipated by more than sixty years by Lambert, who in 1765 drew up a precisely similar table to that which is now so familiar to us (*Sammlung der Schriften welche den Logischen Calcul Herrn Prof. Ploucquet's betreffen*, p. 212). But in philosophical matters priority of mere statement is surely of but little value; appeal should rather be directed to the use made of a principle and to the evidence of its having been clearly grasped. Taking this test, the merit, such as it is, of the Quantification of the Predicate, must, I should think, be assigned to Ploucquet, and that of the closely connected doctrine of these eight propositional forms to Hamilton. As regards the Quantification, Ploucquet freely uses the distinctively characteristic forms 'No A is some B,' 'Some A is not some B;' and even distinguishes and directs attention to the case in which from two propositions of the form 'All A is some B,' 'All C is some B,' we can conclude that 'all A is all C;' viz. when the 'some B' is the *same* some (*Methodus Calculandi*). He nowhere recognizes the appropriate table of consequent eight propositions, though he was the means of suggesting them to Lambert. As regards mere priority of statement, it may be remarked that

All *A* is all *B*,	Any *A* is not any *B*,
All *A* is some *B*,	Any *A* is not some *B*,
Some *A* is all *B*,	Some *A* is not any *B*,
Some *A* is some *B*,	Some *A* is not some *B*.

I might have termed the view as to the import of propositions now under discussion the Hamiltonian, instead of the class inclusion and exclusion view ; and should have done so but for the fact that it is clearer and simpler to describe a system itself as one understands it, rather than to begin by giving what one cannot but regard as an erroneous expression of that system by some one else. Moreover there are obvious reasons for wishing to keep as free as possible from a somewhat prolonged and intricate controversy. At the same time, I must state my own very decided opinion that the view in question is that which Hamilton, and those who have more or less closely followed him in his tabular scheme of propositions, must be considered unconsciously to adopt.

The logicians in question do not seem to me, indeed, to have at all adequately realized the importance of the innovation which they were thus engaged in introducing ;

another writer, Mr Solly, (*Syllabus of Logic*, 1839,) had also given a similar table, before the time at which Hamilton, by his own assignment of dates, had begun to publicly teach this doctrine. But neither Mr Bentham nor Mr Solly seem to me to have understood exactly the sense in which their scheme was to be interpreted, nor to have attached any importance to it. Hamilton maintains that the scheme of eight propositions is not connected with the quantification doctrine, adding indeed (*Discussions*, p. 162) that "*every* system of logic necessarily contemplated *all* these," both assertions which seem to me incorrect, and the latter paradoxical. (The reader interested in this subject will of course be acquainted with the controversy begun originally between Hamilton and De Morgan in 1846 ; continued intermittently in the *Athenæum*; and concluded in the *Contemporary Review* in 1873. There are several historic references also in Hamilton's *Logic*, (II. 298, and Prof. Baynes's *New Analytic*).

nor, it must be added, the utter inadequacy of the means they were adopting for carrying it out. What they were really at work upon was not merely the rearrangement, or further subdivision, of old forms of proposition, but the introduction of another way of looking at and interpreting the function of propositions. The moment we insist upon 'quantifying' our predicate we have to interpret our propositions in respect of their extension, that is, to regard them as expressing something about the known mutual relations of two classes of things to each other. The view of the proposition must be shifted from that of stating the relation of subject and predicate, or of object and attribute, to that of stating the relation of inclusion and exclusion of two classes to one another.

The question therefore at once arises, How do the eight verbal forms just quoted stand in relation to the five which we have seen to be in their own way, exhaustive? As this is a very important enquiry towards a right understanding of the nature and functions of propositions, I shall make no apology for going somewhat into details respecting it. As regards the first five out of the eight, the correspondence is of course complete, if we understand that the word 'some' is to be understood, as here, to distinctly exclude 'all[1].' But then, if so, what account is to be given of the remaining three out of the eight? Only one account, I think, can be given. They are superfluous or ambiguous equivalents for one or

[1] Though his language is not always free from ambiguity this is, on the whole, the sense I understand Hamilton to adopt. Sometimes he is quite explicit; *e. g.* "Affirming *all men are some animals*, we are entitled to infer the denial of the propositions *all men are all animals, some men are all animals.*" *Logic*, Vol. II. p. 283. The reader will understand that I am not advocating this sense of the word, but merely pointing out that if we propose to adopt a certain division of propositions this sense will best serve our purpose in the way of distinguishing them.

more of the first five. This may need a moment's ex
planation. By calling the first five complete and unam
biguous we mean, as already remarked, that if one of these
propositions were uttered, but one form of diagram could be
selected to correspond with it; and conversely, if one of the
diagrams were pointed out, it could only be referred to one
form of verbal expression. But if we were given one of the
latter three to exhibit in a diagram we could not with
certainty do so. Take for instance the proposition 'No A is
some B.' If we proposed thus to exhibit it we should find
that diagrams (2) and (4) are equally appropriate for the
purpose; whence this proposition is seen to be ambiguous
and superfluous. Similarly its formal converse the proposition
'Some A is not any B,' is equally fitly exhibited in diagrams
(3) and (4) and therefore appropriately in neither. Conse
quently it also must be regarded as needless in our scheme.
The case of the remaining proposition, 'Some A is not some
B' is still worse. It is equally applicable to all the first four
of our five distinct possible cases, and therefore, as making
no distinction whatever between them, is almost entirely
useless to express the mutual relation of classes.

The ambiguity affecting these three last forms is, it need
hardly be remarked, reciprocal. That is, so long as these
three are retained in the scheme, we should not know, on
a diagram being presented to us, which proposition was
meant to be exhibited; any more than we can draw the
diagram when a proposition is stated. Diagram (3), for
instance, might under these circumstances be read off indiffe
rently as 'Some A is all B,' 'Some A is not any B,' or 'Some
A is not some B'

It may perhaps be replied that there is still a use in
retaining forms of proposition which thus refer ambiguously
to two or more actual class relations, in addition to those forms

which refer unambiguously to one only. It may be urged that if we do not know which of the two is really applicable, though one or the other must certainly be so, there is an opening for a form which covers both of them. I do not think that this will do. In the first place there is the objection that the employment of terms in their extensive signification implies that we are expressing their actual relation to one another in the way of inclusion and exclusion, and not our imperfect knowledge of that relation. At any rate this seems to be so when we make use of diagrams of this kind, for the circles must either cut one another or not do so; we cannot express a diagrammatic *doubt* whether they do or not. We may feel a doubt whether they should do so or not, but we must make them do one or the other.

An attempt is sometimes made in this way by the device of marking a part of one of the circles with a dotted line only. Thus 'Some *A* is not *B*' would be exhibited as follows :—

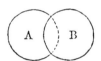

(as, for instance, is done, amongst others, by Dr Thomson in his *Laws of Thought*). The dotted part here represents of course our ignorance or uncertainty as to whether the *A* line should lie partly inside *B*, or should entirely include it. But surely, if we are thus ignorant we have no right to prejudge the question by drawing one part inside, even as a row of dots. What we ought to do is to draw *two* lines, one inter secting *B* and the other including it. Doing this, there is no need to dot them; it is simpler to draw at once in the ordinary way the two figures (3) and (4) above, and to say frankly that the common 'Some *A* is not *B*' cannot distinguish between them. In other words this form cannot be adequately represented by one of these diagrams; it belongs to another propositional theory. Ueberweg (*Logic, Trans.* p. 217), has thus represented propositions of this kind by alternative diagrams, as well as by a scheme of dotted lines.

But there is a more conclusive objection than this last. If we were lenient enough to admit the three latter Hamil tonian forms on such a plea as the one in question, we should be bound in consistency to let in a good many more upon exactly the same grounds. Take, for instance, the first two, 'All *A* is all *B*,' 'All *A* is some *B*.' We often do practically want some common form of expression which shall cover them both, and this was excellently provided by the old *A* proposition 'All *A* is *B*,' which just left it uncertain whether the *A* was all *B*, or some *B* only. Perhaps this is indeed the very commonest of all the forms of assertion in ordinary use. Hence if once we come to expressing uncertainties or am biguities we should have to insist upon retaining this old *A*, not as a substitute for one of the two first Hamiltonian forms, but in addition to them both. Similarly we should require a form to cover the first and the third. Or again, whilst we are about it, we might desire a form to cover all the first four; for we might merely know (as indeed is often the case) that *A* and *B* had some part, we did not know how much, in common. What we should want, in fact, would be a simple equivalent for 'Some or all *A* is some or all *B*;' or, otherwise expressed, a form for merely denying the truth of 'No *A* is *B*.'

The Hamiltonian scheme has, no doubt, a specious look of completeness and symmetry about it. Affirmation and denial, of some and of all of the subject and predicate, give clearly eight forms. But on subjecting them to criticism, by enquiring what they really say, we see that this completeness is illusory. Regard them as expressing the relations of class inclusion and exclusion, (and this I strongly hold to be the right way of regarding them, though quite aware that it is not the way in which they commonly are regarded), and we only need, or can find place for, *five*. Regard them as expressing to some extent our uncertainty about these class relations, and we want more than eight. This exact group of eight seems merely the outcome of an exaggerated love of verbal symmetry [1].

If indeed our choice lay simply between the old group and the Hamiltonian, the old one seems to me far the soundest and most useful. One or more of those four will express almost all that we can want to express for purely logical purposes, and as they have their root in the common needs and expressions of mankind, they have a knack of signifying just what we want to signify and nothing more. For instance, as above remarked, we may want to say that 'All *A* are *B*,' when we do not know whether or not the two terms are coextensive in their application. The old form just hit this off. An obvious imperfection in the Hamiltonian scheme is that with all his eight forms he cannot express this very common and very simple form of doubtful statement, by means of a single proposition. He can express the less common state of doubt

---

[1] De Morgan appears to have entertained a similar view, for, after describing the five propositional forms above, he adds "these enunciations constitute the system at which Hamilton was aiming" (*Camb. Phil. Tr.* x. 439).—This, and two other papers in the same volume contain the fullest and acutest criticism of the Quantification doctrine which I have anywhere seen. The best compendious account of his own view and criticism of Hamilton's view, is, I think, in the article "Logic" in the *English Cyclopædia.*—Hamilton (*Discussions*, p. 683) has made an attempt to represent his eight forms diagrammatically, on Lambert's linear plan. He offers only six diagrams, and as much as admits that one of these is superfluous. See also his *Logic* (II. 277) where the eight propositions are illustrated by four circular diagrams.

between the two, 'All *A* is some *B*' and 'Some *A* is some *B*,'
by one of what I have termed his superfluous forms, viz., by
his 'Some *B* is not any *A*,' for it exactly covers them both.

So long as we confine ourselves to the five propositions
which correspond to the five distinct diagrams, we are on clear
ground. These rest on a tenable theory as to the import of
propositions sufficiently to give them cohesion and make a
scheme of them. That theory is, as above explained, that
they are meant to express all the really distinct relations
of actual class inclusion and exclusion of two logical terms,
and none but these.

The advantages of this form of propositional statement, if
few, are at any rate palpable and unmistakable. Each form
has a corresponding diagram which illustrates its exact
signification with the demonstrative power of an actual
experiment. If any sluggish imagination did not at once
realise that from 'All *A* is some *B*,' 'No *B* is any *C*,' we could
infer that 'No *A* is any *C*,' he has only to trace the circles,
and he sees it as clearly as any one sees the results of a
physical experiment. And most imaginations, if the truth
were told, are sluggish enough to avail themselves now and
then of such a help with advantage.

But whilst this is said it ought clearly to be stated under
what restrictions such an appeal may fairly be made. The
common practice, adopted in so many manuals, of appealing
to these diagrams,—Eulerian[1] diagrams as they are often
called,—seems to me very questionable. Indeed when it is
done, as it generally is done, without a word of caution as to the
important distinction between the implied theories about the
import of propositions, it seems to me that there can be
no question as to its being wrong. The old four propositions

[1] A brief historic notice is given in the concluding chapter about the
employment of diagrams in Logic.

A, E, I, O, do not exactly correspond to the five diagrams, and consequently none of the moods in the syllogism can in strict propriety be represented by these diagrams[1]. We may sometimes see Celarent represented thus :—

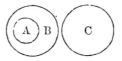

But this is too narrow. The Affirmative represented here is not 'All *A* is *B*,' but 'All *A* is *some B*' To represent Celarent adequately in this way we should have to append also the diagram,

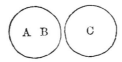

representing 'All *A* is all *B*' 'No *B* is *C*,' and to say frankly that we can only know that one of these diagrams will re present our syllogism; we do not know which[2].

Of course this inability to represent each syllogistic figure by one appropriate diagram will not always affect their cogency as illustrations. Any one can see in the above instance that one diagram will practically take the place of the other; and so it would in *Barbara*, but not in every instance, as we shall presently shew more in detail. But none the less must we remember that the systems of pro-

---

[1] The *rejected* mood 'No *B* is *C*,' 'No *A* is *B*,' with the consequent inability to draw any conclusion at all, can be thus exhibited; because the Universal Negative is the only form common to the two schemes.

[2] If it be urged that the upper diagram is the general one, including the lower as a special case, the answer is two-fold. First, that this would be tantamount to a rejection of this scheme of propositions; and second, that even so we should not meet the case of syllogisms involving particular propositions, as the reader will see if he tries thus to exhibit, say, *Disamis*. (See further on. for more illustration of this point.)

positions are really based on distinct theories, and we have con sequently no right thus without warning to use the diagrams of one system to represent the propositions and syllogisms of another.

What then is the number and nature of the Syllogistic Figures, if we may still call them such, which we should have to adopt if we adhered with strict consistency to this pro positional theory now under discussion ? The matter is not one of much importance in itself, but it deserves con sideration as serving to impress upon the reader what are the true representative characteristics of the diagrams with whose appearance he is already so familiar ; and I will therefore go into it with more detail than would otherwise be needed[1].

As I apprehend the matter then the problem of the Syllo gism is this :—Given three terms combined into two propo sitions, how many really distinct pairs can be made out of them which shall yield a necessary and unambiguous conclusion ? Of course this needs some explanation as to what is to be considered really distinct. On this point logical con vention has decided, (1) that the order of the premises is at our option and therefore affords no ground of distinction. (2) That the difference between subject and predicate is

[1] When the substance of this chapter was first written out for *Mind* I was unable to ascertain that any attempt had been made to reconstruct the syllogistic figures upon this propositional scheme. I have since found that almost exactly the same results as are given here had been already obtained by F. A. Lange, in his admirable *Logische Studien*, though from a somewhat different point of view. Hamilton (*Logic*, II.

p. 475) has given a table of valid Syllogistic Moods adapted to his own complete scheme of propositions. It is also printed in Dr Thomson's *Laws of Thought*, p. 188. Mr Ingleby also (*Outlines of Logic*, 1856), as a disciple of Hamilton, has discussed the problem with more fulness, but his results are naturally widely different from mine, since he too admits all the eight forms as standing on an equal footing.

not to be meddled with, and therefore does yield a distinction. (3) That negative subjects and predicates are not to be introduced, the negation being confined to the copula[1]. Given then three terms X, Y, Z, our range of liberty extends to making universal or particular, affirmative or negative, propositions out of them; and then arranging them so that the term which occurs twice over, (the middle term), shall be subject of both, predicate of both, or subject of one and predicate of the other. This yields sixty-four possibilities, from nineteen only of which can a necessary conclusion be drawn.

Take then the properly corresponding conditions for the scheme now under discussion, and see what we are led to. The very similarity of the conditions leads to differences in application. To begin with, we recognize five forms of proposition instead of four, but then in turn we recognize no distinction between subject and predicate. Hence we have only twenty-five possible combinations of premises, instead of sixty-four to submit to examination. Again there is another very important ground of distinction arising out of the fact (already adverted to) that on this scheme 'some' does not include 'all,' but is incompatible with it. That is to say the two conclusions 'Some X is Z' 'All X is Z' are not here compatible with one another, but contradictory. These points will come out better in the course of the following discussion.

Make then an arrangement of all the possible combinations of premises with a view to determining how many of them will lead to certain and unambiguous conclusions.

[1] The rejection of this third convention, with the consequent free introduction of negative subjects and predicates, is one of the most marked characteristics of De Morgan's System.

They will stand as follows :—

I.	II.
All *Y* is all *Z*,	All *X* is all *Y*,
All *Y* is some *Z*,	All *X* is some *Y*,
Some *Y* is all *Z*,	Some *X* is all *Y*,
Some *Y* is some *Z*,	Some *X* is some *Y*,
No *Y* is any *Z*.	No *X* is any *Y*.

Now combine each of the first column with each of the second, and take the results in detail :—

1.   All *Y* is all *Z*, All *X* is all *Y*. This yields the conclusion, All *X* is all *Z*. [See Figure (1), p. 21.]

2.   All *Y* is all *Z*, All *X* is some *Y*. This yields the conclusion, All *X* is some *Z*. [Fig. (2).]

3.   All *Y* is all *Z*, Some *X* is all *Y*. This yields the conclusion, Some *X* is all *Z*. [Fig. (3).]

4.   All *Y* is all *Z*, Some *X* is some *Y*. This yields the conclusion, Some *X* is some *Z*. [Fig. (4.)]

5.   All *Y* is all *Z*, No *X* is any *Y*. This yields the conclusion, No *X* is any *Z*. [Fig. (5.)]

6.   All *Y* is some *Z*, All *X* is all *Y*. This yields a valid conclusion, but may be rejected on the ground that it is formally identical with No. (3), merely substituting *Z* for *X*, and *vice versa.*

7.   All *Y* is some *Z*, All *X* is some *Y*. This yields the conclusion, All *X* is some *Z*. [Fig. (6.)]

8.   All *Y* is some *Z*, Some *X* is all *Y*. It may seem as if the conclusion that common logic would draw 'Some *X* is *Z*,' ought to yield us something here. But the peculiar signification of 'some' forbids a conclusion; for any one of the four (with us, not merely distinct but mutually hostile) propositions 'All *X* is some *Z*,' 'Some *X* is all *Z*,' 'All *X* is all *Z*,' 'Some *X* is some *Z*,' are equally compatible with the premises. Hence no single conclusion is admissible.

9.   All Y is some Z, Some X is some Y. The state of things here is similar to that in the last case. We reject the syllogism, on the ground of its admitting of two mutually inconsistent conclusions 'All X is some Z,' and 'Some X is some Z.'

10.   All Y is some Z, No X is any Y. Rejected on the same ground as the last two, inasmuch as it admits of three mutually hostile conclusions. Common logic agrees with us in this rejection, because two of the possible conclusions, viz.: 'No X is any Z,' 'Some X is some Z,' are also recognized by it as hostile, whereas in cases (8) and (9) it recognized no such hostility.

11.   Some Y is all Z, All X is all Y. Admissible in it self, but dismissed on the ground of its formal identity with (2).

12.   Some Y is all Z, All X is some Y. Rejected (as in common logic) because *any* of the five possible conclusions is compatible with the premises.

13.   Some Y is all Z, Some X is all Y. Formally identical with No. (7).

14.   Some Y is all Z, Some X is some Y. Rejected as leading to three possible conclusions. Common logic concurs here.

15.   Some Y is all Z, No X is any Y. This yields the conclusion, 'No X is any Z.' [Fig. (7.)]

16.   Some Y is some Z, All X is all Y. Formally identical with (4).

17.   Some Y is some Z, All X is some Y. Rejected as leading to three conclusions: formally identical with (14).

18.   Some Y is some Z, Some X is all Y. Common logic would treat this as *Disamis,* with conclusion 'Some X is Z;' but we have to reject it, because we do not know whether the some X is 'all Z,' or 'some Z,' which with us are conflicting conclusions. Formally identical with (9).

19. Some Y is some Z, Some X is some Y. Rejected as admitting of five possible conclusions.

20. Some Y is some Z, No X is any Y. Rejected as admitting three conclusions.

21. No Y is any Z, All X is all Y. Formally identical with (5).

22. No Y is any Z, All X is some Y. Formally identical with (15).

23. No Y is any Z, Some X is all Y. Common logic would conclude 'Some X is not Z,' but since this proposition covers three of our distinct forms, we have to reject the syllogism as leading to no certain conclusion. Formally identical with (10).

24. No Y is any Z, Some X is some Y. This case corresponds to the last; we reject it on the same ground. It is formally identical with (20).

25. No Y is any Z, No X is any Y. Rejected as admitting of five possible conclusions. Common logic of course concurs in this rejection, since it interprets universal negatives exactly as we do.

It will be seen therefore that we should admit seven forms or 'moods' of syllogism as distinct, and only seven. They are thus exhibited in diagrams:—

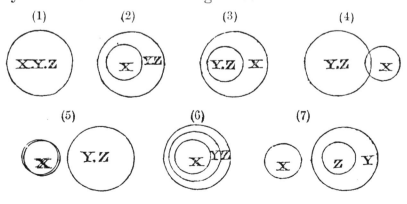

A study of these figures will, I think, convince any one, independently of detailed investigation, that they represent all the ways in which each of two figures, say circles, can stand in relation (relation, that is, of the five specified kinds) to a third such figure, so that their mutual relation to each other shall be unambiguously determined thereby. And this mediate and unambiguous determination is exactly what I understand that the syllogism proposes to effect.

So much then for this second scheme of propositional import and arrangement. In spite of its merit of trans parent clearness of illustration of a certain number of forms of statement, it is far from answering our purpose as the basis of an extension of Logic. Its employment soon becomes cumbrous and unsymmetrical, and possesses no flexibility or generality. Fortunately there is another mode of viewing the proposition, far more powerful in its applications than either of those hitherto mentioned. It is the basis of the system introduced by Boole, and could never have been invented by any one who had not a thorough grasp of those mathematical conceptions which Hamilton unfortunately both lacked and despised. The fact seems to be that the moment we quit the traditional arrangement and enumera tion of propositions we must call for a far more thorough revision than that exhibited on the system just discussed. Any system which merely exhibits the mutual relations of two classes to one another is not general enough. We must provide a place and a notation for the various combinations which arise from considering three, four, or more classes; in fact we must be prepared for a complete generalization. When we do this we shall soon see that the whole way of looking at the question which rests upon the mutual relation of classes, as regards exclusion and inclusion, is insufficient. There is a fatal cumbrousness and want of symmetry about it which renders it quite inappropriate for any but the simplest cases.

The way of interpreting and arranging propositions which has to be substituted for both the preceding (for the purpose of an extended Symbolic Logic), is perhaps best described as implying the occupation or non-occupation of compartments. What we here have to do is to conceive, and invent a notation for, all the possible combinations which any number of class terms can yield ; and then find some mode of sym bolic expression which shall indicate which of these various compartments are empty or occupied, by the implications in volved in the given propositions. This is not so difficult as it might sound, since the resources of mathematical notation are quite competent to provide a simple and effective symbolic language for the purpose. What we can afford to say about this scheme, here, is of course merely preliminary, since many questions will arise which will demand discussion and illustration in the following chapters. Enough, however, may easily be said to bring out clearly its bearing on the par ticular subject which has just been discussed, viz. the number of distinct forms of proposition which ought to be recognized. The view which is here taken is still distinctly a *class* view rather than a predication view ; but, instead of regarding the mutual relation of two or more classes in the way of inclusion and exclusion, it substitutes a complete classification of all the sub-divisions which can be yielded by putting any number of classes together, and indicates whether any one or more of these classes is occupied ; that is, whether things exist which possess the particular combination of attributes in question.

A fair idea of the meaning, scope and power of this system will be gained if we begin with two class terms X and Y, and consider the simple cases yielded by their combination.

It is clear that we are thus furnished with four possible cases, or compartments, as we shall often find it convenient to designate them; for everything which exists must certainly

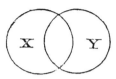

possess both the attributes marked by X and Y, or neither of them, or one and not the other. This is the range of possi bilities, from which that of actualities may fall short; and the difference between these two ranges is just what it is the function of the proposition to indicate. We will confine our selves at present to intimations that such and such compart ments are *empty*, since this happens to be the simplest alter native. Now how many distinct cases does this system naturally afford?—we must approach it, let us remember, without any prepossessions derived from the customary divi sions and arrangements.

We should naturally be led, I think, to distinguish fifteen different cases on such a system as this, which would fall into four groups. For there may be one compartment unoc cupied, which yields four cases; or two unoccupied, which yields six cases; or three unoccupied, which yields again four cases; or none unoccupied, which yields but one case. *All* cannot be unoccupied, of course, for we cannot deny both the existence and the non-existence of a thing; or, to express it more appropriately on this scheme, given that a thing exists it must be put somewhere or other in our all-comprehensive scheme of possibilities.

As this whole scheme will be thoroughly worked out in future chapters, I will only call attention here to the nature of the four simplest out of these fifteen cases. Writing, for simplicity, x for not-x and y for not-y, these four would be thus represented :—

$$xy - 0, \text{ or No } x \text{ is } y,$$
$$xy = 0, \text{ or All } y \text{ is } x,$$
$$xy = 0, \text{ or All } x \text{ is } y,$$
$$xy - 0, \text{ or Everything is either } x \text{ or } y.$$

On this plan of notation xy stands for the compartment, or class, of things which are both x and y ; and the equation $xy = 0$ expresses the fact that that compartment is unoc cupied, that there is no such class of things. And similarly with the other sets of symbols.

A moment's glance will convince the reader how entirely distinct the group of elementary propositions thus obtained is from that yielded by either of the other two schemes ; though, starting from its own grounds, it is just as simple and natural as either of them. One of these four is of course the universal negative, which presents itself as fundamental on all the three schemes. Two others are universal affir matives, but with the subject and predicate converted. But the fourth is significant, as reminding us how completely relative is the comparative simplicity of a propositional form. On the present scheme this is just as simple as any of the others ; but in the traditional arrangement it would probably obtain admittance only as a disjunctive, since that arrange ment hates the double negation ' No not-x is not-y' and does not like even the simpler 'All not-x is y.' Indeed on hardly any other view could such a verbal statement as this last be considered as elementary, since almost every one would have to put it into other words before clearly under standing its import.

We might easily go through the eleven remaining cases referred to above, but to do so would be an anticipation of

future chapters.   It may just be noticed, however, in passing,
that the emptying out (as we may term it) of two compart
ments does not necessarily give a proposition demanding
a greater amount of verbal statement than that of one only
does.   For instance the combination $xy = 0$, $xy = 0$, expresses
the coincidence of the two classes x and y; it is ' All x is all y.'
That of xy and xy yields the statement that x and y are
the contradictory opposites of one another, that x and
not-y are the same thing, and consequently y and not-x.
These and other results of this system will call for attention
hereafter.

The full merits of this way of regarding and expressing
the logical proposition are not very obvious when only two
terms are introduced, but it will readily be seen that some
such method is indispensable if many terms are to be taken
into account.   Let us introduce three terms, x, y and z; and
suppose we want to express the fact that there is nothing in ex
istence which combines the properties of all these three terms,
that is that there is no such thing as xyz.   If we had to put
this into the old forms we should find ourselves confronted with
six alternative statements, all of them tainted with the flaw of
unsymmetry; viz. No x is yz, No y is xz, No z is xy, and
also the three converse forms of these.   No reason could be
shown for selecting one rather than another of them; and if
we attempted to work with the symmetrical form ' There is
no xyz ' we should find that we had no supply of rules at hand
to connect it with propositions which had only x, y, or z, for
subject or predicate.

If we tried the second propositional theory we should
only reduce the above six unsymmetrical alternatives to
three; three being got rid of by our refusing to recognize
that conversion makes any difference in the proposition.   But
the same inherent vice of a choice of unsymmetrical alterna-

tives would still confront us.   No reason could be given why we should say that the class x excludes the class yz, rather than that the class y excludes that of xz, or z that of xy.   Common language may be perfectly right in tolerating such alternatives; but a sound symbolic method ought to be naturally cast in a symmetrical form if it is not to break down under the strain imposed by having to work with three or more terms.   This requires us to avoid such forms as 'the class x excludes that of yz,' as well as all the statements of the common Logic, and to put what we have to express into the symbolic shape $xyz = 0$.   The verbal equivalents for this are, of course, that there is no such thing as xyz, or that the compartment which we denote by xyz is empty.   There are theoretical reasons for regarding the latter form as the most rigidly accurate and consistent.

It deserves notice that ordinary language does oc casionally recognize the advisability of using symmetrical ex pressions of this kind, though the common Logic shows no fondness for them.   We should as naturally say, for example, that 'cheapness, beauty and durability never go together,' or that 'nothing is at once cheap, beautiful, and durable,' as we should use one of the forms which divide these three terms between the subject and the predicate.   But this latter plan is what would be adopted presumably by the strict logician, by his arranging it in some such form as 'no cheap things are beautiful-durable.'   It need not be remarked that popu lar language, though occasionally making use of such sym metrical forms, has never hit upon any general scheme for their expression, and would be sadly at a loss to work upon more complicated materials.   Especially would this be the case where negative predicates or attributes had to be taken into account as well as positive.   However what we are here concerned with is the insufficiency of the ordinary logical view rather than the occasional ingenuity of popular expression.

In these remarks I have endeavoured to keep rather closely to the enquiry suggested at the outset; that, namely, of the number of fundamentally distinct logical forms, and the foundation on which each different arrangement must be understood to rest. It seems quite clear that no attempt can be made to answer this question until we have decided, in a preliminary way, what view we propose to take of the proposition and its nature. There is no occasion whatever to tie ourselves down to one view only, as if the import of propositions were fixed and invariable. Very likely other views might be introduced in addition to the three which have been thus examined, though these appear to me to be the only ones with which the student is likely to have to make much acquaintance.

Each of the three stands upon its own basis, yields its appropriate number of fundamentally distinct propositions, and possesses its own merits and defects. The old view has plenty to say for itself, and for ordinary educational purposes will probably never be superseded. It is very simple, it is in close relation with popular language, and it possesses a fine heritage of accurate technical terms and rules of application. Its defects seem to me to be principally these :— that it does not yield itself to any accurately correspondent diagrammatic system of illustration; and that its want of symmetry forbids its successful extension and generalization.

The great merit of the second plan, or that of class inclusion and exclusion, is its transparent clearness of illustration. We may be said thus to *intuite*[1] the proposition. This

---

[1] F. A. Lange (*Logische Studien* p. 9) maintains that such intuitions of space lie at the bottom of our logical axioms exactly as they do in the case of our mathematical axioms.

has indeed caused a most unwarranted amount of employment of its diagrams by those who do not realize that its five distinct forms of proposition cannot be properly fitted in with the four of the traditional scheme. This clearness is however almost its only merit. It possesses little more of symmetry, or consequent adaptability to generalization, than the former, and it is considerably removed from popular forms of expression. I regard it in fact as a sort of logical *blind alley*, inasmuch as it does not seem to lead out any where further, that is, not to admit of any generalization. Above all, as it insists upon exhibiting the *actual* relations of the two classes to one another, it has no power to express that degree of ignorance about these relations which many propositions are bound to do, if they are to state all that we know, and nothing but what we know, about the relation of the subject and predicate to each other. (Hamilton's eight propositions seem to me an inconsistent and partial attempt to remedy this latter defect, in so far as the last three of his forms are concerned.)

The third scheme is, of course, in comparison with the others, an artificial one, and possesses the merits and defects which might be expected in consequence. It is couched in too technical forms, and is too far removed from the language of common life, for it ever to become a serious rival of the traditional scheme on the ground appropriate to this latter. For symmetry, however, and the power which comes of symmetry, nothing can for a moment be put into competition with it, as will abundantly appear in the course of the following chapters.

The following comparative table will aid the reader in keeping in mind the distinctions insisted on in the course of this chapter.

In the first column the five possible distinct objective class relations are exhibited. In the second column stand the groups of ordinary propositions requisite for the purpose of unambiguously expressing these relations. In the third, we

(i) Diagrammatic	(ii) Common Logic	(iii) Quantified	(iv) Symbolic
	All A is B All B is A	All A is all B	$A\bar{B}=0$ $\bar{A}B=0$
	All A is B Some B is not A	All A is some B	$A\bar{B}=0$ $\bar{A}B=v$
	All B is A Some A is not B	Some A is all B	$\bar{A}B=0$ $A\bar{B}=v$
	Some A is B Some A is not B Some B is not A	Some A is some B	$AB=v$ $A\bar{B}=v$ $\bar{A}B=v$
	No A is B	No A is any B	$AB=0$

express these relations by single propositions with quantified predicates, and a special interpretation of '*some.*' In the fourth we represent them symbolically. (As regards the signification of the letter v I am anticipating here. As will be shown in chap. VII., $AB=v$ means 'There is A which is not B,' or 'AB is something,' *i.e.* is neither 0 nor 1.)

In the above arrangement the last three columns are forced into following the lead of the first. To see into what shape they will throw themselves when this pressure is removed, I add another arrangement; in which they, so to say, think of nothing but following out their own bent and framing themselves as simply and symmetrically as possible. In this case the second column contracts into the familiar four propositions; the third, when regarded as consisting of verbal statements unchecked by diagrams, shows a decided inclination towards mere grammatical symmetry, and will tend to spread out into Hamilton's (redundant) eight-fold scheme; whilst the last yields its own compendious table to be explained in a future chapter.

II.	III.	IV.
	All A is all B.	$xy = 0, v, 1.$
All A is B.	All A is some B.	$xy = 0, v, 1.$
Some A is B.	Some A is all B.	$\overline{x}y = 0, v, 1.$
Some A is not B.	Some A is some B.	$xy = 0, v, 1.$
No A is B.	No A is any B.	
	No A is some B.	
	Some A is not any B.	
	Some A is not some B.	

CHAPTER II.

In Symbolic Logic we are concerned with two kinds of symbols, which are commonly described as standing respec tively for *classes* and for *operations*. It should be remarked, however, that these two kinds cannot be very sharply dis tinguished from one another, inasmuch as each to some extent implies the other. Thus a class may be almost always described as the result of an operation, namely of an operation of selection. The individuals which compose the class have been somehow taken from amongst others, or they would not be conceived as being grouped together into what we call a class. Similarly what we call operations always result in classes ; at least all the operations with which we are here concerned will be found to do so. The mere signs of operations never occur by themselves, but only in their appli cations, so that practically we never encounter them except as yielding a class, and in fact almost indistinguishably merged into a class[1]. For purposes of exposition, however, it

---

[1] Popular usage does not seem perfectly clear upon this point even in mathematics, since it is frequently overlooked that what we commonly see expressed are not operations but *results* of operations. Thus $\sqrt{2}$ stands for a number pure and simple, that is, for the number which when squared

will be necessary to make the distinction, since those logical operations by which classes are governed, and which we shall presently discuss, being less familiar to the reader than the direct symbols for simple classes, will demand far the greater share of our attention.

The former kind of symbols, namely those which stand for classes of things, need occupy us but a very brief space here, since we may presume that the reader has already become familiar with them elsewhere. Nothing is more usual than to put such general symbols as X and Y in place of the con crete subjects and predicates of our propositions. In fact it is necessary to do this when we wish to judge of any kind of general rule upon its merits, and to keep clear of individual circumstances and of misleading associations. Hence we adopt the practice of putting single letters to stand for whole classes of individuals, in other sciences, as in stating Law cases, and indeed in some of the circumstances of ordinary life.

What indeed the logical student may have to do in this direction is not so much to acquire new associations as to divest himself temporarily of some old ones. For instance we have, strictly speaking, no concern whatever within the limits of our enquiry with such distinctions as those between deno tation and connotation, between essential and accidental attributes, or even with that between subject and predicate. Not of course that we would for a moment imply that such

will yield 2. We imply this when we say $\sqrt{2} = 1.41...$, for of course we could not equate an operation to a numerical result. That is, $\sqrt{2}$ denotes a mere number but indicates at the same time the operation by which that number is justified. Exactly so in Logic. We must under- stand xy, $\dfrac{x}{y}$, &c. strictly to denote mere classes, but to indicate by their form the nature of the operation by which the classes in question are to be justified or obtained, as described in the course of this and the following chapter.

distinctions as these are unimportant. Quite the reverse; the study of them furnishes decidedly the most valuable edu cational advantage to be derived from the Common Logic. We omit them solely in order to keep our own Science homogeneous and symmetrical. I wish to insist upon this point strongly because it has been so much overlooked. Symbolic Logic is not a generalization of the Common Logic in all directions alike. It confines itself to one side of it, viz. the class or denotation side,—probably the only side which admits of much generalization,—and this it pushes to the utmost limits, withdrawing attention from everything which does not develope in this direction. Moreover, inasmuch as it is a purely Formal Science, the resolve to fit it in with the problems of Induction, or to regard it as an introduction to the Principles of Science in general, seems to me a grave error, and to result merely in the attempt to combine hetero geneous materials.

We shall find it convenient therefore to say that we regard the literal symbols, x, y, z, &c., as standing simply for classes of individuals, no matter how these classes are deter mined. For instance, it is of no consequence, for our purposes, whether the things which we select to denote by x and y are actually marked out to us by a substantive or an adjective; by reference to their essential or their accidental attributes; by a general connotative term, by a merely denotative term, or by some purely arbitrary selection of a number of individuals. Of course, such classes must be somehow distinguished or distinguishable from others, or the symbols would not be significant. If I am to make use of the terms x and y to any purpose, I must obviously have some means of making it clear to myself and to others which things are x and which are not, which are y and which are not. But all discussion as to *how* this is done, and all analysis of the grounds and processes of doing it, deeply interesting as such discussions are when philosophically regarded, must just now be relegated to Common Logic, to Grammar, or to Psychology.   With us, x and y regarded as class terms must be considered as having mere denotation, as standing for certain assignable individuals or groups of individuals[1].

Suppose, for instance, I make the assertion, "The Philo sophical writers whom I have in view are the a posteriori school, the first editor of the Edinburgh Review, and the Mills."   Here I have occasion to allude to four classes, as we may term them.   The first is indicated by a many-worded term 'the philosophical writers whom I have in view.'   The class here, it will be observed, is partly determined by the connota- tive terms 'philosophical writers,' but these are identified in some way known perhaps only to myself; for possibly no one else may at the moment know *how* I recognize or keep in mind this group, or what are the common characteristics which I detect throughout it.   When therefore I put a sym bol, say w, to represent this many-worded term, such symbol does not exactly correspond to any distinct kind of class term recognized in Logic.   Again, as regards "the a posteriori school"; here we have a connotative general name of the familiar kind; this we equally represent by a symbol, say x. "The first editor of the Edinburgh" is partly a mere proper name, partly connotative, partly limited arithmetically.   And

---

[1] The above account will do as a preliminary one, but the reader will find in the sequel that it needs modi- fication or enlargement in two re- spects. First (as explained in ch. vi.) it is imperatively necessary to regard these classes as *hypothetical, i. e.* to lay it down that the employment of a class term does not imply that there are actual existent members of it. Secondly the ordinary conception of a class, as consisting of a plurality of individuals, will need enlargement; it must cover the case, *e.g.* of the truth or falsity of a single proposition, amongst other things (this is explain- ed in ch. xviii.).

finally "the two Mills" is purely denotative, the class being marked out by a proper name only. But on our system all these important distinctions have to be let drop out of sight. The classes, whether plural or individual, are all alike re-presented denotatively by literal symbols, w, x, y, z; and accordingly we equate (as will presently be explained) the first group and the last three. We express the given state ment in some such form[1] as $w = x + y + z$.

So much then at present as regards symbols of classes. We must now turn to consider the symbols of operations[2]. In other words, given that we have got our classes thus designa ted before us, in what various relations can they be supposed to stand towards one another? How can they be combined or otherwise worked upon?

[1] Prof. Jevons has endeavoured to rk out a symbolic system of Logic which the symbols are to stand for ie *meaning* of the terms and not for heir extension. Amongst other evils of such a plan it leads up to the catastrophe of having to maintain "that the old distinction of conno-tative and non-connotative names is wholly erroneous and unfounded," and that "singular, proper, or so-called non-connotative terms, are more full of connotation or meaning in intent or quality than others, in-stead of being devoid of such mean-ing." (*Pure Logic*, p. 6.) It is really impossible to carry out such a view as this; 'particular propositions,' (with which however we fortunately have but little to do) simply refusing in many cases to be interpreted other wise than in extension, and violence being demanded thus to interpret uni versal propositions when 'accidental.'

F. A. Lange (*Logische Studien*, p. 56), has spoken of the "heilloseste Ver-wirrung" which has been introduced in this part of the subject since the old scholastic logic of com prehension began to give way, but inconsistently, to a logic of extension. This latter he considers to be essen-tially the modern view; it is certainly the view we must take in the gene-ralized Symbolic Logic.

[2] The introduction of these sym-bols marks the real turning point in Symbolic Logic. The distinction was long ago noted by Leibnitz, and by Lambert. The latter (*Neues Or-ganon*, II. 26, 27) distinguishes be tween "Zeichen der Begriffe", and the "Verbindungskunst der Zeichen." He admits not having (in that work) carried out the latter, but having used letters to express concepts, and words to express their conditions and rela-tions.

There would appear to be three distinct modes in which we might approach the consideration of this part of the subject. (1) We might resolve to take, as our starting point, the ordinary forms of language; either in their rude shape as exemplified in common speech, or as they appear after they have been shaped by the logician; and enquire what divisions and arrangements these naturally suggest. Or, (2) we might start by borrowing a set of symbols which have been already adopted in another science (say mathematics), and, taking these provisionally as the basis of our arrangement, see whether we could conveniently, by analogy or generalization, extract any sort of logical interpretation out of them. Or, (3) we might resolve to start anew for ourselves, by ascertaining what are the really distinct processes, in the way of mutual relations of classes, which we actually have occasion to employ in thinking and reasoning.

There appear to be strong objections to the two former plans. The first, which might seem in some respects the most natural, is rendered impracticable by the extreme laxity and consequent confusion of popular language on almost every point where logical distinctions are involved. Such characteristics of language are intelligible enough when we remember its historic development, and the varied purposes which it has to fulfil besides that of mere logical predication. But they naturally interpose serious difficulties across the path of the logician. If we attempt to carry out a scientific arrangement of valid and distinct meanings by examining the various phrases through the medium of which our meanings are popularly expressed, we shall find that we have chosen a very troublesome path. Nor have we had as much aid from the ordinary logician here as we might have fairly expected. Several technical points of importance,—of which one, viz. the mutual exclusiveness or otherwise of alternatives, will almost immediately come under our notice,—could be mentioned, upon which either the logician has no settled convictions of his own, or, if he does entertain any, he has scarcely made any serious attempt to guide and establish popular usage into accordance with them.

The objection to the second course, indicated above, is that it is not strictly a logical one. We do not want here to concern ourselves with mathematical relations and symbols, at least not primarily, but with logical relations and their appropriate symbolic representations. Doubtless we shall soon find that the symbolic statement of the latter kind of relation may be conveniently carried out by the use of symbols borrowed from mathematics. But this is a very dif ferent thing from starting with these, and trusting to being able to put some logical interpretation upon, say, *plus* and *minus*, or upon the signs indicative of multiplication and division.

The course therefore which it is here proposed to adopt, is the following. We shall begin by examining successively the principal really distinct ways in which classes or class terms practically have to be combined with one another for logical purposes. We shall then proceed to discuss in each case the various words and phrases which are popularly employed to express these combinations, enquiring whether they may not be briefly and accurately conveyed by help of such symbols as those of mathematics. It must however be once for all insisted on, that our procedure is to be logical and not mathematical. For suggestions indeed, coming whether from mathematics or from any other source, we shall be grateful, (the sign for division is suggested in this way, as will be shown in the next chapter). But our determination and justification of the requisite processes must be governed solely by the requirements of logic and common sense. Of course if symbols which were originally designed for one purpose, are found to work conveniently in some other application, various interesting and important questions are raised. Accordingly we may hereafter have to discuss such questions as these :—how it comes to pass that a set of symbols will thus answer two very different purposes as well as they do; within what limits such extensions may be relied upon as trustworthy, and so forth.

I.   In the first place, then, we often require to group two or more classes together, so as to make one aggregate class out of them. We do not want to sink their individualizing characteristics, so as to reduce them to one miscellaneous and indistinguishable group ; but leaving their respective class distinctions untouched, to throw them together, for some special purpose, into a single aggregate. We want to talk or think of them as a whole. Besides making assertions, for instance, about clergy, lawyers and doctors separately, I may want to make assertions about all three classes together, under the title, say, of the learned professions.

There ought not, one would think, to be much opening here for doubt and confusion. What however with the ambiguities of popular language, and the disputes of rival modes of symbolic statement, a little cloud of confusion has been stirred up. The possibility of this has arisen mainly from a want of proper care in clearly distinguishing between the various questions at issue[1].

---

[1] Three distinct questions are involved, which ought to be discussed apart. *First* the question of fact as regards our logical operations : do we actually require thus to aggregate class groups in distinct ways?

Secondly, the verbal question, partly grammatical, partly one of logical usage, as to the interpretation of alternatives : Can we specify, context apart, in which of the three possible senses '*A* and *B*' and '*A* or *B*'

The difficulty arises as follows. Are the classes, which we thus propose to group together, mutually exclusive or not? If they are, then all is plain enough. And often this is the case, owing to one cause or another. The classes may, for instance, be contradictories, like 'citizen and alien'; or con traries, like 'good and bad'; or distinct on material grounds, as 'British and American'; or may be separated off from one another by some known distinctions, (distinctions, as remarked, about the grounds of which our Logic does not much concern itself). In these cases there can be no opening to confusion.

More often however the classes will not be mutually exclusive, but will more or less overlap one another; so that the same individual may belong to both of them. When this is so, three distinct cases may present themselves, between which we must clearly distinguish.

(1) To begin with, there being members common to two classes we may have it in view to *exclude* these from our aggregate. In physical problems it may happen that one or other alone of two causes will produce a certain effect, but that the two together will either neutralize each other, or by their excess produce something else. Or, to take a familiar example of another kind, we might have it in view to announce the pardon of two classes of offenders, but expressly wish to exclude the aggravated cases which fell under both heads.

(2) The more frequent case, however, is that in which the common members are included in our formula, so to say,

are to be interpreted? *Thirdly,* the question of symbolic procedure: can we make our symbolic system equally powerful and elegant without marking *formally* whether or not our alternatives are exclusive? The first question is discussed in the text above, the second a few pages further on, whilst the third is mainly reserved for the final chapter. (These three questions are, so far as I can see, hopelessly confused together by Prof. Jevons; the statements of the *Pure Logic* being mostly repeated without verbal altera tion in both editions of the *Principles of Science.*)

by a double right. Whenever we are discussing mere
qualifying characteristics, without introduction of any quan
tifying circumstances, it would be taken for granted that
the members of both classes are of course included.

(3)   But there is still a third possible case for examina
tion.   May we ever want to reckon this common part *twice
over?*   In numerical applications of our formula, or whenever
considerations of quantity are in any way introduced by
them, it seems to me quite clear that we may have to
do so.   And since the simple forms of language indicative
of class aggregation are meant to be of general application,
many cases might be conceived in which they do thus
doubly reckon the common members. This has been too
hastily objected to by urging, for example that if we take all
the cattle and all the beasts of burden from a promiscuous
assemblage of animals, we do not think of counting the
common part, viz. those which fall under both designations,
twice over.   Of course we do not, because the word "take" is
one which in most of its applications negatives the possibility
of repeated performance. A thing taken once may be
considered to be taken altogether.   A still better instance in
support of this view, so far as material considerations are
concerned, would have been found in the proposal to *kill* the
members of both of these classes; for some of the beasts
of burden having been put an end to whilst we were dealing
with the cattle, would certainly not need any further atten
tion.   On the other hand it would be easy to find instances
in which the same form of class aggregation by no means
denies, but rather suggests, this double counting. Suppose,
for instance, we found, by putting together two Acts of
Parliament, that 'all poachers and trespassers are to be fined
20 shillings': is it quite certain that poachers who trespass,
could not be fined 40 shillings? This is, I apprehend,

a question for the lawyers to decide[1]. But the language is, to the common understanding, certainly ambiguous, which is sufficient for our present purpose. Or, if postmen and parish clerks were authorized to apply for a Christmas box of five shillings, does anyone suppose that postmen who happened to be parish clerks, would not apply for ten shillings altogether; and is it quite certain that their claims would be rejected?

On the whole therefore it seems clear that we must at least recognize all these three varieties of simple class aggregation as actually likely to occur, and that we must also admit that popular language does not distinguish clearly between them. It uses, or might use, the same form for all three, leaving it to the context to decide which of them is intended in any particular case.

There is, however, for logical purposes, a broad distinction between them. The last is not strictly a logical mode of aggregation, or rather it is one, not of Pure Logic, but of Applied. The sorts of classes and class relations which we require as a basis of Logic, must lend themselves to every kind of application, qualitative as well as quantitative. But the last mode, in which the surplus is reckoned twice, seems to be confined to applied Logic; that is, to some kind of numerical application of our class terms, as in the instances given above. This mode therefore may be said to be practically rejected by all logicians, but there is a very important difference in respect of the mode which they adopt for

[1] There seems to be no general rule here. On enquiring of good authorities whether, for instance, if it were enacted that auctioneers and hawkers should take out a licence, those who belonged to both classes would require *two* licences, I was told that it would probably be decided by such considerations as whether the conditions of the two licences were the same, whether they were issued by the same authority, were imposed in the same Act, and so forth.

rejecting it.   Boole preferred what we will call the strict plan of *formally* excluding any duplicate counting.   He wrote his alternatives (as will presently be indicated) in the form '*A* and the *B* which is not *A.*'   Others, who have more or less adopted his system, have employed the looser form of writing '*A* and *B*,' assuming it to be understood as a matter of course that the *A* which happens to be *B* is not to be reckoned twice.   The main grounds for preferring the former plan cannot be assigned here, since they introduce important questions of symbolic procedure.   But simply on the grounds now before us I should choose the former.   If indeed it were quite certain that the designation '*A* and *B*,' never counted *AB* twice over, there would be something to be said in favour of taking this for granted in Logic, and writing it accordingly.   Inasmuch however as this does not seem to be the case, it is decidedly better to mark our meaning by the very form of our symbolic arrangement, and to make it formally clear that there is to be no such double reckoning. It involves somewhat more trouble to adopt this plan; but saving of trouble is of very little importance in Logic, compared with the habit of keeping necessary distinctions prominently before us.

In order not to break the thread of connection at this point I will just remark at once that these three meanings may be thus indicated on the system here adopted :—

$$A \text{ not-}B + B \text{ not-}A, \quad A + B \text{ not-}A, \quad A + B.$$

In the first we exclude the *A B* members; in the second we simply include them, that is we count them once like their neighbours; in the third these *A B*'s must be considered to be counted twice over.   But inasmuch as this last would introduce alien considerations of a numerical character we shall as a rule reject that form.   If ever it makes its appearance, as representing a class, in the statement of our premises, it must be understood that A and B are in that case so obviously exclusive by their very signification (*i. e.* materially exclusive) that such a form cannot lead to error. It is somewhat briefer, and, if it be rather slovenly to adopt a form which strictly counts a part twice over, at least there can be no mistake in consequence, if it be known that such a part does not exist.

We must now take some notice of the attempts of popular language to express the above meanings. That it can do this, by using words enough for the purpose, is obvious ; but there is something almost bewildering in the laxity, in the combined redundancy and deficiency, of our common vocabulary in this respect. Broadly speaking we employ two conjunctions, 'and' and 'or', for thus aggregating classes ; these terms being practi cally synonymous in this reference, and both alike leaving it to be decided by the context whether or not they exclude the common part. Often there *is* no such part, the terms being known to be exclusive of one another ; but if there be such, and the context does not make our meaning plain, we often add a clause 'including both', or 'excluding both', or something to that effect, in order to remove all doubt. (The third of the recently mentioned cases, being comparatively exceptional, and hardly likely to occur except in some kind or other of numerical inference or application, may be left out of consideration.)

Thus, 'Lawyers are either barristers *or* solicitors', 'Lawyers consist of barristers *and* solicitors', must be taken as being equivalent statements. They both alike state that the class of Lawyers is made up of, or co-extensive with, the two classes of 'barristers' and 'solicitors'. Whether a barrister can be a solicitor they do not give the slightest hint. Nor if such be the case do they unequivocally inform us whether these com-

mon members are to be included or not ; though as inclusion
is the far more usual case this would be very strongly assumed
in the absence of any statement to the contrary.

There is, of course, a slight difference between the signi
fication of these two particles. The word 'lawyers', when
identified with 'barristers *and* solicitors', being taken some
what more collectively, and when identified with 'barristers
or solicitors' somewhat more distributively, as logicians say.
Hence when our subject is an individual a real distinction will
be introduced by the use of one term rather than the other.
Thus to say of any person that 'he is deceiver or deceived', is
by no means the same thing as to say that 'he is deceiver and
deceived'.   But the distinction here seems merely forced
upon us by the necessity of the case and not by the nature of
the grouping of the two classes.   The individual cannot, like
a class, be split up into two parts ; accordingly his 'collective'
reference to two classes forces us to conclude that one person
at least must be common to both classes, that one deceiver
must be deceived ; whereas his 'distributive' reference to the
two classes carries no such implication with it.   This must
rank of course amongst the many perplexities and intricacies
of popular speech, but it does not seem at variance with the
statement that regarded as mere class groupings, independent
of particular applications, '*A* and *B*', '*A* or *B*', must as a rule
be considered as equivalent.

In addition to these words, *and* and *or*, we have a variety
of other words and phrases at our occasional service ; such as,
'as well as', 'also', 'not excepting', and so forth,—all of which
serve the same purpose of aggregating class terms together so
as to make them represent a single whole.   But *how* they
aggregate them, in respect of this matter of inclusiveness,
must be a matter of interpretation and of reference to the
context.

II.   The next way in which we have to consider the mutual relation of classes is when one is *excluded* from another. It is often convenient to begin by taking account of some aggregate class, and then proceed to set aside a portion of it and omit it from consideration. This process is the simple inverse of that discussed above, and the difficulties to which its expression has given rise spring from corresponding causes. Three cases may be noticed in order.

(1)   One of the classes may be included within the other (or within one or more of the others, if the group consists of several). In this case the omission or exclusion cannot give rise to any perplexity, but is perfectly simple and intelligible.

(2)   Again, if the classes are mutually exclusive of one another, the omission of either from the other is equally simple, but unintelligible. The direction to omit the women from the men in a given assembly has no meaning. At least it will require some discussion about the interpretation of symbolic language in order to assign a meaning to it.

(3)   But if the two classes are partly inclusive and partly exclusive of one another, we are landed in somewhat of a difficulty. What for instance, would be meant by speaking of "all trespassers omitting the poachers"? If we interpreted this with the rigid stringency with which we treat symbols, we should have to begin by deducting the common part, viz. the poachers who trespass, from the trespassers; and should then be left with an unmanageable remainder, viz. the poachers who did not trespass, and who could not therefore be omitted.

Popular language is of course intended to provide for popular wants, and must be interpreted in accordance with them. Hence a laxity of usage is permitted in its case which could not be tolerated in the case of symbols. Accordingly when we meet with such a phrase as that in question, we take it for granted that any such uninterpretable remainder is to be disregarded, and we understand that 'trespassers omitting poachers' is to be taken to signify 'trespassers, omitting such trespassers as poach.'

Here too we have a variety of phrases at command to convey the desired meaning. The word most frequently used for this purpose is perhaps 'except', as when we say 'Lawyers, except Chancery barristers'. In this case we specify the sub-class to be omitted, but sometimes we can express our meaning better by specifying the portion which is not to be omitted, as when we say 'Lawyers, provided they are Chancery barristers', which means that we are to except all who are not so. Besides these phrases we have a number of others to choose from, such as, 'omitting', 'excluding', 'but not', 'only if not', and so forth.

III. Our third logical operation in dealing with classes consists of selecting the common members from two or more overlapping classes. This is the statement of the process in respect of denotation,—the only side of terms, as previously remarked, with which we are properly concerned. If however we choose to express the same thing in respect of connotation we should say that given two sets of attributes as distinctive of certain groups, we propose to confine ourselves to the attributes which occur in both groups. It is obvious that such a mode of class relation will as a rule result in a restriction or limitation of the numbers of things taken into account. This clearly must be so unless the two classes happen to be coincident, owing to our having really two names for the same group ; or unless one class is entirely included in the other, in which case the combination of the two is equivalent to the neglect of the wider one. In this latter case we have limited the wider class, but have left the narrower one with its limits unaltered.

The way in which common language indicates this opera
tion is very commonly by simple juxtaposition of the terms
involved. This plan is always admissible when one term
is a substantive and the other an adjective, and not unfrequently in other cases also; though as the logician, when
he employs ordinary language, has to act in concert with
the grammarian, he naturally finds his freedom of expression
rather hampered.

But though the readiest way of naming the part common
to two assigned classes is by simple juxtaposition of the
respective names,—as when we say 'black men' to mark
those individuals who are both black and men,—it is far
from being the only way. Here, as elsewhere, the resources
of language are only too copious and varied for the logician.
We have quite a collection of popular phrases at disposal,
differing from one another not so much in what they logically
assert as in what they are conventionally understood to
imply in addition. Sometimes this implication may be
so strong that it is difficult to say where mere suggestion
ceases and actual logical predication must be considered
to begin. Thus it comes about that such words as *and*,
but, accordingly, together with a host of others, are all
employed to express the process of selecting the common
part in two overlapping classes. 'Zulus are savages and
cunning', 'are savages but cunning', 'are cunning but
savages', 'being savages are cunning', must all be understood
as indicating exactly the same kind and degree of class
limitation. They all alike assert that the class 'Zulu' is
contained somewhere within the common part of the
classes 'savage' and 'cunning'; or, if we prefer so to put
it, that they possess the attributes distinctive of these
two terms. Where they differ from one another is not
in respect of what they assert but in respect of what they

imply; the first containing no further implication, the second implying the independent proposition that 'most savages are not cunning', the third that 'most cunning people are not savage', and the fourth that 'most, or all, savages are cunning'. But when we come to write them down, we should be forced to reject all these suggestions, and to express them each alike in the form 'All Zulus are savage-cunning'.

Again; in common speech, adjectives are often ambiguous by not distinguishing whether they are predicative of a whole class or merely selective out of it. When I read of "those who claim the black-skinned Hindoo as a brother" I cannot be certain whether this phrase picks out certain Hindoos only, by this characteristic, or whether it is meant to inform us that all Hindoos possess the characteristic. As in so many other cases we do not know what exactly is meant to be implied beyond what is directly stated.

The following simple sentence is one of many which might be offered to illustrate the combined redundancy and deficiency of common speech in the expression of these class relations:—"The proper recipients of charity are those who are poor but honest, or sick and old, and those who are young if they be orphans". Here we are simply treating as an aggregate class the three classes describable as 'poor-honest', 'sick-old', and 'young-orphan', each of these three being the common part of two overlapping classes. But the various words used to connect our class-terms seem almost as if they were chosen at hazard. For the purpose of expressing aggregation or addition we have used *and* and *or*; and for that of expressing the selection of a common part we have used *and, but*, and *if*.

We have now enumerated and described the three

principal logical operations which are concerned with the mutual relations of our class terms. They are, I think, the only operations of the kind which would naturally and spontaneously present themselves to the mind. There is, it is true, a fourth operation which will have to be dis cussed in the next chapter, but it is not by any means an obvious one[1]. Instead of being forced upon our notice like the above three, not only by logical necessity but by the requirements of daily speech and thought, it rather comes to us by way of our symbols. Its very existence may be said to be suggested by the wish to make our symbolic scheme complete and symmetrical. We will there fore set it aside for the present, until we have discussed the appropriate symbolic language for the three operations which are so familiar to us.

When we look about, in order to choose our symbols, those of elementary mathematics naturally offer themselves. Any that we shall need are very simple and almost univer sally familiar, so that it seems at any rate worth while to try if they will answer our purpose. Not of course that we propose to use them in the same sense as that primarily imposed upon them. On the contrary, the signification they will have to bear has been already definitely settled for them in the foregoing discussion, and this distinctly varies from their natural or primary signification. Even where the analogy is closest, as in the aggregation of classes above described, we are not engaged in a process of *addition*. The process we have to perform may be best described, in familiar words, as that of throwing several compartments into one; but we have no thought of counting individuals

---

[1] I allude here, not to the process of *equating*, indicated by (=) and dis- cussed presently, but to the logical analogue of *division*.

or in any way adding up numbers. We do not 'add' together the English, French, Germans, and so forth, in order to make up the Europeans. Of course such a process of class aggregation may be made a *basis* of numerical calculation, but then so it may of many other operations with which it is in no way to be confounded. I cannot see that we are justified in any case in considering that there is more than an analogy, sometimes indeed a very close one, between these operations of Logic and those of mathematics. Certainly the employment of the same symbols must not be construed into an admission that this is so.

I. To begin with the operation of aggregating two or more classes into one. This seems to be so naturally represented by the sign for addition, that one can hardly avoid writing down some such expression as $x + y + z$ to represent the class made up of x, y, and z. No other formal or symbolic justification for it seems to be called for than these, —that the order of the terms thus connected is entirely indifferent, and that the aggregation of two groups is equivalent to the aggregation of the detailed classes which compose them; that is, we must accept the commutative and associative laws. Whatever sense we put upon the sign we must secure that $x + y$ and $y + x$ shall have precisely the same signification, and that $(x + y) + (z + w)$ is equivalent to $x + y + z + w$. It is so in mathematics, and it must be so in Logic too if the symbol is to answer its purpose. That this condition is secured in Logic is obvious; for the order in which we group our terms is perfectly immaterial, and is recognized as being so in the common usage of *and* and *or*. Indeed common language has so thoroughly appreciated this fact that it does not seem to have prepared any pitfalls here against which the logician has to be on his guard. In whatever order we arrange the 'Jews, Turks, infidels, and heretics,' we cannot extract any difference of signification out of the combined group[1].

We must however clearly understand that in adopting this sign (+) we have to some extent committed ourselves in the matter of the mutual exclusiveness discussed a few pages back. For wherever we meet with such a form as $A + B + C$ in mathematics it is always supposed that A, B, C, are mutually exclusive, whether the symbols stand for things or for operations; or that, if they are not, the common parts must be considered to have been taken twice over. It is never tolerated that they should overlap one another and leave it to us to make the correction by omitting what would otherwise be doubly reckoned. Accordingly, if we wish to be quite consistent, we ought to do the same in Logic. That is, we must take care to ascertain that the terms which we thus connect are mutually exclusive of one another. If we happen to know that this is already the case, on either formal or material grounds, then there is no harm in our writing $x + y$ at once. But if this be not known, then we must take care to *make* them exclusive, which is readily done by expressing it as '$x + y$ not-x.' (Of course if we want to omit the common part altogether, we should put it 'x not-$y + y$ not-x.')

The necessity of thus expressing ourselves has been

---

[1] The systematic employment of this sign (+) for this particular purpose of class aggregation dates, I apprehend, from Boole. Of course the sign itself had been introduced into Logic long before. Thus Leibnitz (*Specimen demonstrandi*, Erdm. p. 94) writes $A + B$ to mark the addition of attributes or notions to form a more complex notion, in which he has been followed by others, *e. g.* Twesten (*Log.* p. 25) and Hamil-

ton (*Log.* I. 80), but this is an interpretation in intension. The sign was also used by Ploucquet to mark the combination of assertions or premises, and by Maimon and Darjes to stand for affirmation in contrast with negation. Maimon however used another sign (|) in a case of exactly the same kind as that which we now mark by (+), as in, $a + b \mid c \mid d$, for 'a is either b or c or d' (*Versuch einer neuen Logik*, p. 69).

objected to on various grounds, which seem to me decidedly insufficient, but which will be discussed in a future chapter. It doubtless involves somewhat more trouble in writing down our formulæ. But the extra trouble thus entailed is after all but slight, and, as pointed out in the preface, mere expedition in the performance of the work is not by any means an important consideration in Symbolic Logic. On the other hand, there may be urged in its favour, the high advantage of keeping real distinctions present to the eye by means of the formulæ we employ; the greater harmony thus secured with the analogous steps in Mathematics; and a certain considerable increase of symbolic power, which (as will be shown in future chapters) we are thus enabled to acquire.

II. The deduction, omission, or subtraction, (it will be seen that we can hardly help resorting at once to mathe matical terms here) of one class from another is expressed with equal convenience by aid of the symbol $(-)$; so that $x - y$ will stand for the class that remains when x has had all the ys left out of it. The only point here that seems to call for symbolic justification is the ascertainment of the fact that the well known mathematical rule, about *minus* twice repeated producing *plus,* is secured in Logic. That is, we must ascertain that it is so, both in the processes we actually perform, and in the language we use to describe them. And this may be established by a single suitable example. Thus if we describe the persons who may remain in a captured town as 'all the inhabitants except the military, but omitting from these the wounded'; the wounded military are understood to be put back, by virtue of the two 'omissions', into the same position as the non-military ;—pro vided, of course, that there are only two alternatives in the case. It is just a case of $x - (y - z) = x - y + z$. So the rule holds in Logic.

In using this symbol we must remember the condition necessarily implied in the performance of the operation which it represents. As was remarked, we cannot 'except' anything from that in which it was not included; so that $x - y$ certainly means that y is a part of x. This is quite in accordance with the generalized use of the symbol in mathe matics where it is always considered to mark the undoing of something which had been done before. Not of course that it must thus refer to the immediately preceding step, but that there must be some step or steps, in the group of which it makes a part, which it can be regarded as simply reversing. The expression $x - y + z$ will be satisfactory, provided either x or z is known to be inclusive of y, or if both combine together to include it[1].

III. The third logical operation, namely that of restric tion to the common part of two assigned classes, may be represented by the sign of multiplication. That is, $x \times y$, or xy, will stand for the things which are both x and y.

The analogy here is by no means so close as in the preceding cases, but the justification of our symbolic usage must still be regarded as resting on a simple question of fact: *i.e.* do we in the performance of the process in question, and

[1] Leibnitz (*Specimen demonstran-di*) employed this sign, but his view of Logic being one of 'comprehension', $A - B$ meant, with him, the omission of the attribute B from the notion A; not the exception of B as a class from A as a class. As already remarked, the sign $(-)$ was frequently employed to mark logical negation, as by Maimon and Darjes. The earliest such use that I have noted is by Lambert:—"In dieser Absicht liesse sich das Bindwortchen ist durch das Zeichen $(=)$, das *nicht* durch das arithmetische Verneinungszeichen $(-)$ ausdrücken......Kein A ist M wäre $A = -M$" (Lambert's *Briefwechsel*, I. 396:—This is not Lambert's own notation). There is also a suggestion in this direction in Leibnitz's *De arte combinatoria* (Erdmann, p. 23), "Quemadmodum igitur duo sunt Algebraistarum et analyticorum prima signa $+$ et $-$, ita duæ quasi copulæ *est* et *non est.*"

in the verbal statement of it, act under the same laws of operation in each case, logical and mathematical alike? The answer is that we do so up to a certain point, but not beyond.

For instance the *commutative* law[1], as it is termed, viz. the indifference of the order of the symbols, prevails; xy and yx, English Protestants and Protestant English, being precisely the same class. So does the *distributive* law, that every element of the one multiplier shall combine with every element of the other, that *e.g.* $x(y+z) = xy + xz$, and $(x+y)(z+w) = xz + xw + yz + yw$. Of course we have to make our way here through various grammatical obstacles, but allowing for them it is clearly true that we do thus combine and distribute our terms, so that 'English and French soldiers and sailors', is the same as 'English soldiers, and English sailors, and French soldiers, and French sailors'. When however we say that this commutative law holds in common speech, we must remember that the idiosyncracies of language insist upon exceptions here as elsewhere; and on the same ground, viz. the necessity of compressing a quantity of implication into our sentences, in addition to the direct assertions they contain. Thus when x implies y we al ways use the form yx, rather than xy. For instance one would not direct a legacy to those old servants "who are destitute and alive"; but to those "who are alive and destitute".

It will be equally obvious that if $x = y$ then $zx = zy$, that is, that we may 'multiply' equivalent terms by the same factor. For (as will be more distinctly insisted on presently) $x = y$ means that the individuals which go by the names x and y are the same; consequently it comes to

---

[1] The introduction of these technical terms appears to be of recent date. Hankel (*Vorlesungen*, p. 3) says that *distributive* and *commutative* (in this particular sense) were introduced by Servois in Gergonne's *Annales* v. 93 (1814); and *associative* by Sir W. R. Hamilton.

exactly the same thing whether we select the z's from them, under their name of x or their name of y. In each case alike we get the same result.

Where we depart from mathematical usage, or rather restrict the generality of its laws, is in the following respect. As a rule, xx (or x^2) is different from x. If x represent a number, then x^2 is greater or less than x, according as x is greater or less than 1; if x represent a line, then x^2 represents an area, and so forth. But in Logic x^2 must equal x, or rather any number of self multiplications must leave the significance of a term unaltered, *i.e.* $x = xxx\ldots\ldots$ That this is so as an operation, is obvious, for the selection of the common part of two classes, when these classes happen to be the same, is reduced to the simple repetition of this one part. And that the same is true as regards the laws and usages of common speech must also be admitted. Or rather, it must be admitted under some exceptions; for there are signs of divergence towards the mathematical rule here, when we are dealing with *comparative* terms. Thus, even in English, 'great great' does not mean quite the same as 'great' alone; and in some languages, as Italian for instance, adjectival repetition is really almost like mathematical multiplication, increasing or diminishing the effect according as the term is in itself an augmentative or diminutive. If this conventional rule prevailed universally in respect of all, or even most terms, the logician would have to give way to the grammarian here, with the result of having to abandon Symbolic Logic, as a distinct formal science from Mathematics[1]. As it is, however, we feel at liberty to set aside this 'comparative' usage as an

---

[1] Any one who has read Algebra will see the importance of this restriction in the processes of logical calculation. It reduces every logical equation to the *first degree*. Hence any equations with any number of terms are resolvable by the expenditure of sufficient time and trouble.

irregularity, and to lay it down universally that xx shall be considered the same as x.

It may be pointed out that this is not so much an infringement of mathematical laws as a special restriction of them. In fact there is one case in which the same rule does hold in mathematics, that is when x stands for *unity*. In that case $xx - x$ obviously[1].

So far then seems plain. It must now be enquired what, on the suppositions thus made, will be the proper mode of representing certain important and limiting classes with which we shall often have to deal. How, for instance, shall we represent "all things" :—or rather, to speak more correctly, how shall we represent the 'universe of discourse' with which we may happen to be concerned ;—about the nature of which universe we shall have something more to say hereafter ? It may at first occur to the reader that the most appropriate way of representing such a huge and miscellaneous assemblage as this would be by the sign for *infinity*, since mathematics has such a sign at its disposal. We might resolve so to represent it if we pleased[2]; but, if we did, we should soon find that we were acting inconsistently with the plan we have just

---

[1] There was a much freer employment of this sign for multiplication, than of that for addition, by the earlier symbolists. This was probably owing to two causes: partly, that here the comprehensive and extensive views come so much more nearly to the same thing; but more to the fact that popular language had already familiarized men with the juxtaposition of *words* to express the same results which the logician expresses by juxtaposition of *letters*. For instance Leibnitz uses the form AB for "A that is B", (*Erd.* p. 102) and similar forms are of constant occurrence in Ploucquet's logical writings. But note how the latter describes them :—"Durch *mb* will Ich keine form der Multiplication sondern eine Associirung der Ideen verstanden haben", a very different conception this from that of the common part of the extension of m and b. (*Samm-lung.* p. 254.)

[2] It has indeed been so represented by more than one symbolist. (See on, ch. VIII.)

adopted of indicating combined attributes or overlapping classes by the sign of multiplication. When once that plan is adopted we are inevitably bound in consistency to make the symbol for unity, or 1, stand for the universe. That this is so can very readily be shown. For what does our x stand for? It comprises *all things* which are x. In other words, one way of describing and getting at x is to say that we combine, or take the common part of, the universe and x, just as 'English men' may be got at by taking the common part of the classes which are English and which are men. We do not say that this is the only way of getting at it, but it is one way and there fore our results must be consistent with so reaching it. Now the only known symbol which when combined, in accordance with the rules for multiplication, with any symbol x, will always still give us x, is unity. Hence the one universal class must be represented by the sign for unity, so that $1 \times x$ shall always equal x.

The interpretation of the commutative law in the case of $x \times 1 = 1 \times x$ deserves a moment's attention. If we regard it as a process of selection rather than as the indication of a result (which is not however the best way of regarding it) we should say that $x \times 1$ may be described as the process of selecting from the whole universe those things which are x. So $1 \times x$ will be the selection from x of all those things which belong to the universe, which of course leaves x unaffected.

On the same principles a non-existent class, or, as we shall often find it convenient to describe it, an empty compart ment, will be fittingly represented by the sign for nothing, or 0. This looks natural and plausible enough; but it is well to point out that it follows strictly from what has hitherto been laid down. For if xy stands for the things which are both x and y, then $0x$, or 0, will stand for those which are both nothing and x; in other words for the non-existent, or for any empty class.

The sign of subtraction supplies us in the same way with a suitable expression for the logical contradictory of any class x, viz. for the class 'not-x'. For since not-x comprises everything which the universe contains except what is x, we should write it symbolically[1], $1 - x$. Now combine x and $1 - x$, and what do we thus indicate? The class of things which are at the same time x and not-x. Of course this is bound to equal *nothing*; *i.e.* $x(1-x) = 0$. This supplies a link of consistency with some of our previous assumptions. For 'multiply out' $x(1-x)$, as in algebra, and we have $x - x^2$ or $x - xx$; which as just remarked, is to be equal to zero, and this necessitates that x and xx, or x^2, shall be identical with each other, which we already know that they must be.

One or two examples may be added in illustration of the employment of our symbols, and of the restrictions to which they are subject. Suppose we have the expression 'English and French Poets and Orators'. Following the indications already given we might propose to write it down symbolically $(a+b)(c+d)$, thus combining the four terms by the signs respectively of addition and of multiplication. Multiplied out, the latter becomes $ac + ad + bc + bd$. Now the original verbal statement, when fully expressed in its details, is equivalent to English poets and English orators and French poets and French orators, that is, the symbolic process of multiplication gives exactly the same combinations of terms that are obtained in common discourse ; the two corresponding step for step, as of course they are bound to do.

In this case the condition of accurate expression previously alluded to, about the mutually exclusive character of our terms, does not obviously make itself perceptible, but that is because correction is tacitly made where required, when the

---

[1] For the sake of brevity we shall commonly write x for $1 - x$, or not-x. It is an abbreviation introduced and frequently employed by Boole.

symbols are translated into words.   Since a and b, standing
for French and English, are already exclusive, no correction is
required.   But c and d, standing for poets and orators, *do*
overlap, and therefore $c + d$ does *symbolically* count this
common part twice.   We mentally make a correction at
this stage.   But working symbolically we come upon the
same repetition again in the final form $bc + bd$.   Here again
we make a correction of the true symbolic import of this
expression, without any symbolic warrant, but merely to
secure what we know to be meant; accordingly we conclude
that the orator-poets are only to be reckoned once.   Symboli
cally we have no right to do this, for we ought to have
written our terms down in the form of mutual exclusion.
But the needed correction is so tacitly and readily made
that we are hardly conscious of requiring to appeal to it.

In other cases the necessity of making this correction,
when translating our symbols into words, is forced upon our
attention.   Suppose, for instance, that instead of combining
two distinct groups, like $(a + b)\,(c + d)$, we combine the same
twice over.   Taking, as before $c + d$ to stand for the poets
and orators, what is denoted by $(c + d)\,(c + d)$?   Clearly
this is only a slightly more complicated case of $xx = x$, viz.
$(c + d)\,(c + d)$ must $= (c + d)$.   But when multiplied out, of
course, $(c + d)\,(c + d)$ yields, (on our symbolic plan) $c + 2cd + d$.
That is the common part cd, and the fact of its being counted
twice over, is here forced obtrusively upon our notice.   We are
reminded of the fact (equally true in the former case, though
it escaped notice there) that we had no symbolic right to use
the expression $c + d$ unless c and d were mutually exclusive.
In that case $cd = 0$, and the redundant term does not occur to
trouble us.

In order not to multiply examples needlessly we will take
one more which involves the sign of subtraction, and see how

that answers when worked out. Take, for instance, $(a - b)$ $(c - d)$ and see what it might stand for in common language, both in its present shape and as it would become when multiplied out in detail. The following would be a fairly corresponding verbal expression :—'Barristers (excepting foreigners) who are graduates, but not of Dublin'. What does this mean ? It seems quite clear that all whom we can possibly intend to except from the barristers are foreign barristers, not foreigners in general, and that all whom we except from the graduates are Dublin graduates. In other words this process of exception or subtraction always presupposes that the class excepted is a part (formally or materially) of the class from which it is excepted. We are therefore warranted in writing our symbols $(a - ab)$ $(c - cd)$ or $a (1 - b) c (1 - d)$, and in re garding both this and the verbal statement as being com pounded of four terms, two of them positive and two of them negative.

But the question was not so much whether the two expressions corresponded as they thus stood, but whether the result of multiplying out the symbols could be translated step by step in its details and shown to correspond to the results of ordinary thought. Those symbols, when treated by the ordinary rules, yield the result, $ac - acd - abc + abcd$. Is there any thing in the statement about the barristers corresponding to all this ? Certainly there is, for these symbols as they thus stand in detail, are literally translatable into the words 'Graduate barristers, omitting Dublin graduate barristers, omitting also foreign graduate barristers, but adding on Foreign Dublin graduate barristers'. If we go through this we shall see that it expresses exactly the con templated class, but with one important proviso. This proviso is that the expression 'omitting' here is not to be taken in its loose popular signification, by which its application is tacitly understood to be limited to the range of the term which precedes it, but in its strict symbolic signification in accordance with which we may *omit too much*, and therefore find it necessary to add on a term to correct this excess. This, of course, is the real meaning of the final term *abcd*. Common language left to itself, would have compendiously expressed the details in the form $ac - acd - abc$, that is, would have put it ' Graduate barristers, omitting those of Dublin and the foreign ones'. The accurate language of symbols requires us to insert a final term which common language had rejected for the sake of brevity.

The above examples are fairly illustrative of a number which might be offered. They will serve to explain some of the main points of our system of Symbolic Logic. We see that we may employ the sign of addition (+) for the aggregation of classes, provided we make our classes mutually exclusive (which common logic does not in general do, preferring to leave this point unexpressed, and tacitly to make any correction and alterations which are necessary). We may employ the sign of subtraction (−) for the exception of one class from another, provided the excepted class is included in the other (common language appears so uniformly to take this for granted that we may consider it as really intending this limitation, though its terms do not formally imply it). And we may employ the sign of multiplication (×) for the results of selecting the common members of two classes. (This process is so simple that common language does not seem to have become loose or inaccurate here, except in so far as it puts an occasional intensifying effect upon the act of repetition of comparative terms ; a perfectly natural intensification, but one which we find ourselves compelled to reject.)

To one point, which has been already noticed, attention

must be very persistently directed, as any vagueness of apprehension here will be fatal to the proper understanding of symbolic reasoning. It was seen in the last example that, in translating a common phrase into symbols, we felt justified, or rather bound, to ask ourselves what exactly that phrase must be understood to mean, instead of just proceeding to put it into symbols as it stood. We may say in fact that we were resolved to give an *idiomatic* translation and not to resort to a bald and literal substitution of terms. 'Lawyers excepting foreigners' was accordingly interpreted, on this ground, to refer to what was left after foreign lawyers, not foreigners in general, were left out of account. Accordingly we translated it into our symbols as $a - ab$, and not $a - b$, for we knew that the former was what we meant. But in the converse case, that is when we were translating back from the language of symbols into that of common life, we had no right to do anything of this kind. Symbols have no tacit limitations or con ventional interpretations other than that which has been strictly and originally assigned to them. Accordingly if I meet the symbolic expression $a - b$, where a stands for lawyers and b for foreigners, I have no right to regard this as a popular lax expression, in which only a part of b instead of the whole is to be subducted. I must take it as signi fying (whatever that may mean) the subduction of *all* foreigners from the lawyers; and I must look out for, and in this case shall find, the introduction of another term which will set matters symbolically straight, by just neutra lizing the surplus subduction ; common language on the other hand sets matters straight by interpreting the subduc tion in its own sense, and then just neglecting the required additional term.

It comes therefore to this. We may translate *into* the

language of symbols almost as we please, for we are the only ultimate judges of what we really mean to signify by our words. But having once done so, and laid down rules for working with our symbols, our further control of them ceases. We must translate out of these symbols into the language of common life in exact accordance with their assigned meaning. Otherwise we shall find that one correction and modification after another will be called for.

IV. The only remaining mathematical symbol to which we will at present direct attention, and almost the only other one which we shall have occasion to adopt, is the sign (=) of equality. Here too we must not trust too much to acquired associations. What this symbol generally means in mathematics is identity (or indistinguishable similarity) in respect of some one characteristic only in the various things which it connects together ; this characteristic being in most cases the number of *units* involved. These may be units of space, or time, or mass, or acceleration, or what not. Thus in the case of a falling body, $v^2 = 2fs$ means that the square of the number of units in the velocity is the same as twice the product of the number of units of force and space. But in logic this is not so. The sign of equality here indicates absolute identity in all respects, except nomen clature, of two or more classes. The identity indeed is so complete, that all that needs pointing out is how we can talk of two distinguishable classes in such a case. The answer of course is that a 'class' is merely our way of grouping or *outlining* things, and is indicated and retained by the imposition of names. The very same individuals therefore may belong to more than one class ; in other words, may have more than one single name or combination of names assignable to them. It is in this sense only that we can talk of the identity of all the members of two or more classes. Such identity is what we mark by the sign of equality (=).

Here, as in the case of our other symbols, we must turn to see by what sort of contrivances popular language succeeds in conveying its meaning. As usual it is vague, and shows both defect and redundancy, the signification being controlled by innumerable conventions and implications. One way of expressing this identity is by mere predication. If in answer to the question, What are triangles? I reply, 'triangles are plane figures included by three straight lines' I clearly mean that every thing referred to by the one name is also referred to by the other; that is, that the individuals in these classes are identical. This is however rather a lax form of speech, for the copula 'is' (or 'are'), by itself, properly implies nothing more than predication. The stricter form for expressing this identity of classes is by some such words as "consists of", or "comprises"; and even these may sometimes need the addition of some other clause such as "and includes no others" in order to remove all ambiguity, and to make it plain that we contemplate a case of identity of classes, and not merely of the inclusion of one class within another. Again the word "means" implies this identity, and implies it somewhat strictly. It does not properly speaking *state* it; for the two things which we thus connect in our pro position are not so much two classes of individuals, as the significance of some word on the one hand and the things it refers to on the other. But it certainly carries with it this complete identity of classes. When I say that 'ghost' means a disembodied human spirit, I imply that the class of things, real or imaginary, referred to by one name is identical with that referred to by the other name.

Symbolic Logic may therefore fairly be said to take an ultra-nominalistic view of this subject. The expression

$x - y$ simply tells us that the class of things of which x is a name is composed of the very same members as that of which y is a name. And $xy = a + b$ tells us that the class of things, of which both the names x and y simultaneously hold, is identical with the class of things covered by the two names a and b. This implies however, in strict propriety, that the classes a and b are mutually exclusive ; if they are not so we should do well to write our equation in the form $xy = a + b \,(1 - a)$ or $xy - b + a \,(1 - b)$.

CHAPTER III.

SYMBOLS OF OPERATIONS (CONTINUED).

THE INVERSE OPERATION, $\frac{r}{r}$; OR SYMBOLS OF DIVISION.

WE have now seen our way clearly enough to the performance, and symbolic expression, of three distinct logical operations upon classes, viz. :—

1. A direct operation closely analogous to the addition of ordinary arithmetic and algebra, and suitably symbolized by the familiar sign (+).

2. The inverse operation to the above, and therefore closely analogous to subtraction, and which may be suitably symbolized by the sign (−).

3. A direct operation very remotely analogous to multiplication, and which we have seen could (with one restriction in respect of usage) be expressed by the usual signs for that process, viz. (×) or simple juxtaposition of the terms.

The question therefore at once suggests itself whether there may not be a fourth operation which shall be the inverse of the third, as the second was of the first. This suggestion, it must be admitted, comes to us rather by way of the symbols than by way of the actual logical process itself.

5—2

In this it is unlike the first three. As regards them we saw that it was quite impossible to think and speak about classes of objects without having these three operations forced upon our notice : in fact, they are so familiar to us that our trouble arises rather from a confusing redundancy, than from any lack, of phrases to express them. The symbols are therefore an afterthought to express results and operations to which we are already accustomed, though their introduction is a powerful means of economizing time and thought.

We now take a different course. We might conceive the symbols conveying the following hint to us : Look out and satisfy yourselves on logical grounds whether there be not an inverse operation to the above. We do not say that there is such, though we strongly suggest it. If however you can ascertain its existence, then there is one of our number at your service appropriate to express it. In fact, having chosen one of us to represent your analogue to multiplication, there is another which you are bound in consistency to employ as representative of your analogue to its inverse, division,—supposing it to exist.

A few words of reminder as to the nature of an inverse process[1] may not be out of place here, especially as the application of this term, just above, to subtraction may suggest too simple a notion of its general nature. The relation of Interest to Discount, as theoretically treated

---

[1] The reader who can do so with profit is strongly recommended to consult the works of some of the more philosophical mathematicians for a discussion of the distinction in question. It is the symbolic language of mathematics only which has yet proved sufficiently accurate and comprehensive to demand familiarity with this conception of an inverse process. See, for instance, Boole's *Differential Equations*, ch. xvi. There is an admirable discussion of some of the general characteristics of the symbolic language of Mathematics in De Morgan's *Double Algebra*. Also in Hankel's *Vorlesungen über die complexen Zahlen.*

in elementary works on arithmetic, will furnish a familiar instance. Take a sum of £100, and put interest upon it at 5 p. c. for a year ; and call this the direct process. The result will of course be £105. But now suppose that we had been asked instead to find a sum such that, when a year's interest was added on to it, we should obtain £100, we should have been called upon to perform the inverse to the above. The result of course is £95. 4s. 9d. In this case it will be observed that the inverse process is just as definite as the direct, that is, there is but one sum possible such that, with the interest added on, it shall yield the given amount. In mere arithmetic this is generally so. To subtract 5 from 20, or in other words to find a sum that, with 5 added on to it, it shall become 20, can only result in 15. So it is with multiplication and division, and with the calculation of logarithms, powers, and so on.

As a rule, however, what are called inverse operations are indefinite. Instead of there being only one starting point such that the performance of the direct process would carry us from it to the desired result, there may be a plurality of such starting points, or even an indefinite number of them. Thus in Trigonometry the calculation of the sign of a given angle is definite :—e.g. $\sin 45^\circ = \dfrac{1}{\sqrt 2}$. But the calculation of the angle whose sign is given is indefinite :— thus $\sin 135^\circ$ is also $\dfrac{1}{\sqrt 2}$, or generally, $\sin^{-1} \dfrac{1}{\sqrt 2} = (2n + \tfrac{1}{2}) \pi + \dfrac{\pi}{4}$. It is to this class of indefinite inverse operations that the logical process which we indicate by the sign of division will be found to belong.

In strictness these terms *direct* and *inverse* are purely relative, and of indifferent application ; that is, whichever of a suitable pair of processes we may choose to call direct, we may call the other its inverse. But the fact that the one process is very frequently definite whilst the other is indefinite, makes such an important practical distinction between them, that we are in the habit of applying the term absolutely to the latter ; and we speak of *the* inverse process, whilst we call the definite one the direct process[1]. It is in this sense that we shall call the logical process which will be indicated by the sign of division, an inverse operation.

It should be remarked that the inverse rule merely indicates a result, giving at the same time a test by which that result is to be verified, but that it does not describe in any way the process by which it is to be obtained. It does not even assure us that there is any known method of obtaining it. It says in effect : Find something, which, when operated on in a certain way, will yield a certain result, but it does not tell us *how* we are to set about finding that something. As Boole says (*Differential Equations*, p. 377), "It is the office of the inverse symbol to propose a question, not to describe an operation. It is, in its primary meaning, interrogative, not directive[2]."

To find then the inverse of xy, that is of the direct operation of x upon y, or y upon x, we must recall what that

---

[1] Even where both processes are definite, one of them may be much more difficult of performance than the other, or even impracticable. Thus it is easy enough to calculate the fifth power of a given number, but we have no arithmetical rule for calculating a fifth root. There seems some disposition to apply the term 'inverse' in an absolute sense to such cases also as these ; viz. where no rule of operation can be given, and where in consequence we can only test a proposed result by means of the corresponding or direct process.

[2] It surprises me that one who had so clearly stated the nature of an inverse operation in mathematics should never have proposed, so far as I know, any corresponding explanation in Logic.

operation is. It is, generally speaking, one of *restriction*[1]; it is the act of confining the attention to the common members of the two classes x and y; so that to operate upon x by means of y is to restrict the class x by exacting the condition of being y also. What then will be the inverse of this, represented symbolically by $\frac{x}{y}$? Not, as some might be tempted to reply at once, the mere *taking-off* of this y-restriction from x, but rather the finding of a class such that, *when the y-restriction is imposed upon it,* it shall be brought down exactly to x.

What then is the description of the desired class, and can it be determined by ordinary logical considerations? Certainly it can, provided we set to work methodically by examining all the possible cases in order. When we do so, we see that such a class must certainly contain the whole of x. As regards what is not-x it certainly cannot contain the y part, (or yx), for, if it did, this part would not fulfil the condition of reducing to x on imposition of y. As regards what is neither x nor y, it may take as much or as little as it pleases, that is, a perfectly indefinite portion for any such portion will satisfy the condition, by disappearing on combination with y and leaving us x only. The full description therefore of the desired class is given by saying that it comprises the whole of x, and a quite uncertain part of xy, namely of what is neither x nor y. If we like to put

---

[1] We call it restriction, because this is the usual result; but in special cases the class thus determined will clearly not be narrowed. For instance, if x and y are identical in extent, then xy has the same range as either x or y. (If 'all x is all y' then xy is no more restricted than x or y simply.) Or again, if x is already included in y, then xy will be no narrower than x, but will coincide with it; so that it is only y that is restricted by the process. If all men are lung-breathers, the lung-breathing men are no narrower a class than the men in general.

a peculiar symbol (v) to represent perfect uncertainty, we should write down the class symbolically as $x + vxy$.

The test of the correctness of this result is found, as in the case of other inverse operations, by simply performing the direct process upon it, and seeing whether we are thus led back to our original starting point. Thus if we multiply this expression, $x + vxy$, by y, it must yield x. It is true that at first sight we seem to get a different result, viz. xy instead of x; but the difference is soon found to be apparent only, inasmuch as xy and x are in this case the same.

As the point here touched upon is very important in symbolical reasoning, I must call careful attention to it, though its full significance will only come out in a future chapter. The fact is simply this, that the very stating of such a problem presupposes a condition, or makes an assumption as to the mutual relations of x and y. To ask for a class such that on restriction by y it shall reduce to x necessarily implies that all x shall be y, as otherwise the process could not possibly be performed. If there were any part of x that is not y this part would of course disappear on restriction by y · that is, a part of x would have disappeared from our result, whereas the question demanded that we should be left with the whole of x on our hands and nothing else. Accordingly when we are asked to perform the inverse process indicated by $\dfrac{\overset{\sim}{}}{y}$ it is necessarily assumed that 'all x is y,' or that x and xy are the same. The symbolic expression of the desired class may therefore be written down indifferently $x + vxy$ or $xy + vxy$. The 'proof' of the result is that either of these expressions when multiplied by y reduces to xy, that is, to x, as the problem demands.

It will be observed therefore that we may speak of the expression $\dfrac{\overset{\sim}{}}{y}$ as standing for a certain logical class. It is particularly necessary to call attention to this. I regard it as an essential part of our scheme that this symbol, like all others which are admissible into Logic, represents a class or class-group of some kind or other. The class may be complicated in its determination, that is, it may require a number of terms to assign it; and it may, in certain directions, be indefinite in regard to its limits, as in the above example, but it is never anything else than a true logical class or conceivably assignable group of individuals.

The reason for laying such stress upon this point is that the contrary view is very widely assumed. It is generally maintained that the sign of division is uninterpretable upon Boole's system, and by implication upon any other system of Symbolic Logic[1]. Of course if we suppose that the sign stood for nothing but ordinary division, so that $\frac{x}{y}$ meant 'divide x by y'; then it must clearly be admitted that such a sign would be meaningless in Logic. But then, for that matter, so would xy if it meant 'multiply x by y'; for

---

[1] I admitted this uninterpretability myself (in an article in *Mind* for October 1876) more than I should now be disposed to do. At least, I could not then see my way with certainty to any other than that *interrogative* explanation which is discussed on the next page, and therefore assumed that we must admit the fraction $\frac{}{y}$ as being an uninterpretable stage in the process of deduction. But that essay was little more than a brief account of Boole's actual method; and not being then concerned with the re-investigation of his principles I was content in various directions to take them temporarily for granted. It seems clear that Boole himself so regarded it, for he says expressly (p. 69) "the chain of demonstration conducting us through intermediate steps which are not interpretable to a final result which is interpretable." And, further on, "The employment of the uninterpretable symbol $\sqrt{-1}$ in the intermediate processes of Trigonometry furnishes an illustration of what has been said." (I need hardly say that I do not here accept the uninterpretability of the symbol $\sqrt{-1}$.)

Logic makes no direct use of either of these operations. But if we say, as we should rather say, Do the inverse of that logical process which you have elected to indicate by the sign of multiplication, then it lends itself readily enough to a comparatively simple interpretation. The required interpretation is merely this :—the expression $\frac{x}{y}$ stands for a class, viz. for the most general class which will, on imposition of the restriction denoted by y, just curtail itself to x. But to this expression we must remember to attach the condition, that this presupposes that 'all x is y,' as otherwise no such class as that which is desired could possibly exist.

The above is one way of approaching these inverse processes, and it seems the most immediate way. But as the conception is decidedly unfamiliar, it will be well to look at it from more than one point of view. As it happens there is another way of being led into the use of fractional forms in Logic. It is somewhat more circuitous, but the advisability of employing such forms to indicate inverse operations is, if anything, even more obvious on this plan than on the one already examined.

It has been shown that when we try to solve the inverse problem we find that it necessarily presupposes a condition of relation between x and y. Suppose we start with the explicit assertion of a condition, by asking the question, 'If z which is y is the same as x, what is z in general'? we shall find that we are doing exactly the same thing as asking for the inverse of xy. For express this condition symbolically and it stands $zy = x$. Now suppose that we proceed to treat our symbols in reliance upon the belief that the process corresponding to division could be performed, or rather, that when indicated it could be submitted to explanation. We should go on to conclude that $z = \dfrac{}{y}$; in other words, we should be led on to use and interpret that symbolic form which we have just been discussing immediately and at first hand.

It is in this manner, it may be remarked, that these fractional forms will almost always originate in practice. We have some term given to us qualified or limited by a condition, and we are asked to determine all that we can about it without such condition. But whether the process be called for directly, or, as here, in consequence of a stated condition, it is always essentially the same. We have assigned to us a restricted class, and a restricting class, and we are called upon to determine with the utmost generality the class which on combination with the latter will reduce to the former.

A simple concrete example will serve to make this plain. For instance, given that Peers are the same as English Aristocrats, what are aristocrats in general?—the answer to be given of course in terms of *peer* and *English*. Aristocrats, when restricted by the class *English*, become *peers;* what can we say about them when subject to no such restriction? A little reflection would lead to one or two exclusions. They cannot be non-English peers, for it is definitely implied that there can be none such; nor again, from the meaning of the terms, can they be non-aristocratic English. But they must certainly include all the peers. Hence they can only be described generally as including 'all peers, together with a perfectly indeterminate number of what are not English nor consequently peers.' That is, symbolically, if $yz = x$, then $z = x +$ possibly any portion of what is neither x nor y. If, as before, we put v as indicative of this kind and degree of indeterminateness, we should write it $z = x + vxy$. (It is also clear here that $x = xy$; that is, that 'peers' are the same as 'English peers', so that we might equally write it $z = xy + vxy$, as already pointed out.)

We have gone thus minutely into the discussion of this question, because the requisite conceptions are decidedly unfamiliar even to logicians[1]; but there can surely be no mental exercise more beneficial than that of generalizing to the utmost the processes we perform, and realizing clearly such distinctions as that between direct and inverse operations. Of course if the inverse process of class-expansion were as important in common thought and speech as the direct process of class-restriction is, it would become desirable to adopt some simple verbal expression for indicating it. Just as we now write 'English aristocrat' as a brief expression for the restricted class common to the two classes, so we might write $\dfrac{\text{Peer}}{\text{English}}$ as a brief expression for the expanded class obtained by the above mentioned process, namely for the class 'peers, together with (possibly) any portion of what are neither peers nor English'. We need be no more suspected of wanting to divide the peers by the English in this case than of wanting to multiply the English by the aristocrats in the other. We should be using nothing but convenient linguistic forms for operations which we had occasion to perform. As a matter of fact, since we hardly ever do have to perform the latter process, except as a deliberate logical exercise, no necessity for the introduction of such a verbal device has arisen. But we must not forget that our symbols are simply a substitute for our terms

---

[1] A word of warning may be offered to those logicians who happen to be anti-mathematicians. It is of no use rebelling against the introduction of these processes on the ground that they are not logical. They must be introduced, and indeed are so, though in a very rudimentary stage, (as will be shown in a future chapter) even in the common Logic. What is wanted is that they should be discussed in their full generality.

or words, and therefore any scheme of thought and language which can find a rational use for the symbolic form $\frac{r}{y}$, might conceivably find it desirable to introduce such a form as $\frac{e\ r}{\text{English}}$ into ordinary language, in order to express its current wants.

The mathematician may be interested in noticing that the logical process indicated by $\frac{\sim}{y}$ has, in one respect, more analogy with integration than with division. This latter, though an inverse operation in respect to multiplication, is perfectly definite; it can only be answered in one way The direction to find a quantity which multiplied by 4 shall yield 20, is just as definite as the direction to multiply 4 by 5. Only one answer is yielded in either case. But the direction to find a quantity which when differentiated with respect to x shall yield, say, a, is indefinite. It can only be described in the form $ax + c$, where c may be any thing not involving x $(\int a\,dx = ax + c)$. We are bound, that is, to allow for the possible existence of an unknown or indeterminate surplus term which will vanish on the appli cation of the process of differentiation.

The inverse logical process in question has this one characteristic in common with the above, since *it* also yields an unknown or indeterminate term which disappears on application of its corresponding direct process, and for that reason has to be allowed for and inserted. We say that $\frac{x}{y} = xy + vxy$, where the term vxy corresponds to the constant c in the integration. Whatever c may be, $\frac{d}{dx}(ax + c) = a$; and so whatever vxy may be, $y \times (xy + vxy) = xy$. Conse-

quently just as we write $\int a dx = ax + c$, so we must write
$$\frac{x}{y} = xy + v\,\overline{x}\,\overline{y}.$$

There is another explanation which has been offered for this sign of division, and which deserves notice here, as does also the corresponding one for the sign of multipli cation. It is that the former sign represents the process of logical *abstraction* and the latter of logical *determination*[1]. Against the general propriety of this view no objection can be raised, abstraction and determination being of course strictly logical processes, and therefore falling well within the limits of any logical system. This explanation is also on the right track, but it does not seem to me quite to hit the mark.

My main objection to such an explanation is that it rests too much upon the connotative force of the terms we use instead of appealing solely to their denotation. (The grounds for thus defining our terms entirely in regard to their class limits, instead of in regard to their 'meaning', or the attributes

[1] I gather that this is Prof. G. B. Halsted's opinion (*Journal of Speculative Philosophy*, Jan. 1879). A similar view is adopted by Schröder (*Operationskreis*, p. 2) and by his reviewer, Gühring (*Viertel Jahrschrift der wiss. Phil.*, 1878), besides other recent writers.

The explanation in question however is much older than is commonly supposed, having been proposed by Lambert and by G. J. Holland, more than a century ago, in the course of the intercourse which they and Ploucquet carried on together about the principles of Symbolic Logic. Thus Holland says, "If from the concept A the partial concept b is abstracted let the resultant concept be termed R. Then we have $R = \dfrac{A}{b} = ac$ (say . But one is no more dividing here than one is multiplying in Composition" (J. H. Lambert's *Deutscher gelehrter Briefwechsel*, Letter xxviii. 1768). Lambert himself has employed the same notation (*Nov. Act. Erud.* 1765 :—for some account of which scheme in the particular case of negative propositions see Chap. xx.). Lambert has also remarked that Determinations (*Bestimmungen*) may be indicated by the sign of multiplication. (Ploucquet's *Sammlung*, p. 223.)

they imply, is discussed more fully in the next chapter.) It is quite true that the product xy may frequently be described as the process of combining the attributes connoted by x and y and so obtaining a limited or more 'determined' class. But it seems decidedly better to say simply that it represents the members common to these two classes x and y, without reference to their attributes; both because some terms may have nothing but denotation, and because where they have connotation also, this latter element is far less easily determined.

Now though it is true that Abstraction represents a process the reverse of class restriction, and so far corresponds to our 'analogue of Division', yet it seems to do so with such limitations and to presuppose such conditions as to unfit it to be regarded as general enough for our purpose. We cannot for instance abstract an attribute from a term unless such attribute is distinctly implied in the meaning of the term. We can abstract, say, rationality from man, because 'man' means 'rational animal'; but there seems no warrant for saying that we can abstract the property of 'having two eyes', or any other property not included in the connotation. When we use the form $\dfrac{r}{y}$ we assume, it is true, that the class x is included in y, (or that $x - xy$), but this is a far more definite and determinable fact than to decide whether certain attributes are or not included in the connotation of x. To decide that 'all x is y' is often simple enough, but every one knows the delicacy of deciding what is implied in the 'meaning' of x and of y. Similar remarks apply to the logical process of Determination. Indeed it is quite a question whether, with Professor Wundt (*Log.* p. 225), we ought not, in consistency, to go the length of rejecting the Commutative law when we take this view of the process. The determining and the determined are not, so to say, symmetrical; the process of determining A by B is not identical with determin ing B by A. I have therefore preferred to speak of 'class restriction' which is perfectly symmetrical.

Again, Abstraction as I understand it, is limited in another way which unfits it for our purpose. It is re- garded by logicians as yielding a definite class, whereas we require one which shall be to a certain extent and in a certain direction, indefinite. Thus the abstraction of 'ration ality' from 'man' would be considered to give 'animal', because man is defined as rational animal. But on our system $\dfrac{\text{man}}{\text{rational}}$ would represent 'rational man *plus* an uncertain portion of what was not rational nor man'[1]. In both cases we are extending the class man (or rational man), but in the former case we extend it precisely up to the limits of 'animal', whereas in the latter we confess our ignorance of what the limits of the extension ought to be.

All that I feel able to say therefore is that if we had to select recognized logical terms to express the analogues of multiplication and division, Determination and Abstraction would be the best for the purpose. But as things are, these terms are too much connected with the connotative force of common terms, and too much restricted in their acquired signification, for it to be quite convenient thus to appropriate them. To make them fit our purpose we should not only have to confine them entirely to the extension of our classes irrespective of their meaning or intension, but we should have to insist upon assigning to Abstraction an indefiniteness

---

[1] Let $z = $ man, $x = $ rational, $y = $ ani- mal. Then $z = xy$, $\therefore y$, or 'animal', $= \dfrac{z}{x}$, *i.e.* $\dfrac{\text{man}}{\text{rational}} = zx + \overline{vzx}$ as indi- cated above. I cannot find that any logician before Boole had contem- plated the necessity of the indefinite term to be thus added to form the complete result.

of limitation to which it has never been accustomed in Logic[1].

Before concluding this chapter it will be well to call attention to a few generalizations and extensions in the use of our symbols, which will be found to conduce greatly to the convenience and efficiency of their use. Some of these are obvious enough when pointed out. For instance, in the employment of the additive sign (+) we laid it down that in strictness this sign was only to be suffered to connect non-intersecting classes. There was indeed an interpretation which could be put upon instances which did not comply with this regulation, expressible as 'counting the common part twice over'. But such over-reckoning was an arithmetical process rather than a logical; for the basis of a logic of this description can only consist of combinations of classes, none of which ought any more to be counted repeatedly than ought the subject or predicate of any common proposition.

But it is soon seen that there is no harm in passing through such inappropriate expressions, provided we do not admit them into our final results. I may heap up one such term upon another, provided I put in some expression at the end which shall neutralize the surplus. Instances of this, it will be remembered, forced themselves upon our notice in the discussions of the last chapter. Thus $2xy$ is unauthorized by itself, and therefore $(x + y) - 2xy$ cannot, as it stands, be read off into strict logical language. But a

[1] The only other distinct attempt at the systematic introduction of fractional forms into the treatment of Logic that I remember to have seen is by Bardili (*Grundriss der ersten Logik, &c.*, 1800). The signification he there gives to the signs of subtraction and division is however of far too metaphysical and non-logical a kind (in any sense of the word Logic with which we are now concerned) to deserve discussion here. Some account of his system will be found in Erdmann's *Geschichte der neuern Philosophie* (III. 479).

different arrangement makes it irreproachable, for it can be thrown at once into the form $x\,(1-y)+y\,(1-x)$. It then becomes 'x or y, but not both'. These obvious considerations are noticed here, because in complicated class expressions a little trouble devoted to this kind of arrangement will often not only make an expression interpretable which otherwise would not be so, but will greatly facilitate our processes of reduction and so forth.

The same remarks apply to the use of the subtractive sign. We cannot intelligibly deduct except from a class which obviously contains that which is to be deducted. But there is no harm in beginning with one or more negative terms, provided we set matters right before we have done by the insertion of the requisite terms from which they could have been deducted. It should be observed that in doing this we are only carrying out more boldly and consistently what common language has already recognized as convenient. Thus we might say that 'except hotel keepers, muleteers and such persons, the Swiss are an agreeable people' though in perfect strictness we could not 'except' from what had not been already laid down. Symbolic Logic does nothing more than carry out fully and consistently this right of regarding the order of our terms as indifferent in this respect. We may group them as we please, provided the aggregate is capable of falling into an intelligible arrangement. Thus $xy + xz + yz - 3xyz$ is really only another way of 'saying' in symbols, $(1-x)\,yz + (1-y)\,xz + (1-z)\,xy$; which is itself a way of saying, in words, 'whatever belongs to two and two only of the three classes x, y, and z'. This is therefore merely an extension of the right which even common language has found it expedient to claim in certain cases and to a partial extent.

The next simplification or generalization to which I will

call attention is less obvious, at least in some of its applications. The reader will remark that throughout our explanation of the symbolic forms xy and $\dfrac{x}{y}$ we have never said anything to imply that x and y must be merely single logical terms. We have spoken of them as representing logical classes; and our explanation, being a purely logical one, will therefore cover the case of x and y representing any kind of logical class. In the case of the 'multiplication' of terms, indeed, this is readily recognized, and we have had examples in point in the last chapter. All that remains therefore is to call attention to a few peculiar or limiting cases which result from such an admission.

When we combine classes which are composite in their character, that is, which are built up of a plurality of terms, we generally, whilst restricting the actual limits of the class, increase the number of terms by which it is expressed. Thus $(a + ab)(c + cd)$, or the class[1] common both to 'a and b' and to 'c and d', is assigned by the four elements $ac + acd + abc + abcd$. This class is presumably narrower than either $a + ab$ or $c + cd$, but it contains twice as many terms. Some times however such a process of combination will cause a number of elements to cancel one another and disappear, and so the resultant class may be simpler in symbolic expression as well as narrower in actual extent. Thus combine $(a + ac)$ with $(ace + ace)$ and we have merely $ace \cdot$ that is, in words, the class common to 'what is a, or neither a nor c' and to 'what is ac and not e, or ce and not a' is simply 'ac that is not e'.

It is quite possible that the two classes thus combined may contain no common part at all, in which case the process of multiplication results in zero. When classes are thus

---

[1] The abbreviation a for $(1 - a)$ will be ordinarily adopted in future.

mutually exclusive, indeed, this may be the simplest way of proving the fact. Thus, for instance, $(ace + ace)$ $(ace + ace)$ $= 0$, for there are no members common to both.

This simple extension of our right thus to combine classes is so familiar to students of symbolic Logic that it may be left to the natural course of example and discussion to afford the requisite illustration and explanation. But in the case of the inverse operation, $\dfrac{m}{y}$, it seems to have been strangely overlooked that exactly the same generalized use is ad missible. How important the saving is, as compared with current modes of working out problems, will only become apparent in a future chapter, but a few examples may be given here in illustration. Thus, in accordance with the general formula,

$$\frac{m}{y} = x + v \cdot \bar{x}y \quad (\text{with } x = xy)$$

we may deduce

$$\frac{a\bar{c} + \bar{a}c}{1 - c} = ac + ac + ve\,(1 - ac - ac).$$

The verbal description of this is that the most general ex pression of 'the class which, on restriction by taking only that part of it which is not e, shall just be reduced to a only or c only of the two a and c', is 'a or c only, together with "we know not what" of that which is e, but not a only or c only'.

Many other forms might be suggested, some of which will look very strange to those whose associations with fractional forms are confined to division and to representation of ratios. Thus the form $\dfrac{0}{1 - xy}$ — yields easily enough $0 + v \cdot xy$, or $v \cdot xy$. The explanation of this is simple enough, it being merely a roundabout way of stating the familiar Law of Contradiction. We are asked to assign the class such that its combination with $1 - xy$, or not-xy, shall give *nothing*.

The answer of course is that 'xy, or any part whatever of xy' will be thus exclusive of 'what is not xy', and this is therefore the most general assignment of the class in question.

The only caution to be kept in view here is that both the numerator and denominator of our fractional form shall be intelligible class expressions. We have no right, for instance, to put together such a form as $\dfrac{x \quad y}{w \quad z}$ unless we mean to imply that both y and z are parts of x. A formula will indeed be given in a future chapter which is competent to deal with such expressions as these, and to force an explanation out of them. But so long as we confine ourselves, as at present, to simple logical explanations, we must not try to make the expression work beyond the limits within which we can clearly accept and interpret it. So long as x and y are logical classes, but only so long, may we regard $\dfrac{\tilde{x}}{y}$ as equivalent to $x + v . xy$, and as implying also the condition $x - xy$. If, within these limits, we find the formula lead to falsity or absurdity, it can only be that we were asking a question which was in itself in some way false or absurd.

It may be pointed out here that, in Logic, any fraction and its reciprocal will be found to yield the same form. Thus $\dfrac{1}{y} = \dfrac{y}{w} = xy + v\,xy.$ Of course their *value* is not the same,— that is, in other words, their logical import,—for the conditions yielded respectively by them are different. In $\dfrac{\tilde{x}}{y}$ the condition is $xy = 0$, and in $\dfrac{x}{w}$ it is $xy = 0$; that is, the relations of x and y to each other are different according as one or other of these fractions is written down and an explanation called for it.

The only remaining generalization which we shall find it

convenient to introduce into Logic is the mathematical term *'function'*. There is nothing in this which should raise any alarm. We are doing absolutely nothing more than making use of a somewhat wider generalization of the same kind as those with which the ordinary logician is already familiar, and which form one of the main distinctions between his language and that of common life. We are accustomed to put an X or a Y to stand not for this or for that subject or predicate only, but for subjects and predicates generally; and so we put *Barbara* or AAA to stand for one particular form of argument whatever its matter may be. This does well enough for such simple terms and propositions as the common Logic mostly has to do with; but when we come to grapple with more complicated terms and propositions we shall find a need for some corresponding advance in our technical language. We want some kind of expression which shall stand for any class-group or class-equation, however complicated these may be, provided only they involve some given term as one of their constituent elements.

For instance:—'Every XY which is either A or B,' 'No AB which is not X, is Y':—here we have respectively a class-group and a class-equation, both of which involve the term X. They are of course already in what is called an abstract form, as compared with the concrete language of ordinary life; but inasmuch as they both involve the common element X, we may make a higher abstraction out of them in respect of this element. We do this in calling them both 'functions of X'. Writing them respectively, $xy\,(a + ab)$, $abxy - 0$, we may use the common form $f\,(x)$ to stand for them both. We can, of course, mark the fact that the latter is an equation by writing it $f\,(x) = 0$, and this it will generally be convenient to do.

Technical language is, it must be remembered, called for by technical uses. The reason why we want a common form for such various expressions is to be sought in the fact that we propose to subject them all alike to certain common operations. Ordinary Logic finds no occasion to do this, and therefore finds none to take note of that common element in them which gives ground to such operations, and which we indicate by the expression $f(x)$ or 'function of x'.

This necessity for the performance of common operations is of course the reason why we call such an expression a function of x rather than of anything else. It will commonly involve other terms besides x, and therefore be a function of them also. The sole reason why we single out one element and regard it as $f(x)$, is that x, and not one of the other terms, is the common element in virtue of which we propose to operate upon it and to which alone therefore we pay attention for the time being.

It may be added that, on the view adopted in this book, $f(x)$ never stands for anything but a logical class. It may be a compound class aggregated of many simple classes; it may be the class indicated by certain inverse logical operations; it may be composed of two groups of classes declared equal to one another, or (what is the same thing) their difference declared equal to zero, that is, a logical equation. But however composed or derived, $f(x)$ with us will never be anything else than a general expression for such logical classes of things as may fairly find a place in ordinary Logic.

CHAPTER IV.

ON THE CHOICE OF SYMBOLIC LANGUAGE.

In the last two chapters we have shown how the familiar symbols of mathematics may be used to express logical relations and processes. The ease and accuracy with which they do this will to many minds afford a complete justifica tion of their employment for this purpose, but as repeated and violent protests[1] have been raised in various quarters against introducing them into Logic, a short chapter of justi fication may conveniently be inserted here.

That a language of symbols of some kind or other is needed must I think be taken for granted. Such a language indeed is already admitted into the ordinary logic just as far as that science is supposed to need it: and, on the same ground, if more of it is wanted more of it must be called for. If we are to handle such classes, for instance, as that composed of "A which may be both B and C, but not one only of the two except when it is either D or E or both", what arguments can be urged for trying to work with this cumbrous verbal expression except such as would tell equally against con densing some verbose statement into the form 'All X is Y'? And as the reader knows by now, what we have to be

---

[1] *e.g.* Spalding's *Logic*, p. 50.   T. S. Baynes's *New Analytic*, p. 150.

prepared to do is to manipulate groups of terms such as that just offered. Of course if we had only proposed to go over the familiar ground again in new words, and were asking for a fresh array of symbols in which to exhibit Conversion, Opposition, the Syllogism, and so forth, such a demand might reasonably be protested against. It is indeed true that most of the earlier symbolists did not propose to do more than this, but considered that the transformations they effected would receive their crowning justification when they could show how we might go in detail through all the moods of the syllogism and exhibit them clothed in symbolic language. Probably many logicians still believe that nothing more than this has even yet been attempted, but it would really be a waste of time to stop to argue deliberately against such a misapprehension as this, after what has been said in the pre ceding chapters.

The question therefore is considerably narrowed. Our choice lies between taking the language of mathematics as far as this will serve our purpose, or inventing a new one, for there is certainly no existent rival to the former. That is, there is no complete system of symbolic language, devised for any other science, which would practically answer our purpose. (The notation of chemistry has, I presume, no advocates here.) It must be admitted that the choice here is not altogether without difficulty.

The prevalent objections to employing mathematical symbols rest mainly upon an entire misapprehension of their nature and existent range of interpretation. Something has been already said on this subject in the Introductory Chapter, so that a few words will suffice here. The objectors who protest against the introduction "of relations of number and quantity[1]" into logic, and who reject the employment of the

---

[1] Spalding's *Logic*, p. 50.

sign $(+)$ "unless there exists exact analogy between mathe matical addition and logical alternation[1]", cannot, it would appear, get rid of the notion that mathematics in general are of the nature of elementary arithmetic. We must again remind the reader of the wide range of interpretation which already exists within the domain of mathematics : how the sign $(+)$ starting with addition in ordinary arithmetic, has, in algebra, come to cover the case of subtraction ; and has continued to extend its range of application till in Quaternions, A and B indicating both the magnitude and the direction of two steps, $A + B$ will indicate the net result produced by taking successively first one and then the other of these steps. How again the sign $(\times)$ has similarly extended its interpretation; beginning with true multiplication of integers, it has embraced fractions and negative quantities within its rules, and has continued extending its signification till it too has become transformed in Quaternions. So that finally $A \times B$ may mean, not multiplication, but amongst other things a certain rotation of a line through an angle. Simi larly the sign $(=)$, when applied to vectors, denotes both equality of length, and parallelism of direction[2].

---

[1] Jevons's *Principles of Science,* p. 68.

[2] The mathematical reader is recommended to consult a paper by Mr Spottiswoode on "Some recent generalizations of Algebra" (*Proc. of London Math. Soc.* Vol. IV. p. 147). He there says:

"In the majority of systems proposed, the distributive and associative principles have been adopted [certain exceptions being mentioned even here] and starting from this basis a variety of laws of multiplica- tion might be laid down. The following apparently comprise the principal systems now in use:—

(1) The commutative principle might be adopted, so that

$\iota_1, \iota_2, \ldots$ being the units, $\iota_1 \iota_2 = \iota_2 \iota_1$; and the actual value of such a product might be the subject of any other arbitrary assumptions. Such an algebra might be called commutative.

(2) The commutative principle being suspended, the following relation might be adopted: $\iota_1 \iota_2 = -\iota_2 \iota_1$, expressive of what might be called

It is clear that these considerations decidedly blunt the edge of much of the objection in question. It is no longer a case of shifting a term or sign from one precise and rigid signification to another, but that of extending in a new direction the signification of signs which have already proved themselves able and willing to undergo a succession of very important extensions.

Another objection, and in some respects a more reason able one, against the practices of the symbolic logician, would be directed not at the *interpretation* he puts upon the symbols but at his meddling with their actual *laws of operation.* It may be urged that we do not use these mathematical signs consistently, that is, that we put special restrictions upon their laws of operation which are not admitted in mathe matics :—that, for instance, we maintain that x^2, as also every higher power of x, is the same as x itself, and that, as a con sequence of this, we cannot adopt the plan of striking out common factors from the numerator and denominator of a fraction. This is so : we do depart in these respects from the ordinary practice of the mathematician in most of his depart ments. But here again a little reflection upon what is already admitted somewhere or other in mathematics will weaken such an objection. Do we depart wider from the primary traditions of arithmetic than the Quaternionist does? It is a question if we can be said to depart so far, for at least we still adhere[1] to the 'commutative law' that $xy - yx$, whilst he finds it necessary to reject it and assigns a different interpretation to these two expressions. With him they are, generally speaking, not equivalent.

the alternative principle ". Two other possible cases are then mentioned.

In comparison with all this free handling the symbolic logician really shows the caution, and even timidity, which is becoming in an amateur.

[1] Wundt (*Logik*, p. 225) has been already mentioned as a solitary exception here. See Ch. III. p. 80.

There being therefore already so considerable a license in these respects admitted amongst mathematicians, there is not so much fear that the logician will unsettle the minds of men, or introduce misleading associations, if he decides to employ their symbolic language in the way which he thinks will suit him best. It is a mere balance of opposite advantages, there being something to be said for and against each side. It must be remembered that there are but very few signs which we find it convenient to borrow: in fact only the following:—four symbols for operations, viz. $+$, $-$, $\times$, $-$; the sign of equality viz. $(=)$ and two symbols for quantities, viz. 1 and 0:—these being for the most part just those oldest and most general symbols which have already undergone the widest transfer or generalization of interpretation. The abbreviated expression for *function,* viz. (f), need hardly be formally included in the list, since we can scarcely be con sidered to change or extend its signification.

The reason which makes me decide in favour of the plan of employing the symbols of mathematics is briefly this. The introduction of any new set of symbols is in itself a very serious evil. Symbolic language ought if possible to be used with mechanical facility, which presupposes a considerable amount of practice. Every one who has learnt a system of shorthand knows what a length of time elapsed before it ceased actually to frustrate its only object by causing rather than avoiding trouble. Now the *interpretation* of our symbols is only occasional whilst their *employment* is by comparison constant. Interpretation is demanded at the primary step of writing down our data, and at the final step of reading off the answer, but in all the path between the start and the finish we are not really obliged to think of interpreting our formulæ at all. · Accordingly when the alternative is before us of inventing new symbols, or only assigning some new meaning to old and familiar ones, experience and reason seem decisively in favour of the latter plan. Certainly the experience of the mathematicians appears to tell in this direction, which ought to count for much. When they have to denote a new conception or a new law of operation, of course they may want a new symbol for it. But when the law of operation is the same, or even partially the same, they continue to use the old symbol even though the signification may have undergone a very considerable change. To take then one of the simplest instances : which is easiest, to use the familiar sign ($+$) as we have always been accustomed to use it, bearing in mind, as we do so, that $x + y$ does not mean *addition* of x to y (an early prejudice which the mathematician has long laid aside), or to invent a new symbol ($\cdot\vdash$) where we have to learn anew both the laws of operation and the signification ?

Whilst then we shift the signification of the symbols we retain their laws of operation as far as possible unchanged. Indeed the only change we venture to make is of the nature of special limitation rather than of actual alteration. Thus to identify x^2 with x is admissible in certain cases even in mathematics, for instance when $x = 1$; and to forbid division by x is also admitted, in case $x = 0$. We can hardly be said therefore to transgress universally binding usage. As an illustration of what must be called the false use of such symbols a practice which has the sanction of several good names must be noticed, that, namely, of employing $+$ and $-$ to mark respectively affirmation and denial. The analogy on which this usage is founded is very slight, amounting indeed to little more than the fact that two denials (in the case of contradictions) result in re-affirmation, just as ($-$) twice repeated yields ($+$). But the commutative law is here rejected, for if $X + Y$ means that 'All X is Y'

we must clearly refuse to identify this with $Y + X$. Again if we express 'if S, then not P' by $(+ S - P)$, we might be tempted, following familiar usage, to regard this as equivalent to $(- P + S)$ which would be, of course, to fall into a familiar fallacy[1]. The fact is, as was abundantly illustrated in the preceding chapters, that the contrast between affirmation and negation, important as it is on a predicative view of logic, becomes quite superficial when we adopt a thoroughgoing class view. We have therefore no right here to use such a pair of symbols as $(+)$ and $(-)$ to indicate it.

Those who propose a new notation commonly, and not unnaturally, assume that it is to supersede all others. But those who approach it as strangers know that the odds are decidedly that it will only prove one more of those many attempts which perplex and annoy the lecturer, historian, and critic. Hence we may fairly use the argument, dear to

---

[1] As indicated above, the actual usage here is various. Maimon made $+$ and $-$ equivalent respectively to 'is' and 'is not', so that '$a + b$' meant 'a is b', and '$a - b$' meant 'a is not b'. As Darjes used them they might be best rendered by 'posit' and 'sublate', for he affixed them to each term. Thus $+ S - P$ meant 'posit S and we sublate P'. Drobisch's use is sounder, as he seems to confine them to mark propositions as wholes: thus $+ u, - u, + p, - p$, stand respectively for what are commonly indicated by A, E, I, O. But in all cases alike the usage seems to me faulty and misleading.

For downright grotesque perversion of mathematical terms some of the non-mathematical logicians are unequalled. Many readers must have been puzzled by Hamilton's symbolic equivalent for the Law of Contradiction. "This law is logically expressed in the formula,—what is contradictory is unthinkable. $A = \mathrm{not}$-$A = 0$, or $A - A = 0$" [*Logic*, I. 81:— Is this, by the way, an attempt at rendering a passage in Bachmann (*Logik*, p. 43), "Reine position und negation, setzen und aufheben, $(+ A - A)$, in einem Denkakte unmittelbar verbunden, vernichten sich, weil sie einander rein entgegengesetzt sind $(A - A = 0)$"?]. Mr Chase again (*First Logic Book*) making $+$ and $-$ do duty for affirmation and negation employs the negative particle as well, writing e.g., *Cesare*, thus:

No $Z - Y$,
All $X + Y$,
No $X - Z$.

those in authority, that if we loosen the sanctions of orthodoxy heresies will multiply. Only those whose professional employ ment compels them to study a number of different works have any idea of the bewildering variety of notation which is already before the world. A new notation is not like a new fact or theory from which, so to say, the passer-by may learn something. It is meant for habitual use, and thus practically aims at the exclusion of all rivals. No doubt it would be rank intolerance to forbid such new attempts, but an attitude of slight social repression towards them may serve to check too luxuriant a growth of new proposals[1].

There are two subordinate advantages in employing an already widely-used and familiar set of symbols. One of these is in their occasional *suggestiveness*. Take for instance that inverse process to class-restriction which was explained in the last chapter. It is not by any means an obvious process, and though perfectly intelligible in itself it is not at all likely that it would have suggested itself to the mind except by way of the symbols. We are very familiar with

[1] In order to gain some idea of what has been from time to time proposed in this way, the reader may turn to the final chapter of this volume where he will find a detailed account of over twenty distinct nota- tions for that simplest of all proposi- tions:—the Universal Negative.

The following illustrations may be given here. The same *meaning*,— the distinction between a term and its contradictory;—has been variously symbolized as follows:

A a (De Morgan, Jevons),
a a (Boole, R. Grassmann),
a a' (Delboeuf, Maccoll),
a $1 - a$ (Boole),

a a_1 (Shroder),
a $- a$ (Segner),
a na (Maass),

whilst the same *symbols*:—capital and small letters respectively :—have been made to do duty for the fol- lowing meanings :

The class A and its contradictory (De Morgan, Jevons),

The class A distributed and un- distributed (Ploucquet),

The concept and its extension (Maass, *Logik*, p. 100),

The determined and the determin- ing concepts (Wundt, *Logik*, p. 223),

Universal and particular proposi- tions (Gergonne).

the particular inverse process of Division in relation to Multiplication, and when we use the latter sign to denote class-restriction the enquiry seems forced upon us to deter mine what there is in Logic corresponding to the former. The moment we write down $xy = z$, we can hardly refrain from writing also $x - \dfrac{z}{y}$, and then the interpretation of the latter is forced upon us. Every mathematician knows what a fertile source of new theorems is the attempt to ascertain the analogues to such and such a familiar process in some other branch of analysis. Of course we must not permit such hints as these to be anything more than hints, for every logical rule must be established on its own proper grounds, but even hints may be of great value.

It may be remarked that the analogy just mentioned was seized from the first by logical symbolists; (as was shown, in the last chapter, in the case of Lambert and Holland). As they interpreted the step indeed, viz. as denoting Abstraction, the logical process was one which was already quite familiar, so that very likely the symbolic step was first suggested and justified by the logical. As *we* feel bound to interpret it, however, viz. in respect of extension or denotation, the case is very different. As just remarked, the step is not an easy one to grasp, and it is very doubtful if we should have been able to see our way to it without the help of the slight pressure in the right direction afforded by our wish to justify and explain a familiar symbolic procedure.

Again it seems really important to impress upon the mind of the student certain characteristics of symbolic language. The distinction between the mere laws of opera tion, and the interpretation of them, is apt to be overlooked, and this will very likely be still more the case if we insist upon introducing a new notation for one special class of interpretations.   We may thus lose our appreciation both of the generalized extent over which the same laws of operation can prevail, and the very various though connected signi fications which this extent of application will serve to cover.

Various other ways have been adopted in order to prevent any confusion between the special logical usage of symbols and the ordinary mathematical usage of the same, and yet not to lose sight of the common properties.   Thus Mr C. S. Peirce has proposed[1] to differentiate the logical use by the insertion of a distinguishing mark (a comma underneath). Instead of writing $a + a = a$, with Professor Jevons, in order to represent the fact that logical 'addition' does not double the number of the common members, he writes it $a + a = a$. This would be interpreted to mean that 'the (logical) ad dition, or aggregation, of a to a is (logically) equivalent to the class taken simply.'   So again, as a consequence, if we know that a and b are mutually exclusive we have the formula $a + b = a + b$; for in this case the results of the logical and the arithmetical additions correspond.

Or again, an entirely new set of symbols might be introduced, intended to be applied not to logic separately in contrast with mathematics, but made so general as designedly to cover both.   Among those who have actually offered something in this way, of a logical kind, may be noticed H. Grassmann.   He proposes the symbol $\frown$ to denote 'con nection' (verknüpfung) in general, and $\smile$ to denote its inverse, so that $a \smile b$ denotes the form which when joined by $\frown$ to b will yield a.   He does not indeed in his definition refer to anything outside the domain of mathematics, but his language seems intended to be perfectly general: "By a

---

[1] *(Proc. of American Acad. of Arts and Sc.* 1867.)

general science of symbols [Formenlehre] we understand
that body of truths which apply alike to every branch of
mathematics, and which presuppose only the universal con
cepts of similarity and difference, connection and disjunction"
(*Ausdehnungslehre*, p. 2). As a result of this generalized
use we shall have to notice, in another chapter, a curious
anticipation, in certain respects, of one detail in Boole's pro
cedure.

It is to this generalized symbolic language, such as we
are here employing it, that some writers have applied, by a
revival of an old word, the term *Algorithm*. Thus, for
example, Delbœuf entitles his work, written on the same
kind of subject as this, "Logique algorithmique." There is
no objection whatever to the word, but I have preferred
to speak of "Symbolic Logic" as being more familiar in our
language : 'symbolic' as I understand it, being almost exactly
the equivalent of 'algorithmic.'

There is also another old term which will be familiar to
readers of Leibnitz and Wolf,—characteristic,—which seems
to me to cover much the same ground as Algorithmic and
Symbolic : the word is thus defined by Wolf (*Psychologia
empirica*, § 294 *seq.*) "Ars characteristica appellatur ea quæ
explicat signorum, in rebus aut earundem perceptionibus
denotandis, usum. Ars hæc adhuc in desideratis est."......"In
Algebra istiusmodi signa habemus pro quantitatibus   sed
desiderantur talia in philosophia pro rerum qualitatibus."...
"Ars illa quæ docet signa ad inveniendum utilia et modum
**eadem combinandi eorumdemque combinationem certa lege
variandi, dicitur Ars characteristica combinatoria. Vocatur**
a Leibnitzio etiam speciosa generalis."......"Si quis mente
perpendit qualis numerorum in Arithmetica, magnitudinum
in Algebra, syllogismorum in Logica, notio præsupposita
fuerit antequam characteristica ad numeros magnitudines et

syllogismos applicari potuerit, et quamdiu in Arithmetica atque Algebra commodi desiderati fuerunt characteres; is difficultatem artis characteristicæ combinatoriæ generalis haud difficulter æstimabit."

These extracts seem to indicate a tolerably clear appreciation of the end to be aimed at in constructing a generalized symbolic logic but the discussions on this subject are much mixed up with the wider question of a general philosophical language. As the reader very likely knows, this problem was keenly discussed in the seventeenth and eighteenth centuries and occupied the attention of Leibnitz more or less throughout his life. Speaking from a very slight acquaintance[1], I should say that what was mostly contemplated by the writers in question was more what we should now call either a universal language, or a general system of shorthand, than a logic. I mean that they do not attempt any analysis of the reasoning processes; and that the words or symbols proposed by them do not stand perfectly generally for any classes whatever, like our x and y, but specially for such and such well-known classes as are already designated by general names; they differ, in fact, as language does and should differ from logic.

[1] I refer here to such works as the *Ars magna sciendi* of Athan. Kircher (1631)'; Bp. Wilkins's often mentioned *Essay towards a real character and a philosophical language* (1668) and Dalgarno's *Ars signorum* (1661). A discussion of Leibnitz's speculations and attempts in this direction will be found in Trendelenburg's *Historische Beitrage*, III. 1—48. Lambert, who took much interest in this subject, has discussed many of the special sets of symbols appropriate to particular arts and sciences. Of course the growth of international telegraphy, and other causes, have greatly varied the relative importance of the schemes known to him. (*Neues Organon. Semiotik.* §1. Von der symbolischen Kenntniss ueberhaupt.)

CHAPTER V.

DIAGRAMMATIC REPRESENTATION.

THE majority of modern logical treatises make at any rate occasional appeal to diagrammatic aid, in order to give sensible illustration of the relations of terms and pro positions to one another. With one such scheme, namely that which is commonly known as the Eulerian, every logical reader will have made some acquaintance, since a decided majority of the familiar treatises make more or less frequent use of it[1]. Such a prevalent use as this clearly makes it desirable to understand what exactly this particular scheme undertakes to do and whether or not it performs its work satisfactorily.

As regards the inapplicability of this scheme for the purposes of a really general Logic something was said by implication in the first chapter, for it was there pointed

---

[1] Until I came to look somewhat closely into the matter I had no idea how prevalent such an appeal as this had become. Thus of the first sixty logical treatises, published during the last century or so, which were con-sulted for this purpose:—somewhat at random, as they happened to be most accessible :—it appeared that thirty-four appealed to the aid of diagrams, nearly all of these making use of the Eulerian Scheme.

out how very special and remote from common usage is the system of propositions for which alone it is an adequate representation. To my thinking it fits in but badly even with the four propositions of the common Logic to which it is usually applied, but to see how very ineffective it is to meet the requirements of a generalized or symbolic Logic it will be well to spend a few minutes in calling the reader's attention to what these requirements are.

At the basis of our Symbolic Logic, however represented, whether by words by letters or by diagrams, we shall always find the same state of things. What we ultimately have to do is to break up the entire field into a definite number of classes or compartments which are mutually exclusive and collectively exhaustive. The nature of this process of sub division will have to be more fully explained in a future chapter, so that it will suffice to remark here that nothing more is demanded than a generalization of a very familiar logical process, viz. that of dichotomy. But its results are simple and intelligible enough. With two classes, X and Y, we have four subdivisions; the X that is Y, the X that is not Y, the Y that is not X, and that which is neither X nor Y. And so with any larger number of classes. How then are these ultimate class divisions to be described?

For one thing, we can of course always represent the products of such a subdivision in the language of common Logic, or even in that of common life, if we choose to do so. They do not readily offer themselves for this purpose, but when pressed will consent, though failing sadly in the desired symmetry and compactness. The relative cumbrousness of such a mode of expression is obviously the real measure of our need for a reformed or symbolic language. We must not however forget that we are not dealing with mathematical conceptions which common language will hardly avail to

describe, but only with logical classes which can be com
pletely and unambiguously determined by the traditional
modes of speech. However complicated the description of
any given class may be we could always build it up by means
of X and not-X, Y and not-Y, and so forth; whether X and
Y remain as letters, or be replaced by concrete terms such as
substantives and adjectives.

But it need not be insisted on that we require something
far more manageable and concise than this, if we wish to deal
effectively with really complicated groups of propositions.
For this purpose nothing better can be employed than
letters such as we use in algebra. This is done of course to
some extent in ordinary Logic, the only innovation upon
which we have to insist being that of introducing equally
concise symbols for negative terms. We could never work
with not-x, in that form, and must therefore look about for
some substitute. The full significant substitute is, as already
shown, $1 - x$, and this will often have to be employed. But
this is too cumbrous for actual calculation. Of the various
substitutes that have been proposed for not-x we shall make
a practice of employing x.

The reader will see at once how conveniently and briefly
we can thus indicate any desired combination of class terms,
and, by consequence, any desired proposition. Thus xyz
represents what is x, y, and z; xyz what is x, but neither
y nor z; $xw(yz + yz)$ stands for 'what is not x, but is w; and
is also either y but not z, or z but not y', and so forth. The
significance of such expressions, when built up into proposi
tions, will be fully discussed in a future chapter.

That such a scheme is complete there can be no doubt.
But unfortunately, owing to this very completeness, it is apt
to prove terribly lengthy. The powers of 2 soon mount up;
so that a pair of terms will yield 2^2 combinations, three will

yield 2^3, or 8, and so on; the total number doubling every time. Of course in any particular proposition or problem we shall most likely not require to make appeal to more than some of these constituents, perhaps only to a few of them. But the existence of all has to be recognized, and a notation provided for every one of them. Moreover it is always possible that a problem may be so stated as to demand an explicit reference to a great number, or even to all. Suppose for instance a proposition were given involving five terms, and we were told to enumerate all the ultimate combinations denied by it, we should have a certain number of class terms on our hands; and if to this were added the enumeration of all the combinations which were not denied, we should have all the rest of the total of thirty-two before us.

This then is the state of thing which a reformed scheme of diagrammatic notation has to meet. It must correspond in all essential respects to that regular system of class sub division which has just been referred to under its verbal and its literal or symbolic aspects. Theoretically, as we shall see, this is perfectly attainable. Indeed up to four or five terms inclusive it works very successfully in practice; where it begins to fail is in the accidental circumstance that its further development soon becomes intricate and awkward, though never ceasing to be feasible.

I. On the proposed scheme we have to make a broad distinction, not recognized on the common scheme, between the representation of terms and the representation of proposi tions. We begin with the former. What we propose to do is to form a framework of figures which shall correspond to the table of combinations of x, y, z, &c. All that is necessary for this purpose is to describe a series of closed figures, of any kind, so that each successive one shall in tersect all the compartments already produced, and thus

double their number. That this is what is done with the
letter symbols is readily seen. Thus with two terms, x and
y, we have four combinations; $xy, \bar{x}y, x\bar{y}, \bar{x}\bar{y}$. Introduce the
term z, and we at once split up each of these four into its z
and its not-z parts, and so double their number. Provided
our diagrams are so contrived as to indicate this, they will
precisely correspond, in every relevant respect, to the table of
combinations of letters.

The leading conception of such a scheme is simple
enough, but it demands some consideration in order to
decide upon the most effective and symmetrical plan of
carrying it out in detail[1]. Up to three terms inclusive,
indeed, there is but little opening for any variety; but as
the departure from the familiar Eulerian conception has to
be made from the very first, it will be well to examine the
simplest cases with some care. Our primary diagram for two
terms is thus sketched :—

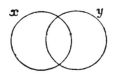

On the common plan this would represent a *proposition*,
and is indeed commonly regarded as standing for the proposi
tion 'some x is y'; though (as was mentioned in the first
chapter) it equally involves in addition the two independent

[1] A brief historic sketch is given in
the concluding chapter of some previous attempts, before and after Euler,
to carry out the geometric notation
of propositions. I tried at first, as
others have done, to illustrate the
generalized processes of the Symbolic
Logic by aid of the familiar methods,
but soon found that these were quite
unsuitable for the purpose. Though
the method here described may be
said to be founded on Boole's system
of Logic I may remark that it is not
in any way directly derived from him.
He does not make employment of
diagrams himself, nor does he give
any suggestions for their introduction.

propositions 'some x is not y', and 'some y is not x', if we want to say all that it has to tell us. With us however it does not as yet represent a proposition at all, but only the framework into which propositions may be fitted; that is, it indicates only the four combinations represented by the letter compounds, xy, $x\bar{y}$, $\bar{x}y$, $\bar{x}\bar{y}$.

Now suppose that we have to reckon with the presence, and consequently with the absence, of a term z. We just draw a third circle intersecting the above two, thus :—

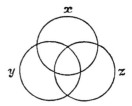

Each circle is thus cut up into four parts, and each common part of two circles into two parts, so that, including what lies outside them all three, there are eight compartments. These of course correspond precisely to the eight combinations given by the three literal symbols; viz. xyz, $x\bar{y}z$, $x\bar{y}z$, xyz, $\bar{x}yz$, $\bar{x}yz$, $\bar{x}yz$, $\bar{x}\bar{y}z$. Put a finger upon any compartment, and we have a symbolic name ready provided for it; mention the name, and there can be no doubt as to the compartment thereby referred to.

Both schemes, that of letters and that of spaces, agree in their elements being mutually exclusive and collectively exhaustive. No one of the ultimate elements trespasses upon the ground of any other; and, amongst them, they account for all possibilities. Either therefore might be taken as a fair representative of the other.

This process is capable of theoretic extension to any number of terms. The only drawback to its indefinite extension is that with more than three terms it is not possible to use such simple figures as circles, for four circles cannot be so drawn as to intersect one another in the way required. With employment of more intricate figures we might go on for ever. All that is requisite is to draw some continuous figure which shall intersect once, and once only, every existing subdivision. The new outline thus drawn is to cut every one of the previous compartments in two, and so just double their number. There is clearly no reason against continuing this process indefinitely.

With four terms in request the most simple and symmetrical diagram seems to me that produced by making four ellipses intersect one another in the desired manner;—

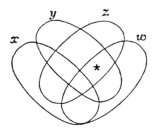

It is obvious that each component class-figure (say y) is thus divided into eight distinct compartments, producing in all 16 partitions; that these partitions are all different from one another in their composition, and so mutually exclusive; and moreover that they leave nothing unaccounted for, and are therefore collectively exhaustive. And this is all that is required to make them a fitting counterpart of the 16 combinations yielded by x, y, z, w, and their negations, in the ordinary tabular statement.

With five terms combined together ellipses fail us, at least in the above simple form. It would not be difficult to sketch out figures of a horse-shoe shape which should answer the purpose, but then any outline which is not very simple and easy to follow fails altogether in its main requirement of being an aid to the eye. What is required is that we should be able to identify any assigned compartment in a moment. Thus it is instantly seen that the compartment marked with an asterisk above is that called *xyzw*. The simplest diagram I can suggest for five terms is one like this, (the small ellipse in the centre is to be regarded as a portion of the *outside* of *z*; i.e. its four component portions are inside *y* and *w* but are no part of *z*).

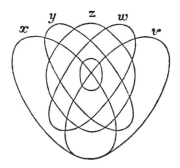

It must be admitted that such a diagram is not quite so simple to draw as one might wish it to be; but then consider what the alternative is if one undertakes to deal with five terms and all their combinations;—nothing short of the disagreeable task of writing out, or in some way putting before us, all the 32 combinations involved. As compared with *that* the actual drawing of such a figure as this is surely an amusement, besides being far more expeditious; for with a little practice any of the diagrams we have thus offered might be sketched in but a minute fraction of the time required to write down all the letter-compounds. I can only say for myself that having worked hundreds of examples, I generally resort to diagrams of this description, in order to save time, to avoid unpleasant drudgery, and to make sure against mistake and oversight. The way in which this last advantage is secured will be better seen presently, when we see how these diagrams are to be used in the representa tion of propositions as distinguished from that of mere terms or classes.

Beyond five terms it hardly seems as if diagrams offered much substantial help, but then really what occasion have we often to trouble ourselves with problems which would intro duce any more than that[1]? Although however diagrammatic illustration fails to keep pace with true symbols, or letters, in respect of symmetry and simplicity, we must remember that they are really in strict correspondence with one another. No combination of class terms could be invented or expressed either in symbols, or in common language, which could not be made sensible to the eye by a suitable diagrammatic construction.

We have endeavoured above to employ only symmetrical figures, such as should not only be an aid to reasoning, through the sense of sight, but should also be to some extent elegant in themselves. But for merely theoretic purposes the rule of formation would be very simple. We should merely have to begin by drawing any closed figure, and then proceed to draw others subject to the one condition that each is to intersect once, and once only, all the existing subdivisions produced by those which had gone before. There is no need here to exhibit such figures, as they would probably be distasteful to any but the mathematician, and he would see his way to drawing them readily enough for him self[2].

---

[1] If we wanted to use a diagram for *six* terms (x, y, z, w, v, u,) the best plan would probably be to take *two* five-term figures, one for the u part and the other for the not-u part of all the other combinations. This would give the desired 64 subdivi- sions. Of course this loses the advantage, to some extent, of the *coup d'œil* afforded by a single figure.

[2] It will be found that when we adhere to continuous figures, instead of the discontinuous five-term figure

A number of deductions will occur to the logical reader which it may be left to him to work out in detail. Some of them may be briefly indicated. For instance, any two compartments between which we can communicate by crossing only one line, can differ by the affirmation and denial of one term only, e.g. $xyzw$ and $xy\bar{z}w$. Accordingly, when two such come to be compounded, or as we may say, 'added' together, they may be simplified by the omission of such term; for the two together make up all xyw. Any compartments between which we can only communicate by crossing two boundaries, e.g. $xyzw$ and $x\bar{y}z\bar{w}$, must differ in two respects: it would need *four* such compartments to admit of simplification, the simplification then resulting in the opportunity of dropping the reference to *two* terms. For instance, $xyzw$, $x\bar{y}zw$, $xyz\bar{w}$, $x\bar{y}z\bar{w}$, taken together, amount simply to xw. In talking thus of crossing boundaries it must be remembered that to cross the same one twice is equivalent to not doing so at all, so that to do so three times is the same as doing so only once; it merely puts us outside if we were inside before.

II. So far then this diagrammatic scheme has only been shown to represent classes or terms, we have now to see how it can be worked so as to represent propositions. The best way of introducing this question will be to enquire a little

given above, there is a tendency for the resultant outlines thus successively drawn to assume a comb-like shape after the first four or five. If we begin by circles or other rounded figures the teeth are curved, if by parallelograms then they are straight. Thus the fifth-term figure will have two teeth, the sixth four, and so on, till the $(4+x)^{th}$ has 2^x teeth. There is no trouble in drawing such a diagram for any number of terms which our paper will find room for. But, as has already been repeatedly remarked, the visual aid for which mainly such diagrams exist is soon lost on such a path. But it must be remembered that their theoretic perfection, as regards the exclusiveness and exhaustiveness of the component portions, is unaffected by their intricacy.

more strictly whether it is really *classes* that we thus repre
sent, or merely *compartments* into which classes may be put ?
The question is by no means an idle one, though its full signi
ficance will not be apparent until we have discussed the nature
of Hypotheticals and the import of propositions generally.

The only accurate answer is that our diagrammatic sub
divisions, or for that matter our symbols generally, stand for
compartments and not for classes. We may doubtless regard
them as representing the latter, but if we do so we should
never fail to keep in mind the proviso, "if there be such
things in existence." And when this condition is insisted
upon, it seems as if we expressed our meaning best by saying
that what our symbols stand for are compartments which may
or may not happen to be occupied.

The reason for insisting upon this distinction is to be
found in the absolute impossibility of ascertaining, until we
have fully analysed our premises, whether or not any particu
lar combination is possible. We must be prepared to make
provision for any number of terms, and it is impossible to
foresee whether the existence of such and such a class is
compatible with the data. We have a notation for each ; its
place is ready for it; but will it be found there or will the
place be empty ? Common Logic, dealing as it does with
seldom more than two or three terms at a time, can evade
the consequent difficulty, or can make tacit suppositions
which will help to solve it in most cases. But with us the
possible contingencies are far too numerous to be foreseen
and provided against.

Take, for instance, the following group of premises, which
are by no means of a very complicated nature :—

> All x is either both y and z, or not y,
> All xy that is z is also w,
> No wx is yz.

It would not be easy to detect, from mere inspection of these data, that though they admit the possible existence of such classes as xz and yz, they deny that of the class xy. But since, as they stand, xy is the subject of one of them, we could not consistently admit such a conclusion unless we re strict the force of that premise to what it *denies;* i.e., unless we confine ourselves to saying that it just destroys the class $xyzw$, or 'x that is y and z but not w', and does nothing else. We find in fact that to consider ourselves bound to *maintain* the existence of all the subjects and predicates, instead of merely *denying* the existence of the various combinations *destroyed*, would sadly hamper us in the manipulation of complicated groups of propositions[1].

It would of course be pedantically at variance with ordinary usage to insist upon never speaking of anything but compartments. I shall therefore freely use such expres sions as 'the class $xyzw$', and so forth. But when we thus speak in the course of our analysis it must always be under stood that we do so without prejudice for or against the existence of such a class. The compartment necessarily exists, because it is purely formal, but it must be left to the data to decide whether or not it is occupied. However we like to phrase it, this distinction between an ideally perfect scheme of notation or classification, which will meet every requirement, and its limitation by one possible class after another being proved incompatible with our data, must always exist. A complete enumeration of compartments is one thing, but it is quite another to be able to prove that there is a class of things to put into any one of them.

---

[1] The grounds for thus inter- preting the import of a proposition will be fully discussed in the course of the next chapter, and rules will be offered, dependent upon this analysis, for reading off any given proposition into its constituent denials.

Our diagrams very readily lend themselves to mark this distinction, and the plan of doing so is nothing but the representation of propositions. The full justification of the particular method here adopted must be reserved for the next chapter, but the present will be the best connection for giving a general description and illustration of it. What we do then, is to ascertain what classes are negatived by any given proposition, and proceed to put some kind of mark against them in the diagram. For this purpose the most effective means is just to shade them out. For instance the proposition 'all x is y' is interpreted to mean that there is no such class of things in existence as 'x that is not-y', or xy. All that we have to do is to scratch out that subdivision in the two-circle figure[1], thus :—

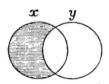

If we want to represent 'all x is all y', we take this as adding on another denial, viz., that of xy, and proceed to scratch out that division also; thus

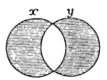

On the common plan we should have to begin again with a new figure in each case respectively, viz., for 'all x is y' and 'all y is x'; whereas here we start with the same general

---

[1] Other logicians (*e.g.* Schroder, *Operationskreis*, p. 10; Macfarlane, *Algebra of Logic*, p. 63) have made use of shaded diagrams, but simply to direct attention to the compartments under consideration, and not, as here, with the view of expressing propositions.

outline in each case, merely modifying it in accordance with the varying information given to us.

We postulate at present that every universal proposition may be *adequately* represented by one or more denials, and shall hope to justify this view in its due place. But it will hardly be disputed that every such proposition does in fact negative one or more combinations, and this affords an ex cellent means of combining two or more propositions together so as to picture their collective import. The first proposition empties out a certain number of compartments. In so far as the next may have been tautologous it finds its work already done for it, but in so far as it has fresh information to give it succeeds in clearing out compartments which the first had left untouched. All that is necessary therefore to a complete diagrammatic illustration is to begin by drawing our figure, as already explained, and then to shade out, or in some way distinguish, the classes which have been successively abolished. This will set before the eye, at a glance, the whole import of the propositions collectively.

How widely different this plan is from that of the old-fashioned Eulerian diagrams will be readily seen. One great advantage consists in the ready way in which it lends itself to the representation of successive increments of knowledge as one proposition after another is taken into account, instead of demanding that we should endeavour to represent the net result of them all at a stroke. Our first data abolish, say, such and such classes. This is final, for, as already intimated, all the resultant denials must be regarded as absolute and unconditional. This leaves the field open to any similar accession of knowledge from the next data, and so more classes are swept away. Thus we go on till all the data have had their fire, and the muster-roll at the end will show what classes are, or may be, left surviving. If therefore we simply

V. I.   ᴏ

shade out the compartments in our figure which have thus
been successively declared empty, nothing is easier than to
go on doing this till all the information furnished by the data
is exhausted.

As another very simple illustration of the contrast between
the two methods, consider the case of the disjunction, 'All *x*
is either *y* or *z*'.   It is very seldom even attempted to represent such propositions diagrammatically, (and then, so far as
I have seen, only if the alternatives are mutually exclusive),
but they are readily enough exhibited when we regard the
one in question as merely extinguishing any *x* that is neither
y nor *z*, thus :—

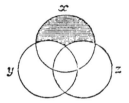

If to this were added the statement that 'none but the
x's are either *y* or *z*' we should meet the statement by the
abolition of *xy* and *xz*, and thus obtain :—

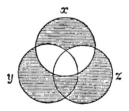

And if, again, we erase the central, or *xyz* compartment,
we have then made our alternatives exclusive ; i.e., the *x*, and
it alone, is either *y* or *z* only.

Now if we tried to do this by aid of Eulerian circles we
should find at once that we could not do it in the only way
in which intricate matters can generally be settled. viz., by

taking them step by step, making sure of each as we go on.
These familiar figures have to be drawn so as to indicate at
once the final outcome of the knowledge furnished. This
offers no difficulty in such exceedingly simple cases as those
furnished by the various moods of the Syllogism, but it is
quite a different matter to handle the complicated results
which follow upon the combination of four or five terms.
Those who have only looked at the simple diagrams given by
Hamilton, Thomson, and other logicians, in illustration of the
Aristotelian Syllogism, will have very little conception of the
intricate task which would be imposed upon them if they
tried thus to illustrate equations of the type that we must be
prepared to encounter.

As the syllogistic figures are the form of reasoning most
familiar to ordinary readers, I will begin with one of them,
though they are too simple to serve as effective examples.
Take, for instance,

No Y is Z,

All X is Y,

$\therefore$ No X is Z.

This would commonly be exhibited thus:

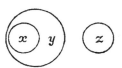

It is easy enough to do this; for in drawing our circles we
have only to attend to two terms at a time, and consequently
the relation of X to Z is readily detected; there is not any of
that troublesome interconnexion of a number of terms simul
taneously with one another which gives rise to the main per
plexity in complicated problems. Accordingly such a simple
example as this is not a very good one for illustrating the

method now proposed; but, in order to mark the distinction, the figure to represent it is given, thus:

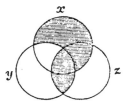

In this case the one particular relation asked for, viz. that of X to Z, it must be admitted, is not made more obvious on our plan than on the old one. The superiority, if any, in such an example must rather be sought in the completeness of the pictorial information in other respects—as, for instance, that, of the four kinds of x which may have to be taken into con sideration, one only, viz. the xyz, or the 'x that is y but is not z', is left surviving. Similarly with the possibilities of y and z: the relative number of these, as compared with the actualities permitted by the data, is detected at a glance.

As a more suitable example consider the following—

> All x is either y and z, or not y,
> If any xy is z, then it is w,
> No wx is yz;

and suppose we are asked to exhibit the relation of x and y to one another as regards their inclusion and exclusion. The problem is essentially of the same kind as the syllogistic one; but we certainly could not draw the figures in the same off hand way we did there. Since there are four terms, we sketch the appropriate 4-ellipse figure, and then proceed to analyse the premises in order to see what classes are destroyed by them. The reader will readily see that the first premise annihilates all 'xy which is not z', or xyz; the second de stroys 'xyz which is not w', or $xyzw$; and the third 'wx

which is yz', or $wxyz$. Shade out these three classes, and we see the resultant figure at once, viz.

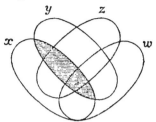

It is then evident that *all xy* has been thus made away with; that is, x and y must be mutually exclusive, or, as it would commonly be thrown into propositional form, ' No x is y.'

I will not say that it would be impossible to draw Eulerian circles to represent all this, just as we draw them to represent the various moods of the syllogism ; but it would certainly be an extremely intricate and perplexing task to do so. This is mainly owing to the fact already alluded to, viz. that we can not break the process up conveniently into a series of easy steps each of which shall be complete and accurate as far as it goes. But it should be understood that the failure of the older method is simply due to its attempted application to a somewhat more complicated set of data than those for which it was designed. But these data are really of the same kind as when we take the two propositions 'All x is y', 'All y is z', and draw the customary figure. *When* the problem, how ever, *has been otherwise solved*, it is easy enough to draw a figure of the old-fashioned, or "inclusion-and-exclusion" kind, to represent the result, as follows,

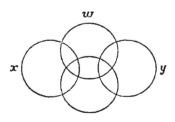

but one may safely assert that not many persons would have seen their way to drawing it at first hand for themselves[1].

One main source of aid which diagrams can afford is worth noticing here. It is that sort of visual aid which is their especial function. Take the following problem :—' Every x is either y or z ; every y is either z or w ; every z is either w or x ; and every w is either x or y : what further condition, if any, is needed in order to ensure that every xy shall be w?' It is readily seen that the first statement abolishes any x that is neither y nor z, and similarly with the others ; so that the four abolished classes are xyz, yzw, zwx, and wxy. Shade them out in our diagram, and it stands thus :—

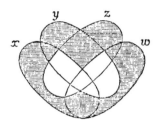

It is then obvious that, of the surviving component parts of xy, one only (viz. $xyzw$) is not w. If, then, this be destroyed,

---

[1] Even then we have said more in this figure than we are entitled to say. For instance, we have implied that there *is* some x which is w, and so forth. The other scheme does not thus commit us; for though the extinction of a class is final, its being let alone merely spares it conditionally. It holds its life subject to the sentence, it may be, of more premises to come. This must be noticed, as it is an important distinction between the customary plan and the one here proposed. The latter makes the distinction between rejection and non-rejection — such non-rejection being provisional, and not necessarily indicating ultimate acceptance. The former has to make the distinction between rejection and acceptance; for the circles must either intersect or not, and their non-intersection indicates the definite abandonment of the class common to both. Hence the practical impossibility of appealing to such diagrams for aid in representing complicated groups of propositions.

all xy will be *w* ; that is, the necessary and sufficient condition is that 'all *xyz* is *w*.'

In the same way the implied total abolition of any one *A* class is thus made extremely obvious. Take, for example, the following premises, and let us ask quite generally for any obvious conclusion which follows from them :—

(Every *y* is either *x* and not *z*, or *z* and not *x* ;

{ Every *wy* is either both *x* and *z*, or neither of the two ;

(All *xy* is either *w* or *z*, and all *yz* is either *x* or *w*.

It will be seen on reflection that these statements involve re spectively the abolition of the following classes, viz :— (1) of *yxz, y.xz* ; (2) of *wy.xz* and *wy.xz* ; (3) of *xywz* and *yz.xw*. Shade out the corresponding compartments in the diagram, and it presents the following appearance—

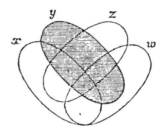

It is then clear at a glance that the collective effect of the given premises is just to deny that there can be any such class of things as *y* in existence, though they leave every one of the remaining eight combinations perfectly admissible. This, then, is the diagrammatic answer to the proposed question.

It will be easily seen that such methods as those here described readily lend themselves to mechanical performance. I have no high estimate myself of the interest or importance of what are sometimes called logical machines, and this on two grounds. In the first place, it is very seldom that intricate logical calculations are practically forced upon us ; it is rather we who look about for complicated examples in order to illustrate our rules and methods. In this respect logical calculations stand in marked constrast with those of mathematics, where economical devices of any kind may sub serve a really valuable purpose by enabling us to avoid other wise inevitable labour. Moreover, in the second place, it does not seem to me that any contrivances at present known or likely to be discovered really deserve the name of logical machines. It is but a very small part of the entire process, which goes to form a piece of reasoning, which they are capable of performing. For, if we begin from the beginning, that process would involve four tolerably distinct steps. There is, first, the statement of our data in accurate logical language. This step deserves to be reckoned, since the variations of popular language are so multitudinous, and often so vague and ambiguous, that they may need careful con sideration before they can be reduced to form. Then, secondly, we have to throw these statements into a form fit for the engine to work with—in this case the reduction of each proposition to its elementary denials. It would task the energies of a machine to deal at once, say, with any of the premises employed even in the few examples here offered. Thirdly, there is the combination or further treatment of our premises after such reduction. Finally, the results have to be interpreted or read off. This last generally gives rise to much opening for skill and sagacity; for though in such examples as the last (in which one class, y, was simply abolished) there is but one answer fairly before us, yet in most cases there are many ways of reading off the answer. It then becomes a question of judgment which of these is the simplest and best. For instance, in the last example but one, there are a quantity of alternative ways of reading off our conclusion; and until this is done the problem cannot be said to be solved. I cannot see that any machine can hope to help us except in the third of these steps; so that it seems very doubtful whether any thing of this sort really deserves the name of a logical engine.

It may also be remarked that when we make appeal, as here, to the aid of diagrams, the additional help to be obtained by resort to any kind of mechanical contrivance is very slight indeed. So very little trouble is required to sketch out a fresh diagram for ourselves on each occasion, that it is really not worth while to get a machine to do any part of the work for us. Still as some persons have felt much interest in such attempts, it seemed worth while seeing how the thing could be effected here. There is the more reason for this, since the exact kind of aid afforded by mechanical appliances in reasoning, and the very limited range of such aid, do not seem to be generally appreciated.

For myself, if I wanted any help in constructing or employing a diagram, I should just have one of the three-, four-, or five-term figures made into a stamp; this would save a few seconds sometimes in drawing them; and we could then proceed to shade out or otherwise mark the requisite compartments. More help than this would be of very little avail. However, since this is not exactly what people understand by a logical machine, I have made two others, in order to give practical proof of feasibility.

For instance, a plan somewhat analogous, I apprehend, to Prof. Jevons's *abacus* would be the following:—Have the desired diagram (say the five-term figure with its thirty-two compartments) drawn on paper and then pasted on to thin board. Cut out all the subdivisions by following the lines of the different figures, after the fashion of the children's maps which are put together in pieces. The corresponding step to shading out any compartment would then be the simple removal of the piece in question. We begin with all the pieces arranged together, and then pick out and remove those which represent the non-existent classes. When every one of the given premises has thus had its turn, the pieces left behind will indicate all the remaining combinations of terms which are consistent with the data. I have sometimes found it convenient, where the saving of a little time was an object, to use a contrivance of this kind. There is no reason to give a drawing of it, since any one of the figures we have hitherto employed may really be regarded as such a drawing.

Again, corresponding to Prof. Jevons's logical machine, the following contrivance may be described. I prefer to call it merely a logical-diagram machine for the reasons already given; but I suppose that it would do very completely all that can be rationally expected of any logical machine. Cer tainly, as regards portability, nothing has been proposed to equal it, so far as I know; for though needlessly large as made by me, it is only between five and six inches square and three inches deep. It is intended to work for four terms; and the following figures will serve to show its construction :—

I.   II.

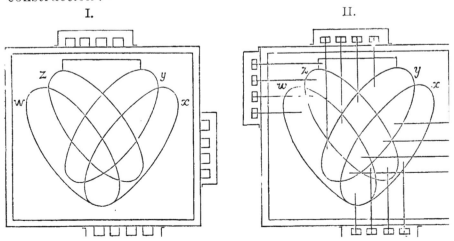

The first figure represents the upper surface of the instru ment. It shows the diagram of four ellipses, the small irregular compartment at the top of them being a re presentative part of the outside of all the four class-figures; that is, this compartment stands for what is neither x, y, z, nor w, or $xyzw$. The second figure represents a hori zontal section through the middle of the instrument. Each of the ellipses here is, in fact, a section of an elliptical cylinder, these cylinders intersecting one another so as to yield sixteen compartments. Each compartment has a wooden plug half its height, which can move freely up and down in the compartment. When the machine is ready for use each plug stands flush with the surface, being retained there by a pin; we therefore have the appearance presented in fig. 1. When we wish to represent the destruction of any class, all we have to do is slightly to draw out the appropriate pin (the pins of course are duly labelled, and will be found to be conveniently grouped), on which the plug in question drops to the bottom. This, of course, is equivalent to the shading of a subdivision in the plane diagram. As the plugs have to drop independently of one another, a certain number of them, it will be seen, have to have a slot cut in them, so as to play free from the pins belonging to other plugs. When the plugs have to be returned to their places at the top, all we have to do is to turn the instrument upside down, when they instantly fall back, and on pressing in the pins again they are retained in their place. The guards outside the pins are merely to prevent them from being drawn entirely out.

The above seems all that is necessary to say about the nature and employment of logical diagrams. Their use under any circumstances has been objected against by some purists, but not on grounds with which readers of such a work as this are likely to sympathize. Thus Dr Mansel declares against them altogether (*Prolegomena*, p. 55,) on the ground that they are an attempt to visualize those concepts which while they remain such must be necessarily incognizable by any faculty of sense, and solely accessible to the understanding. Those who adhere to the material view of Logic will of course be but little influenced by such an objection. What we are concerned with is classes of objects, actual or possible, and these may very fairly be represented by circles or other closed figures. Such figures must necessarily include or exclude any part of the extension, just as the class must, and by shading or otherwise marking the figure we can duly indicate whether or not such a class must be pronounced actually non-existent. And this is all that can possibly be expected of any such figure.

That letters are the truly appropriate instruments of calculation must of course be maintained. They alone can be strictly called symbols, and we must be capable of carrying out every process by means of them. But I shall make constant appeal to diagrams also ; both for purposes of mere illustration, and occasionally because they will really afford much briefer modes of proof. We shall use them in fact much in the same way as 'geometrical proofs' are so frequently employed in physical investigations. The ob jection to them is not that they are in any way inappropriate to Logic, but that like other kinds of pictorial language they are too cumbrous for general purposes.

Of course we must positively insist that our diagrammatic scheme and our purely symbolic scheme shall be in complete correspondence and harmony with each other. The main defect of the common or Eulerian diagrams is that such correspondence is not secured. In fact, as was shown in the first Chapter, those diagrams not only do not fit in with the ordinary scheme of propositions which they are employed to illustrate, but do not seem to have any recognized scheme of propositions to which they could be consistently affiliated. The forms of common language are of course peculiar to no system whatever, and therefore can work in with any possible logical scheme, though they like some, such as ours, less than others. But symbolic and diagrammatic systems are to some extent artificial, and they ought therefore to be so constructed as to work in perfect harmony together. This merit, so far as it goes, seems at any rate secured on the plan above described.

CHAPTER VI.

ON THE IMPORT OF PROPOSITIONS, AS REGARDS THE ACTUAL EXISTENCE OF THEIR SUBJECTS AND PREDICATES.

A CHAPTER must be devoted here to the discussion of a connected group of topics, which, though assuming decidedly more prominence in Symbolic Logic, are by no means properly confined to it. They should, in fact, have been so thoroughly treated elsewhere, and decided one way or the other, that a mere reference here would have sufficed instead of a somewhat elaborate explanation and justification of the view to be adopted. Many logicians, if not a majority of them, have however passed the subject by entirely, interesting and important as it is from any speculative point of view. This is probably owing to the prevalent acceptance until lately of the Conceptualist theory of Logic, to which, at least when rigidly adhered to, such topics as we now propose to enter on are unfortunately somewhat alien.

The simplest way perhaps of introducing the subject now to be discussed is by raising the question whether, when we utter the proposition 'All X is Y', we either assert or imply that there are such things as X or Y, that is, that such things exist in some sense or other? Or again, when we state the proposition 'All X is all Y'; here is a proposition with somewhat more of predication involved in it, does it make more, or more precise, implication as to this particular point of there being any X or Y?

One caution at the outset, in order to avoid misapprehension. Any discussion about the 'existence' of such and such things will create an impression in some minds that we propose to enter on some kind of metaphysical enquiry. Such fears are altogether groundless. It must be clearly understood that we intend to discuss the question entirely on scientific or logical ground, without digression toward considerations which are more appropriate to metaphysics. As to the nature of this existence, or what may really be meant by it, we have hardly any need to trouble ourselves, for almost any possible sense in which the logician can understand it will involve precisely the same difficulties and call for the same solution of them. We may leave it to any one to define the existence as he pleases, but when he has done this it will always be reasonable to enquire whether there is anything existing corresponding to the X or Y which constitute our subject and predicate. There can in fact be no fixed tests for this existence, for it will vary widely according to the nature of the subject-matter with which we are concerned in our reasonings. For instance, we may happen to be speaking of ordinary phenomenal existence, and at the time present; by the distinction in question is then meant nothing more and nothing deeper than what is meant by saying that there are such things as antelopes and elephants in existence, but not such things as unicorns or mastodons. If again we are referring to the sum-total of all that is conceivable, whether real or imaginary, then we should mean what is meant by saying that everything must be regarded as existent which does not involve a contradiction in terms, and nothing which does. Or if we were concerned with Wonder-

land and its occupants we need not go deeper down than they
do who tell us that March hares exist there. In other words,
the interpretation of the distinction will vary very widely in
different cases, and consequently the tests by which it would
have in the last resort to be verified; but it must always
exist as a real distinction, and there is a sufficient identity
of sense and application pervading its various significations
to enable us to talk of it in common terms. No logician who
utters a proposition of the form 'All X is Y', can reasonably
refuse to say *Yes* or *No* to the question, Do you thereby
imply that there is any X and Y?

The clearest way perhaps of stating the line of discussion
here adopted is by claiming the two following postulates. I
state them explicitly and call attention to them because they
are not familiar to logicians, if indeed they have ever been
definitely enunciated.

(1)   That we must be supposed to know the nature and
limits of the universe of discourse with which we are concerned,
whether we state it or not. If we are talking of ordinary phe
nomena we must know whether we refer to them without limit
of time and space; and if not, within what limits, broadly
speaking. If we include the realms of fiction and imagination
we must know what boundaries we mean to put upon them.

(2)   That we must come furnished with some criterion of
existence and reality suitable to that universe. That is, all
our assertion and denial must admit, actually or conceivably,
of *verification*. Put the propositions 'All X is Y', 'No X is Y',
into the forms $XY = 0, XY = 0$, and the statements 'There is
no XY', 'There is no XY', must admit of verification and
be intelligible, without any necessary digression into meta
physics.

Take the following comparison by way of illustration.
The question whether or not a certain statement has been

published clearly requires us to know exactly what books are to be appealed to, as decisive in the matter. But it is equally clear that the point can be settled whatever the books thus chosen may be. The maximum known stature of man could be decided as unequivocally by appeal to Swift as to Quetelet if we know what exactly are the things we are talking of. The verification of a statement can be carried out by appeal to a novel or a scientific work, to a fairy tale or a blue-book, provided we know what our authorities are.

Here, as on several other occasions in this work, we are in face of three very distinct questions which we must prevent from getting entangled more than is absolutely unavoidable. The first is one of popular usage; the second is one of ordinary logical legislation and usage; and the third is one of convenience and consistency in the working out of the Symbolic or Generalized Logic. The first two of these do not much concern us here, for we have had to repudiate once for all any bounden obligation to either the language of common life, or that of the common logic. They must therefore be passed over much more slightly than they deserve. It is however impossible to neglect them altogether, since it is only by realizing the difficulties which meet us in both of those quarters that we can appreciate the weight of argument in favour of the conclusion which I am about to state.

I. The first question then is merely one of custom or usage: what do ordinary persons think and understand on this point? It is quite impossible to answer this question off hand; partly owing to the immense number and variety of the popular forms of assertion, and partly to the multitudinous associations contained in them, these varying from the barest suggestion up to implication scarcely short of direct assertion. To the best of my judgment we should have to decide somewhat to this effect.

The Universal Affirmative. Broadly speaking, All X is Y does imply directly that there are X's, and consequently indirectly that there are Y's[1]. If any non-mathematician were told that all rectangular hyperbolas have their asymptotes at right angles to one another, he would assume unhesitatingly that there are such things as rectangular hyperbolas, that they exist in the domain of mathematics. And so with most other of the things about which we have occasion to make affirmative assertions. The main ground for this assumption seems to be the very obvious one that the practical exigencies of life confine most of our discussions to what does exist, rather than to what might, or once did, but does not now; and that here as elsewhere, where one thing is the rule and another the exception the *primâ facie* presumption is in favour of the former. People do not in general talk about what they believe to be nonentities. They do not, for instance, without warning describe the qualifications for an office which they suppose does not exist, nor do they state the attributes of a substance which is nowhere, within the scope of their enquiry, to be found.

This seems to be the rule; but there are some admitted classes of exceptions. For instance, assertions about the *future* do not carry any such positive presumption with them, though the logician would commonly throw them into precisely the same 'All X is Y' type of categorical assertion. 'Those who pass this examination are lucky men' would certainly be tacitly supplemented by the clause 'if any such there be.' So too, in most circumstances of our ordinary life, wherever we are clearly talking of an ideal. 'Perfectly

[1] The reader must keep in mind that we are not discussing the question whether every separate word, that is, substantive or adjective, has things corresponding to it; but only whether single words, or groups of words, when forming subjects and predicates of propositions, are to be so understood.

conscientious men think but little of law and rule', has a sense without implying that there are any such men to be found.   Other classes of cases will probably occur to the reader, but the broad conclusion remains that when we are speaking of facts within our power to verify we do not without warning predicate of non-existent subjects.   And the subject of the proposition being thus established, it follows clearly that that of the predicate must be so too.

The Particular Affirmative and Negative.   The same as sumption seems to rule here, but in a more unqualified manner, owing to the fact that most of the exceptions admit ted there could have no place here.   An assertion confined to 'some' of a class generally rests upon observation or testi mony rather than on reasoning or imagination, and therefore almost necessarily postulates existent data, though the nature of this observation and consequent existence is, as already remarked, a perfectly open question.   'Some twining plants turn from left to right', 'Some griffins have long claws', both imply that we have looked in the right quarters to assure ourselves of the fact.   In one case I may have observed in my own garden, and in the other on crests or in the works of the poets, but according to the appropriate tests of verifi cation, we are in each case talking of what *is*.

The Universal Negative.   So far as I can judge it seems that we very commonly make the same assumption as before in regard to the subject, but do not do so equally strongly as regards the predicate.   'No substance possesses a temperature below -280^0 centigrade' (I must again remind the reader that we are considering the subjects and predicates as wholes, not the separate elements of which they may be composed). Since nothing but substances is supposed to possess a temperature at all, this negatives the existence of the predi cate altogether.   The exceptions here seem of much the same kind as in the case of the Affirmative, and perhaps more frequent; but owing to the general reluctance of men to quit the ground of fact altogether, I presume that where the subject does not exist we should generally find that the predicate does: e. g. 'No perfectly wicked character is to be found in fiction.' As an instance of a possibly non-existent subject of a negative proposition, take the following:—'No person condemned for witchcraft in the reign of Queen Anne, was executed.' I have verified this, say, by searching all the records of executions within the time specified. There would surely be no impropriety in my publishing the fact before ascertaining, by records of trials, that there were any persons so condemned. The disproval of this fact, which would be equivalent to showing that the subject had no existence, would at most show that I had been hasty. It would not make the proposition itself invalid. Where the sentence can stand equally well in the converted form it seems that we decidedly prefer that the subject should be a reality. Thus the two propositions 'No unpardonable sins are sins', and 'No sins are unpardonable sins', are logically equivalent. The objection would of course be raised in either case that what is really meant is that there are no such things as un pardonable sins, and that it would therefore be best to say so at once; but whereas the former proposition strikes every one as absurdly stated, the latter is at most awkwardly stated. The ground of this distinction seems to me to lie in the natural dislike to a non-real subject of such a proposition where it can be avoided.

Any account of popular phraseology which is thus confined to the accepted four fundamental forms of logical predication is of course very imperfect, but we have no space to enquire as to the import of other forms. They seem to carry the most various degrees of implication with them.   Thus, 'None but X are Y':—No one on hearing this would be shocked if the speaker went on to say 'And I do not believe there are any X's.'   But the logician would commonly phrase this statement as either 'All Y are X', with the consequent implication that there are Y's and X's, or, 'No not-X are Y', with the consequent implication that there are not-X's.   This does not seem to be quite what the ordinary mind contemplates in such a phrase.

II.   We must now see what the logicians have to say upon the matter.   The most direct way of deciding this point would be to listen to their own assertions, but here unfortunately we shall obtain very little help indeed. Most of the treatises written by English authors, if I am not mistaken, entirely omit all reference to the subject; at least I can find no sort of critical examination of it[1].

---

[1] In several English treatises the question is raised as to whether a *class-term* postulates the existence of things corresponding to it, i. e. whether the class must be actual or merely potential.   But this question, though doubtless connected with the one before us, is quite distinct.   All that here concerns us is whether a *whole subject or predicate*, as such, consisting perhaps of a complex of terms, demands such a postulate.

Even those who have more nearly approached our present point of view have done so under two limitations which render most of their discussion irrelevant to our purpose. For (1) they have only (so far as I see) touched upon the case of universal affirmative propositions. And (2) they have mostly assumed that the contrast demanded was always the same, viz. that between phenomenal or sensible existence on the one hand and the region of the imaginary on the other (see, for instance, Mill's *Logic*, I. ch. VIII. where he discusses the dragon and its flame-breathing characteristic).   I want to make the question perfectly general. Take what test we please of existence, and what universe of discourse we please, and we ought to be prepared, when A and B are anyhow connected in a proposition, at least to face the question whether there 'is' or 'is not' an AB.   No one who considers such a question as beside the mark can be considered to assert or deny intelligently.

Even Mansel seems to admit this much when he says (*Prolegomena*, p. 67) "When I assert that A is B,...[I mean] that the object in

There are indeed two distinct opinions which have been advanced more or less by way of implication, which as representing to my thinking each of them a reduction to absurdity, but in opposite directions, deserve a short notice.

✓ For instance, it is sometimes stated or implied that subjects and predicates have no reference whatever to the phenomenal existence or non-existence of things corresponding to them. This is presumably the view of the rigid conceptualists; at least it is not easy to put any other construction upon much that they say. Mansel repeatedly maintains that we are concerned with concepts only and their mutual relations to one another. On this view it might be urged that we are uniformly certain of the existence of the idea or concept in our own minds, and uniformly uncertain (from a logical point of view) of any phenomena corresponding to it. It seems impossible to carry out this view consistently. We may, by a shift, adhere to it in the case of essential properties ;—thus when we say that 'all honest men are deserving of respect' we may maintain that we are thinking merely of groups of attributes present to our mind, and that 'deserving of respect' is found amongst those which compose the characteristics of 'honest men'. But how can we adhere to this in the case of accidental attributes, which hardly any one ever thought

---

which the one set of attributes is found is the same as that in which the other set is found."

Of English writers De Morgan is the only one who has entered fully on the subject, deciding in favour of the implication of existence (*Formal Logic*, p. 111. *Syllabus*, p. 10. *Eng. Cyclopaedia*, p. 344). Herbart is the best known philosopher perhaps who has supported the opposite view

(*Einleitung*, § 53), in which he is followed by Sigwart (I. p. 95), and Beneke (*Logik*, p. 77). See also Ueberweg (*Logic*, §§ 68, 69, 85) and C. S. Peirce (*Journal of Spec. Phil.* 1868). But since these writers have (generally speaking) expressed their views subject to the limitations indicated above, I cannot with certainty claim them as for or against my own view.

of putting into the subject till he heard the assertion made ? So too with particular propositions. These certainly imply actual observed or recorded occurrences.

Even if we insist upon turning everything about us into a concept when we have to deal with general propositions, we shall not find it so easy to carry this out elsewhere, for Proper names and Individual propositions have a good deal of vitality about them which resents and resists this process of conversion into the state of a concept. And if, with Mansel, we are resolutely consistent in making no exception here, what are we to say to Existential propositions? We are always liable to encounter these, and terms whose essence (in old language) is to exist. They will still persist, in spite of our efforts to make away with them, and so stalk about with the glaring incongruity of a living body amongst the world of shades composed of our concepts.

It may be remarked that this question is intimately connected with that of Hypotheticals. As all the more consistent logicians who have adopted this view have re cognized (e.g. Herbart, Beneke, Sigwart) we thus do away with the distinction between the hypothetical and the categorical. That this must be so can be illustrated by a very simple example :—'If there are any X which are Y then they are Z', this is clearly hypothetical. But it may be phrased, without the slightest change of meaning, 'All XY, if such there be, are Z'; and this is identical in form with the ordinary categorical 'All A is B' when we accept it with the tacit proviso ' All A, if there be any.'

This rejection of the Hypothetical, as a distinct form, will not be any sacrifice to us, for it is (as will be fully shown in a future chapter) a marked characteristic of this generalized Logic to abandon that distinction. But it is important as showing the really serious nature of the difficulty from the point of view of the ordinary Logic. How those writers who adopt the hypothetical interpretation explicitly[1], or those who adopt it implicitly by enunciating a theory[2] which necessarily implies it, can still retain the distinction between Categorical and Hypothetical as anything more than one of expression, is to me unintelligible.

Another view, equally extreme in the opposite direction, has been hinted at by Prof. Jevons; viz. that *every* term, and its contradictory, must alike be claimed as represented in fact, at least when they occur as subject or predicate of a proposition. Even such a view as this, if deliberately maintained and supported by reasons, would claim respectful consideration. As however it is merely doubtfully advanced in a note, with a very inadequate idea apparently of its consequences or its relation to ordinary opinions upon the subject, I prefer to approach it by another path[3].

Most logicians, I apprehend, entertain an intermediate view more nearly in accordance with the conclusions of common sense and common language as indicated above. In any complete treatise on Formal Logic it would be necessary to enter into this question somewhat fully, so as to ascertain in what direction the weight of judgment and reason must be considered to lie. Historical discussion however of this kind being alien to the object of this volume it will be better to approach the subject in a somewhat different way ; namely, by enquiring what can be elicited from the universally accepted rules of Logic. This will also have the advantage of indi-

---

[1] e. g. Spalding (*Logic*, p. 104) "*X* is *Y*, has logically no more meaning than this: if *X* is and if *Y* is, then *X* is *Y*."

[2] I refer of course to the thorough going Conceptualists. Mansel, indeed, is more consistent, rejecting the distinction of hypothetical by maintaining that "All formal thinking is, as regards the material character of its objects, problematical only" (Aldrich, p. 236).

[3] See Jevons's *Pure Logic*, p. 65.

cating those difficulties in the subject, the desirability of avoiding which has induced me to accept the doctrine to be presently explained.

Perhaps the most conclusive evidence from this source is to be found in the accepted rules of the syllogism. For instance, 'All Y is Z' 'All Y is X', would not enable us to conclude as we do, 'Therefore some X is Z', if the propositions had to be interpreted 'All Y, *if there is any*, is Z.' They must certainly be interpreted 'All Y, and there is such, is Z.' Since however no special assumption is announced in the case of *Darapti* we must fairly conclude that *all* uni versal affirmatives postulate the presence, so to say, of actual representatives of their subjects, and consequently of their predicates.

This is all very well to begin with, but observe to what length it will lead us if we accept also other commonly received rules. For instance, are we to be allowed to contraposit propositions? If so we get at once into implications about negative terms. From 'All X is Y' we are commonly allowed to derive 'All not-Y is not-X.' But this being a universal affirmative must indicate that there are instances of not-Y and not-X, as well as of Y and X. This is certainly very remote from the popular view, which never thinks of insisting that X and Y must not only exist but must also abstain from comprising all existence. The popular interpretation of this form of proposition is surely conditional only, and equivalent to 'All not-Y, if there be any, is not-X.' Then again as regards negative propositions. From 'No X is Y', we obtain without hesitation, 'All X is not-Y.' Consequently the *negative* proposition also must refuse merely possible subjects and claim them as existent[1]. And since

[1] These remarks apply mostly to the handling of modern logicians. It is well known that the older lo gicians rather avoided these negative

the universal negative is simply convertible, what holds of its subject must also hold of its predicate. Here again we are at variance with the popular view, which seems to recognize a dis tinction in this respect between the subject and the predicate.

It really seems then as if the commonly accepted rules of Logic, when pressed to their conclusions, would force us into that extreme view noticed by Prof. Jevons. But none the less it seems to me a reduction to absurdity. It involves not only a needless departure from all popular conviction and association, but, if adhered to, it would terribly hamper us in all our logical predication. Are we never to assert anything or deny anything about X or Y unless we are certain not only that there are things which are X and Y, but also things which are not X, and not Y? The former condition might not be any great hardship, but the latter would extremely curtail our customary right of denial. Far rather than submit to such restraint we should abandon the claim to contraposit our propositions, or in any way to extract negatives out of positives. Probably also we should think it best not to hold out for the right to simply convert a universal negative proposition. Otherwise we should hardly have elbow-room left in which to assert or deny with any sense of freedom.

---

subjects and predicates, and that the rules of the syllogism were not devised for their employment. For instance several logicians have noticed that the rules against draw- ing a conclusion from two negative premises were only valid under the supposition that we might not thus introduce a fourth term under the guise of a negative term. Thus both Ploucquet (*Sammlung*, p. 78) and Darjes (*Weg zur Wahrheit*, p. 227) have given concrete instances which may be expressed by the letters 'No A is B', 'No A is C', and have shown that if we were allowed to phrase them in the form 'All A is not-B', 'All A is not-C', we might draw the con- clusion 'Some not-C is not-B.' But knowing under what restrictions the common rules were drawn up, they did not therefore charge these rules with being incorrect.

Such difficulties as those just mentioned encounter us within the field of ordinary Logic, and amongst the simple propositions with which it commonly has to deal, but they would be but the beginning of our troubles in the wider field of Symbolic Logic. We then have to deal with a number of propositions simultaneously. involving perhaps half a dozen or more of terms, two or more of such terms being sometimes combined into a single subject or predicate [1]. We should soon find that it was simply impossible to tolerate a system in which either assertion or denial were permitted to carry along with it the implication of the existence of things corresponding to the subject or predicate. Any group of such propositions would form a very precarious structure, for it might be discovered on careful analysis that taken together they demanded the annihilation of one or other of the subjects or predicates involved in them. The discovery of such a result would instantly involve the rejection of the whole group as involving mutual inconsistencies, the solution of which was nowhere furnished in the data.

For instance, take the group,

$$\begin{cases} \text{All } x \text{ is either } y \text{ and } z. \text{ or not } v, \\ \text{All } xy \text{ is } w \text{ or not } z, \\ \text{No } wx \text{ is } yz. \end{cases}$$

There is certainly nothing intrinsically amiss with any one of these propositions, and on the rational and simple

[1] Professor Bowen (*Logic*, p. 144) has seen the difficulty in the case of these complicated subjects and predicates. He makes a special exemption in the case of, say, XY, as a subject; terming the proposition a 'limitative' one, and reading the subject 'X if it be Y.' Subjects so compounded he considers do not postulate any existence, but take their place amongst hypotheticals. As stated above, a generalized system of logic cannot recognize any distinction between one and the other of these forms of proposition.

explanation to be presently offered they will harmonize together perfectly. But taken together they demand, and are satisfied by the condition 'No x is y', or 'There is no such thing as xy.' But xy is the subject of one of them, and this fact would therefore (if we admit the implication now under discussion) positively put a veto upon such a conclusion. In that case we should have nothing else to do than to dismiss the whole group of propositions together as involving an inconsistency somewhere, though we could not tell where; for we should have no right to assign the fault of the inconsistency to one of the propositions rather than to another.

Finally, as a climax to all this, we must remember that the scope of our propositions has to be limited to a certain universe of discourse. This consideration immensely aggravates the burden of all these restrictions; for it would force us in consistency to ascertain, not only that there are X's and Y's somewhere or other, but also that these as well as their contradictories prevail within the sphere, perhaps a very narrow one, which constitutes the universe of our discourse for the time being. For it is certainly to this only that our premises apply, and in reference to which their import must be interpreted.

III. There is however another view open to us which will, I think, avoid all the difficulties above mentioned, together with others which will present themselves in the course of our discussion. Or perhaps one ought rather to say that we may succeed in this way in removing all such portion of the attendant difficulty as arises from real uncertainty and ambiguity of meaning, for though this comprises much the larger part of our trouble it certainly does not exhaust it. The view now to be explained is, I think, almost necessarily forced upon us by the study of Symbolic Logic, though when it has been once realized it will be found to apply also to the ordinary interpretation of the proposition.

Every universal proposition may of course be put into a negative form : this is familiar to every logician, the distinction of our system being that this negative side of a proposition is more consistently and uniformly developed and provided with a suitable symbolic notation. Now if we adopt the simple explanation that *the burden of implication of existence is shifted from the affirmative to the negative form;* that is, that it is not the existence of the subject or the predicate (in affirmation) which is implied, but the non-existence of any subject which does *not* possess the predicate, we shall find that nearly all difficulty vanishes[1]. This may need a little explanation and justification. Take the proposition 'All x is y.' There being two class terms here, there are, as has been so abundantly explained, four ultimate classes, viz. xy, x not-y, y not-x, and not-x not-y. Now what I shall understand the proposition 'All x is y' to do is, not to assure us as to any one of these classes (for instance xy) being *occupied*, but to assure us of one of them (viz. x not-y) being *unoccupied*. That is, instead of regarding the *affirmative* form as being the appropriate and unambiguous form, we regard the corresponding or equivalent *negative* form as possessing these attributes. Whether there be any x's or y's we cannot tell for certain, but we do feel quite sure that there are no such things existing as 'x which is not y.'

The example on p. 139, showed the necessity of some

---

[1] I wish to insist once for all that I am not proposing to *deny* that any assigned proposition can have these implications, but merely to maintain that in the Symbolic Logic, as a means to generalization, they should not be regarded as any part of the proposition. Admit them by all means wherever desired; but as a distinct implication, to be distinctly indicated.

such understanding as this. A solitary proposition may make positive implications without any mischief, but if it is to com bine harmoniously with other propositions it must lay aside all such claims, for they will very possibly lead to conflict and disappointment. Whereas if it confine itself to its negative implication, it will make a contribution to the net knowledge furnished by the other propositions, which can be set aside by nothing short of a direct contradiction in terms.

It comes to this therefore, that in respect of what such a proposition affirms it can only be regarded as conditional, but that in respect of what it denies it may be regarded as abso lute. The proposition 'All x is y' may be written, and for the purposes in hand is much better written, 'No x is not-y' $(x(1-y)-0$, or, more briefly $xy=0$, as will be more fully explained hereafter) that is, it empties the compartment xy, or declares the non-existence of a certain combination, viz. of things which are the combination of x and not-y. But it does not tell us whether there is any y at all; or, if there be, whether there is also any x, or whether the two together make up the total of the things with which we are concerned. All these facts it leaves quite uncertain, carefully limiting itself (so far of course as existence of the things is concerned) to the single negation of there being any xy. Now we know that our symbols are subject to the universal condition repre sented by $1=xy+xy+xy+xy$ · or, put into words, that everything must be either xy, or x not-y, or y not-x, or not-x not-y. When therefore we have thus expunged one of these as not existing, we have three alternatives left: and we know that some one, or some two, or all three of these must be re presented amongst existences, but we do not know which of these cases may hold good.

The import therefore, as regards existence, of the Universal Affirmative is very plain. Whatever it does in the way of predication, in the way of implication of existence it just denies one combination and no more, leaving the other com binations untouched, as it should do. Now let us couple another proposition to the former, by asserting that 'All y is x', as well as 'All x is y.' We see at once what results. The second proposition empties out the class xy, as the former did xy; that is, it declares the non-existence also of things which are y and not-x. Before, the positive possibilities were three in number, now they are reduced to two; for it is implied that everything must be either both x and y or neither of the two. Carrying this process one step further, we see that three such propositions would be requisite to establish un equivocally the existence of any one of the four classes. If we expunge xy also, we are then reduced at last to an asser tion of existence, for we have now declared that xy is *all*, viz. that within the sphere of our discussion everything is both x and y.

The positive assertion in this last case is of course of a peculiar kind. We are not merely told that a certain class is represented, but that it is represented to the exclusion of all else. It is the sole survivor after all else has been ex punged. It may therefore be very fairly asked whether there is no simple form for declaring that such and such a class *is* represented, and for declaring nothing more? There is such a form, but it will have to be sought in the *particular* pro position, and not in the universal. I do not mean that this is naturally understood to be signified by such propositions, but that they will readily lend themselves to such an inter pretation with very little violence, and are the only ones that will do so. This will be fully explained in the next chapter, but in order to round off the present discussion I will give a few lines of indication of what is meant. The formula $xy = 0$ expresses, as we have seen, that the class in question is absent; whilst $xy - 1$ expresses that it is not only present, but present to the exclusion of all else. Now invent an intermediate form $xy = v$, where v is to stand for a class of which we merely know this, that it is intermediate between 1 and 0, viz. between all and nothing. The most natural and simple way of reading off such a proposition would be 'xy is something', corresponding to the other forms 'xy is all' and 'xy is nothing'; or 'there is xy.' This seems to me to be very nearly the signification of the familiar form 'Some x is y' of our ordinary Logic, with the important difference, however, that it is free from all ambiguity as to there being any x and y, for it is expressly understood to tell us that this is so[1].

When therefore we meet with the proposition 'all x is y' I shall understand it to be interpreted as follows : (1) negatively and absolutely, 'there are no such things as xy', or (2) positively but conditionally, 'If there are such things as x, then all the x's are y.' And owing to the superior brevity and absoluteness of the negative form, we shall make it our ordinary rule to write down such a proposition symbolically in the form $xy = 0$.

The foregoing results may be summed up by saying that whereas it is quite certain that common usage does make various assumptions as to the existence of the subject and the predicate separately, and quite certain that the Symbolic Logic (as here interpreted) does not[2], the state of the law on this point in the common Logic is full of perplexity.

[1] This, I think, partly meets the objection which has been raised against Boole's system by Mr A. T. Ellis, viz. that "an algebra of 0 and 1 can correspond only to a logic of *none* and *all*," whereas we need room for 'some' as well (*Proc. R. Soc.* vol. **xxi**. 497).

[2] The *symbolic* right for which I contend can be expressed in a few words. It is merely this:—that any logical element whatever may be put equal to either 1 or 0, subject only to the condition that the sum-total of all such elements shall $= 1$.

Much of the above discussion will perhaps appear rather dry and far-fetched, but we shall soon find that it will lead to some interesting and unexpected applications. We will begin by examining the mutual relations of two contradictory propositions of the customary kind. Take the two following, which in technical language are termed 'contrary' the one to the other: 'All x is y', and 'No x is y'. It will sound rather oddly at variance with ordinary associations to ask if these two propositions are compatible with one another, that is, if they can both be admitted simultaneously? It need not be said that we have no intention of trespassing on to any of the ground appropriate to transcendentalism, but are prepared to discuss the question in a perfectly matter of fact way. The reply of ordinary Logic would doubtless be an emphatic negative; and this reply would be valid enough from the point of view of predication, provided we look no further than that. But if we take a wider, and I should say a sounder view, we shall readily see that there is no reason whatever against our accepting both these propositions. Look at them from the class or compartment point of view, and we see at once that 'All x is y' simply empties out xy, whilst 'No x is y' empties out xy. There is no harm in this, no suggestion whatever of any conflict or inconsistency here. These two negations (for as such we regard them both of course) when combined together are simply tantamount to denying the existence of x at all:—an existence which no one had been supposed to assert:—that is, the always implied hypothesis 'x, if x exist' is here declared not to be admitted.

To the mathematician, or to any one trained in a mathematical way of looking at things, the admission of such a result as this would not even put the slightest strain upon the language which he is in the habit of using. Nothing is more familiar to him than the practice of dealing with some unknown quantity during a continued process of reasoning, and then finding as a conclusion that this unknown quantity (say a root of an equation) is equal to nothing :—that is, not that it must at last be *made* nothing, but that we must now recognize that that was the value which belonged to it all along, under the given conditions of the problem. This possibility of complete material destruction is what his symbols must always be prepared to face as something which may at any moment be declared to be their lot. The only caution which he has to keep in view is that of looking back to see that he has not unconsciously transgressed certain rules (*e.g.* division by the unknown quantity, in case this quantity was equal to nothing). If therefore we combine together two of these contrary propositions we must merely be prepared to interpret the combination as implying that there is no such thing as the subject of them : whether or not there be anything corresponding to their predicate is not thus determined.

In ordinary Logic this difficulty seems to have evaded notice[1], doubtless owing to the fact that ordinary Logic seldom or never has to deal simultaneously with more than two propositions and the conclusion from them ; these propositions being moreover very simple ones. Therefore any direct and glaring contradiction, such as that in question, could hardly present itself, for it would at once strike the attention, and the premises would have been reconsidered.

[1] There is a suggestion in this direction :—as of what indeed in Logic is there not a suggestion?—by Leibnitz. After saying that from '*a* is *b*' '*c* is *d*' we can deduce that '*ac* is *bd*', he applies it to the case of *a* and *c* being incompatible "Circulus est nullangulus. Quadratum est quadrangulum. Ergo circulus-quadratum est nullangulus-quadrangulum. Nam haec propositio vera est ex hypothesi impossibili" (*Specimen demonstrandi*, Erdmann, p. 99). The only distinct notice that I have met of the subject discussed above is in an interesting and highly suggestive article by Mr C. S. Peirce in the *Journal of Spec. Phil.* for 1868.

But any extended System of Logic, which ventures to deal
with combinations of several complex propositions, must
make up its mind how to deal with this measure of contra
diction and of what would commonly be regarded as in
compatibility.   Suppose, for instance, that we have three or
four propositions, involving possibly half a dozen terms, no
untrained acuteness would be capable of detecting at a
glance whether or not they involved amongst them this
measure of contradiction.   The example given on page 139 is
a case in point.   There are only three propositions in it, in
volving four terms; but who would undertake to say at once,
on looking at it, what was the only solution of it?   We must
always be thus prepared to find that the non-existence of one
or more of the classes involved in the combination, as subject
or predicate, is all that is required to harmonize them satis
factorily with one another.   Suppose we put together several
Acts of Parliament, Rubrics or Canons Ecclesiastical, or rules
of some club, it might so happen that they turned out, on
comparison, to be in this way irreconcilable with one another.
No doubt if this were found to be the case in practice
we should take it as a sign that the rules needed remodelling.
But if we chose to stick to them as scientific statements, and
to treat them as we should treat such statements if given
us through a set of equations, it might well be that the
irreconcilability would disappear at once on our abandoning
some class which we were in no way pledged to retain.
The confusion would have only arisen from the fact that we
were trying to dispense with the universal and necessary, but
tacit, proviso that the various classes with which we deal are
only referred to conditionally, 'if they exist'; and that in the
case in question some of them did not exist[1].

[1] Prof. Jevons maintains as already
remarked, that we are not to allow
this extinction either of any simple
class or of its contradictory.   Thus

The only sort of contradiction amongst our propositions which we really have cause to fear, that is, the only one which we must peremptorily decline to admit under any interpretation, is one of a much more thorough going kind than the common contradiction of ordinary predication. It would be one which tried to empty and to occupy a com partment simultaneously; either directly, as if we persisted that there is xy and that there is not xy, or indirectly, as if we set about denying the existence of all the four classes xy, xy, xy, and xy. It must not be replied here that in admitting this we are reintroducing the just rejected doc trine that such propositions as 'All X is Y' and 'No X is Y' are absolutely incompatible. The two cases are not in reality parallel. In the latter case we were able to make the reply:—By all means let us admit both the propositions simultaneously, provided they are offered to us under the tacit condition that there may not really happen to be any such thing as an X, a condition which in this case we should require to make use of. But when we are dealing with what I have called compartments rather than classes, that is with formal instead of material divisions, no such reply

of the example:

$$\left\{ \begin{array}{l} a - b + b \\ \imath - \cdot cd \\ \bar{a} - 0 \\ a\ddot{u} = \bar{v}cd \end{array} \right.$$

(the notation is mine) which de-mands $a, b, c, = 1$ to satisfy it, he says "we find that there cannot be any a at all without contradiction, what-ever may be the meaning of this result. It means doubtless that the premises are contradictory" (*Pure Logic*, p. 64). It means simply that 'everything is a' (and also b and c), a

perfectly admissible conclusion. To reject such a conclusion is to con-found the formal possibilities of our notation with the material conditions of our data. Such a principle of rejection is difficult enough to adhere to within the range of ordinary pro-positions, but in the case of the extended propositions of the Sym-bolic Logic it would become simply suicidal. Who and what are a and b, I should like to know, that they are to be suffered to refuse treatment to which ab submits as a matter of course?

is available.   The compartment is formal and necessary; we
can never admit the assumption that it may possibly not
exist.   *Things* exist indeed (in the sense of that term which
has been already fully explained); this amount of assumption
we certainly do make.   And these things must either possess
any assigned attribute or not possess it; which is equivalently
expressed by saying that they must certainly fall into one
or other of these compartments.   The analogous retort
therefore here, in order to be effective, would have to be that
there *are* no things whatever, at least within the universe in
question.   If any one likes to maintain that this really
might be so, on the psychological theory of matter and
mind, before any sentient or perceptive beings came into
existence I will not stop to dispute it.

We must now turn to another somewhat similar topic in
which the same kind of considerations present themselves.
On the same grounds on which we have to demand a
discussion and revision of the meaning and consequences
of 'contrariety' in propositions, when they are found in
combination, we must also in consistency demand a recon
sideration of what is to be understood by the 'dependence'
and 'independence' of propositions.   Here, as in the last case,
the question is really presented to us in ordinary Logic and
not in Symbolic only, though it does not assume any serious
aspect within the range of the former.   The simple forms of
dependence indeed with which the common system mostly
has to deal deserve only a passing glance by way of intro
duction.   'All A is B', and 'Some A is B'; 'No A is B' and
'Some A is not B' are obviously dependent in the sense that
the second member in each pair is included in, or inferrible
from, the first.   In the same way 'X is neither Y nor Z',
includes within it 'X is not Y', and so on with similar simple
examples.

But if we admit that hypothetical interpretation of all Universal propositions, which is under discussion in this chapter, we shall readily see that once started on that track we cannot stop so soon as this. Just as 'inconsistency' had to contract its boundaries within the limits of what was in a sense rigidly formal, so will 'dependence' have to extend its boundaries up to the same limits. Here too the mathe matician, and the mathematically minded, will find nothing strange or perplexing. All that is required is that we should adhere rigidly to the assigned meaning of our symbols, and never suffer ourselves to give way to one of those pernicious 'understandings' or 'implications' which are of course inevi table in ordinary speech. Our x and y are undoubtedly symbols standing for classes, but they emphatically refuse to commit themselves to saying that such classes are to be found.

Take the extremest case possible of apparent indepen dence between negative propositions, for instance, 'No A is B', 'No C is D.' Are even these really independent of one another in the sense of not possessing any common implications? Not if the existence of the subjects and predicates of the pro positions is only hypothetically implied, as we have agreed shall be the case. For though neither of these two propositions can be certainly shown to cover any part of the ground occupied by the other, yet they *may* prove to do so for anything that we can tell to the contrary. Hence there is one common conclusion that can equally be deduced from either of them, and accordingly, to that extent, we must not speak of them as independent. This common conclusion is of course, 'No AC is BD.' For if no A whatever is B, it is clear that this must hold of the A that is C, viz. of AC. Similarly, if this AC is no D whatever, it clearly cannot be the D which is B, viz. BD. We may infer therefore (expressing ourselves very fully and cautiously) 'No AC (if such there be) is BD

(if such there be).' But this interpretation is, as we have seen, that under which it was agreed that such a simple and categorical negative as 'No X is Y', was to be accepted.

We need hardly remark that no logician will have any occasion to feel himself troubled by material difficulties in any of these cases. If from 'No men are green', 'No horses are red', we should shrink from drawing the conclusion 'No men-horses are green-red', on the ground of its absurdity; we must remember that from 'No Americans are monar chists', 'No capitalists are unselfish', the not irrational con clusion that 'No American capitalists are unselfish monar chists', would only stand upon the same footing of provisional acceptance. Both alike are unassailable in so far as they deny, and on our interpretation they are far too cautious to do anything but deny.

All this becomes very clear and straightforward when regarded in the light of our symbols. 'No A is B' simply blots out the occupants of the compartment AB, as 'No C is D' blots out those of CD. But AB, as a compartment, must contain the four divisions made by C and D, any of which *may* be occupied ; just so CD contains those made by A and B, which may equally be occupied and have accordingly to be reckoned with. The subdivision $ABCD$ being therefore contained within both AB and CD it is clear that the original propositions are to that extent not independent of one another. If we were determined to make the second proposition certainly independent of the first we should have to limit its range by the insertion of another clause. We must phrase it 'No C *which is not* AB, is D.' When they are so phrased each proposition keeps itself entirely clear of the ground occupied by the other, and nothing is denied twice over. Of course in such a simple example as this it is easy to see by inspection what is the common part, in other words, what is the amount of dependence of the two propositions. But when we have to deal with groups of propositions and considerable numbers of terms no acuteness would suffice without the aid of systematic rules. It is one of the characteristics of Boole's system that it furnishes such a rule, so that by a simple and regular procedure every fragment of surplusage involved in the whole group of propositions is at once detected and brought to light. It was the fulfilment of the require ments for avoiding such surplusage of statement as this that Boole contemplated when he discussed some of the conditions of a perfect language. What was supposed to be demanded was a system of statements which should be complete and symmetrical; which should leave no gaps between any of them unaccounted for (except of course where we are really in ignorance) and which should never interfere with one another by the possibility of their being found to go twice over the same ground.

The reasons for adopting this interpretation of the import of propositions will only become appreciated after the examination of a number of examples, but enough has already been said to afford a fair justification. It is not for a moment maintained that this view is entirely in accor dance with popular impressions ; though if the choice were between it and that which seems consistently deducible from the rules of ordinary Logic, the former ought, I think, to have the preference on this ground. For if the ordinary person would be disturbed, after hearing that 'All X is Y', by the admission that perhaps there were no X's, he would be still more disturbed if required to admit that there were certainly things which were not X and not Y, as well as X and Y. Moreover, as it happens, we can readily rectify even this divergence from popular association. I only

say that 'All X is Y' shall, in the absence of express
assurance, be taken as equivalent to 'There is no X which is
not-Y.' If such assurance be given, it is to be regarded
as an independent assertion and be dealt with as such.
Of course this would complicate matters, and as it hampers
the freedom and generality of our rules we shall make
a practice of avoiding it. But examples can readily be given,
and some will be given, to show how the admission of any
such intimation into our data would lead to modification
of our inferences.

CHAPTER VII.

SYMBOLIC EXPRESSION OF ORDINARY PROPOSITIONS.

HAVING thus cleared the ground in respect of the general existential import of our propositions, we are now in a posi tion to complete the discussion upon which we entered in the first chapter, viz. as to the best mode of expressing symboli cally the familiar propositions of ordinary Logic.

I. The Universal Affirmative, 'All x is y.' We have seen that we are involved in numerous perplexities if we permit this form of proposition to imply the existence of either x or y. It can therefore best be understood in the conditional sense that if there be x s and y's then all the x's must be y. How are we to put this meaning into our symbols? Three equivalent forms have been suggested, one of them negative and the others positive.

(1) The negative expression is the one referred to repeatedly in the course of the last chapter. We simply frame it, $xy = 0$; viz. 'No x is not-y.' This seems to cover unambiguously all the meaning which we want it to cover, and nothing besides. It is equally true whether x is the whole of y or only a part of y. Again if there be no y,

then not-y being 'everything' there can of course be no x; but if there be y there need not consequently be any x. Also if y be 'everything', then of course the x, if there be any (which is not necessary), must be y. This simple negative form therefore carries naturally with it all the signification which, as we have seen, should be read into the Universal Affirmative, and no more than that.

(2) The form adopted by Boole is $x = vy$, where v is to be regarded as an indefinite class symbol. At least this is the form with which he starts in order to express such propositions, the form which he deduces as a conclusion from his rules of operation being the unfamiliar one, $x = \frac{0}{0} y$. The nature and justification of the rules by which this latter mathematical form is deduced will occupy our attention hereafter, but the meaning of the symbol can be easily assigned. In mathematics $\frac{0}{0}$ represents the *absolutely indefinite* in respect of numerical magnitude, standing for anything between 0 and infinity. We might propose to take it then in Logic in exactly the same sense, with the one necessary restriction that our universe ranging (symbolically) only from 0 to 1, instead of from 0 to ∞, we must keep within those narrower limits. In that case $\frac{0}{0}$ would be absolutely indefinite between 0 and 1, that is, it would denote a class which may be anything between '*nothing*' and '*all*', inclusively. But although if we thus borrowed the symbol at once as a suitable sign of the indefinite, we might offer a fair defence of our choice, it must be insisted on that we are in no way whatever dependent upon a second-hand interpretation here. The symbol has a rigid logical significa-

tion of its own. Just as $\frac{x}{y}$ denotes the class which on restriction by y will reduce to x, so does $\frac{0}{0}$ denote the class which on restriction by 'nothing', that is by our taking none of it, will reduce to nothing. But clearly *any* class whatever will do this, so that $\frac{0}{0}$ stands for any logical class whatever. That is, it is perfectly indefinite.

It must be clearly understood therefore that if we put v as an equivalent for $\frac{0}{0}$, this v is by no means a substitute for the 'some' of ordinary logic, since it includes 'nothing'; still less for the 'some' of ordinary language, since it includes 'all.' It is the more necessary to call attention to this since Boole himself has repeatedly treated this v as equivalent to 'some', which I can only regard as an oversight. There is, in fact, no exact equivalent in our language for this form $\frac{0}{0}$, and it should therefore be preferred to the symbol v, for the double reason that this latter requires a more special definition thus to fix its meaning, and that we shall want it in a somewhat more natural signification when we come to treat of particular propositions. Moreover the very unfamiliarity of such a symbol in Logic, as $\frac{0}{0}$, calls attention to the various implications which we are to admit into, or exclude from, the meaning of the proposition $x = \frac{0}{0} y$, or 'All x is y', better than a mere arbitrary letter like v can do. But the prejudices which it is likely to excite are so violent that I must confess to not having always had the courage to press its just claims to employment.

Before passing on to discuss an alternative form a difficulty must be signalled here. We say that $x = \frac{0}{0} y$ (this $\frac{0}{0}$ being absolutely indefinite within our limits) represents the Universal Affirmative, and that only. Now $\frac{0}{0}$ includes 0. Hence in this limiting case the proposition would stand $x - 0y$. The inexperienced reader might translate this into 'All x is *no* y', and thence take it as the equivalent of 'No x is y.' In other words he might conclude that this way of symbolizing the Universal Affirmative had broken down, since it was found to include the Universal Negative also. This would be a mistake, involving the same play on the word '*no*' as the familiar problem, which it is said took Whately's fancy, about 'no cat' having more legs than 'a cat.' The equation $x = \frac{0}{0} y$ identifies the whole of x with an uncertain portion of y; when $\frac{0}{0} = 0$ it identifies this whole with a part of y which is *nothing,* in which case of course x itself $= 0$. 'All x is no y', if we are to use the phrase in this case, refers the x still to 'a part' of y, but *declares that part to have vanished;* it does not refer it to any part of not-y, and this last would be necessary in order to identify it with the Universal Negative[1].

(3) There is a third form, viz. $x - xy$, which was probably first employed by Leibnitz[2]. It is discussed by Ploucquet[3], and is occasionally made use of by Lambert[4]. In no effective way does it differ from the form last discussed; and though not primarily employed by Boole as representative of the proposition, is constantly presenting itself in the course of his analytical processes.

This form is best known at present from its systematic employment by Prof. Jevons. In supporting the use of it against $x = vy$, he objects to this latter on the odd ground of its indefiniteness;—indefiniteness, that is, in respect of the

---

[1] It was just at this point that an ingenious scheme by Holland (Lambert's correspondent: see on, ch. xx) went wrong. He proposed $\frac{S}{p} = \frac{P}{\pi}$ as a general propositional form, in which p and π are to lie between 1 and ∞. This of course is the exact equivalent of $vS = vP$ when v lies between 1 and 0, as on Boole's notation. He then examines the nine cases yielded by putting p and π respectively equal to unity, greater than unity, and equal to infinity. But when he gets $S = \frac{P}{\infty}$ or $S = 0P$, he does not translate it as he should, 'All S is the same as *no P*', i.e. is *nothing;* but simply 'All S are not P, i.e. 'No S are P.' Similarly $0S = 0P$ is translated, not as absolutely indefinite, but as 'All not-S are all not-P.' This is to confound $0S = 0P$ with $S = P$.

[2] *Difficultates quædam logicæ.* 'Omne A est B; i.e. equivalent AB et A.'

[3] *Sammlung, &c.* p. 262.

[4] *Sammlung,* p. 212; *Log. Ab.* I. 23.

extension of the predicate; this characteristic being the very thing which it is bound to possess if it is to coincide with the ordinary proposition[1]. He declares that he will "throughout this system of Logic dispense with such in definite expressions." If it were really the case that we thus introduce greater definiteness of statement it would seem to be a conclusive objection against the form in question, instead of an argument in its favour, for the proposition would be suffered to express more than it has any right to express. A little consideration will however show that the two forms are in every way exactly equivalent. For, starting with either $x = vy$ or $x = \frac{0}{0} y$, multiply each side by the factor y, and we have $xy = 0$: that is $x (1-y) = 0$, or $x = xy$. On the other hand if we start with $x = xy$, and eliminate y (by a process to be hereafter explained) we are led at once to $x = \frac{0}{0} y$ or $x = vy$.

These three forms then are exactly equivalent and convertible one with another. Which therefore, it may be asked, is the best for our purpose? So far as there is any difference, the distinction lies between (1) on the one hand, and (2) and (3) on the other; though this is merely the distinction between the negative and its corresponding

---

[1] *Principles of Science*, p. 41. Others also have failed to see the substantial identity of the two forms. Thus A. Riehl, in a highly laudatory review of the *Principles of Science*, says, 'Boole employed the indefinite symbol v for denoting a partial identity; whilst Jevons makes the definite signification of such an identity visible by his notation' (*Vierteljahrsschrift fur wiss. Phil.* 1877). The same idea is repeated further on in words which, consider-ing what they assign to Hamilton, I quote verbatim : "Hamilton und Boole schreiben diese Urtheile in der Form $X = vY$, allein diese Bezeich-nung lasst unbestimmt welcher Theil von Y, X sei." The notion, that we can in this way secure greater defi-niteness of statement, is really nothing but an old joke expressed in general symbols :—'What functions does an archdeacon perform? archidiaconal functions.'

positive form. As between these we must make our choice according to circumstances, sometimes one and sometimes the other happening to be the most convenient in the statement of a problem. As between (2) and (3) the preference should in strictness be given to (2), at any rate as the primary form of statement. It is to be preferred on the ground that it more prominently calls attention to the indefiniteness in respect of the distribution of the predicate which, as we have seen, the form $x - xy$ somewhat tends to conceal. As a primary statement the form $x - xy$, for 'All x is y', should be rejected alike by the logician and the mathematician; for the former shrinks as much from introducing the term to be defined into a definition, as the latter does from offering an implicit equation in place of an explicit when this latter is available.

It should be observed that, though these two latter forms are thus exactly equivalent, we shall often find that in the process of working there are reasons for preferring one or other of them. Thus, in dealing with the simpler kinds of statement, we shall generally find that $x = xy$ is an easier and less confusing form to deal with. But then it cannot be very readily used unless the term on the left is single. Thus $xy + y + zxy = \frac{0}{0} W$, if we wish to state it as a single proposition, would have to be written out in the form $xy + y + zxy = (xy + y + zxy) W$; nor would the amount of symbols demanded for its expression be economized by breaking it up into three distinct propositions.

II. The Universal Negative: 'No x is y.' About this there is less difficulty. When I say that ' No x is y', it will be admitted, I apprehend, that it ought strictly to be a matter of indifference to me whether x and y exist or not. If either or both of them be wanting the proposition is certainly rendered none the less significant for it is only the combination of the two that I am concerned to deny. If I were told to kill a dog I should certainly have a difficulty in executing the order in case no dog were found alive ; but if I were simply told to make certain that no dog was in the garden, my task should surely be rather simplified than otherwise on my finding that there was neither dog nor garden in existence.

Accordingly there would seem to be little opening for difference of opinion that the way to express such a pro position should be $xy = 0$. Boole preferred to write it, at least as an initial step, in the form 'All x is not-y', $x = v(1 - y)$. I can see no advantage in such a plan ; for, besides being more cumbrous, it sets astir all those difficulties about the existence of the subject and the predicate, which it is our desire to avoid and which the simpler negative form lets well alone. He was doubtless influenced by feelings of logical conserva tism: since such a form preserves at least the semblance of a subject and a predicate, instead of combining them into one and denying the existence of this combination.

III.   So much for Universal propositions, the treatment of which is comparatively easy.   We now come to particular propositions, and at once ground on serious difficulties ; in fact it would not be too much to say that their adequate representation has proved a sore vexation to every thought ful symbolist.   Part of the difficulty is one of mere ambiguity and affects the language of logic and of common life alike. What does 'some' mean ? what cases does it cover ? This depends upon whether we take it as 'some, it may be all', or 'some only.'   With the former explanation 'some x is y' covers the four following cases :—' All x is all y', 'All x is some (only) y', ' Some (only) x is all y', ' Some (only) x is some (only) y':—in fact it only excludes the case 'No x is y.'   With the latter explanation it would include only the last two of these four cases.   The former is the ordinary logical expla nation, and shall be adopted here.

When this obstacle is surmounted we come upon certain symbolic difficulties of representation of a much more serious kind. We shall best see the nature of these by examining their source. Does then the Particular Proposition give us any assurance of the existence of its subject and predicate? It seems clear to me that we must in this respect put it upon a different footing from the Universal Affirmative, and say that it does give us such an assurance, on the ground that if it did not do so it would have absolutely nothing certain to tell us. Whatever shade of doubt of this kind may hang over x and y in ' All x is y ', one thing at any rate is certain, viz. that we thus extinguish xy; and from this we may deduce the hypothetical affirmative form. But when the proposition ' Some x is y ' comes to be affected in the same way, it is paralyzed at once. It can extinguish no class and establish no class, and has therefore no categorical information to give the world. But that this characteristic of really establishing something must be admitted, and indeed made prominent in such propositions, was, I hope, fully made out in the last chapter. And this is borne out by popular usage, for such propositions have, so to say, a tone of reality and of sober fact about them which cannot always be claimed for universals.

Boole's formula is $vx = vy$, where v is to be regarded as an indeterminate class-term. This is seen at once to be obnoxious to various objections. For one thing it is cumbrous and awkward compared with the form to be presently advocated, viz. $xy = v$. But the main difficulty, to my thinking, is in the interpretation to be assigned to this term v. We may call it an ' indeterminate ' symbol, as Boole repeatedly does, but we cannot afford to let it really be so, or the proposition, as we have just seen, will break down and have no message to give us. We must expressly stipulate therefore that v shall not equal *nothing*. But thus to introduce a symbol v,

to speak of it as if it was like any other class term, to com
pound it with other such terms and commute it at will,
and yet to subject it to special and peculiar restrictions of
value unknown to any other of our class symbols, is to say
the least very awkward and questionable.   If indeed we really
wanted to represent entire indefiniteness it would be better
not to use the letter v for the purpose.   We have already
made acquaintance with a symbol which aptly signifies such
indefiniteness.   So if we wish to see how $vx = vy$ would look,
when v was unrestricted, we had best write it at once $\frac{0}{0} x = \frac{0}{0} y$,
and make what we can of it [1].

My own conviction is that we shall not, in this way, make
much of the symbolic treatment of particular propositions;
the fact being that they are, in their common acceptation,
too quantitative for us.   What Symbolic Logic works upon
by preference is a system of dichotomy, of x and not-x, y and

[1] In his *Pr. of Science* (p. 41)
Prof. Jevons declares, as already remarked, that he shall dispense with
such indefinite expressions as 'some'.
("This can readily be done by substituting one of the other terms.   To
express the proposition ' All A's are
some B's ' I shall not use the form
$A = VB$, but $A = AB$".)   Unfortunately this is *not* what can be done in the
case of a really particular proposition, as is exemplified by Jevons
himself a few pages on, in treating
the proposition 'some nebulæ do not
give continuous spectra'.   He says
at once, "treating the little word *some*
as an indeterminate adjective of selection, to which we assign a symbol
like any other adjective, let A = some,
B = nebulæ, &c." (p. 85).

This, since it gives the form

$AB = AC$, for 'some B is C', is merely
Boole's $vx = vy$ over again ; or rather
it is that form with one exception
which here assumes a certain importance.   It was shown in the last chapter
that Prof. Jevons had adopted a sadly
hampering restriction by declaring
that no simple class-term was to be
equated to either 0 or 1.   As a general restriction on our symbolic procedure this would be suicidal,—in
fact it cannot be adhered to,—but
in this special case it comes in ser-
viceably, or rather half of it does.
By forbidding the value $A = 0$, in
$AB = AC$, we save 'some' from being
'none'; and this is well.   But by
forbidding $A = 1$, we prevent ' some '
from being ' all ', both in subject and
predicate, and this is by no means
what we intend to imply.

not-*y*, and so forth.   The sort of propositions therefore that suit us best are those which yield two alternatives only, such as individual propositions :—*A* is *B*, *A* is not-*B*, and so on.   But the particular proposition, in its common acceptation, slips in between these two and says '*Some* of the *A*'s are, or are not, *B* '.   And this we cannot conveniently represent symbolically.   Of course if these 'some' were indicated by a genuine class-term we could express them at once; they would then be marked off by *C* or *D*, and would become the *CA*, or the *DA*, or whatever it might be.   But it hardly needs pointing out that we have then quitted the particular and taken to the universal again, for the *CA* is by no means the vague 'Some *A* '.   If by 'some men have curly hair' I mean that *black* men have, I had better substitute 'black' for 'some', and so make a universal of it.   But this completely alters the kind of proposition.   'Black men' are the objects common to the classes 'black' and 'man':—in contrast with this let us try to put ourselves in the position of taking the common part of the class 'man' and the class 'some'.   The word 'some' marks, and most appropriately marks, those cases in which we are wholly without any other selective class-term which we could substitute for it: *e.g.* 'some throws of a penny will give heads', where it is impossible to sub stitute any more definite term for 'some'.   The device by which we evaded, or thought we evaded, the indefiniteness of the predicate in 'All *A* is some *B* ', by saying that the *A* is *AB*, fails us entirely in the case of true particulars.   We cannot conceal our ignorance in the case of 'Some *A* is *B* ', where both subject and predicate being in the same predica ment of uncertainty neither can aid or prompt the other[1].

[1] There is another form which has been adopted for particular pro- positions by Professor Delbœuf and Mr J. J. Murphy.   Thus the latter writes 'some *x* is *y*' in the form $x - q = y - p$ (*Relation of Logic to*

Another illustration may be offered to show how alien is the ordinary sense of 'some' from the customary symbolic treatment. We know that not-A always means the *rest*, after A has been excepted ; so that A and not-A together make up 'all'. Accordingly, if 'some' be marked by a class-term like any other substantive or adjective, 'not-some' ought to mean 'all except that some'. We shall have instances hereafter of this treatment of a really indeterminate class-term, when it will appear that $\frac{0}{0}$ and $1 - \frac{0}{0}$ are pre cisely equivalent in their signification. But it would surely be doing unnecessary violence to common usage to insist upon using the word 'some' here, and so to maintain that ' not-some' also meant 'some' instead of, as by invariable usage, meaning ' *none* '. Turn it how we will, language and common sense rebel against the attempt to put 'some' on the same symbolic footing as any other substantive or adjective, by assigning it an exactly analogous class symbol.

My own view is that we shall best succeed with these troublesome propositions by taking account of quite another side of their character. To secure as much as possible of the current signification of the particular affirmative, and to express this clearly in symbols, we shall do best to write

Language. See also *Mind*, no. v). The meaning of this is, that, since x and y must have some part in common, if we deduct the ' x that is not-y' (call it q) from x, and the ' y that is not-x' (call it p) from y, the remainders will coincide. The objection to this form seems to me to lie mainly in the conditions by which it must be propped up, for we must insist that q shall be contained in x, and p in y : facts which the symbols themselves do not indicate.

When these conditions are secured, this exception by 'subtraction' becomes identical with exception by 'multiplication'; that is, the formula may be written $x\,(1 - q) = y\,(1 - p)$ which is formally identical with Boole's $vx - vy$. And then finally we encounter here, as there, the question as to what are the limiting values to be admitted for the term employed in subtraction or multipli cation.

it in the form[1] $xy = v$. In so writing it we must observe that v is not a strictly indeterminate class symbol, but is taken as excluding the value 0, or *none*:—whether it is also to be taken as excluding the value 1, or *all*, is not of so much importance, and will be briefly noticed presently.

What we thus lay the stress on is the *existential* character of such propositions. The expression $xy = v$ may be read off in words as ' xy is something', *i.e.* is not nothing ; or, more colloquially, 'There is xy', or ' x and y are sometimes found together'. The last two of these forms are of quite familiar occurrence in the language of common life, and would, I think, be naturally accepted as equivalents of the logical particular affirmative. Similarly, when we want to express the particular negative we adopt the form $xy = v$. This

---

[1] It deserves notice that Boole did adopt this form in his earlier work (*Math. Analysis of Logic*, p. 21) but afterwards rejected it in favour of $vx = vy$. But in neither context can I find any discussion of the real difficulty which arises when we are called upon to decide the limits of indefiniteness to be assigned to v. It may be remarked that Leibnitz with his usual penetration, had observed that particular propositions could be thus expressed. He says (*Difficultates logicæ;* Erd. p. 102) that he had formerly adopted the following scheme : ' Omne A est B...seu A non B est non-ens : Quoddam A non est B...seu A non B est ens : Nullum A est B, erit AB est non ens : Quoddam A est B, erit AB est ens'. So far as it goes this exactly coincides with the arrangement adopted above. But he seems to have rejected it to some extent afterwards, owing to the consequent difficulties about the *conversion* of propositions. But I find his discussion of the subject very intricate and obscure.

In quite recent times the same arrangement substantially has been adopted by Professer F. Brentano (*Psychologie vom empirischen Standpunkte*, 1874), but he does not extend it beyond the four familiar propositions. He announces it as a startling novelty which is to spread dismay among orthodox logicians. Like some other symbolists he springs to the conclusion that the new mode of notation is to supersede altogether the traditional one; instead of being, as I should say, an alternative method, not necessarily hostile to the old one, but far more suitable for the treatment of complicated problems and broad generalizations.

would with equal readiness be thrown into the familiar colloquial statements, 'There are such things as x's which are not y', or 'x's which are not y do occur sometimes'.

We have thus noticed two forms of particular statement, one of these being our substitute for the ordinary affirmative and the other for the ordinary negative of the logical treatises. But it is obvious that when we lay aside logical convention in our arrangements, symmetry and consistency will call for two more such forms. To make our system complete in this department we must exhibit it thus :—

$$xy = v,$$
$$x\overline{y} = v,$$
$$\overline{x}y = v,$$
$$\overline{x}\,\overline{y} = v.$$

The first three of this list belong to forms already discussed and familiar,—the third being merely 'Some y is not x', against the 'Some x is not y' of the second ; they are therefore formally identical. But the fourth is not a familiar form, at least in logical treatises. It would commonly be expressed as 'Some not-x is not y', or 'There are things which are neither x nor y', or 'x and y do not comprise everything'.

This form of expressing symbolically the particular proposition though not new, cannot be considered familiar, and therefore a little more discussion of it will not be out of place. That it cannot be considered quite to coincide with the popular view must be admitted, though I doubt if such departure is wider than in the case of the common Logic. But as regards this latter I can never feel very sure, not having been able to determine what its usage may be. If some logician will undertake to resolve the difficulties indicated in the last Chapter (pp. 133—140), laying down rules which shall be consistent with some view of the nature of general names and propositions acceptable at the present day, I feel sure that every thoughtful reader will be grateful to him.

As regards the relation of this scheme to the conventions of popular speech, the case seems to me as follows. In all universal propositions,—including of course those with complex subjects and predicates—there is one constant element present, and one only, viz. a denial. This we preserve, writing 'All A is B' and 'No A is B', in the forms $AB = 0$, $A\bar{B} = 0$. In addition to this there is an element which is not constantly present, viz. one of implication as to the existence of A and B. This we reject, or rather we say that when required it must be separately called for. Similarly, in all particular propositions there is a constant element, viz. the affirmation of existence. Accordingly we write 'Some A is B', and 'Some A is not B', in the forms $AB = v$, $A\bar{B} = v$. But along with this there are many implications, partly connected with the word 'some' as meaning 'not all,' partly with other words which though excluded from Logic are abundant in common speech, such as 'many', 'most', &c. All these convey information, not merely as to the existence of the AB and $A\bar{B}$, but as to the *amount* of it present; and all these implications we reject.

The only point at which we come into serious conflict with well grounded associations is in refusing to deduce the particular from the universal. From 'All A is B', we cannot infer 'Some A is B'; for if the one merely destroys $A\bar{B}$, and the other merely saves AB, and if these two classes are entirely distinct (as of course they are) then the two propositions clearly do not come into contact with one another at any point. I have purposely emphasized this objection in order to bring out the characteristics of this mode of treatment, but the difficulty is not so formidable as it may seem. Popular thought, when cautioned, would surely agree with us even here. Many universal propositions, or what the logician would treat as such, might be proposed from which every one would feel that it was very hazardous to infer a particular. We do not infer 'Some A is B' merely from 'All A is B', but from this proposition taken with its rider, 'and there is A, and B'; the inference therefore falls to the ground as soon as we agree to exclude this rider from forming any necessary part of the proposition.

Whenever the existence of the subject and predicate is claimed · and duly expressed, the inference follows on the symbolic notation as readily as on any other. 'All A is B, and there is A' would be expressed: $AB = 0$, $AB - v$; and 'Some A is B' would merely be the latter part of this expression repeated again, viz. $AB = v$. In other words the function of the particular affirmative on this principle is that of supplying and distinctly formulating the implication which common thought often makes as a matter of course [1].

[1] Herbart's view about the mode in which existential propositions are connected with categoricals is curious, and, though not the same as that described above, comes in contact with it at several points. He considers (*Einleitung*, § 63) that the scope of the predicate in affirmation is limited and conditioned by that of the subject. Therefore the greater the depth and the less the breadth of the subject notion, the less will be the breadth of the predicate. Now conceive the limiting case in which the subject *disappears*, so that we have in its place merely 'it is', or 'there is', connected with a predicate. We cannot suppose the predicate to have vanished too, or there would be no proposition (it would be the baffling result $0 = 0y$, as the limiting value of $x = xy$). On the contrary, the predicate being then unrestricted and unconditioned, stands by itself, and the sentence takes the form of an existential proposition. 'Jene verwandelt sich in das zeichen von diesem wenn fur ein Pradikat das Subjekt fehlt, und es entsteht auf dieser Weise ein existential Satz.' Elsewhere (*Hauptpunkte der Logik*) he compares the condition of the predicate when the subject vanishes to that of the second member of the equation $S = x^a$, when $a = 0$, and we have $S = 1$.

I cannot accept this account of the process, and the whole discussion is as usual too much cast into 'Begriff' language to fit in

This must suffice for the present treatment of these troublesome propositions. All symbolists, I think, however satisfactory they may consider their own solution of the difficulty to be, are practically agreed in having very little to do with them in the course of their work. And quite rightly so. Indeed I greatly question whether, if the Symbolic Logic had been developed before the Aristotelian had ac quired so firm a hold upon us, such propositions would have been admitted at all. To exclude them from our rules would only be a slightly greater encroachment upon the full freedom of popular speech than has been already brought about by the exclusion of such terms as ' many', ' most', and others of a somewhat quantitative character. Particular propositions, in their common acceptation, are of a somewhat temporary and unscientific character. Science seeks for the universal, and will not be fully satisfied until it has attained it. Indefi niteness indeed in respect of the predicate cannot, or need not, always be avoided ; but the indefiniteness of the subject, which is the essential characteristic of the particular proposi tion, mostly can and should be avoided. For we can very often succeed at last in determining the 'some'; so that instead of saying vaguely that ' Some A is B', we can put it more accurately by stating that ' The A which is C is B', when of course the proposition instantly becomes universal[1].

readily with such a purely class theory as ours. But the passage deserves notice as one of the ex tremely rare instances, till recently, of the examination in Logic of one of those limiting cases with which every mathematician is so familiar.

[1] If we could *always* do this, particular propositions might of course be suppressed altogether; and this is possibly what Prof. Jevons

means in the passages criticized above. But neither usage nor scien tific requirements permit such an assumption. 'Some B' does not necessarily mean 'the B which is marked out by the possession of some common attribute A'. There may be no such common attribute what ever so far as we know, (as in the instance of the throws of the penny offered above) except that which is

Propositions which resist such treatment and remain in curably particular are comparatively rare: *their* hope and aim is to be treated statistically, and so to be admitted into the theory of Probability. The relative importance of really particular propositions is, I think, vastly exaggerated in the common syllogistic treatment, where nearly half the members are particular. But this is almost unavoidable owing to the extreme narrowness of that scheme. We cannot afford to be very scrupulous in what we reject when we are thus confined to three terms and propositions, and are not allowed to resort to negative subjects and predicates. Accordingly we have to welcome there what the symbolist with his abundant resources may well afford to dispense with[1].

We can now in conclusion exhibit a complete scheme of propositional forms as suggested by the capabilities and requirements of our symbolic method. We will suppose two terms only, x and y ; these lead to the following forms :—

$$
\begin{array}{lll}
xy = 0, & xy = v, & xy = 1, \\
x\overline{y} = 0, & x\overline{y} = v, & x\overline{y} = 1, \\
\overline{x}y = 0, & \overline{x}y = v, & \overline{x}y = 1, \\
\overline{x}\,\overline{y} = 0, & \overline{x}\,\overline{y} = v, & \overline{x}\,\overline{y} = 1.
\end{array}
$$

The significance of these various forms will be quite plain from what has been already said. They must be regarded as elementary statements, and as containing all the elementary statements attainable with two class-terms.

mentioned in the predicate, in which case the conversion of it into a universal would merely result in an identical proposition. (The additional difficulties introduced by denying the values 0 and 1 to any simple class term are extraneous to the subject.)

[1] The alternative which every symbolist has to face here may be concisely expressed thus :—If he admits the values 0 and 1 as possible to every class term, how does he express the conventional sense of particular propositions? If he denies these values how does he express *any* proposition of a complex kind? I accept the former, and meet the difficulty by admitting a third value v for propositions which are incurably particular.

(1)   In the first column we declare that such and such a compartment is empty, that is, that the corresponding class is unrepresented in our universe.   This grouping of such propositions of course differs considerably from the customary one. The first of the four is always naturally couched in a negative form in ordinary language and logic, whereas the second and third generally appear as affirmatives.   The fourth again has no precise logical equivalent, the exactest popular equivalent being 'There is nothing but what is either x or y'.   I call attention the more expressly to this point as it enforces the opinion, laid down in the introductory chapter, that there can be no absolute arrangement of propositional forms.   The number and grouping of our forms must depend upon the fundamental view we take as to what should be the import of a proposition.

(2)   In the second column we declare that such and such a compartment is occupied, that is, that the class *is* repre sented.   The only trouble here is in settling the degree of indefiniteness to be assigned to v.   Fortunately for us, in such a notation as this, there are almost no acquired as sociations to be attended to, so we may define freely accord ing to our judgment.   That being so, it would seem best to lay it down that v shall be perfectly indefinite, except that it excludes 0 and 1.   This of course makes the second column intermediate between the first and the third.   The exact meaning of this form of proposition is that a portion, and a portion only, of the things in our universe are found to belong to the class in question ; the remainder of them being distributed in some way, we know not how, amongst the other three conceivable classes.   The particular propositions of ordinary logic are best assigned to this class ; for, though not always precise in their signification, yet when they are made precise they most naturally take up the meaning here assigned.

(3) In the third column we declare that the compart ment is not only occupied, but occupied to the exclusion of all else; that that class, and that class only, is represented. Here we make a complete departure from the familiar forms of ordinary logic, no one of its recognized propositions coin ciding with anything in this column. Popular language would express $xy = 1$ in the words 'Everything is both x and y', whilst $xy - 1$ would stand as 'Everything is neither x nor y', or 'Nothing is x, and nothing is y'.

We might of course easily express all three columns in the generalized form $xy = w$, provided we make w perfectly general; that is, regard it as a general term standing, as the case may be, for any of the values $0, v, 1$. We shall have occasion to treat it so when we come to the consideration of the Aristotelian syllogism in a future chapter.

It must be observed that every one of the above forms readily gives rise to a corresponding alternative. This result follows symbolically from the fundamental formula connecting our class terms, $xy + xy + xy + xy - 1$; or, logically, from the fact that every existing thing must belong to one or other of the four classes thus indicated. In this case since the propo sitional forms with which we are concerned are of the simplest character, dealing with one sub-class only, the corre sponding alternative will be somewhat complex, for it will have to deal with the remaining three classes.

There is no need to go in detail through all the applica tions of this principle, as the reader will find it easy enough to work them out for himself, but it will be well just to take one from each column as a sample. For instance $xy = 0$ yields the alternative $xy + xy + xy = 1$, the two forms being precisely equivalent and convertible. Put into words this amounts to saying that it is exactly the same thing to assert that 'No x is y', or that 'Everything is either x and not y,

y and not x, or neither x nor y', which of course it is. The second column yields a somewhat different kind of alterna tive. From $xy = v$ we deduce $xy + xy + xy = 1 - v$. Now $1 - v$ has exactly the same significance as v, for this was defined to be indefinite between 0 and 1 exclusively. Hence the alternative form might equally be written

$$x\overline{y} + \overline{x}y + \overline{x}\,\overline{y} = v.$$

The meaning of this is easily assignable, for just as $xy = v$ meant 'There are such things as xy', so the longer alternative means 'There are such things as either xy, xy, or xy'. It is of course a very indefinite, and not very useful, form, for it simply assures us that one or more of three classes, we know not which, is represented.

There only remains the corresponding alternative in the third column. This yields a slightly different result from either of the foregoing ; for we thus obtain, not a disjunctive of a positive kind, but a series of categorical negatives. That is, if $xy = 1$, then $xy + xy + xy$ must equal 0, a conclusion which as will be shown hereafter necessitates the three separate conclusions $xy = 0$, $xy = 0$, $xy = 0$. Logically this is clear enough, for if 'Everything is xy , then certainly ' Nothing is xy, xy or xy'; that is, to crowd everything into one compart ment is to cause every other compartment to lie empty.

This will be a convenient place for noticing the charge which has been repeatedly brought against Boole's system,— and presumably against every analogous system of Symbolic Logic,—that it is forced to adopt the Hamiltonian doctrine of the Quantification of the Predicate. Thus Mr Lindsay says, " The doctrines contained in this New Analytic of logical forms lead directly to the theories of Boole and Jevons. A leading characteristic of the doctrine of the Quantification of the Predicate, and other recent theories of a similar kind, is the attempt to assimilate all propositions to the type of

mathematical identities...[1]"; and Prof. Jevons goes further by
declaring that "Dr Boole, employing this fundamental idea
[of Quantification] as his starting-point," arrived at such and
such results[2].

The assertion that Boole's system is in any way founded
on the doctrine of the Quantification of the Predicate, is, in
fact, not directly hostile to that doctrine,—is so astonishing
that one is inclined to suspect some lurking confusion of
meaning. So I will just remark that what I understand by
the doctrine is this:—Whereas the ordinary forms of proposi
tion leave it uncertain whether we are speaking of the whole
predicate, or part only, in affirmation, and decide that we must
be speaking of the whole predicate in negation; we thus
leave four possibilities unrecognized: that in fact we *may* think
the predicate either as a whole or as a part, and *must* think
it as one of the two, in both affirmation and negation alike.
Moreover, since what exists in thought should be expressed
in words, a really complete scheme of propositions demands,
and is satisfied by, eight forms. There is surely no doubt that
this is the sense in which Hamilton, and his authorized ex
ponent Prof. Baynes, understood the doctrine.

Now though it seems hard upon ordinary predicates thus to
charge them with secretly quantifying, it may be brought
against them that at least they have nowhere denied that
they do so. But with Boole's system it is otherwise. If the
wit of man had sought about for some expression which
should unequivocally and even ostentatiously reject this
unfortunate doctrine, what better could be found than $x - \frac{0}{0}y$

---

[1] *Translation of Ueberweg's Logic,*
p. 568:—I am not sure to what extent Mr Lindsay is responsible for
this part, as it is actually contributed
by another writer, Prof. W.R. Smith.

[2] *Substitution of Similars,* p. 4:—

Boole himself expressly states that he
takes the four old forms of proposition "with little variation from the
Treatises of Aldrich and Whately."
(*Math. Anal. of Logic,* p. 20.)

for such a purpose ? So far from quantifying the predicate, by specifying whether we take *some* only or *all* of it, we select a form which startles the ordinary logician by the un customary language in which it announces that it does not at all mean to state whether some only, or all, or even *none* is to be taken. The negative equivalent, $xy = 0$, is just as resolute not to commit itself on this point; whilst, as I have pointed out, $x = xy$ is a precisely synonymous expression. It is diffi cult to conjecture how these symbolic forms could be thus connected with Hamilton's doctrine, unless by a hasty con clusion from the fact that both systems adopt the equational form.

We have thus discussed categoricals with sufficient ful ness, and have touched incidentally upon disjunctives. It will readily be seen why we have not found occasion to say more about the latter kind of proposition. The reason is that on our system they do not differ from categoricals in any re spect of serious importance. The only difference in them is that their subjects or predicates, or both, are composed of two or more class terms instead of one only. To the common logic this may involve a real distinction, but on any class view it is of no significance, since these groups composed of two or more classes are really classes all the same. In $xy - 1$ we declare that a single class constitutes the universe, whilst in $xy + xy + xy = 1$, we declare that three such classes collectively constitute it ; but this difference does not essen tially alter the kind of proposition.

Suppose, for instance, we are given $x + y = a + b$, (x and y, as also a and b, being supposed exclusives). Categorically described, this declares that the members embraced col lectively by the two former classes are identical with those so embraced by the two latter. It then really forms only one proposition. Or we might express it in two pair of ordinary disjunctives by saying 'Every x is either a or b', and 'Every y is either a or b'; adding the corresponding assertions about every a and b being either x or y. Or we might make a more complicated proposition with disjunctive subject and predicate, by saying that whatever is either x or y is either a or b, and vice versa. Some licence of phraseology is allowed on every system; even the common universal affirmative may be read as ' All x is y', or ' Every x is y'; what we do is to insist that this licence shall be rather wide. Provided the class facts asserted remain unchanged, we claim to make almost any verbal statement about them that we please.

The nature of the Hypothetical Proposition and the desirability or otherwise of assigning it a special symbolic form will be best reserved for a future chapter.

A few examples of propositions are added, in order to illustrate the use of our symbolic expressions, as explained in the course of this and preceding chapters. The reader will observe that we purposely employ sometimes one, and some times another, of the various alternative forms of the Univer sal Affirmative which were noticed at the commencement of this chapter.

1. ' Men who are honest and pious will never fail to be respected though poor and illiterate, provided they be self-supporting, but not if they are paupers'. As explained, the various particles here used must all alike be replaced by the mere symbols of connection, so that the proposition may be phrased as follows:—All honest (a), pious (b), poor (c), illiterate (d), self-supporting (e), are respected (f); and no honest, pious, poor, illiterate, self-supporting paupers (g) are respected.

$$\begin{cases} abcde\,(1-f) = 0, \\ abcdefg \qquad -0. \end{cases}$$

Of course when, as here, a whole group of terms presents

tself which does not demand analysis into its details, we may substitute a single letter for the group. Thus we might replace *abcde* by a single letter.

2.   'No x can be both a and b; and, of the two c and e, every x must be one or other only'. This may be written in one sentence,

$$x = x\,(1 - ab)\,(ce + ce),$$

or in two, separately,

$$\begin{cases} xab & = 0, \\ x\,(ce + ce) = 0. \end{cases}$$

In the one case we make a single Affirmative out of the proposition; in the other we couch this in the form of its two constituent elements of denial.

3.   'Every a is one only of the two x and y, except when it is z or w; in the former of which cases it is both x and y, and in the latter case neither of them'. This may be expressed in three sentences :

$$\begin{cases} a, \text{ that is neither } z \text{ nor } w, \text{ is } x \text{ or } y \text{ only,} & azw = \tfrac{0}{0}\,(xy + xy), \\ a, \text{ that is } z, \text{ is both } x \text{ and } y, & az - \tfrac{0}{0}\,xy, \\ a, \text{ that is } w, \text{ is neither } x \text{ nor } y, & aw = \tfrac{0}{0}\,xy, \end{cases}$$

or, in one sentence, and without the express sign of indefinitude, $a = a\,\{zw\,(xy + xy) + zwxy + zwxy\}.$

4.   As an example of translating symbols into words take the following :—

$$a + a\,(1 - ce).$$

Here ce stands for what fails to be c and fails to be e, so that $1 - ce$ stands for all that does not so fail. Hence the given expression may be read off, 'Anything which is a; or even not a, provided that in this case it does not fail both to be c and to be e'.

An alternative symbolic statement here would be $1 - ace$,

(since $a + a = 1$). It might then be read off, 'All that does not fail to be a, c and e'.

5. 'Every member of the Committee (x) is a Protestant (a), and either a Conservative (c), or Liberal (e); except the Home Rulers (y), who are none of the three'.

$$x = x\left\{\overline{y}a\,(c + \overline{c}e) + y\overline{a}\,\overline{c}\overline{e}\right\}.$$

If we are supposed to know that Conservative and Liberal are exclusives, we may put $c + e$ for $c + ce$. The best way perhaps of interpreting the symbolic sentence here is just to substitute the significant words, when it would stand:— Every member of the Committee is a member of the Committee who is not a Home Ruler, (and then he is a Protestant, and either a Conservative or a Non-Conservative Liberal), or he is one who is a Home Ruler, and then he is neither Protestant, Conservative, nor Liberal.

6. $xy + xy + z\,(xy + xy).$

This may be read off, 'x or y only; or, provided there be z, both x and y or neither of them'. An alternative symbolic statement would be $1 - z\,(xy + xy)$, which might be read, 'All excepting what is not z, but is both or neither x and y'.

7. As an illustration of the symbolic signification of particular propositions we may take the following :—'Every ab is either x or y only, and it is known that there are some a which are x and some b which are not y'.

If the latter clauses were omitted, the sentence would be written simply :—

$$ab = \tfrac{0}{0}\,(x\overline{y} + \overline{x}y).$$

This would merely obliterate the two classes $abxy$ and $abxy$, leaving the remaining 14 classes perfectly indeterminate, subject to the formal condition that one at least of them must be represented. Now the statement 'Some a is x', or, 'There *are* such things as ax', puts a check upon the destruc-

tion of ax, insisting that some one at least of its four consti
tuents (or rather three, since $abxy$ is gone) shall be saved.
But it does not tell us which of them is thus rescued.
Similarly, 'There is b which is not y' saves some one at least
of the three surviving elements of by.   On the diagrammatic
scheme this would be carried out by our taking a note, so to
say, that the whole compartments ax and by were not to
be shaded out in any case.

CHAPTER VIII.

THE UNIVERSE OF DISCOURSE.

We have had repeated occasion to refer to the Logical Universe of Discourse in the foregoing chapters, but the present will be the best opportunity for completing what it is necessary to say upon this point. As in other parts of our subject, there are three main topics of enquiry before us; for, in trying to rearrange things in accordance with the principles of Symbolic Logic, we cannot afford to pass over either the conclusions of unassisted common sense, or the rules and assumptions of the logicians.

As regards then the popular way of thinking, the question of course is this. When we make use of names and resort to reasonings, what limits of reference, if any, do we make? What is the range of subject matter about which we con sider ourselves to be speaking? I think we must answer that as regards negative terms we always make very considerable restrictions, and that as regards positive terms we only some times make them, and then comparatively slight ones[1]. The

[1] True negative names of the type 'not X' are not very frequent in popular speech, but are mainly an invention of the logician. Still they

limits of positive terms are generally settled very readily : we all know what is in most cases meant to be included under the name 'black'. But what does 'not-black' include? Does it apply to all things without exception to which the colour black cannot be applied; including, say, the Geological Glacial Period, the sources of the Nile, the claims of the Papacy, the last letter of Clarissa Harlowe, and the wishes of our remote posterity? Clearly not : some kind of limit, more or less restricted, is generally understood to be drawn ; but where exactly it may be traced must depend upon the nature of the subject and the associations of the speaker.

This distinction between the application of positive and that of negative names is in great part of a comparatively verbal character. It is not because a name is negative that we commonly have to refer to a part only of its denotation, but because certain classes are tolerably definite and often have to be referred to as a whole, that we confer a positive name upon them, the heterogeneous multitude outside falling to the share of the corresponding negative name. But of course, when we have got this comparatively definite name, it does not follow that we must in every case refer to the whole of it, especially when it is itself a somewhat extensive

do occur sometimes both in subject and predicate, when the classes indicated by them happen to be narrower, or more conveniently assigned, than those indicated by the corresponding affirmative names:—*e.g.* 'What is not conceivable is no fit subject of instruction'. Of course if we class with these, as I think we must, such names as 'inhuman', 'unnatural', and so forth, what is here said about the very great restriction with which their extent is commonly interpreted, is indisputably true. (We must remember to keep clear of the Quantification dispute here. In such a proposition as 'some contractions are involuntary', the question now before us is not as to how much of the whole extent of the 'involuntary' is *present in thought* in the proposition, but rather as to what we are to consider *is* that whole extent when we come to reflect upon what has been said.)

one.   Hence we constantly make assertions about 'all men' without the slightest intention of being bound by our words beyond a reference to a comparatively small selection of mankind.

The same general question is sometimes practically raised in another form by enquiring whether we have any pairs of terms in our language which are strictly contradictories. That we have plenty of formal contradictories, such as good and not-good, human and inhuman, &c., is obvious enough ; but what is here sought for is rather a pair of material con tradictories, which shall be logically contradictory in their current use and application.   The reply must be, as above. that language being relative to human wants every pair of contradictories is restricted to some tolerably well understood universe.   Such restriction is commonly more constant in the case of material than in the case of formal contradictories; for each of the pair being a so-called positive, and a natural instead of an artificial term, each carries its customary limitation of signification with it : thus British and alien are equivalent to British and not-British, provided we under stand that we are talking only of human beings.   Not-British being an artificial word its range of application may be very variable, but legal and customary usage have decided much more rigorously to what objects the word 'alien' shall be rightly applied.

We must now notice briefly what the ordinary logician has to say upon the matter.   The use of this word universe was first made familiar by De Morgan[1], but the conception itself is one that is suggested at more than one point in the traditional treatment.   For instance the doctrine of a *summum genus* is connected with the present enquiry; involving,

[1] *Camb. Phil. Tr.* viii. 380.   He speaks there of "inventing a new   technical term ".

as it does, the necessity of some restriction upon the extent
of the class which we take into account. But where the
need of some restriction of the kind seems mostly felt is in
the discussions about the nature of 'infinite' or indefinite
terms and propositions. I have no wish to enter into that
Serbonian bog further than one not brought up in those parts
may venture with safety, and will therefore merely refer to
the form in which this doctrine was held by a very eminent
thinker who was but little restrained by traditions of the
past. Students of Kant will remember the three-fold divi
sion of propositions which he makes, in respect of their quan
tity, into positive, negative, and infinite. Verbally, of course, -
it is easy enough to say that we must either assert that A is $qu.$
B, or deny that it is B, or (couching the latter in affirmative
form) assert that A is not-B; and we may readily admit that
there is some conventional difference of signification between
these various cases. But is there any difference whatever, of
which logic should take account, between the last two? On
any rigid class view of the nature of predicates it is
impossible to extract more than two divisions; for, that to
exclude a thing from a boundary is to include it somewhere
outside that boundary, that to deny that any thing has a
given attribute is to assert that it has not that attribute,
seems indubitably clear. I suppose that the idea underlying
the distinction is this. When we deny that A is B we think
of A as a whole, and B as an attribute and therefore as a
whole, so that the judgment is finite in both terms. But
when we say that A is not-B and try to consider this not-B
as an attribute, we have forced upon our notice the vague
amplitude of its extent; and therefore, when we do not
make appeal to a limited universe, we must recognize that
the judgment is in respect of its predicate an infinite or
indefinite one.

Whether I am right or wrong in this last remark it will equally serve to call attention to the view which the Symbo lic logician is bound to adopt. Taking, as we do, a strict class view of the nature of propositions we meet the difficulty by flatly denying that the class not-X need be more 'infinite', or in any way more extensive even, than X. The notion that it is so is simply a survival from the traditions of common speech and is one of which the symbolist should rid himself as speedily as possible. Not-X is of course always the contradictory of X, but there is no reason to suppose that the former symbol is more appropriately applied to classes which are essentially negative or are popularly regarded as such[1]. There may be practical reasons of convenience for thus assigning our symbols, but as far as any reasons of principle are concerned we might exchange X and not-X all through our logical processes without the slightest change of symbolic significance. There is nothing to hinder us from putting not-X to stand for the few and highly specialized members of some narrow class, and X for the innumerable and heterogeneous individuals which do not belong to it.

When thus regarded, the conception of a universe is seen to be strictly speaking extra-logical; it is entirely a question of the *application* of our formulæ, not of their symbolic statement. It is quite true that we always do recognize a

[1] I cannot therefore agree with Prof. Wundt when he says (*Logik*, 233) that 'Boole's view rests upon the wide spread logical error according to which the concept non-A is referred to the infinitude of the concept world'. (It seems to me that Prof. Wundt's treatment of his subject is in several places somewhat marred by his not having shaken off the language and tone of conceptualism.)

It deserves notice that one of the earliest writers to apply symbolic notation to Logic, — Segner, — has called attention to this indifferent symbolic application of X and not-X. Employing $(-)$ to mark the contra-dictory, he says that if we like to put X for *non-triangulum* then $-X$ will stand for *triangulum*. (*Specimen Logicæ*, p. 71.)

limit, sometimes express but more often tacit, as to the extent over which not-X is to be allowed to range; and also that we not unfrequently do so in respect of X itself, so long as these expressions are set before us in words and not in symbols only. Between them, X and not-X must fill up the whole field of our logical enquiry; they can leave nothing unaccounted for there. But when the question is asked, How wide is that field? the only answer that can be given is, just as wide as we choose in any case to make it. Whether the practical imposition of these limits does most to curtail the range of X or of not-X is of no significance, for this will depend upon the arbitrary assignment of our symbols in the stating of our premises.

This limitation of our universe, tacit or avowed, may take a variety of forms. In this respect Boole's view has, I think, been misunderstood by some writers (as by Mr Macfarlane)[1]. He seems to think that Boole just drew, as it were, a definite outline to mark the limits, and then con sidered himself bound to·take every kind of logical entity to be found within those bounds. I cannot perceive that that was his view, and certainly I should reject any such interpre tation myself. The limits of application of our formulæ seem to me in every respect open to our own choice. They may take the form of any order or plane of existences, as well as that of any boundary line on such a plane. For instance, we are applying, say, the terms European and not-European. We may extend our universe so as to embrace

---

[1] "It appears that what Boole means by the universe of discourse is not the objects denoted by a Universal Substantive, but a definite part of the whole realm of things,—a limited portion of the physical universe, with all the entities which are or can be imagined to be in it, whether mental or physical, ponderable or imponderable, atomic or complex" (*Algebra of Logic*, p. 6).

the sum-total of logical existence, in which case European includes things other than men, and not-European includes the unlimited myriads of entities which people that hetero geneous domain. Or we may restrict it to *man*, in which case not-European is limited to men of other quarters of the world. Or it is equally open to us, in the case of any special example, to confine it to the British House of Commons, in which case European is limited to some 650 persons, and not-European is non-existent. That is, in this last case, European is logically 'all', and not-European is 'nothing'.

'All' and 'nothing' therefore, in any application of our formulæ, are to be interpreted in accordance with the limits which we may decide to lay down at the outset of the particular logical processes in question. The *all* of some reference may, as it happens, be absolutely all, in the sense that the widest extension of our universe would not yield any more of it. Thus no extension of the universe beyond *man*, would yield any other specimens of 'rational animal' than those which are human. And the *nothing* of some reference may merely mean nothing *there*, whereas the term may apply to any number elsewhere, possibly to 'all' else that exists. All applications of our logic are, as remarked, at our free choice; we might limit our application of the terms 'good' and 'not-good' to the London cabs with odd numbers, and every logical rule will hold valid as well as if we had selected a less absurd sort of universe.

It has been said above that this question of the Universe only arises when we *apply* our formulæ. Now diagrams are strictly speaking a form of application, and therefore such considerations at once meet us when we come to make use of diagrams. I draw a circle to represent X; then what is outside of that circle represents not-X, but the limits of that outside are whatever I choose to consider them. They

may cover the whole sheet of paper, or they may be con
tracted definitely by drawing another circle to stand as the
limit of the universe; or, better still, we may merely say
vaguely that the limits of the universe are somewhere out
side the figure but that there is not the slightest ground of
principle or convenience to induce us to indicate them.

The settlement of the Universe being therefore a question
of application merely it can never be indicated by our
symbols, for these must in themselves be perfectly general.
They know nothing of any kind of limit except what is
purely formal.   When it is asked, What are the limits of
not-x? the symbolic answer is invariably the same, 'all that
is excluded from x is taken up by not-x'.   It is only when
we go on to enquire what is meant by 'all' that the question
of a limit comes in, and this is a practical matter involving
the interpretation of our data.   Hence, for instance, we ought
not to say that in the expression $zx = zy$, we necessarily mean
that "in the universe z, all x is the same as all y".   That we
may make z our universe in this case, as in any other, is
indisputable, and, if we do so, then the above is the true
explanation of the statement; but there is nothing in the
statement to compel us to make it there, or to do more than
suggest to us to do so.   On the contrary, the employment of
any symbol z immediately intimates not-z, and unless we are
told (on material grounds), or decide for ourselves arbitrarily,
that there shall be no not-z, we should naturally infer that
the universe will find place for something of that sort.   The
statement $zx - zy$ would, on a diagram, be thus repre
sented :—

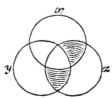

(for we must simply regard 'zx which is not y' and 'zy which is not x', as being abolished). It is clear that within the universe of z, x and y coincide; but then so they may also to some extent outside it, to say nothing of there being also a place provided outside for what is x alone, and y alone, and neither of the two. Similarly we can see that within the universe x, z is but a portion of y; and that within the universe y, z is but a portion of x[1].

I cannot therefore agree with Mr Macfarlane (*Algebra of Logic*, p. 29) that "Every general proposition refers to a definite universe, which is the subject of the judgment... For example, 'All men are mortal' refers to the universe 'men'. 'No men are perfect', refers to the same universe". I prefer to say that there is no indication here of what the universe may be; this being a matter of private interpreta tion or application, in no way suggested by our symbols. Moreover, on the symbolic system it is universally admitted that the distinction between subject and predicate is lost: why then are we to consider that 'no x is y' has x as its universe rather than y?

The outside of our Universe itself is of course simply disregarded. It must not only not exist in the sense of being affected by negative attributes only, but in that of having no attributes whatever, positive or negative. It contains no compartments even, which we can speak of as either empty or occupied. We simply do not suffer our minds to dwell upon it. The outside of any particular universe may in fact be considered to stand in much the same relation to all

---

[1] This may be exhibited symboli- cally thus:— Put $z = 1$, then $x = y$. That is, when z is made 'all', x and y are co-extensive. Similarly put $x = 1$, and we have $z = zy$, or 'All z is y'. It is clear that in making these changes we have interfered with the statement as originally given to us. That statement in no way called for these restrictions, though it lays itself open to them.

possible logical predication that the field of 'view' at the *back* of our heads stands to all possible colours.

The fact that we thus regard the real extent of that sum total of things which makes up our Universe as a matter of application, rather than as anything which can be considered formal, is another reason for representing it by *unity*[1]. This fitly indicates its perfectly general character. The standard expression $xy + x\bar{y} + \bar{x}y + \bar{x}\bar{y} = 1$ declares that the four classes on the left make up 'all'. If any one presses for further information as to what this 'all' may be, we reply that this is a part of the data and therefore to be postulated by the logician, as given to him, not a formal principle to be supplied by him.

---

[1] The main grounds for choosing *unity* for this purpose were given in Chap. II. They were connected with the particular processes of 'multiplication' and 'addition' adopted in our logical system. Some writers, who do not accept these processes exactly as we do, have employed other symbols instead. For instance R. Grassmann (*Begriffslehre*) makes use of the letter T. Adopting as he does the non-exclusive plan of expressing alternatives (some further account of this plan is given in Chap. XIX.) he writes $a + T - T$, in order to express the fact that the universe, since it includes a, cannot be increased by any addition of a to it. If we are to admit such a formula at all, I certainly think that less violence is done to acquired associations by writing $a + T = T$ than by writing $a + 1 = 1$. The companion formula however, $a \times T = a$, is less convenient than $a \times 1 - a$. Those who adopt the symbol ∞ for the Universe (Wundt, *Logik*, p. 233, Prof. C. S. Peirce, *Am. Ac. of Arts and Sciences*, 1870; *Am. Journal of Mathematics*, Vol. III.), have in consistency, on the same non-exclusive scheme, to face the results $a \times \infty = a$, $a + \infty = \infty$. Prof. Pierce in fact does not shrink from their employment in this way.

CHAPTER IX.

ON DEVELOPMENT OR EXPANSION.

THE process called sometimes Development, and sometimes Expansion, is the most fundamental and important with which we shall have to concern ourselves. In fact when the nature and results of this process are fully under stood the main task of Symbolic Logic is grasped. Both of these terms (Development and Expansion[1]) possess some symbolic propriety, as will be seen when we come to give rules for the performance of the operation in question; but on merely logical grounds such an expression as 'continued dichotomization', or 'subdivision', would seem to be more appropriate.

Every one who has read a treatise on Logic is familiar with the fact that any assignable class admits of dichotomy,

---

[1] The objection to these two terms is that they do not readily offer any appropriate *correlatives;* whereas when we regard the operations themselves, we see that the splitting up of a class into its ulti- mate elements, and the recombi- nation of these elements into a single group, are inverse operations to one another. 'Subdivision' and 'Aggregation', though not without objection, seem to satisfy this condi- tion of standing as convenient cor- relatives.

or division into two parts, x and not-x respectively, whatever quality x may stand for. One or other of these two parts may of course fail to be actually represented, but both cannot thus fail; in other words, these may be regarded, as already remarked, as compartments into one or other of which every individual must fall, and into one or both of which every class must be distributable. At this point common Logic mostly stops in practice. It is clear however that we have thus made but a single step along a path where indefinite progress is possible. Each of the classes or compartments thus produced equally admits of subdivision in respect of y, whatever y may be; and so on without limit. The subdivision in respect of one class term (x) gives two classes, x and not-x; that in respect of two terms gives four classes; with three we obtain eight, and so on. Stating the results with full generality, we see that with n terms thus to combine and subdivide we have a complete list of 2^n ultimate classes.

This dichotomous scheme is of course absolutely complete so far as it extends. It contains the provision or the raw materials for the statement of every purely logical proposition which can possibly be framed by employment of the terms in question. It may therefore be regarded as a sort of framework for all possible propositions involved in, or expressible by, the given terms. If, for instance, we have two terms x and y, then the four sub-classes indicated by xy, xy, xy, and xy, comprise all the elements which can possibly be needed or employed for the purpose of constructing propositions out of the terms x and y. This was explained in a preceding chapter where we drew up, on this suggestion, a scheme of elementary forms of propositions. To these we might have added many more by combining the elements two and two, or three and three together.

Of course this dichotomous subdivision of terms is not Logic, but rather a substructure of logic. It is an orderly process for assigning all the elements which we can need in our reasonings, and the performance of it is therefore rather a preliminary to reasoning than reasoning itself. It is however an absolutely necessary preliminary when we are going to occupy ourselves with complicated propositions or groups of propositions, and we shall accordingly proceed to discuss it.

The process of subdivision thus indicated is, as a rule, easy enough to carry out by mere inspection, unless we are concerned with complicated class expressions. Suppose for instance, to begin with a very simple example, that we had the class group $xy + xz$ to deal with in this way. It is clear at once that the term xy admits of no further sub division of this kind, as regards either x or y; for it is xy most unmistakeably, and can therefore yield no term of the not-x or not-y description. Accordingly the only sub division open to it is in respect of z, so we divide it into the parts which are, and which are not z, viz. into xyz, and $xy\bar{z}$. Similarly xz admits only of subdivision in respect of y, and yields the terms xyz and $x\bar{y}z$. And here of course the process stops, for we are only supposed to have the three terms x, y, and z, before us. Indeed they are the only terms entering into the given expression. Accordingly the result of the process is given by $xyz + xy\bar{z} + xyz + x\bar{y}z$.

So much of what has to be said on the subject of this Development has already been anticipated in previous chap ters, that it really does not seem that much more expla nation is called for at present. We shall consider it almost at once indeed, in its wider symbolic aspect, when it assumes a form which is very far from being familiar and obvious; but just at present I prefer to look at it in the light of

ordinary logical considerations. Such simple remarks as
remain to be said under this head may be gathered up
as follows :—

I. It will be observed that in the above example we
only developed the expression $xy + xz$ in respect of the class
terms actually involved in it, viz. x, y, and z. There was
however no necessity for thus confining ourselves ; every
subdivision which we reached might have been still further
subdivided, if we wished, in respect of a, b, c, or any other
succession of letters regarded as representing class terms.
The reasons for not doing this are however obvious. Nothing
is, or could be, gained in this way. Any degree of sub
division is useful which turns upon class terms about which
definite suggestions are given to us, that is, which enter
into the data of the problem before us. But to go on
subdividing beyond this point, by introducing terms about
which no suggestions are given to us, can be nothing but an
idle exercise of our rules of operation.

Of course each component element of the expression which
is given to us to develop will be treated in respect of terms
which *it* does not contain ; otherwise indeed there could
be no development. Thus xy did not involve z, nor did
xz involve y. The rule is that every element must be
developed in respect of every term which we may have to
take into account, that is, which the whole expression before
us involves. Hence follows one very important conside
ration. We shall often find *unity* entering amongst our
symbols ; and this, being a class term, must admit of de
velopment like any other. No term visibly occurs in it, but
representing as it does the sum-total of all things, all con
ceivable classes must be contained in it. Hence unity must
be developed, in any given case, in respect of *all* the class
terms involved in the expression in which it occurs. Take

for instance, $1 - xy - xy$. Here two terms (x and y) occur in combination. When we develop 1 in respect of these two, we obtain $xy + xy + xy + xy$. The other two terms in the given expression are already in their ultimate state of subdivision. Hence the whole expression when developed resolves itself into $xy + xy$. As it happens here, this is actually a simpler and shorter result than it was before development. As a rule the reverse is the case, this process of subdivision generally multiplying the number of final terms; to such an extent indeed when the terms are numerous as to make the statement of the result very tedious and complicated.

II. Every class other than unity, howsoever composed, must be logically *less* than unity. This follows from the very meaning of our symbols; for 1 stands for 'all things', and x stands for a limited selection from all, viz. for such of them as are x. Hence no class term, or group which can constitute a class, will contain *all* the elements which have to be referred to in the process of developing it. Some will contain more of these ultimate elements, others will contain less, but the development of unity alone can contain them all. Some indeed may already happen to be given in their lowest terms and so admit of no further development. Thus if we took xyz and developed it with respect to the three symbols which it contains, we should merely get the same result over again, every other combination vanishing from the development. The example above, viz. $xy + xz$, developed into four ultimate subdivisions only, the other four not appearing in the final result.

III. If the original class group which was given to us to be developed contain none but mutually exclusive terms, no element in the development will appear more than once in our result. But if the original statement was faulty in this respect the fault will appear immediately in the development, by one or more of their elements having some other factor than unity;—2, 3, or so on. Take for instance $x + y$ and develop it; it will yield the result $xy + xy + 2xy$. This of course is nothing but the question of overlapping classes, and the proper form of expression of an alternative, discussed in Chap. II. The process of development is in fact the suitable mode of testing whether or not any given expression, constituting a group of classes, is correctly and accurately drawn up in this respect. So simple and obvious a redundancy as that in $x + y$ can be detected at a glance, but one in which the overlapping part is very special and limited could hardly be discovered without this methodical process of subdivision into all the ultimate elements. Thus $1 - x + yz + xyz$ yields, after development, the term $2xyz$ indicating that as it thus stood the element representing 'things that are y and z but not x' is counted twice over. It must therefore be regarded as an instance of faulty expression. Had it stood, instead, $1 - x + xyz + xyz$, no fault could have been found with it in this respect, as all the class terms would have been mutually exclusive. (We here take $1 - x$ as a simple class term.)

Up to this point in our investigation of the process of Development, we have resorted to no other considerations than such as are suggested by ordinary Logic, and are perfectly explicable within its province [1]. Since everything must be either x or not-x it stood to reason that every class which did not expressly by its form belong to one or other of these two divisions alone, must be capable of being split up into two parts one of which belongs to each. And this

---

[1] It deserves notice that Lambert had got as far as this in Logic: *e.g.* "Man drücke die eigene Merkmale des a durch $a|b$ aus, und die eigene Merkmale des b durch $b|a$; so hat man $a|b + b|a + ab + ab = a + b$' (*Log. Abhandlungen*, I. 11).

process, once commenced with some one class term as the dividing element, could be continued with another, and so on indefinitely, or until all the class terms assigned in the data were exhausted.

What we now propose to do is not to trust to mere acuteness to carry out this process, but to ascertain whether we cannot give a perfectly general symbolic rule of operation for effecting it. This was one of the grand steps of generali zation introduced by Boole. Take then for examination a group of class terms a trifle less simple than those given above, for example $x + y + xyz$, and suppose we develop this with respect to x. The first and third of these terms remain unchanged, for since they involve x they cannot yield any not-x part. The second term splits up into xy and xy. The whole expression thus becomes $x + y\ (x + x) + xyz$. Now the rule of formation is readily seen in this case, and it is one which will equally apply to all other cases. It is this. Every term in the given expression which involves either x or x is left as it stands, and every term which does not involve x is multiplied by the factors x and x, i.e. is sub divided into these two parts; these being then added to gether to form the result. Of course, in a sense, all the terms are left unaltered in value; for subdivision, when all the elements are retained, leaves the aggregate undis turbed. But then to resolve the total class into its elemen tary parts and to retain all these parts before us, is just the very process which we are proposing to carry out.

As thus deduced, the Development took the form $x + y\ (x + x) + xyz$. Now this may be differently arranged, if we pick out separately and group together the x and not-x parts, for it then becomes

$$(1 + y + yz)\, x + y\bar{x}.$$

When put into this form we see that the following rule

of operation for obtaining the development may be laid down. 'Write 1 for x all through the given expression, and multiply the result so obtained by x: then write 0 for x all through it, and multiply this result by x. The sum of these two results is the full development of the given expression with respect to x.'

This rule of operation lends itself to an extremely brief and simple symbolic expression, for the whole of it is conveyed at once by the statement, 'the development of $f(x)$ is $f(1)\,x + f(0)\,x$'. This is the rule given by Boole almost at the commencement of his work, and which plays so large a part in his method[1]. As regards the true logical interpretation of it we shall have more to say hereafter, but at present I will merely give a word or two of explanation of its symbolic construction as it thus stands. It need not be added, after what has been already said, that $f(x)$ is to be regarded as being merely a perfectly general symbol for any class, or group or arrangement of classes, which involves x in it. The symbol $f(1)$ stands, as usually in mathematics, for this same class group when it is altered by changing every x in it into 1, and leaving every other letter unaltered; whilst $f(0)$ stands for the same class group when x is changed into 0 and no other change made. Hence the expression $f(1)\,x + f(0)\,x$ must be regarded as being merely a symbolic representation of the rule of operation given above.

In the above investigation we were only supposed to subdivide the given class expression in respect of *one* of the terms involved in it, viz. x. It is equally open to us however to proceed further in the same course of subdivision. Pre-

---

[1] Boole gave only formal proofs of this rule. Thus, assume $f(x) = ax + bx$. Putting $x=1$ and 0 respectively, we have $a = f(1)$, $b = f(0)$; Hence $f(x) = f(1)\,x + f(0)\,x$. He then applies it at once to the development of a fractional expression. (*Laws of Thought*, p. 72.)

sumably the given expression was built up of a number of class terms aggregated together, such as x, y, z, &c. ; of which terms we have only taken one into account. Now it must be remembered that the result of this first operation will be of precisely the same general character as the original expression with which we started. We were supposed to start with a class expression, indicated by $f(x)$; and we get from it another class expression ; indicated by $f(1) x + f(0) x$. The only difference between them is that the latter is more subdivided than the former, having been broken up in respect of one of its component elements, viz. x.

Whatever therefore we did to the former expression we may repeat in a similar way upon the latter. We cannot of course develop the latter again in respect of x, for that has been already done. We may apply the rule to it indeed if we like, but it will leave us exactly where it found us, for we shall merely have the same result repeated unchanged, and so on as often as we chose to continue the process. But if we treat it the second time in respect of some other class term involved in it, say for instance y, then we shall be really carrying out the process of subdivision one stage more. We suppose then that $f(1) x + f(0) x$ involves y; that is to say, that the class symbol y, amongst others, enters into $f(1)$ and $f(0)$ as it did into $f(x)$, for it must be remembered that it was only x which was meddled with by being turned into 1 and 0 respectively, the other class symbols being left untouched.

We want then to develop $f(1) x + f(0) x$ in respect of y. We might proceed by the process which we first started with, but it will be simpler to adopt at once the symbolic process which was seen to yield the same result. The rule which it gave was to write 1 for y all through and multiply by y, and then write 0 for y all through and multiply by y, and add these together. This rule applied to $f(1)$ gives us $f(1,\ 1)y + f(1,0)y$; where $f(1,\ 1)$ stands for what $f(x)$ becomes when y as well as x is put equal to 1, and $f(1,\ 0)$ stands for what $f(x)$ becomes when x is put $=1$, and $y=0$. Similarly $f(0)$ develops into $(0,1)y + f(0,\ 0)\ y$, where $f(0,\ 1)$ is $f(x)$ with $x=0$, and $y=1$, and $f(0,\ 0)$ is the same expression with both x and $y=0$. Hence the whole result thus obtained is

$$f(x) = f(1,\ 1)\,xy + f(1,\ 0)\,x\overline{y} + f(0,\ 1)\,\overline{x}y + f(0,\ 0)\,\overline{x}\overline{y}.$$

Of course we need not stop here. If there was a third class term z in the original expression, this must appear in one or more of the factors $f(1,\ 1)$, $f(1,\ 0)$, &c. Hence the process of development or subdivision may be repeated a third time, yielding 8 possible ultimate elements; and so on again and again, until we have taken every class term or symbolic letter in the original expression into account.

In this expression, as will be more fully pointed out presently, the factors $f(1,\ 1)$, $f(1,\ 0)$, &c. are not logical class terms involving x, y, &c., at least not when the Development is fully completed; for by that time every x and y has been changed into 1 or 0, and has accordingly disappeared from the result. Hence these expressions are, symbolically, purely *numerical* quantities; whilst logically, they are, as will be shown, directions to take into account the whole, an uncertain part, or none, of the class to which they are prefixed as factors. Thus, in this case, xy denotes a class; $f(1,\ 1)$ tells us whether or not that class is to be included; and so on all through.

It need not be remarked that the process is a tedious one, owing to the multitude of terms involved, but except in this respect it is as simple and easy as anything well can be. Tedious as it is however, it, or some equivalent of it, is unfortunately inevitable, granted the desirability of the end aimed at. That is to say, if we really want to determine all the mutual relations of four terms and their contradictories,—and many problems may demand this,—then we have no other course but to examine in detail all the 2^4 or 16 ultimate subdivisions thus produced. Hence if problems of this kind had more than a speculative interest (which they can very seldom have) any mechanical means for aiding us in this process would be most valuable. Some account of such machines was given in the fifth chapter.

The point therefore at which we have at present arrived is this. By perfectly simple and intelligible logical steps we can break up a composite class into all the elementary classes of which it consists; and we can show that identically the same result can be obtained by the symbolic rule of operation, ' for $f(x)$ write $f(1) x + f(0) x$ '.

We must now look about to see under what sort of restrictions such a rule as this is obtained, and whether any of these restrictions are removable.

I. To begin with ; is it necessary that the class group which we thus develop should be stated in its rigidly accurate form in which it consists solely of an aggregate of mutually exclusive terms? By no means ; in fact one use of Development is to detect whether or not the component elements do thus overlap one another. Treat $x + y$ in this way and it becomes $2xy + xy + xy$, thus reminding us that the common part is xy. There are indeed objections both of principle and of method, to suffering any class terms which are not mutually exclusive to enter into our logical statements, but these objections do not in the slightest way affect the validity of this process of Development.

This will indeed be obvious if we remember that Development is nothing but subdivision into its ultimate class elements, and that all that is meant by insisting on mutual exclusiveness is the avoidance of the double counting of the

overlapping part; this being so, every doubly counted ele
ment in the development must necessarily stand out in relief
from amongst the others by being multiplied by the factor
2. Similarly if it is counted thrice over. Thus develop
$xy + xz + yz$ and we have $xyz + xyz + xyz + 3xyz$, thus
reminding us that each of these three terms involves one
part peculiar to itself, and one (xyz) common to all three.

There is however a far more important extension than
this to be considered in the application of our formula. Have
we a right to apply it to *uninterpretable* expressions, either at
first hand or in the process of passing through such ex
pressions in case we are led to them? There is no doubt that
Boole held this opinion himself, nor, I presume, that the
same view has been held by many, if not most, of those who
have accepted and used his formulæ. He regarded this rule
of Development, apparently, as a sort of engine potent
enough to reduce to a series of intelligible logical terms
expressions which as given to us had not a vestige of
intelligible meaning in them. He appeals, in justification of
this rather startling procedure, to the practice of the mathe
maticians ; especially to their employment of the symbol
$\sqrt{-1}$, as offering an analogy and justification for this corre
sponding step in Logic.

If we were forced to adopt this view a very difficult
enquiry would have to be entered on. We should have to go
rather deeply into the question as to the nature of reasoning,
and the limits within which it may be relied on,—discussing
indeed the question whether and how far the processes of ma
thematics do really offer what can be called uninterpretable
steps,—an enquiry which I should prefer to let altogether
alone. Fortunately however it does not appear that any
discussion of this kind is really called for, at least not on the
principles adopted in this work. It is to *fractional* forms

only, such as $\dfrac{m}{y}$, that it is ever proposed to apply our formulæ in any supposed uninterpretable application of this kind,—for it would be a mere sportive misapplication of them to think of making them treat such expressions as $\sqrt{x}$, log x, and so forth,—and to fractional forms we have seen that a very easy logical explanation could be given.

The general justification and explanation therefore of the application of our rule $f(x) = f(1)\,x + f(0)\,x$ to expressions of which $\dfrac{m}{v}$ is the simplest type, ought not to offer any difficulty. We have already explained these expressions, in detail, by purely logical considerations, so that all that remains at present is to compare the results thus obtained with those deducible from the formula for Development. The reader will remember that we discussed two slightly different ways of approaching the form $\dfrac{r}{y}$, (the one being a somewhat more direct and immediate way than the other,) but that in each case alike that form stood for a *logical class*. It only differed in fact from such a form as xy, in respect that the desired class was more remotely indicated by an operation instead of being directly set before us as a result; and that, the operation by which it was to be procured being an inverse one, it was consequently indefinite in some respects as to its limits. But none the less was it a logical class. On my view therefore the distinction in question is by no means one between the interpretable and the uninterpretable, for the whole range of our discussion belongs to the former category. It is merely one which may be described *sym bolically* as that between integral and fractional forms, and *logically* as that between direct and inverse processes. And this distinction, though by no means a profound one in principle, is sufficiently important in its results to deserve separate consideration here.

We shall therefore apply our formula to $\frac{x}{y}$ with no more hesitation than for example to $x + xy$. When we do so, developing it in accordance with the rule

$$f(x, y) = f(1, 1)\, xy + f(1, 0)\, x\overline{y} + f(0, 1)\overline{x}y + f(0, 0)\, \overline{x}\overline{y},$$

we obtain

$$\frac{x}{y} = \tfrac{1}{1}\, xy + \tfrac{1}{0}\, x\overline{y} + \tfrac{0}{1}\overline{x}y + \tfrac{0}{0}\, xy \; \ldots\ldots\ldots\ldots \; (1)$$

The result obtained by purely logical considerations in the third chapter, it will be remembered, was

$$\frac{r}{s} = xy + v.\,xy, \text{ with the attendant condition } x - xy \quad (2).$$

A very little comparison will show the complete identity of these two results. The first term is the same in each, for $\tfrac{1}{1}$ is of course the same as 1, the logical sense of which has been already settled. So is the third, the only difference being that we had before simply omitted it as not occurring, whereas here it is expressly noticed and rejected. The fourth term again is identical in each case, or may fairly be considered so. Our factor v stood for 'a perfectly uncertain portion, some, all or none': it was proposed in despair of finding any suitable logical word which should possess the same degree of indefiniteness, for of course *some*, in its recog nized significations, would not answer our purpose. Now this is exactly the well known meaning of $\tfrac{0}{0}$ in mathematics, which indicates perfect indefiniteness[1]. So much is this the case that but for the wish not to excite prematurely the fears

---

[1] In each case the indefiniteness extends over the whole admitted range. In mathematics that range extends from 0 to ∞, with us from 0 to 1; so that there is this degree of difference in the application in the two cases.

and prejudices of the timid we would have appealed to it at once instead of using the symbol *v*, but for the future we shall feel perfectly at liberty to resort to it[1]. There still remains one term, the second, which the formula gives in the peculiar shape $\frac{1}{0}$ $x\bar{y}$. This term we had omitted, though not on the ground on which $\bar{x}y$ was omitted,—viz. that we were not to include it in $\frac{\sim}{y}$,—but on the ground that *there was no such class.* Which ever way we express it, whether in the shape $x = xy$, or $xy = 0$, we saw that the condition that there is no xy in existence was necessarily presupposed in the mere

---

[1] It may be remarked that there is a very curious anticipation of this logical fractional form by H. Grassmann, when he expresses the result of a generalized process of division in the form $C + \frac{\wedge}{\smile}$, C being a particular value of the quotient and $\frac{\wedge}{\smile}$ a term which will ordinarily vanish but must be admitted as a symbol. He does not apply it to Logic, nor work it out in detail, but his explanation is worth giving:—'If $B \cdot C = A$, we have the quotient in the form $\frac{-}{}$. Now any value which substituted for C satisfies this equation may be re garded as a particular value of this quotient. Every such value will admit of being produced by addition from the value C, and indeed the portion to be added to C when multi plied by B must give *zero* if the product is to remain equal to A, and any such added portion will leave the product equal to A. Now we may represent generally such a por-

tion as when multiplied by B will yield 0, by $\frac{\wedge}{\smile}$; and we may say that if C is a particular value of the quotient, and B the divisor, then the complete value of the quotient will be $C + \frac{\wedge}{\smile}$' (*Ausdehnungslehre*, p. 213). I have not quite grasped his meaning in the rest of the explana nation; but the fact that he general izes the process indicated by division, by admitting a surplus term (an indefinite one, observe), which will vanish on 'multiplying' again by the divisor, is clear, and this consti tutes a striking analogy to the form $\frac{x}{y} = x + \frac{0}{\smile} \bar{y}$. It must be remembered that this latter also might be written $x + \frac{\wedge}{\cdot}$, since $\frac{\wedge}{-} y$ is really the same as $\frac{\wedge}{y}$. In fact, Grassman stopped short with $\frac{\wedge}{y}$, whilst Boole developed this into $\frac{\wedge}{-} \bar{y}$, or its equivalent $\frac{\wedge}{\smile} xy$.

proposal to accept and interpret the expression $\overset{\sim}{}$. Now the meaning of $\frac{1}{0}$ in mathematics is *infinity*. What then is meant by offering us, in a simple class expression, a term multiplied by infinity ? Surely that there is no such class in existence, for this is the only way of escaping the consequent absurdity. On this view then the two expressions above given agree in all their details, as we might expect that they would agree.

In speaking thus, however, we must not be understood to be merely borrowing from mathematics. It has been already shown (p. 155), that $\frac{0}{0}$ has a strict logical signification, representing the class of which if we take 'no part' we obtain 'nothing', and is therefore perfectly indefinite. Similarly with the other factorial expressions just introduced. Thus $\frac{1}{1}$ stands for a class such that 'all' of it = all that is, and is therefore 'all' itself, viz. 1. So $\frac{0}{1}$ stands for the class 'all' of which = 0, and must therefore = 0. And $\frac{1}{0}$ attempts symbolically to represent a class such that when we take 'none' of it we yet obtain 'all', and thus represents an impossibility.

It may be remarked that the same inference as to the non-existence of the affected class would have to be drawn if any other definite factor than 1 or 0 had presented itself. For a class rightly expressed, that is, only once counted, cannot have as one of its constituent elements a portion which is twice or oftener reckoned. This would really be to compare disparate things, and would be an absurdity equal to assigning a length in acres. So, if we met the expression $z = x + 2xy$, where z was a simple class term, it would necessarily require that $xy = 0$.

So far then it is clear that the application of our general symbolic formula to such expressions as $\overset{\sim}{-}$ does nothing more

than could have been secured by familiar logical conside
rations. Why then resort to it at all? For two reasons. In
the first place though we *can* get at the full result with
out it, it is highly improbable that we *should* do so. With
out a perfectly orderly rule of procedure which should direct
our attention to every possible class in turn, and pronounce
not merely upon its inclusion and exclusion, but also on
its rights of existence under the data assigned, it is hardly
possible but that some should be omitted. This, of course,
might be secured by any method even of the most tentative
kind which took the whole table of possible combinations of
the terms as its guide, and insisted on considering them each
in turn in relation to the given premises. But there seems
to me a far more important reason than this for advocating
the use of formulæ such as that in question. As this was
insisted on in the Introduction, I will merely call attention to
it again in a few words here. The speculative advantages to
be gained by really comprehensive logical theorems far
outweigh any mechanical saving of trouble which they may
secure. To understand the nature of an inverse operation as
such; to generalize as far as possible familiar processes;
to acquire an intelligent control of symbolic language, as dis
tinguished from a mere mechanical facility in using it,—
which can only be done by constantly interpreting its
results, especially in limiting cases, and checking them by
comparison with the results of intuitively evident processes,—
these and such as these are the great merits of a proper
study of Symbolic Logic. It is well worth while to take
some trouble in understanding $f(x)$ and the processes per
formed upon it, in order to secure such advantages as
these.

We have now given a complete explanation of this
formula in its application to those fractional forms of which

$\dfrac{\cdot\cdot}{y}$ — may be taken as a sample; that is, to forms in which both the numerator and the denominator are themselves intelligible class terms as they stand. But it must be noticed that we shall often have to apply it, and shall find it applied successfully, to expressions which are not so simple as this.

For instance, take the expression $\dfrac{z-x}{w}$. The numerator of this, or $z - x$, is not a properly stated class term, for we cannot take x from z unless we know that x is a part of z, and no such information is here given to us. But the formula resolves it at once into $xz + \frac{0}{0} \, \bar{x}z$. How is this ? The reader will very likely guess at the solution for himself, especially if he appeals to the help of a diagram. But we must defer the explicit discussion of it until we have entered more thoroughly into the meaning and interpretation of logical equations in the next two chapters. For the present therefore much of what we say must be considered to be limited to those expressions in which both numerator and denominator could be interpreted if they stood alone. They probably form the great majority of the logical fractions we shall encounter in practice.

The reader will remember, in accordance with what was said in Chap. III., that when x and y are each of them strict class expressions there is no need to take the trouble of analyzing them into all their components elements. We may write down at once $\dfrac{X}{Y} = XY + \frac{0}{0} X\bar{Y}$. Thus $\dfrac{x \cdot y}{z \cdot w}$ involving, as it does, four terms, would expand by strict employment of the formula into 16 elements. This would be troublesome enough, and, what is worse, the process of 1 and 0 substitution is so intricate that we should be very likely to make a slip in performing it. So it is well to remember that we may write it down at once in the form

$$(x + xy)(z + zw) + \tfrac{0}{0}(1 - x - xy)(1 - z - zw),$$

or
$$(x + xy)(z + zw) + \tfrac{0}{0}\, xyzw.$$

And then, if we like, we may expand this, which is a far simpler business. Of course we must remember to add the im plied condition (corresponding to $XY = 0$) which here becomes
$$(x + xy)(1 - z - zw) = 0$$

or
$$(x + xy)\, zw = 0, \text{ viz. } xzw = 0,\ xyzw = 0.$$

In the development of $\dfrac{\tilde{\ }}{\smile}$ we found that the only numerical multipliers of the various class elements which showed them selves were 1, 0, $\tfrac{0}{0}$ and $\tfrac{1}{0}$;—each of these being equivalent to a representative of a class, or a direction to take or leave a class. It may be enquired here whether there are any other possible factors besides these, or whether we have thus got specimens of all the possible factors? For an answer we must look to the process by which these results were obtained.

(1) First take the case in which we start with a directly interpretable class group, say for instance $x + y - xy$. What sort of numerical factors for our class terms can we get in this case? Our only means of getting such factors, remember, is by putting x and y, each in turn, equal to 1 and 0 (these factors being given by substitution in such expressions as $f(1, 1)\, x$, as described above). It is clear at once that such a process can yield us 1 and 0, and cannot yield $\tfrac{0}{0}$ and $\tfrac{1}{0}$. And if the class-expressions to which it is applied are in their strict shape, that is if their terms were all mutually exclusive, it can *only* yield 1 and 0; for any substitutional arrangement of 1 and 0 for x and y, which caused one of these terms not to vanish, would cause every other one to vanish. This follows from the very meaning, symbolically, of mutual exclusiveness.

But, if their terms are not mutually exclusive, then, two or more of them overlapping, we may get such factors as 2, 3, 4, or in fact any factor higher than 1. Thus, e.g., if we develop $x + y + xy$ (which may be taken as a blundering expression for 'x or y or both'), in which the element xy is counted three times over, we should find this definitely pointed out in the results of the development, by xy showing as $3xy$. Whereas, in the development of $x + y - xy$, which can be so arranged that the terms *are* mutually exclusive $(x + xy)$, the factor of xy is unity; viz. it occurs as simply xy.

We are led then to this conclusion. Expand any expression which consists of a group of class terms; and if this expression is such that it can be thrown into the strict form of an aggregate of mutually exclusive and positive class terms, then the ultimate elements yielded by the development will either appear simply and singly, or vanish entirely. That is, they will show only the factors 1 and 0. But if they were not mutually exclusive to begin with, and could not be arranged so as to be so, then the elements must appear affected with other signs than 1 and 0, such as -1, ± 2, ± 3, &c.: the negative signs showing that the original expressions were not merely badly phrased by non-exclusiveness, but were also unmeaning, by asking us to deduct when nothing was given from which to deduct. A moment's reflection upon the logical significance of the process, viz. that development or expansion is nothing but subdivision into ultimate elements, will show that these results are the only ones which could be expected or justified.

(2) Now consider the remaining, and only remaining case which it has been agreed to admit; that is, the inverse case when we have a fraction such as $\dfrac{x}{y}$ where the numerator and denominator are both of them class groups of the kind just described. The only difference here is that both this

numerator and denominator can now yield those numerical factors, and no others, which either of them by itself could have yielded when it stood as a simple non-fractional class group. Naturally this lets in a larger range of possible numerical factors; for though the expressions x, y, and so forth, can only yield 1 and 0, it is clear that such an expres

sion as $\frac{m}{y}$ can yield these, and also $\frac{0}{0}$ and $\frac{1}{0}$.

First consider the former of the two cases noticed above, viz. that in which each class group composing numerator and denominator is duly composed of mutually exclusive terms only. Here since each of these separately can (as above shown) yield us only 1 and 0, the combination of the two into a fractional form can yield us only the four forms 1, 0, $\frac{0}{0}$, $\frac{1}{0}$. These four were, as a matter of fact, yielded by the develop-

ment of $\frac{m}{y}$.

Secondly, when either or both of these numerators and denominators had non-exclusive terms entering into it; we saw that, in addition to furnishing such numerical factors to the class elements as 1 and 0, they might also furnish any other numerical factor as well, according to the degree and nature of their defective statement. The only complica tion that is thus produced is that the final elements or subdivisions of such an ill-expressed fractional form may possess other numerical factors, positive or negative, besides the true typical four 1, 0, $\frac{0}{0}$, $\frac{1}{0}$. We shall have to take some notice of such irregular results as these hereafter. At present I will pass them over, for they may generally be avoided by strict attention to the phrasing of our formulæ in the first instance.

If it be asked here, as it very fairly may, *why* the two peculiar factors $\frac{0}{0}$ and $\frac{1}{0}$ thus come into existence when we develop fractional forms, but not when we develop what may be called, by contrast, integral forms, the answer will readily be found by examining into the process by which they are obtained. (In saying this we are supposed to be asking for a *logical* explanation, since the mere symbolic answer is obvious at a glance:—for clearly fractions like $\frac{0}{0}$ and $\frac{1}{0}$ can only be obtained from a fractional expression, by the process of 1 and 0 substitution.)

The answer is this: When we are developing an integral form, that is, a mere group of class terms, there can be no *indefiniteness* about this proceeding. Now $\frac{0}{0}$ is the sign of entire indefiniteness, and cannot therefore be required here. Of course if there was an indefinite term in the original class group it will reappear in the subdivision:— thus, for instance, $x + \frac{0}{0}y$ would clearly yield terms with this indefinite symbol prefixed to them:—but if the original group was definite it can only be divisible into one set of ultimate class elements, every one of which must necessarily appear. There can clearly be no opening for uncertainty about a true process of dichotomy. Again, as regards $\frac{1}{0}$. This we saw implied a proposition or statement. It gave an independent relation between the class elements, declaring that such a class was non-existent. For anything of this sort also there can be no opening in a mere class or group of classes.

With fractional forms the case is of course different. In whatever way $\dfrac{\sim}{y}$ be reached;—whether as a direct proposal indicated in that shape, or as obtained indirectly from such a statement as $zy - x$;—it makes a postulate. It accepts x and y under a condition, and this condition can of course be stated in a proposition. But every proposition is a material limitation of the formal possibilities of expansion; it extinguishes one or more of the classes yielded by mere dichotomy or subdivision. Thus though xy is a mere class, $\dfrac{\tilde{x}}{y}$ is a class with a condition attached; and it is this condition which, leading to the abolition of one or more classes, gives an opening for the directive symbol $\frac{1}{1}$ which orders the suppression of such classes.

So with the other symbol $\frac{0}{0}$. Our fractional form $\dfrac{\tilde{x}}{y}$ indicates an inverse operation, and one which, as customary in such cases, does not lead to a single definite answer. The reply may very likely be that, within assigned limits, *any* class will answer our purpose. Such an indefinite symbol is therefore distinctly necessary.

It should be noticed that in exceptional cases no demand will be felt for either of these peculiar symbols, the conditions of the problem not giving occasion to them. Thus take the expression $\dfrac{xy + xyz}{x}$. On expansion this yields $xy + xyz + \frac{0}{0}x$, but the usual condition (corresponding to $x\bar{y} = 0$, in the development of the simpler fractional expression $\dfrac{\tilde{x}}{y}$) gives here $(xy + xyz)(1 - x) = 0$, which is identically true. That is, no condition of relation between the symbols is demanded for the performance of the operation in question; it can always be done, whatever relation exists between them. The logical explanation of this is easy to detect; for, x *includes* $xy + xyz$, formally and without further postulate. Hence it must always be possible to find a class such that its limitation by x shall reduce it to $xy + xyz$, which is the inverse operation called for. If it be known that X includes Y, we can always find a multiplier (that is, in logical language, some principle of selection,) which shall reduce X to Y.

Again, as regards the possible absence of terms affected by the indefinite sign $\frac{0}{0}$, take the following example:—

$$\frac{xy + x\overline{y} + \overline{x}\,\overline{y}}{xy + \overline{x}y + \overline{x}\,\overline{y}}.$$

Expand it, and it becomes simply $xy + xy$, the term which would have been affected by $\frac{0}{0}$ vanishing formally. The full logical explanation of this had better be deferred until we have adequately discussed the meaning and interpretation of logical equations, but the symbolic conditions for its occurrence are easily seen. The indefinite factor in $\frac{Y}{Y}$ is of course $\frac{0}{0}X\overline{Y}$; it will therefore vanish whenever $XY = 0$. That is, if X and Y together make up, or more than make up, the total universe (for this is the meaning of $XY = 0$) then the inverse operation ceases to be indefinite [1].

This peculiar symbol $\frac{0}{0}$, perhaps the most distinctive feature in the Symbolic Logic, has been much objected to. We shall have to discuss it again on several future occasions, but enough has now been said to show that it is very far from being borrowed in needless affectation from the mathematicians. If we chose to reject it we should still have to invent some symbol to take its place, and where else is such a symbol to be found which shall really express the full indefiniteness we need? There is no such word in the ordinary logical vocabulary, for 'some' in both its senses ('some, it may be all', and 'some, but not all') excludes *none*, and therefore will not answer our purpose. We saw indeed, in Chap. VII., that $x = xy$ is really, though not very obviously,

---

[1] In which case, indeed, this inverse operation loses all peculiar significance. For, if $XY = 0$, as well as $XY = 0$, then $Y = 1$; so that $\frac{Y}{Y} = XY$ or $\frac{Y}{1} = X$, which is identically true whatever may be the value of X.

the precise equivalent of $x - \tfrac{0}{0}y$; but we could not conveni
ently work with this equivalent in our developments, for
it demands the repetition of the whole of one side of the
equation on the other side. If we tried to employ it as
a substitute for $\tfrac{0}{0}$ in the development of $\dfrac{x}{y}$, viz. $xy + \tfrac{0}{0}xy$, we
should have to write it $\dfrac{m}{y} = xy + \dfrac{m}{y} \times xy$, when the impropriety
of substituting an implicit equation instead of an explicit
becomes glaring. If we object to make use of $\tfrac{0}{0}$ in Logic we
shall simply have to invent another symbol and define it in
precisely the same sense. At least we should have to do this
if we undertook to work the same problems with the same
generality.

The reason why we require this symbol, whereas the
ordinary Logic manages to do without it, must be assigned to
the completeness of the Symbolic System. The ordinary Logic
answers what it can, and simply lets alone what it cannot
answer, whilst what the more general system aims at is
to specify the direction and amount of our ignorance, in
relation to the given data, as explicitly as that of our
knowledge. We take into consideration every class which
any combination of the terms in question can yield, and
enquire what information the data will furnish in reference to
it. As Prof. G. B. Halsted has well said, "The problem may
be very compactly stated:...It is: Given any assertions, to
determine precisely what they affirm, precisely what they
deny, and precisely what they leave in doubt, separately and
jointly"[1].

We are now in a position finally to explain the various

[1] *Journal of Speculative Philosophy*, Jan. 1878. See also the same
journal for Oct. 1878, and Jan. 1879,
in each of which there are some
valuable critical remarks by the same
author on Boole's system.

elements which make their appearance in the development of one of these fractional forms which demand the performance of an inverse operation. If our data have been properly expressed in mutually exclusive terms at the outset, our result must necessarily be comprised in the following form :—

$$X = A + 0B + \tfrac{0}{0}C + \tfrac{1}{0}D,$$

where X, A, B, C, D are aggregates of class elements composed of the various combinations of the class terms x, y, z, &c., and their contradictories.

Here then X, on the left side, is a class term. The succession of expressions on the right side may be taken as a description or definition of X given us in terms of x, y, z, &c. or whatever the symbols of the classes may be. Now what we are told in this equation is that, in order fully to determine X as desired, we must ;—

1. Take the whole of A ; A consisting of one or more class elements. Hence conversely, the whole of A is included in X. Ordinary Logic would express this by saying, 'Some X is A', and 'All A is X'.

2. Exclude from X the whole of the class B:—or, to put it in ordinary language, 'No X is B'.

3. As to the entry of the class C into X; we can, from the given data, determine nothing whatever. All C, or some only, or none of it, may go to the making up of X. To decide this more explicitly, we should require fresh infor mation.

4. As to D, this class is not merely excluded from X, as B was, but may be proved from the given data to be an impossible or non-existent class. The *compartments* referred to in D have of course to be taken notice of, but our data pronounce them by implication to be empty.

There are two questions which may fairly be raised here, and which demand a few moments' consideration.

I. It may possibly be objected that though we have thus determined the relation of X to the four classes A, B, C, D and to all the sub-classes which *they* contain under them, there may yet be other classes, of a similar kind to these, of which we have taken no account, for the possible combinations of x, y, z, &c. and their contradictories are numerous. The reply is that there *are* no other classes possible, for however numerous they may be they are all comprised in A, B, C and D. The very nature of Development insures that every possible combination (logically) of our class terms shall be taken due notice of.

II. But, again, it may be asked, What about the *existence* of these classes referred to in A, B, and C? Must there be things corresponding to these various class terms? The answer to this question is contained in the results of a former chapter (Chap. VI.) and is briefly this. Negation is positive and final; therefore every one of the classes which go to make up D is certainly abolished: there can be no such things as these. Moreover we know for certain (on formal grounds) that some one class at least of those included in A, B, and C, must exist. But beyond this we can only speak hypothetically, as in all positive assertion. If there are any A's then the same things must also be X, thus establishing that there must then be X. The existence of a B, however, or a C, proves nothing about there being X. Conversely, if there be any X, the things which are X must be either A or C, so that one of these is proved to exist, but we cannot tell which.

Illustrations and Examples.

I append a few pages of illustration, purposely choosing for the most part extreme or limiting cases in the application of the simplest formulæ, as these subserve the purpose of explaining the principles of this Development better than others.

Begin with one class term only, x, and see how many forms we can obtain with our $f(x) = f(1) x + f(0) x$. Of what we have called integral forms there are the following four:— 1, 0, x, x; which yield the developments,

$$1 = x + \overline{x}$$
$$0 = 0x + 0\overline{x}$$
$$x = x + 0x$$
$$x = 0x + x.$$

They stand in need of no explanation. Logically, they represent the results of subdividing (or, we should rather say, attempting to subdivide) the four classes, 'everything', 'nothing', 'x', and 'not-x', into their x and not-x parts respectively. Of course only 'everything' can really be so divided.

Of fractional forms with one class term, we have sixteen, since any one of the above four may stand as either numerator or denominator. Of these however the four with unity as denominator are identical with the above integral forms, thus leaving twelve. They should all be carefully worked through for the purpose of obtaining perfect command of the logical meaning and symbolic usage of our various forms. They are as follows:—

1. $\dfrac{1}{x} = x + \frac{1}{0}\overline{x}.$

5. $\dfrac{x}{0} = \frac{1}{0}x + \frac{0}{0}\overline{x}.$

2. $\dfrac{x}{x} = x + \, x.$

6. $\dfrac{0}{0} = \, x + \, \overline{x}.$

3. $\dfrac{0}{} = 0x + {}^{0}\overline{x}.$

7. ${}^{1} = \frac{1}{0}x + \frac{1}{0}\overline{x}.$

9    $\dfrac{1}{\bar{x}} = \frac{1}{\div}x + x$

11. $\dfrac{0}{\bar{x}} = \frac{0}{\div}x + 0\bar{x}.$

10. $\dfrac{x}{x} = \frac{1}{\div}x + 0\bar{x}.$

12. $\dfrac{\bar{x}}{x} = \frac{1}{1}x + \bar{x}.$

We will briefly examine a few of these results in turn; sometimes in accordance with one, sometimes in accordance with the other, of the two ways already pointed out for approaching these fractional forms; that is, either by taking them as immediate demands for the performance of an inverse process, or as stating a conditional proposition which leads to such a demand.

1.   This asks us the question, What is that class which, when restricted by taking only the x-part of it, will yield the class '*all*'? A little reflection will show that the only class of which this can be said *is* 'all'; viz. this is the limiting case in which the imposition of a restriction is merely, as it happens, leaving the class unaltered. (The formula indicates this by the term $\frac{1}{0}x$; reminding us that $x = 0$, viz. $1 - x - 0$ or $x = 1$.)

2.   This is in reality a very familiar old friend of every logician, for it is nothing else than 'accidental conversion' done up in a new dress, and, I would add, far more accurately expressed. No doubt it sounds very unfamiliar, even when put out of symbols into words, if we phrase it as 'What is the most general expression of that class which, restricted by taking only the x-part of it, will coincide with x?' But we shall soon recognize its features if we look at it this way:—Suppose we had given us that $yx - x$, and were asked, What then is y in general? This would have led to $y - \dfrac{x}{x}$, as above, which is asking for y in terms of x. Now it was shown in Chap. VII. that the expression, or rather *an* expression, for the universal proposition 'All x is y' is $x - xy$.

Hence it is clear that to ask for y in terms of x, under this condition (as is done symbolically above), and to ask 'If all x is y, what is y?' are really one and the same question.

Now compare our solution here with the common solution. We say that $y = x + \frac{0}{0} x$, whilst the common answer says simply 'Some y is x'. The advantage of the former seems to be that it so prominently forces on our attention (by the employment of the peculiar symbol $\frac{0}{0}$) several possible cases which the common answer rather tends to obscure from sight. We are reminded for instance that x may be the whole of y (if $\frac{0}{0}$ happens to $= 0$); that it may be a part only (if $\frac{0}{0}$ is intermediate between 0 and 1); or that y itself may be 'all' (if $\frac{0}{0} = 1$). These three alternatives may of course be deduced from the common form of conclusion, but they certainly do not appear very prominently in it, especially considering the ambiguity of the word *some*.

I would also call the reader's attention to the very decisive way in which all those troublesome and perplexing questions, as to what is implicated in the way of the existence of our x and y, are avoided by this way of regarding the subject. Once understand that 'all x is y' is only unconditional in what it *denies* (i.e. in denying that there is any xy); and employ the truly indefinite symbol $\frac{0}{0}$ instead of *some*, and a proposition and its converse will fit in harmoniously with any number of other propositions without inconsistency or demand for fresh assumption. For instance: start with 'all x is y' in the form $xy = 0$, thus blotting out one class. Now elicit x from this, and we get $x = \frac{0}{0} y$ (the reader will easily verify this conclusion as follows: $x = -\dfrac{}{y}$, therefore by development $x = \frac{0}{0} y$). The implication is clear and decisive, and in perfect harmony with the unconditional negation above. We see that if there be x there must be y, and that if there be y there may be x; but that there may be neither one nor the other. Then go on to convert $xy = 0$, or $x - \frac{0}{0}y$, and we get, as above, $y - x + \frac{0}{0}x$. Here the same implications meet us as clearly as before:—if there be any x there must be y, but if there be any y there need not be x (since the y may be contributed by the term $\frac{0}{0}x$). And there need not be either x or y.

As just remarked, the two assumptions upon which this explanation rests are (1) the unconditional negative interpretation of the universal affirmative, and (2) the employment of the perfectly indeterminate symbol $\frac{0}{0}$ in place of the ordinary *some*.

3. This result is best interpreted as follows. Suppose $xy - 0$, viz. 'No x is y', What do we know about y? The equation $y = \frac{0}{0}x$ tells us that y, if it exist, must lie outside x, but that there may be no y at all (if $\frac{0}{0} = 0$); that there may be some y; or that the y may be the whole of x (if $\frac{0}{0} = 1$), in which case x and y are (materially) contradictory opposites.

4. This development must have come about from such a statement as that 'xy is the same as not-x'. We can save this from being nonsense or contradiction (on the principles laid down in Chap. VI.), only by supposing that there is no such class as y, and that x is 'all', for 'all nothing' is the same as 'no all'. The development expresses this condition.

6. This is the development of an entirely indefinite class, and is therefore itself entirely indefinite. The nearest verbal equivalent would be the direction to subdivide 'something' into its x and not-x portions. We could but say that this would yield some x and some not-x. After what has been already said in explanation of this symbol $\frac{0}{0}$ the reader will hardly need to be reminded that we regard it as a strictly interpretable expression. It is the determination (if we may

use the word) of a class which proves to be strictly indeter-
minable.

7.   This is of course an instance of gross misapplication of
our formula.   The universe being 1, the expression $\frac{1}{0}$ is
logically unmeaning as a class term.   The demand which
it makes is that we shall find some class such that when *no*
part of it is taken we shall still have, as a result, *all*; $(0x=1)$.
Our formula resents being told to work upon such an
impossible class as this, in the way that formulæ generally
do resent such a call, viz. by just talking nonsense.   It
responds to the demand by declaring that there is neither *x*
nor not-*x*:—as good a reply as any other under the circum
stances.

As the remaining examples do not raise any interesting
questions except what are contained in such as have been
already noticed we will not go into them any further.   The
reader is however recommended to work through them all in
order to familiarize himself with the interpretation of general
formulæ in critical and limiting cases.

CHAPTER X.

HAVING thus considered the nature of Development or Subdivision, which may be considered an introduction to the central subject of Logic, we must now go on to consider this main subject itself under the heads of *Logical Equations,* and *Interpretation and Solution of Logical Equations.* This latter division may be said, roughly speaking, to correspond to that between Propositions and Reasonings in ordinary Logic, though here as elsewhere our arrangement of the subject is very far from coinciding with the traditional one. We shall devote this and the following chapters to the consideration of these topics.

There are two main principles of interpretation to which we shall have to appeal in the course of this discussion. As neither of them is distinctly recognized in the ordinary Logic, and both are in some respects decidedly alien to the ways of common thought and speech, it will be well to begin by calling prominent attention to them.

(1) The first of these is involved in the view of the Import of Propositions explained and insisted on in the sixth chapter. The comparative novelty of that view as a

systematic doctrine, and its extreme importance for our present purpose, must be the excuse for once more recalling the reader's attention to it.

It was laid down then that propositions must be regarded as having, generally speaking, an affirmative interpretation of a conditional and somewhat complex character, and a negative interpretation which is unconditional and compa ratively simple. That is, what they assert can only be accepted under hypotheses and provisionally, in so far as the existence of the objects is concerned, whereas what they can be made to deny is denied absolutely. This contrast presented itself even in the case of the simple propositions of the common Logic, but when we come to the complicated systems of propositions which we must be prepared to grapple with in Symbolic Logic, it appears to me that without this explana tion we can make no way at all.

It must be frankly admitted that this is not the sense in which the popular mind accepts and interprets propositions. Nor is it, I presume, in accordance with the canons of the common Logic;—and very reasonably not so, on the part of the latter; for using, as this does, forms which are but little removed from those of common speech, it cannot risk so complete a breach with convention as we may freely do who deal mostly with symbols. I speak with reserve however on this point from really not knowing what the law may be.

(2) The other principle to which we shall have to resort may be conveniently introduced by the following question. If any one were to declare to us that his annual income and the acreage of his estate, taken together, amounted to precisely £500 and his daughters, could we charge him on the face of the matter with either falsity or nonsense ? He has adopted an unusual way of speaking, but a solecism need not be without meaning. If we insisted on translating

his words strictly, what sort of construction should we have to put upon them, neglecting all merely conventional impli cations? We should have to say that, since it is impossible to equate heterogeneous things, the only solution which will avoid actual nonsense must be found in the conclusion that his income is £500, and that he has no acres and no daughters.

The second of these principles involves of course an appeal to the first. Admitting that the employment of a logical term does not necessarily carry with it the existence of any corresponding class, we say that these are circumstances under which this admission has to be put in force. Disparate things can only be equated by the assumption that both are then and there non-existent.

There is a slightly different way of looking at the same thing which may make it a little more acceptable. Instead of starting, as above, with the statement $x = y$, where x and y are heterogeneous, put it in the form that if y be taken from x nothing is left. Suppose I say, in reference to some given assemblage of people, Take all the rogues from amongst the lawyers and nobody is left, it is quite certain that this identifies the two classes. This is a necessity of thought or of things; but to this necessity common usage couples an assumption, which ordinary Logic doubtfully accepts, viz. that we must not so speak unless we mean to imply that there are certainly some people present who belong to both categories. Symbolic Logic distinctly rejecting this assumption need not hesitate to accept at the same time the proposition that no lawyers are rogues. In this case, since the subduction of a rogue can no longer remove a lawyer the statement can only hold good on the supposition that there is none of either class present. In other words, whereas the logical equation, $x - y = 0$, necessarily and always implies the identity of x and y, all that we are now doing is to claim the right of extending this to the limiting case in which x and y are both $= 0$; and consequently of inferring that if x and y are known to be mutually exclusive then this limiting case is the only possible one.

It can hardly be maintained that this system of interpretation is much more in accordance with popular convention than the former was. The complaint here would presumably be, not that we were misinterpreting statements, but that we were displaying a pedantic and lawyer-like[1] determination to insist upon an interpretation of a statement which was absurdly put. They are both principles however which are certainly legitimate. No one can say that they actually contradict or defy any known law of thought, or any express enactment of Logic (the latter of them indeed errs, if at all, from excessive adherence to the law). Some assumption or understanding therefore is necessary in reference to both, and it will be found, I think, that no other than that here adopted will prove capable of working in a really general symbolic system. Anyhow we shall make use of them both, and since it is well to do nothing unusual without warning, attention is here prominently directed to them.

But it will be readily seen that the principle we have thus invoked is of wider application. It is not merely true that the statement $x - y = 0$, when x and y are exclusives, leads to $x = 0$, $y = 0$. The same holds good when such mutual exclusives are combined by way either of addition or

---

[1] Not I presume that the lawyers would so determine such a question. De Morgan (*Syllabus*, p. 12) gives the following example on a somewhat analogous point: "An Act was once passed exempting indentures [of apprenticeship] from duty when the premium was under five pounds sterling: the Court of King's Bench held that the exemption did not apply when there was *no premium at all*, because 'no premium at all' is not 'a premium under five pounds.'"

subtraction, and when each of them is multiplied by any numerical factors whatever. That is to say, such an expres sion as $ax \pm by \pm cz \pm$ &c. $= 0$, (so long as x, y, z, &c. are independent class terms) necessarily leads to $x = 0$, $y = 0$, $z = 0$. This follows from the very meaning and employment of our class terms. Really exclusive or independent classes are absolutely powerless upon one another; it is not possible for one to neutralize another and thus to offer an alternative for the common extinction of all. We must not be misled by the analogy of ordinary mathematics, where we add and subtract magnitudes, and where in consequence there are many different ways of adjusting the contributions of the separate items in a total, whether that total be zero or anything else. If any analogy is sought in that direction it must be in the equation to zero of the sum of a number of squares, which involves the separate equation to zero of each element of the total[1]. In Logic, if any kind of aggregate, of the addition and subtraction kind, is declared equal to nothing, the only way out of the difficulty is in the declara tion that each separate element is also nothing : provided, as remarked, that these elements are mutually exclusive[2].

The reader must carefully observe that this is no case of arbitrary assumption or definition on our part. All that we are now doing is to insist upon a stringent interpretation

[1] A still more apposite analogy is offered here, as indeed in some other directions, in the Science of Quaternions. The single equation $xi + yj + zk = \xi i + \eta j + \zeta k$ does not there lead to the indeterminateness of an ordinary algebraic equation, but ne cessitates separately;
$$x = \xi, \quad y = \eta, \quad z = \zeta.$$
And the reason is the same, viz. that we are comparing heteroge neous or disparate things in i, j, k.

[2] The *addition* (when equated to zero) of a number of class terms, it will be observed, would also lead to the same result whether they were exclusive or not. But this is a mat ter of procedure merely, for we could at once put them into such a form : *e.g.* $x + y = 0$ is equivalent to
$$2xy + xy + xy = 0.$$

of the definitions and rules formerly laid down. Indeed we
may say more than this; that we are only insisting upon such
interpretation as must be admitted to be obligatory according
to the forms and regulations of common speech, though
it would naturally be complained of there as pedantic and
over fastidious. If one were to say that on adding the
Englishmen in an assembly to twice the Frenchmen, and
subducting the Dutch three times over, there was nobody
left, could any other conclusion be reached than that there
were neither Englishmen, Frenchmen nor Dutch there?
The original statement was expressed in a very absurd
manner, and we should probably be charged with over-
refining in attempting to make anything whatever out
of it, instead of summarily rejecting it; but admitting that it
is to be interpreted logically, this, and nothing else, is
the conclusion. (It is merely a concrete instance of
$x + 2y - 3z = 0$, where x, y, and z are known to be exclusives:
this leads to $x = 0$, $y - 0$, $z - 0$.)

It will now be seen therefore, that in order to analyze
a logical statement, and to extract from it the sum-total
of what it has to tell us, all that is necessary is to break
it up into a series of mutually exclusive terms the sum
of which is declared equal to zero. If this can be done
without injury or loss of significance, then the information
yielded by the statement can be read off at once in all
its details, in the form of a number of separate denials.
This, it may be pointed out, is the full analytical process; the
subsequent synthetic process, which seeks to build up these
details into new forms and thus fully to interpret them,
will have to be discussed in a future chapter. The full
importance, from a theoretic point of view, of the Rule
of Development explained in the last chapter will therefore be apparent. The desired result, viz. of securing that

some complicated expression shall be broken up into all its ultimate and consequently mutually exclusive elements, is precisely that for which this Rule is devised.

We might begin then at once by appealing to this Rule, and this would be the most complete and perfect form of solution. But an intelligent appreciation of the nature and significance of the step we have to take will better be secured by beginning somewhat more in detail, and with more direct appeal to familiar logical considerations.

I. Take then the simple case of an explicit statement, by which is here meant one in which we have only a single term standing by itself on one side, this being equated, on the other side, to a group of terms. We must suppose that the component elements of the group which constitutes one side are arranged in their due and suitable form, in which they appear as a sum or aggregate of a number of mutually exclusive terms. In fact this is demanded, for there is no meaning in declaring a single class to be identical with a group wherein some of the components are counted several times over.

Take as a specimen,

$$w = xyz + xy + x\,y\,z \dots\dots\dots\dots\dots(1).$$

When this is put into words what it amounts to is simply that we here have a description, definition, or synonyme of any kind (neglecting, as we do, all but the denotative import of our terms, these various expressions are regarded by us as equivalent) of w in terms of x, y, and z. The individuals referred to by w are identical with the aggregate of the individuals referred to by the three terms equated to w. Of course as regards the expression or extension of our knowledge by such a statement, various views may be taken. If all the three terms on the right hand are known in themselves, or through their component elements, then w may be known thereby. If w were known, then we have one condition assigned by which to determine the other elements. If we happen to be equally familiar with both, then the equation may be regarded as a statement of our knowledge. Our particular personal relation to any of our statements is not indeed a matter with which Logic need be supposed to trouble itself.

As regards the verbal statement of such a proposition the reader will observe how entirely it is a matter of our own choice whether we throw it into the categorical, hypothetical or disjunctive form. There may be no such things really as w, xyz, xy, &c.; or some only of these classes may be missing. If we want to avoid any reference to such a contingency,— as common logic mostly does,—then we should put it either collectively by saying, 'the w's are identical with the sum of the things which are xyz, or y and not-x, or x and neither y nor z', or distributively 'every w is either xyz, y and not-x, or x and neither y nor z'. If we wish to call attention to the fact that our terms only hold their life, so to say, subject to the conditions entailed by other propositions as well, then we might say '*if* there be any w it must be either xyz, &c.' The popular expressions which thus cover the ground of a single symbolic statement are very various.

So much for the affirmative interpretations of our equa tion or proposition; let us now look at the negative interpre tation. We begin, as usual, with examining the question on purely logical grounds, before looking at it through the medium of mere symbols. What the statement said was that the whole of w was confined to a certain number of compartments, and conversely that every class of things occupying any of these compartments must be a w. Now, on the system of making a perfectly exhaustive scheme of classification out of our class terms, it is clear that to say w is *within* certain compartments is precisely equivalent to saying that it is *without* certain others. Hence it follows that an alternative or disjunctive affirmative can be broken up into a number of independent negatives. This of course is in no way peculiar to our system; for every one knows that the proposition 'All X is either Y or Z' may be phrased 'no X is (neither Y nor Z)'. What is characteristic of this symbolic Logic is the symmetry and generality with which this procedure is carried out all through.

Now look at this symbolically. What we have to do is to break up the given statement into a series of separate state ments each expressing that such and such a combination $= 0$. There are a variety of ways of doing this. Perhaps one of the most methodical is the following :—Suppose we had the very simple statement $x - y$ we should (as was formerly pointed out) throw this into the two negations $x(1-y) = 0$, $y(1-x) = 0$. Now the same holds true for aggregates of class terms as well as for simple ones, for such aggregation does not destroy or in any way affect their class character istics. Hence the equation $w = xyz + xy + xyz$, may be fully expressed negatively by the two

$$w\,(xyz + xy + xyz) = 0$$
$$w\,(1 - xyz - xy - xyz) = 0$$

The upper of these is already in the form of a sum of ne gations, and therefore breaks up at once into three separate negations. The lower as it stands has one positive and three negative terms, but may be easily put into a form composed of positive terms only. For the three negative terms are collectively a part of 'all', or unity; hence if unity be de veloped in respect of x, y, z, some of the eight elements thus resulting will be neutralized by these three negative terms, and none but positive ones will remain. The result is then

$$w\,(xyz + xy\bar{z} + x\bar{y}z + \bar{x}yz) = 0.$$

When this is added to the similar result in the former equation (those three, by the resolution of xy into xyz, $xy\bar{z}$, yield four ultimate terms) we have the eight following elementary negations:—

$$
\begin{array}{ll}
wxyz - 0 & w\bar{x}yz = 0 \\
\bar{w}.\bar{x}yz = 0 & wx\bar{y}z = 0 \\
w\bar{x}yz = 0 & wxy\bar{z} = 0 \\
\overline{w}x\bar{y}\bar{z} = 0 & w\bar{x}\bar{y}\bar{z} = 0.
\end{array}
$$

I shall go more fully hereafter into the explanation of these eight denials, that is, into the various verbal forms in which their joint force may be expressed. But the reader should understand at once that these eight denials contain amongst them every particle of information yielded by the original statement, or in any way deducible from it.

II. Now consider the case of implicit equations, by which we understand those in which we do not find a single term standing by itself on one side, and declared equal to a certain group of terms on the other side. The following will serve as a simple illustration of what is meant,

$$x\bar{y} + \bar{x}z = \bar{x}y + \bar{y}z.$$

A very little observation will show that the two classes in question can only be made equal to one another upon the conditions expressed by $xyz = 0$, $\bar{x}\bar{y}\bar{z} = 0$. On any other supposition it would be equivalent to the declaration of the identity of the money income with the acreage or family. This is more obvious on subdividing the terms on each side, when they stand

$$x\bar{y}z + x\bar{y}\bar{z} + \bar{x}yz + \bar{x}y\bar{z} = \bar{x}yz + \bar{x}y\bar{z} + x\bar{y}\bar{z} + \bar{x}\bar{y}z$$

or $xyz = \bar{x}\bar{y}\bar{z}$, which of course, as already described, demands the destruction of each of these two classes. Hence the full interpretation of the given statement, in so far as analysis is concerned, is given by these two elements,

$$\left.\begin{array}{l} x\overline{y}\overline{z} = 0 \\ \overline{x}y\overline{z} = 0 \end{array}\right\}.$$

III. In the two classes of cases hitherto discussed, all the terms entered *definitely* into the equations or propositions which involved them. We must now discuss the case in which one or more of the terms are affected by the *indefinite* sign $\frac{0}{0}$. Begin with the simplest of cases, in which a definite class is equated to an indefinite one, for instance

$$w = \tfrac{0}{0}\, xy.$$

This form was examined in Chap. VII. We showed that it is, with reserves and explanations, the best accurate symbolic equivalent for the somewhat ambiguous 'all w is xy' of ordinary Logic, viz. for a form of the ordinary Universal Affirmative. We also considered its negative form in the same chapter, but we must now compare it somewhat more fully with the definite statements above considered. In those cases what we did was to exactly *identify* one class group with another, which gave rise to *two* negations: for we could deny of each group that it had any members outside the other. In the present case we merely say more vaguely that one group is at most contained somewhere within the other, which only gives rise to the single denial that the definite group has members outside the extreme limits of the indefinite one. Hence all that can be elicited from such a form as the one now before us is,

$$w\,(1 - xy) = 0.$$

For xy is the extreme limit of the indefinite class $\frac{0}{0}xy$, when $\frac{0}{0}$ becomes $= 1$. Hence we can assert unconditionally no more than that there can be no w which lies outside xy. Of course, if we like to do so, we can break this up into the

constituent members of which $1 - xy$ is composed, viz.
$xy + xy + xy$. Then the equation resolves itself into
the three denials given by

$$\left.\begin{array}{l} wxy = 0 \\ wxy = 0 \\ wxy = 0 \end{array}\right\}.$$

Now take a somewhat less simple example involving
indefinite terms. Suppose we have

$$w = xyz + \overline{x}y + \tfrac{0}{0}x\overline{y}z.$$

First as regards its significance. This is not, like the
examples we began with, the identification of two class groups
with one another, for the term $\tfrac{0}{0}xyz$ comes in to prevent such
identification. It cannot therefore be regarded as expressive
of a definition or description of w. What exactly it tells us
is this:—That w certainly comprises the whole of the two
classes $xyz + xy$ and that it may or may not take in the
class xyz. The indeterminate sign therefore is a sort of
"look out" to us to be prepared for individuals from the class
so affected. The whole of the class may be wanted ; or, if it
be subdivided, a part of it only, or possibly none at all may
be wanted. This is left altogether indeterminate.

It is clear therefore that we cannot here make quite such
a simple double negation as we did in the former cases.
What we have to do instead is to take account of one limit of
$\tfrac{0}{0}$ (viz. 1) in one denial, and of the other limit (viz. 0) in
the other denial.

We may say with certainty that there is no w which lies
outside $xyz + xy + xyz$, for this represents the extreme limit
of the admissible indefiniteness ; and we may say with
similar certainty that there is no $xyz + xy$ which lies outside
w, for this represents the extreme limit of the indefiniteness
in the opposite direction. These two statements yield us
a pair of negations which do not quite so accurately balance

one another as was the case when we were concerned with definite terms only, for one is less extensive than the other. Put into symbols they stand,

$$w\,(1 - xyz - xy - xyz) = 0$$
$$w\,(xyz + xy) = 0.$$

We might then proceed, by expanding 1 in terms of x, y, and z, to convert the former into positive terms only, and should thus be finally left with a string of separate negations as in the former cases; the only distinction being that owing to the occurrence of the $\frac{0}{0}$ term we get *fewer* of these unconditional negations than we should otherwise obtain, and therefore our materials of information are less abundant.

The difference thus marked in the symbols is equally noticeable in the verbal expression: that is, as regards our powers of conversion and contraposition where these indeterminate terms occur. What we *ought* to say is on the one hand, 'All w is made up of xyz, xy, and (possibly) xyz', and on the other, 'All xyz and all xy are w'. What we may be tempted to say, however, is 'All w is made up of xyz, xy, and *some* xyz', thus omitting the full indefiniteness of $\frac{0}{0}xyz$, or introducing confusion and ambiguity by this word *some*.

Inasmuch as it is always well to examine limiting cases, since principles so often lurk concealed in such holes and corners, it will be well to see what these superior and inferior limits of negation become when we have none but indefinite terms on one side. Recur to the example

$$w = \tfrac{0}{0}xy.$$

The limit of $\frac{0}{0}$ in one direction is 1; thus giving us the negation $w\,(1 - xy) = 0$, viz. that 'No w can lie outside xy'. But the limit on the other side is 0. In this case the whole of the right side of the equation vanishes, and we can make no denial by means of this inferior limit; or rather, in formal strictness, such denial assumes the form 'No $0xy$ lies outside w', which tells us nothing whatever. We are thus reminded again of the distinction between this really indefinite factor $\frac{0}{0}$, and both the *some*, and the undistributed predicate, of ordinary logic. These latter exclude the value 0, therefore we can always make something out of the statement 'All w is xy' in both directions. In one direction the result agrees with our symbolic expression $w\,(1 - xy) = 0$, viz. 'No w is not-xy'. In the other it is generally stated positively, in the form 'Some (*i. e.* not none) xy is w'. The validity of such conversion has been already discussed in a former chapter.

We will now look at a more general method for ex amining the significance of any logical statement. Here, as in every other case, I am more concerned to discuss the question in a way calculated to throw light upon the actual logical meaning of the processes we perform, than merely to bring forward convenient or powerful symbolic devices for reaching our conclusions.

Suppose then that we have any logical equation whatever involving the class terms x, y, z, &c. anyhow combined. It is assumed that what we want to do is to examine the full significance of this equation, that is, to resolve it into all the elementary denials which can be extracted from it.

This process of resolution of an equation into its elemen tary denials is, as already remarked, a work of Analysis. What can be done afterwards from these results by way of Synthesis, that is, by putting them together into the form of affirmative assertions, will have to be considered further on.

Perform the following processes upon the equation :—

1. Bring all the terms over to one side, so as to reduce it to the form $f(x, y, z, \ldots) = 0$.

2. Develop every one of these terms into all the sub divisions attainable by taking all these class terms into account.

3. Equate separately to zero every class term which

finally remains after the development; omitting any that may be affected by the symbol $\frac{0}{0}$, for of these nothing can be made.

(1) With regard to the first process hardly anything need be said. It is best to adopt it in order to prevent confusion by the same terms appearing on both sides of the equation.

(2) One or two points seem to deserve notice in respect to this second step. For one thing it must be observed that none but combinations of $xyz...$ can possibly occur in our result. That is, every term which could occur in the original equation will resolve itself into such combinations. For instance no numerical factor can appear there. If our original equation had been $xy + xy = 1$ we should write it $xy + xy - 1 = 0$. Now since *unity* is a logical term, like any other, it must equally undergo expansion into the elements $xy + xy + xy + xy$. Hence the final result of the equation is $xy + xy = 0$. If our equations or statements had been properly drawn out at first, (and we must in fairness assume so much as this), they could contain nothing but 1 and other class terms. Consequently, after development, none but logical class terms can be found in them.

But though nothing else than these logical class terms can be found in our equation after it has thus undergone development, it does not follow that *all* our possible class terms will be represented in it. On the contrary one or more terms must be missing from it, as otherwise we should be landed in a direct contradiction in terms.

(3) The reason why some of the possible terms must thus disappear is connected with the grounds of this third process, and has been already adverted to once or twice. All the terms, as finally arranged, being mutually exclusive, it is impossible for any one of them to cancel another. Conse-

quently when a group of them is equated to zero this can only be brought about by each separate term being equal to zero, just as when in algebra we get the sum of a number of squares $= 0$. But since our alternatives are collectively exhaustive as well as mutually exclusive, it is a contradiction in terms to suppose them all to vanish :—this, it will be noticed, being our generalized form corresponding to the so-called Law of Excluded Middle.

Suppose for instance, just for illustration, that we write down such a form as this,

$$Axy + Bxy + Cxy + Dxy - 0,$$

one or more of the four factors A, B, C, D, must be supposed $= 0$, in order to avoid contradiction. Suppose that B and C thus vanish, whilst A and D do not. We then have

$$Axy + Dxy = 0.$$

Since it is impossible for these terms to neutralize one another, and by supposition A and D do not $= 0$, the other, or logical class terms, must vanish. That is we conclude

$$\left. \begin{array}{l} xy = 0 \\ \overline{x}\,\overline{y} = 0 \end{array} \right\}.$$

these ultimate denials containing, as before, the full information yielded by the original statement.

It may be asked here, but what if *all* the four factors A, B, C, D, above, had vanished: what could we then conclude ? The answer is that in that case nothing whatever can be concluded. The vanishing of any term from our equation is an indication that our data give us no information about it, and the vanishing of every term is an indication that no information whatever is obtainable. As every mathe matician knows, this is the usual resource of an equation under the circumstances. When there is no information yielded by the data, they will not unfrequently save themselves from misstatement by just reducing to the unmeaning form $0 = 0$. Of course we could not *begin* by writing down such a form as this, in which all the terms should vanish; but it might quite well happen (as we shall see when we come to the study of Elimination) that we should deduce such an equation as an inference. We must then take its collapse and disappearance as an intimation that we were trying to extort from it information which it was not in its power to give us.

One case still remains for notice. We have so far sup posed that the factors (A, B, C, D, &c.) of our class terms were either 0 or 1, that is that they either vanish entirely or present themselves simply and singly. But there is, as we know, another recognized class factor, viz. $\frac{0}{0}$; what is to be made of terms which happen to be thus affected? The answer is that we can make nothing of them when they thus come out as members of a series which is collectively made $= 0$. For instance if we met with such an expression as $xy + \frac{0}{0}xy = 0$, the indefinite term must just be let alone, as completely as if it had vanished by having the multiplier 0. We know that the whole expression $\frac{0}{0}xy$ must disappear, but as this may be owing to $\frac{0}{0}$ being $= 0$, we cannot assign the cause to the other term xy. We can therefore only be sure that the term xy vanishes, in other words can only draw the one denial

$$xy = 0.$$

The point then that we have now reached is this. When any significant logical equation is given to us, drawn up in accordance with the various rules which we have laid down, we can resolve it into a series of separate denials, and such denials contain within themselves the sum-total of informa tion which the equation can furnish. That original equation may have been given to us in a categorical, hypothetical, or disjunctive proposition. Such differences as these are mere

iccidents of colloquial form, which disappear in the process
of accurate and generalized symbolic statement. In every
case alike we ground at last upon a certain number, more or
less, of what may thus be called elementary denials, such as
$ryz = 0$, $xyz = 0$, &c.

What further can be done with these denials in the way of
drawing what would commonly be called affirmative proposi
tions: that is, in what various ways the knowledge they
yield us can be again built up into new forms, will have to be
discussed in another chapter.

CHAPTER XI.

HAVING thus explained the meaning and interpretation of a single logical statement or equation, we must now go on to discuss the case of a system of them. Propositions do not generally present themselves alone, but in groups of two or more, and we have already had repeated opportunities of examining the results of their combination in simple ex amples. But we must now give more definite consideration to the specific question whether a combination of equations differs in any essential way from a single equation; and, if it does, what is the nature, the ground, and the limits of such difference?

The principal misleading influences under which the reader will probably lie here are those introduced by the associations of mathematics. In mathematics a combination of equations differs from a single equation by what may almost be called a difference of kind rather than one of degree only. Generally speaking, a single equation which involves two variables, x and y for instance, admits of an infinite number of solutions; and the answer is so far left entirely indeterminate. When we introduce two equations, so serious a restriction is introduced that we are at once tied down to a single and determinate value for x and y, if the equation were of the first degree. If we try to combine together more than two of such equations, we should find them, generally speaking, in direct conflict with one another. The third would either be simply deducible from the other two, or irreconcileable with them.

In the case of Logical equations however there is nothing resembling all this. There is no intrinsic or necessary difference between the nature and amount of information yielded by one, and that which we obtain from two. Given one equation, the addition of a second to it, involving the same terms, will no doubt, generally speaking, add to our information, but it does not do so by the marked and striking steps to which we are accustomed in mathematics. There is nothing here like the precise assignment of a single point by the intersection of two lines; it is more like the contraction of a circle into one of a smaller radius. We are still referred to a class of some kind, whether we are supplied with one equation or with many; but in the latter case the class is narrowed by the excision, probably, of a number of its various subdivisions.

If the reader recurs to that negative interpretation of a proposition which we have had so often to insist upon, he will see at once why this is so. Start with one equation: this will yield us a certain number of excisions or destructions of possible classes. How many it will thus destroy is of course dependent upon various considerations, such as the relative magnitude of the classes with which it deals. Some however it must certainly destroy, or it would be without any significance or value. Now add on another equation. This will similarly proceed to make some further such clearances. Now unless the second be a mere repetition of the first, or of some part of the first, it must follow that the second will make some clearances amongst classes which had been left surviving by the first. It will in fact add to our materials of information. But this does not represent any intrinsic superiority in the information yielded by the two over that yielded by one; for it must be remembered that the sum-total of the information might equally well have been conveyed by one singly.

It is as if a man were to write one letter, and follow it up by another which adds further details; the two tell us more than either did separately, but there is certainly nothing to prevent him putting all that he said, or even more than that, into a single letter if he had chosen to do so. We could clearly lay down no definite rule about two such letters giving us more information or any new kind or degree of information, than a single one would.

If any doubt is felt on this point, an appeal, symbolically and diagrammatically, to any simple example will serve to make it quite plain. Take the following examples;

$$\begin{cases} w = \tfrac{0}{0}\,(xy + \overline{x}z)\ldots\ldots\ldots\ldots(\alpha) \\ w = \tfrac{0}{0}\,(xyz + \overline{x}\,\overline{z})\ldots\ldots\ldots(\beta) \end{cases}$$

They would be naturally expressed in words, by saying,

    {All w is either x and y, or, if not x, then z.
    {All w is either x, y, and z, or neither x nor z.

I.   Begin by looking at the affirmative side of these two statements and their combination together.

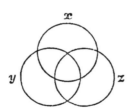

Equation (α) asserts that the whole of the class w is con fined to a portion, (a truly indefinite portion) of the two compartments xy and xz. Similarly equation (β) confines the members of this same class w to the compartments xyz and $\bar{x}z$. It is clear therefore that the two equations when taken in combination confine the class w to the one sub division common to these two assignments, viz. to xyz. To put it into ordinary language, we are told that 'all w is xyz'.

In this case, as it happens, the result of thus combining two distinct determinations of w has been its restriction to a single class, which represents the most definite such logical determination we can obtain. Of course this might have been otherwise; we might have had w assigned, in a dis junctive form to more than one class. No rule can possibly be laid down here as to the limits of such ultimate determi nation.

The reader will observe that in this case the class w was originally referred to two different groups of sub-classes which partially overlap one another, thus restricting w to this common part. It will readily be seen that this must represent the most usual case. For failing this, what else could we have? Either the two groups to which w is re ferred must be entirely distinct from one another, which is tantamount to saying that there is no w at all; or the one group must be entirely contained within the other, in which case the narrower determination completely supersedes the broader.

Of course when, as here, we have a class w thus standing by itself, on one side, and on the other side a group of classes which determines it with more or less definiteness, there is a much shorter method of procedure than that given above. All we have to do is to 'multiply' the two determinations together, when the common elements will stand out as the only survivors. Thus,

$$w = \tfrac{0}{0} (xy + \overline{x}z)(xyz + \overline{x}\,\overline{z})$$
$$= \tfrac{0}{0}\, xyz.$$

for the other three terms of the product disappear, owing to the general symbolic rule $xx = 0$, $zz = 0$.

Had the two groups been identical, this product would have simply repeated either of them. Had they been entirely distinct, the result would have been exhibited in the shape $w = 0$.

II. The same results come out equally distinctly under the negative interpretation of our statements. In fact this is the simplest and most general way of regarding them ; for explicit equations of the kind of which our present example is an instance are but one class of logical equations, whereas we have shown that all logical equations without exception are resolvable into a series of distinct negations. What we ask, under this interpretation, is what subdivisions does each equation blot out, instead of asking what classes it suffers to remain in existence.

By the methods of treatment described in the last chapter we should resolve each equation into all the ultimate denials which it involves, and which together constitute its effective meaning. They would then stand as follows ;—

$$\left\{ \begin{aligned} &w\,(xyz + x\overline{y}z + \overline{x}yz + \overline{x}\,\overline{y}z) = 0 \\ &w\,(x\overline{y}z + xyz + \overline{x}yz + \overline{x}\,\overline{y}z + xyz) = 0. \end{aligned} \right.$$

Now denial, as we have seen, is unconditional and final. All therefore that we have to do is to add up these separate elements, lay aside those which merely repeat what has been already denied, and see what number of classes they succeed in accounting for amongst them. In the case before us, two of the denials are twice repeated, thus indicating that, to that extent, the given equations were not altogether independent of one another. Hence the nine elementary negatives we have obtained are reduced to seven, leaving one and only one surviving, viz. $wxyz$. If this be put into words it may be phrased thus, 'The only w that can exist under the given conditions is the w that is xyz'. This is, as we know, a true interpretation of the familiar Universal Affirmative which was obtained by the other mode of treatment, 'All w is xyz'; so that the two views lead us to the same conclusion.

It appears therefore that the most which a second equation can do is to supplement the information afforded by the first; at least in instances of the kind which we have examined, and which may be taken as fair samples of those which we meet in Logic. As before remarked, there may not even be this supplementary information afforded. If the group of compartments to which the second equation refers the class which we are seeking to determine, be a wider one than that assigned by the first, then it tells us nothing new. Thus $w = \frac{0}{0}(1 - xyz)$ adds nothing whatever to the statement $w = \frac{0}{0}(1 - xy)$; since $(1 - xy)$ is contained in the class $(1 - xyz)$ and is therefore a narrower determination than that which is offered to supplement and restrict it.

Conversely when the new assignment is a narrower group than the old we do not strictly speaking supplement our information, we rather supersede entirely the old assignment. Thus for instance if $w = \frac{0}{0}(1 - xyz)$ had been given to us first, this would be entirely superseded by the equation $w = \frac{0}{0}(1 - xy)$.

Hence the natural and appropriate instances of combination of equations, of this explicit character, will be when the class determination of the one partially overlaps that of the other. Each then contributes something to the other, that is, each in part curtails the limits which the other had assigned. I recall attention to this point because it is so strongly characteristic of that class-view or denotation-view of the import of terms which necessarily pervades this account of Logic. In common Logic when we refer to xy, we as often as not,—probably much oftener,—think of x and y merely as attributes successively imposed upon an object. That is, we think of them in their *connotation;* and, so thinking of them, we make no reference to anything but the *presence* of such attributes:—we do not simultaneously impose the *absence* of these same attributes upon any other objects. We simply think nothing about such absence in reference to any other objects. But when x and y are regarded as classes we cannot but observe that not-x and not-y are themselves just as much classes as those of which they are the contradictories. To say therefore that a thing is xy assigns it as a rule to two overlapping classes: the one assignment cuts off the class xy, and the other cuts off xy, leaving only xy out of the whole contents of x and y together, viz. $xy + xy + xy$.

We gather then that, except for purposes of mere arrangement, such as symmetry or brevity or clearness, it is a matter of entire indifference in how many propositions or equations any given stock of logical information is conveyed. The full significance can always (unlike the case of mathematical equations) be conveyed in the form of a single equation which equates to zero the sum of a number of distinct alternatives.

For instance in the example towards the commencement of this chapter, we saw that all which the two equations had to say could be completely said by one. We might equally take a step in the opposite direction by increasing their number, that is, by breaking them up into smaller contingents. The two, as originally given to us[1], stood thus :—

$$\begin{cases} w = w\,(xy + \overline{x}z) \\ w = w\,(xyz + \overline{x}\,\overline{z}) \end{cases}$$

Now develop each side of the upper one in respect of x, or, in more familiar words, break each side up into its x and its not-x parts. The two sides of the resultant equations must still be equal after this subdivision ; that is, the x part and the not-x part. This follows from the fact that our so-called equation is really the identity of a group of individuals when referred to under two different names or groups of names. Hence the same identity persists when the group is split into two distinct sections, so that the x-parts of the equation and the not-x parts taken separately will each still hold good.

We may therefore substitute for the single equation $w = w\,(xy + xz)$, the pair

$$\begin{cases} wx = wxy \\ w\overline{x} = w\overline{x}z. \end{cases}$$

And for the single one, $w = w\,(xyz + xz)$, the pair

$$\begin{cases} wx = wxyz \\ w\overline{x} = w\overline{x}\,\overline{z}. \end{cases}$$

The combined effect of these four being precisely equivalent in every way to that of the original two, or to the one into which we saw we could compress them.

If we had chosen to make a somewhat different arrangement we might have broken up the two sides in respect of y instead of in respect of x. In that case, as the reader

[1] For variety, and to remind the reader of their exact equivalence, I occasionally adopt the form $w = wX$ ead of $w = \frac{0}{0}X$.

will readily see, we should have got the following group
instead ;—

$$\left\{\begin{aligned} wy &= wy\,(x + xz) \\ wy &= w\overline{y}\,xz. \end{aligned}\right.$$

$$\left\{\begin{aligned} wy &= wy\,(xz + xz) \\ w\overline{y} &= w\overline{y}\,x\overline{z}. \end{aligned}\right.$$

(Attention may be directed here to the second and
fourth of these equations. They refer wy to two contra
dictory classes, viz. to one that is z and to one that is not-z.
This is, as we now know, merely their way of reminding us
that there *is* no such class as wy, or in other words, of
saying that 'all w is y'.)

From what has been said about the interpretation of
equations it follows that logical equations have a sort of self-
righting power about them. In this they are somewhat
distinct from mere class expressions, the correction of which,
when we have reason to believe them badly expressed, can
only be carried out by our guessing what was likely to have
been meant, and then inserting our conjectural correction.
Thus $x + y$, standing by itself, might leave a doubt whether
it was meant for 'x or y or both' (*i.e.* $x + xy$) or whether it
was merely so put because x and y were known to be inde
pendent, and that this was consequently briefer than to write
$xy + xy$.

Now compare the equation $x + y = z$.

We see at once that xy must $= 0$ here, as otherwise a
simple class term z would be partly identified with the
double term $2xy$. Hence the equation may be written in
the correct form, for which it has itself supplied the con
dition :—

$$xy + xy = z \quad (\text{with } xy = 0).$$

So again in the case of $w\,(x + y) = x - y$.
When analysed this leads to the denials $wy = 0$, $wxy = 0$,

$\bar{w}\bar{x}y = 0$. Whence we see that y must $= xy$, so that the statement ought really to have been phrased

$$wx - x\bar{\bar{y}}.$$

It is then intelligible enough, the only misleading features having been the addition of wy (in that form) to wx, and the apparent introduction of a substantive negative term (y) on one side when both the terms on the opposite side were positive. These difficulties are at once removed by the assurance that there *is* no wy, and that $x - y = xy$. What in fact we were originally offered was a piece of very bad sym bolic grammar; this we are able to correct by the conditions of the system, and so can express the statement in the per fectly unobjectionable form, $wx = xy$.

The above remarks become of some symbolic importance in the interpretation of the inverse form $\dfrac{X}{Y}$. We gave a simple enough explanation of it, applicable to every case in which X and Y were possible class expressions in a correct form. But this explanation will not cover every case. For instance $\dfrac{x - y}{x + y}$ cannot be read off in any such simple fashion as this. But if we regard it as, so to say, a piece of symbolic bad grammar, it will become amenable to treatment. We know that it might originate from $w(x + y) - x - y$; that is, 'If w combined with $x + y$ yields $x - y$, what must w be'? Then we have an equation which can be repaired and reconstructed like one of those above considered. For $w(x + y) - x - y$, after resolution and reconstruction stands (as shown on the last page)

$$wx = xy \text{ with } xy = 0.$$

What the expression $w(x + y) = x - y$ asks us, is, to find a class such that on combination with $x + y$ it shall yield $x - y$. It was a foolish question to ask in those words, for we find that the y-part of $w(x+y)$ contributes nothing

(wy being $=0$), and that $x - y$ is really xy, (xy being $= 0$). So the answer is that $w = xy + \frac{0}{0} xy$.

Boole would not have hesitated to take $\dfrac{x - y}{\sim + y}$ as it stands, and develope it into $xy - xy + \frac{0}{0} xy$. So phrased it has no meaning, for we cannot deduct xy from either of the other classes. Accordingly he has to introduce the rule that any term thus affected with a negative factor (or indeed any factor but 1 and $\frac{0}{0}$) must be equated to zero, as we do with those affected with the factor $\frac{1}{0}$. We then find that $\dfrac{x - y}{x + y} = xy + \frac{0}{0} x\bar{y}$ This seems to me to be rather straining the use of our symbols, though it does not amount to real error. Take again the following: $\dfrac{1 - x - y}{xy}$. This when developed yields $- xy + \frac{0}{0} \bar{x}y + \frac{0}{0} x\bar{y} + \frac{1}{0} \bar{x}\bar{y}$. This, like the other forms above, will submit to explanation, but it is certainly very badly expressed. Since $1 - x - y = \bar{x}\bar{y} - xy$, what we are really asking for, is some factor which will reduce xy to $\bar{x}\bar{y} - xy$. Some class term z is wanted, such that $zxy = \bar{x}\bar{y} - xy$. Of course there can be no such class term, for how can a positive term, like xy, be converted into its contradictory $\bar{x}\bar{y}$, or into a negative like $(- xy)$? So the statement escapes nonsense by demanding that xy and $\bar{x}\bar{y}$ shall both $= 0$, and then z may naturally be anything whatever. The value apparently deduced for z, by Boole's symbolic method of expansion, is in fact quite illusory and misleading. It stands indeed in the form $\frac{0}{0} xy + \frac{0}{0} \bar{x}y$; but, (since $xy = 0$ and $\bar{x}\bar{y} = 0$,) $xy + \bar{x}\bar{y} = 1$, so that $\frac{0}{0} xy + \frac{0}{0} \bar{x}y$ is not, (as it clearly ought not to be) any determination at all : it is equivalent to $\frac{0}{0} 1$, viz. it is absolutely indefinite.

This sort of symbolic solecism, as we may term it, commonly takes the form of asking two questions in one,

but asking them in terms which resemble a single ques-
tion. Thus the expression $\dfrac{0}{\dot{w}-\dot{y}}$ yields $\frac{0}{0}xy+\frac{0}{0}\bar{x}y$. Now
$x-y=xy-\bar{x}y$. so that what $\dfrac{0}{x-y}$ asks for is a class such as
shall, when combined with $\bar{x}y-xy$, reduce to 0. But we can
not, as pretended or suggested, deduct xy from $\bar{x}y$. Accord
ingly the question really means 'Find a class such that combi
nation with *either* $\bar{x}y$ or xy shall reduce to 0'. This being
what we meant, the (symbolically) correct grammatical form
would have been $\dfrac{0}{xy+\bar{x}y}$. This would develope at once into
$\frac{0}{0}xy+\frac{0}{0}\bar{x}\bar{y}$.

It may be noticed that these awkward expressions will
often meet us in the solution of problems. Thus take the
statement $wx=wy$ which in that form is quite irreproachable.
If asked to determine w, we might proceed to say $wx-wy=0$,
therefore $w-\dfrac{0}{x-y}$ as above : and then solving this we should
obtain $w=\frac{0}{0}xy+\frac{0}{0}\bar{x}y$. The awkwardness here of course
begins at the step $wx-wy=0$, for we thus use the form of
subtraction or subduction upon terms which do not formally
merit it, though we know that materially, that is, by the con
ditions of the data, they do so. A less questionable plan
would have been to have broken up $wx=wy$ into $wxy=0$,
$w\bar{x}y=0$, which would lead at once to $w(\bar{x}y+x\bar{y})=0$ or
$w=-\dfrac{0}{\bar{x}y+x\bar{y}}$ a form against which no objection whatever could
be raised.

On the interpretation of Equations.

There are few points in the Symbolic Logic about which
acquired views will have to be more completely abandoned

than in reference to the interpretation of logical equations. In the common system we talk of *the* solution as if there were but one; in fact a plurality of possible answers is considered a fatal defect, so that possible syllogistic figures are rejected on this ground alone.

On the symbolic system all this has, at first sight, to be altered. We must be prepared here for such an apparent variety of possible answers that different persons might draw conclusions which appear to have no connection between them. In saying this it is not, of course, implied that conflicting answers could be drawn, but rather that the modes of expression are so various that the same answer substantially can assume a bewildering variety of forms.

This distinction rests upon two grounds; firstly, the fact that we put a term and its contradictory (x and x) on exactly the same footing, whereas the common system seeks always to express itself in positive terms, putting the negation into the predicate. Secondly, there is the obvious difference that whereas but two or three terms are commonly admitted into the former, the latter is prepared to welcome any number.

For instance, take the familiar syllogism, 'all x is y; no z is y; ∴ no z is x. Here it would be said, and very correctly from the appropriate standpoint, that there is one and only one conclusion possible. Now look at it symbolically: We write the statements in the form $xy = 0$, $yz = 0$. Therefore the full combination of the two may be written $xy + yz = 0$, and it may be represented in a diagram thus:

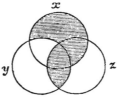

It will be seen at once, even in such a simple case, what

ι variety of possible solutions are here open to us. First take the complete solutions. These fall into the usual distinction offered by the positive and negative interpretation; that is, according as we enumerate all the abolished classes, or all the possible surviving ones. Thus, $xy + yz = 0$ expanded into its details gives four terms to be destroyed, the remaining four being equated to unity.

$$\begin{cases} xyz + xyz + xyz + xyz = 0 \\ xyz + xyz + xyz + xyz = 1. \end{cases}$$

These are the complete alternative answers given in their fullest details. The former states, with negative disjunction, that there is nothing which falls into any one of its four classes; the latter, with affirmative disjunction, that everything does fall into one or other of its four classes.

These ultimate elements we may of course group at will, and thus obtain various simplifications of expression. The former we know will stand as $xy + yz = 0$, the latter will stand as $yz + xy = 1$. They then state respectively that there is nothing which is either yz or xy, and that everything is either yz or xy.

These are the complete statements of the information yielded by the data in an implicit form. Now for the same or a part of the same complete information in an explicit form. We may require to have the account of any one of the six terms x, x, y, y, z, z, as described in the other terms; thus

$$x = \tfrac{0}{0}\, y\bar{z}$$
$$x = z + \bar{y}\bar{z} + \tfrac{0}{0}\, y\bar{z}$$
$$y = x\bar{z} + \tfrac{0}{0}\, \bar{x}\bar{z}.$$

and so on with the remaining terms.

But even this is only a part of the full problem before us. Our complete scheme comprises two further modifications on anything here indicated. For we may want to determine not merely x and x, y and y, z and z, but any possible combination or function of these; and this we may want to determine not as here in terms of *all* the remaining elements, but in terms of any selection from amongst these, after elimination of the remaining elements. These extensions will be duly discussed in their proper places.

The above example will serve to shew how indefinite is the solution of a logical problem, unless some further indications are given as to the kind of solution desired. The sum-total of the facts which are left consistent with the data must necessarily be the same however they may be expressed. But the various ways of expressing those facts, and still more the various ways of expressing selections and combinations of them, are very numerous. Take, for instance, a slightly more complicated example, such as that indicated in the following figure :

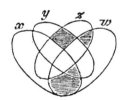

and observe in what a variety of ways the unshaded portion may be described. The figure represents the results of the data;—

$$\begin{cases} \text{All } wx \text{ is } z \\ \text{All } wz \text{ is } x \text{ or } y \\ \text{All } yz \text{ is } w \text{ or } x \end{cases} \text{viz.} \begin{cases} wxz = 0 \\ wzxy = 0 \\ yzwx = 0. \end{cases}$$

One way of course is to say that the surviving classes are all which are not thus obliterated; these being negatively

$$1 - xzw - xyzw - xyzw$$

or, slightly grouped,

$$1 - xzw - xz(yw + yw).$$

Or again, we may put them all positively thus,

$$x\,(wz + \overline{w}z + \overline{w}\,\overline{z}) + \overline{x}z\,(wy + \overline{w}\,\overline{y}) + \overline{x}_\sim$$

or, less completely positive, but briefer,

$$x\,(1 - wz) + xz\,(wy + w\,y) + xz$$

or $$x\,(1 - wz) + x\,\{z\,(wy + w\,y) + z\},$$

each of these symbolic groupings having of course its suitable verbal description. Thus the last may be read 'All x except what is w but not z; and all not-x, provided it be not-z, or, if z, then both or neither w and y'.

The general nature of the problem thus put before us is easily indicated. Suppose there were four terms involved; then our symbolic apparatus provides 2^4 or 16 compartments or possibilities. The data impose material limits upon these possibilities, leaving only a limited number of actualities. That is, they extinguish a certain number and leave only the remainder surviving. In this case out of the 16 original possibilities 12 are left remaining. The full result then of the data is given by enumerating completely either the extinguished compartments or the remaining ones. Either of these enumerations is only possible in one way, provided we do it in detail. But when we want to group these results, for more convenience, into compendious statements, we see that it can be done in a variety of ways.

The number of different combinations which can thus be produced by taking successively one, two, three, and so forth of these sub-classes is enormous, and increases with the introduction of every fresh class term in a way which taxes the imagination to follow. Thus three terms yield eight subdivisions. From these we might make eight distinct selections of one only; 28 of a pair; 56 of three together, and so on. The total number of distinct groups which can thus be produced is $8 + 28 + 56 + 70 + 56 + 28 + 8 + 1$ or 255.

One case, and only one, is excluded necessarily, namely that in which every compartment is erased, for this corre sponds to the one formal impossibility of endeavouring to maintain that every one of our exhaustive divisions is unoccupied: this being, as the reader knows, the symbolic generalization of the Law of Excluded Middle or Third. The arithmetical statement of the total number of cases is readily enough written down. Three terms yield eight sub-classes. viz. 2^3; and these eight sub-classes may be taken as above in $2^8 - 1$ ways, viz. $2^{2^3} - 1$ represents the possible varieties before us. Or expressed generally, if there be n terms we can have 2^n classes, and accordingly $2^{2^n} - 1$ distinct groups o these classes. Of course this expression increases with enormous rapidity as n increases. Four terms thus yield 65,535 possibilities in the way of combination of the elements yielded, and so on.

It may be enquired here if there is no system of classifi cation available for these enormous numbers, so as to make them somewhat less unwieldy to deal with. This is a question which Prof. Jevons has set himself to answer in what seems to me the most original part of his logical inves tigations (*Pr. of Science,* p. 137). The following (see next page) is his table of results for the case of three terms, A, B, C.

For a full explanation of this table and the way to work it, the reader must be referred to the work in question, but a brief indication may be offered here. Suppose, for instance, we had as the result of a set of premises, the conclu sion[1] $ABc = 0$, $AbC = 0$. Suppose also that we wished to reduce this to a single proposition, if possible, of the ordinary type. Since two combinations are destroyed, we turn to

---

[1]   I have employed Prof. Jevons' own notation here, as the table is copied from his work.

the last column, and find that there are three types

Reference Number.	Propositions expressing the general type of the logical conditions.	Number of distinct logical variations.	Number of combinations contradicted by each.
I	$A = B$	6	4
II	$A = AB$	12	2
III	$A = B, \quad B = C$	4	6
IV	$A = B, \quad B = BC$	24	5
V	$A = AB, \quad B = BC$	24	4
VI	$A = BC$	24	4
VII	$A = ABC$	24	3
VIII	$AB = ABC$	8	1
IX	$A = AB, \quad aB = aBc$	24	3
X	$A = ABC, \quad ab = abC$	8	4
XI	$AB = ABC, \quad ab = abc$	4	2
XII	$AB = AC$	12	2
XIII	$A = BC \cdot\mid\cdot Abc$	8	3
XIV	$A = BC \cdot\mid\cdot bc$	2	4
XV	$A = ABC, \quad a = Bc \cdot\mid\cdot bC$	8	5

of propositions which produce this amount of destruc tion, viz. II, XI, XII. Accordingly we know that we are to seek amongst these for the desired proposition which is to sum up our result. Of course this is only a portion of our task, for these are *types* merely, containing a variety of species under them. For instance, $A = AB$ is one of four distinct species; viz. $A = AB$, $A = Ab$, $a = aB$, $a = ab$: and similarly with the others. Accordingly every species of proposition of each type may have to be considered before we finally hit upon the right one. The solution we are in quest of, as it happens, is one of those in No. XII, viz. $AB = AC$. That it will produce the required destructions, viz. those of ABc and AbC, and of these only, is evident. We may therefore regard it as the answer.

The nature and use of such a table as this will be readily

understood now. Given, as the final outcome of our premises, a certain number of subdivisions destroyed, we want to find one or two propositions which shall sum up, that is, which shall contain within themselves these destructions. In the case just noticed, the destructions were those of ABc and AbC, and it was found that the one proposition $AB - AC$ would suffice thus to sum them up. That is, it is a compendious summary of the solution of the problem.

There can be no doubt that much ingenuity and labour has been devoted to the composition of this table :—in fact it involved, as a preliminary, the writing out and the analysis and discussion of every one of the 255 possible cases which we saw might result from the combinations of three terms. Moreover as a classification of the forms of proposition which would produce these various results it seems to me sound and successful on the whole[1]. But regarded as a means of solving an indeterminate inverse problem, that is of discovering the simplest propositions from which the assigned destructions would result, it does not seem to me equally successful. We must remember that even this rather complicated table only includes the consequences of dealing with *three* terms, an unusually small number in even such simple examples as we have employed in this work. With four terms there are 65,535 possible selections of combinations. Prof. Jevons considered that it would take several years of continuous labour even to determine the number of possible types of proposition here; and, though Prof. Clifford solved this part of the question by showing that

---

[1] I differ entirely from some of the assumptions of Prof. Jevons by which the number of admissible combinations is limited. For instance the results are rejected as "inconsistent" whenever they require the simple abolition of any class or its contradictory: e.g. A, B, C, a, b, c. I have already given my reasons for regarding their rejection as arbitrary and unphilosophical.

there were 396 such types, he still considers that such a period would be required to ascertain what these types actually are. With five terms the number of possible selections is 4,294,967,295, and the number of types is one which presumably no man will ever determine.

However valuable the direct and indirect results of classifying and analysing these propositional forms may be, any labour bestowed upon them with a view to actually solving logical problems seems to me scarcely well bestowed. The procedure here appears rather to be of that kind which tact and judgment, aided by graphical methods, will alone suffice to grapple with. It is naturally allied to that class of physical investigations which we deal with by the method of curves. Suppose a quantity of values of some element are given, and we want to determine the law involved in them. What we should do is to draw ordinates corresponding to these values, and trace a curve through their extremities, and then endeavour, by the help of the eye, to detect, at any rate provisionally, what kind of law the curve follows.

In the case of logical problems the corresponding device is one which we have already had frequent occasion to use, viz. that of diagrams. The diagram corresponding to the two destructions of subdivisions *ABc*, *AbC*, is of course:

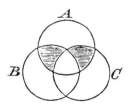

Looking at such a diagram it seems to me that one might readily detect that a good and brief description of the result is that the only *A* which survives is that which is both

17—2

B and C and that which is neither. In the notation above adopted this would be written down $A = A (BC + bc)$. At first sight it may seem that this is a different result from that yielded by the table, but a little observation will show that they are equivalent or alternative forms.

In the course of Chap. v. several examples were given to show the kind of cases for which this graphical method was peculiarly suitable, and in those cases there can hardly be a doubt of the superiority of this plan. On the other hand there are cases in which I can quite suppose that a resort to the table might prove the more certain and efficacious plan. But in admitting even this degree of comparison it must be remembered that it is not credible that such a table should ever be practically resorted to (even if it were ever constructed) for more than three terms, whilst the instances most appro priate to the methods of the Symbolic Logic only *begin* when we take into account four or more terms. An appeal therefore to some kind of graphical aid, the usual resort of science in cases of this complicated character, seems the only hopeful resource before us.

CHAPTER XII.

THIS chapter is entirely devoted to the discussion of examples. In so abstract a subject as this it is not easy to explain principles, at any rate to those who are unfamiliar with the topics in question, except by aid of a variety of concrete instances. This will be a justification for treating the first few examples at considerable length. Had our object been to show the possible brevity of the methods at our disposal most of these examples could have been worked out in a few lines. But, as just intimated, this chapter is intended mainly for beginners.

(1) Suppose we were asked to discuss the following set of club rules, in respect of their formal completeness and accuracy :—

> *a.* The Financial Committee shall be chosen from amongst the General Committee.
>
> *β.* No one shall be a member both of the General and Library Committees unless he be also on the Financial Committee.
>
> *γ.* No member of the Library Committee shall be on the Financial Committee.

Put x to stand for the class constituting the Financial

Committee, y for that of the Library, and z for that of the General. Then the three given rules will stand as follows :—I state them, both in the form most natural to the ordinary Logic, and in the equivalent negative form which is most convenient for our symbolic system.

$$
\begin{array}{ll}
(\alpha) \quad \text{All } x \text{ is } z \\
(\beta) \quad \text{All } yz \text{ is } x \\
(\gamma) \quad \text{No } x \text{ is } y
\end{array}\Bigg\} .
\qquad
\begin{array}{l}
x\bar{z} = 0 \\
\bar{x}yz = 0 \\
xy = 0
\end{array}\Bigg\} .
$$

As the rules were given, they might very likely pass muster. But develop the symbolic expressions by our process of subdivision, or rather develop in this way rules (α) and (γ), for rule (β) already stands in its lowest terms.

They then stand thus :—

$$
\begin{array}{l}
xyz + xyz = 0 \\
\bar{x}yz = 0 \\
xyz + xyz = 0
\end{array}\Bigg\} .
$$

It is now obvious at a glance that the third rule is partially redundant, or at any rate that the first and third together are so ; for they partially overlap each other by both of them denying the same element xyz. Accordingly they would stand better stated without redundancy in the form,

$$
\begin{array}{l}
xy\bar{z} + x\bar{y}\bar{z} = 0 \\
xuz = 0 \\
xyz = 0
\end{array}\Bigg\} ,
$$

in which form they are perfectly distinct and consistent with one another.

Of course when we have thus analyzed and corrected them there are reasons of brevity for seeking to express them in the most compendious form. The best way of effecting this (which it must be observed is purely a matter of tact and skill, for which no strict rules can be given) is to put the first rule back into its original shape, and then to combine the other two into one. As regards the last step: symbolically, we just add the two together; logically, we say that if there can be no yz which is x, and none which is not, then there can be no yz at all. The whole force of the rules therefore is fully expressed by the two equations :—

$$x\bar{z} = 0 \atop yz = 0 \Bigg\} .$$

Or in words,

> All the Financial Committee are on the General Committee.
> None of the Library Committee are on the General Committee.

This example is of course intended to be a very simple one, but it serves to call attention to two points of some importance.

In the first place it brings out clearly one of the objects and uses of the process of Development or Subdivision. When we proceed to break up each separate assertion that is given to us into its ultimate details, it becomes very easy to see whether or not they partially overlap; and if so, whether these overlapping parts are, as usual, simple redundancies, or whether they amount to direct inconsistencies. Such redundancies and inconsistencies would in general be obvious enough at once when they are complete; but when they are only partial, especially when they are expressed in the vague forms of ordinary language, they may very easily escape our notice.

In the second place, it should be observed how free from ambiguity is our symbolic notation, as compared with the expressions of common language, owing to our making no 'implications', but only direct and unconditional statements; at least in the form in which we write our equations down. The symbolic statements, as we saw. are in no sense inconsistent, though they are to some extent redundant. But when we look at the verbal statements we find that these convey misleading suggestions. "No one shall be a member of the Library and General Committees, unless he be also on the Financial":—this does not, it is true, assert that there is such a class of persons as those which form the subject of this proposition, but it would.always be understood most strongly to suggest that there is. The symbolic state ment is quite clear upon this point. It confines itself to denials only, and to these it unconditionally adheres.

(2)   Three persons A, B, C, are set to sort a heap of books in a library. A is told to collect all the English political works, and the bound foreign novels: B is to take the bound political works, and the English novels, provided they are not political: to C is assigned the bound English works and the unbound political novels. What works will be claimed by two of them? Will any be claimed by all three?

Put a for English, then $1 - a$[1] stands for foreign.

b	„	political,	„	$1 - b$	„ „	not-political.
c	„	bound,	„	$1 - c$	„ „	unbound.
d	„	novels,	„	$1 - d$	„ „	not-novels.

The propositions therefore assigning the apportionment of the various books will then stand as follows ; A standing for the books assigned to A, and so on ;—

$$A = ab + (1 - a)\,cd$$
$$B = bc + (1 - b)\,ad\bigg\} .$$
$$C = ac + (1 - c)\,bd$$

[1] a is the abbreviated form, of course; but I purposely choose various forms of expression here.

Now we know that x and y being any class terms, the expression xy stands for what is common to both x and y. Hence to indicate generally the books belonging to A and B, we should write AB; or if, as here, we want to know the classes in their details, we should multiply together the detailed descriptions of them ; that is,

$$\{ab + (1 - a)\, cd\}\, \{bc + (1 - b)\, ad\}.$$

'Multiply' out this product, then, according to the symbolic rules of logic, and we have

$$AB = abc + (1 - a)\, bcd,$$
$$= bc\, \{a + (1 - a)\, d\}.$$

That is, put into words, we have assigned to both A and B the class of books describable briefly as 'bound political works; whether English generally, or foreign novels.' Precisely similar expressions would be yielded for BC, and AC, viz. for the books assigned to B and C, and to A and C.

In the same way if the question be to find what books are assigned to all three persons, we should have to find the details of the expression ABC. This is simpler in its result, since more of the terms neutralize each other; we find in fact

$$ABC = abc.$$

That is, the only books which have been thus assigned to all three are the 'bound English political works'.

(3) The following may be offered as an example of the inverse process corresponding to the sign of division ;—It is found that when all the books in a library, except philosophy and divinity, are rejected, they are reduced to philosophy and protestant divinity; but include all works on those subjects. What is the widest and the narrowest extent, so far as expressible in these class terms, which the library could have possessed under the given conditions ?

What is really asserted here, is, that when the restriction of being confined to 'philosophy and divinity' is imposed upon the books, they are exactly reduced to 'philosophy and protestant divinity'.

Put x for philosophy,

y „ divinity,

z „ protestant,

and let w represent the class, whatever it may be, constituting the library:

Then the data assert, when expresssed in symbolic form,

$$(x + xy)\, w = x + xyz.$$

Here, of course, $x + xy$ is our strict expression for what is commonly described as 'x or y', viz. 'philosophy or divinity'. The combination of $(x + xy)$ with w, by the sign of multiplication, indicates the restriction of w by the stated condition, and this is to be equated to $x + xyz$. The inverse problem therefore is, Find w.

Hence $$w = \frac{x + xyz}{x + xy}.$$

Develop this expression in accordance with the rules, and we obtain,

$$w = x + \overline{x}yz + \tfrac{0}{0}\overline{x}\,\overline{y}.$$

That is, the library must have certainly contained all philosophy and protestant divinity, and may possibly have contained any kind of works which are neither philosophy nor divinity: this latter constituent being left entirely indefinite. Unaided common sense would, I doubt not, have been sufficient to enable many persons to say what the positive and definite part of the answer must be, but it is unlikely that they could feel equally confident about the exact limits of admissible indefiniteness.

The two following are miscellaneous examples of this inverse process :—

(4)   There is a certain class of things from which A picks out the 'x that is z, and the y that is not z', and B picks out from the remainder 'the z which is y and the x that is not y'. It is then found that nothing is left but the class 'z which is not x'.   What can be determined about the class originally ?

Call that class w.   Then the statement amounts to this, symbolically ;—

$$w\,(1 - xz - y\bar{z})\,(1 - yz - x\bar{y}) = \bar{x}z.$$

For A, picking out the $(xz + yz)$ part, reduces it from w to $w - w\,(xz + yz)$, or converts it into $w\,(1 - xz - yz)$; similarly B's selection has the same effect of reducing this by the multiplication of $(1 - yz - xy)$.   This final result is then declared to be exactly equivalent to xz, as above expressed.

On multiplying out, most of the terms in the brackets disappear, and we have

$$w\bar{x}\bar{y} = \bar{x}z$$

or

$$w = \frac{\bar{x}z}{\bar{x}\bar{y}},$$

$$\therefore w = xyz + \tfrac{0}{0}\,(1 - xy)\,(1 - xz),$$
$$= xyz + \tfrac{0}{0}\,(x + xyz) \qquad\qquad .(1),$$

with the condition

$$\bar{x}z\,(1 - \bar{x}\bar{y}) = 0,$$

or

$$xyz - 0 \dots\dots\dots\dots\dots\dots\dots\dots\dots(2).$$

That is, the class must have certainly consisted of 'all z that is neither x nor y' and may have also contained 'anything that is x, or that is y but neither x nor z', but nothing else.   Moreover by the terms of statement 'all yz is x.

I append the diagram, as it may serve to aid conviction. The reader will readily see that if from w as thus composed we make the two assigned selections, there will be left

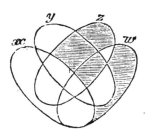

'z that is not x', and that only. This is equally so in whichever order we make the two selections.

(5) Confining oneself to the candidates for a certain examination it was found that the plucked exactly comprised the boys who took Greek and the girls who took Latin. Find the full description of the boy candidates as describable in the other terms thus introduced.

Put x for Latin.

z „ Greek.

w „ boys, $\therefore w$ = girls (these being contradictories

y „ plucked.   in that universe).

The statement is that,

$$y = x\overline{w} + zw,$$
$$\therefore w\,(z - x) = y - x,$$
$$\therefore w = \frac{y - x}{z - x}.$$

The numerator and denominator not being here, separately, as they stand, interpretable class expressions, we adopt the full formula

$$f(x, y, z) = f(1, 1, 1)\,xyz + \&c.$$

Hence $w = xyz + xyz + \tfrac{0}{0}\,(xyz + xyz)$ (1),

with conditions $xyz + xyz = 0$ .... (2).

That is, in words, The boys comprise

		those who take Latin but not Greek, and were not plucked.
the whole of		„ „ „ Greek but not Latin, and were plucked.
an uncertain portion of		„ „ „ Greek and Latin, and were plucked.
		„ „ „ Neither Greek nor Latin, and were not plucked.

With the implied conditions

{ All who took both Latin and Greek were plucked.
{ All who were plucked took either Latin or Greek.

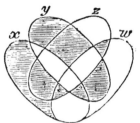

A few moments' attention may be conveniently directed here to the diagrammatic interpretation of the symbol $\frac{0}{0}$. When we look at the four surviving classes which compose the figure w, it might be thought that they all stood upon an equal footing of certainty, and that there was nothing in them corresponding to the sharp distinction represented symbolically by

$$w = x\overline{y}\overline{z} + \dot{x}yz + \tfrac{0}{0}xyz + \tfrac{0}{0}\,\dot{x}\,\overline{y}\overline{z}.$$

But reflection soon shows the difference. The two former are completely describable in terms of x, y, and z. The two latter cannot be so described without making use of w also. But w being the very term to be defined, the admission of it into the definition is equivalent to no determination at all. We may make the semblance of a determination by writing it

$$w = xyz + xyz + wxyz + w\,x\,y\,z,$$

but such avoidance of indeterminateness is altogether delusive.

This class w therefore contains the whole of xyz and xyz, and 'a part' of xyz and xyz. Whether this 'part', or 'some', will really prove to be the whole, or a part only, or even none, will depend upon circumstances. If the given premises are to be regarded as final, and as postulating the existence of all which they do not deny, then this 'part' is really a part only, and the word *some* in its common signification might be substituted for $\frac{0}{0}$.

(6) As an instance of the implied extinction of a whole class, take the following :—

At a certain town where an examination is held, it is known that,

    1.   Every candidate is either a junior who does not take Latin, or a senior who takes Composition.

    2.   Every junior candidate takes either Latin or Composition.

    3.   All candidates who take Composition, also take Latin, and are juniors.

Show that if this be so there can be no candidates there.

Putting x for candidates, a and a for junior and senior, c for those who take Latin, and e for those who take Composition, the data stand thus :—

$$\begin{cases} x = \frac{0}{0}\,(a\bar{c} + \bar{a}e), \\ ax = \frac{0}{0}\,(c + \bar{c}e), \\ ex = \frac{0}{0}\,ac. \end{cases}$$

These resolve at once into the negations

$$\left.\begin{array}{l} xae,\ xac,\ xce \\ axce \\ \bar{a}ex,\ \bar{c}ex \end{array}\right\} - 0.$$

Gathering together the factors of x we have, in slightly different order,

$$x\,\{ae + ae + a\,(c + ce) + ce + ce\} = 0.$$

This accounts for *all* the possible factors of *x*; as would be seen at once by subdividing these terms, when all the eight possible combinations of *a, c, e,* will be found to be represented here with some redundancies. (These redundancies were no part of the original statements, but come from the fact of our having taken more multipliers than were necessary. Thus, in the three obtained from the first statement, *ce* is contained in the other two; and the two obtained from the third have a common part.)

(7) In the last example one whole class was seen to have perished. In such cases, or when the destruction is even more extensive, the results are often more easily interpreted by aid of the diagrams than by relying only on symbols.

For instance,

$$\begin{cases} x = y + z\bar{y}, \\ y = \therefore + z\bar{w}, \\ zw = 0, \\ xw = yzw. \end{cases}$$

Looking out for the appropriate multipliers, as already indicated, the following classes are abolished :—

(1) xyz, xy, xyz.   (2) yzw, yz, yzw.
(3) zw.   (4) $xyw, xzw, xyzw$.

Shade out in the diagram, and it stands thus :—

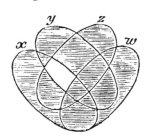

(The outside, or $xyzw$, should also be shaded, to make it complete.)

It is obvious at a glance that all w is destroyed, and that the only surviving compartment is xyz. This would be described verbally in the statements,

(Everything is x, y, and z.
(Nothing is w.

(The same example, with other letters, was discussed in the note on p. 148.)

The next two examples have some historic interest, as representing early attempts at the symbolic solutions of problems.

(8) If x that is not a is the same as b, and a that is not x is the same as c, what is x in terms of a, b, and c? (Lambert, *Log. Abh.* I. 14.)

Since $\quad x = ax + ax, \therefore x - ax - ax, \quad$ or $x - b = ax$.

Since $\quad a - ax + ax, \therefore ax - a - ax = a - c$.

$\quad \therefore x - b = a - c$, or $x = a + b - c$.

(It will be seen, from the terms of statement, that a and b are mutually exclusive; also that c is a part of a. Hence the whole result, as it stands, is really correctly stated, though it apparently involves double counting and inappropriate subtraction.) I append Lambert's solution in his own notation;—

"Man habe $x\,a = b$; $a|x = c$, so ist [by a former result] $ax = a - c = x - b$. Folglich $x = a + b - c$."

(9) If $xy = zw$, is it correct to conclude that $\dfrac{\overset{m}{=}}{} = \overset{m''}{}$? Or,

put into words, if the members common to x and $\overset{\smile}{y}$ are the same as those common to z and w, does it follow that the class which on restriction by z will reduce to x is the same as that which on restriction by y will reduce to w? Lambert more than once assumes that this is so, but it is soon seen (I think) that he was in error. For develop the two expressions $\dfrac{x}{z}$ and $\dfrac{w}{y}$, and we have,

$$xz + \tfrac{0}{0}\overline{x}\,\overline{z} = wy + \tfrac{0}{0}\overline{w}\,\overline{y},$$

with the two conditions,

$$xz = 0, \; wy = 0.$$

Now the equation of two determinate classes implies that everything which falls within one shall also fall within the other. I do not feel perfectly certain about the application of this principle to the case of two classes each of which has an indeterminate addition to it, but on the whole it seems to me to demand that the determinate and indeterminate portions shall be separately equated; i.e. $xz = wy$ and $\overline{x}\,\overline{z} = \overline{w}\,\overline{y}$. It is readily seen that all these conditions, taken together, lead to $x = w, z = y$. The meaning of this is that two logical fractions can only be equated by the identification of both their numerators and their denominators. And this, I think, is what we should expect, inasmuch as we cannot strike out common factors as we should in algebra or arithmetic.

Lambert's error here deserves the more notice, because he had gained a very remarkable grasp of the truth in an analogous, though somewhat simpler case. He most distinctly states that we cannot put logical division on the same footing as ordinary division, by striking out common factors: and this, not because the result would be false, but because it would not be general enough. That is, we ought to have an indeterminate result, instead of a determinate one. His words are,......"Wenn $x\gamma = a\gamma$, so ist $x = a\gamma\gamma^{-1} = a\dfrac{\gamma}{\gamma}$. Aber deswegen nicht allezeit $x = a$; sondern nur in einem einzigen Falle, weil x und a zwei verschiedene Arten von dem Geschlecht $x\gamma$ oder $a\gamma$ sein konnen. Wenn aber $x\gamma = a\gamma$

nicht weiter bestimmt wird, so kann man unter andern auch $x = \alpha$ setzen." That is, $x = \alpha$ is *one* solution of the problem [1].

(10) Express symbolically, 'If x is y, then z is w'. Of course if we were allowed to represent the two clauses *as wholes*, we might replace them by single letters (say α and β), and phrase it, 'If α then β', or $\alpha\beta = 0$. But I assume that all four letters are to be exhibited. Now 'x is y' is expressed $xy = 0$, and 'z is w' is expressed $zw = 0$. What then we want to convey is that if $xy = 0$ then $zw = 0$.

This is readily done if the reader will bear in mind that, on our interpretation of propositions, 'if α then β' merely denies the combination 'α true, β false', viz. denies the combination $\alpha = 1$, $\beta = 0$. Accordingly, just as

$$xy = 0 \text{ denies } \left. \begin{array}{l} x - \\ y \end{array} \right\} \text{ and } z\overline{w} = 0 \text{ denies } \left. \begin{array}{l} z = 1 \\ w = 0 \end{array} \right\}$$

so does $zw\,(1 - x\overline{y}) = 0$ deny $\left. \begin{array}{l} - \\ z\overline{w} = 1 \end{array} \right\}$ which is what we want

to deny. Hence 'If x is y, then z is w' is duly expressed by

$$(1 - x\overline{y})\, z\overline{w} = 0$$

$$\text{or } (xy + \overline{x}y + \overline{x}\overline{y})\, zw = 0.$$

The reader will see, in the annexed diagram, that the assumption of x being y, or $xy = 0$, leads at once to the con-

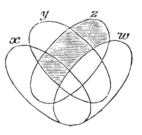

---

[1] The reader will see that $x\gamma = \alpha\gamma$ gives $\alpha\gamma x = 0$, $\alpha\gamma \overline{x} = 0$; whilst $x = \alpha$ gives $\overline{\alpha}x = 0$, $\alpha\overline{x} = 0$. The two will only coincide in case $\alpha\gamma\overline{x} = 0$, and $\overline{\alpha}\gamma x = 0$.

clusion that z is w, or $zw = 0$. (We shall recur to this example again, in connexion with another system of notation, which, in cases of this particular kind, possesses some advantages.)

(11) If a genus A is divisible into the species $x, y, z, \ldots$ and also into $\alpha, \beta, \gamma, \ldots$; and if we know that all x is α, all y is β, all z is γ, and so on; then, conversely, all α is x, all β is y, all γ is z, and so on.

This example is taken from Hauber[1], and can be solved at once under the conditions implied. The species he understands to be mutually exclusive, so that we may write the data,

$$x + y + z + \ldots \qquad = \alpha + \beta + \gamma + \ldots$$
$$\therefore (x - \alpha) + (y - \beta) + (z - \gamma) + \ldots \qquad = 0,$$
$$\text{or } (x\alpha - \alpha x) + (y\beta - \beta y) + (z\gamma - \gamma z) + \ldots \qquad = 0.$$

But 'All x is α' gives $x\alpha = 0$, and so on.

$$\text{Hence } \alpha x + \beta y + \gamma z + \ldots \qquad = 0.$$

That is, under the same implied conditions of mutual exclusion of the species,

$$\alpha x = 0, \ \beta \bar{y} = 0, \ \gamma \bar{z} = 0.$$

Or, 'All α is x', 'All β is y', 'All γ is z', which was to be proved.

(12) Much of the prejudice which still exists against the employment of the symbolic methods in Logic must be attributed, unless I am mistaken, to the extreme length and elaboration with which Boole has generally worked out his results. What he seemed to care for was theoretic perfection of method in the generality of his solution, and consequent certainty of obtaining the desired result, rather than prac-

---

[1] *Scholæ logico-mathematicæ*, 1829. A work mainly mathematical, but containing a variety of good logical hints and generalizations.

tical convenience in working. It may be well therefore to point out in how many cases this tediousness of operation may be avoided. Here, as in mathematics, there are a variety of devices open to us by which particular conclusions may often be obtained with much brevity and ease.

For instance the plan, to which allusion has frequently been made already, of looking out for the appropriate multipliers by which to break up our equations into their elementary denials, will often save much trouble. In such examples as we have already had the reader will probably have detected the nature of this operation for himself, and in no case could it give any trouble to those who have learnt elementary algebra, but for the convenience of others it may be worth while explaining it briefly.

Take, for instance, the following example from Boole (*Laws of Thought,* p. 118,—the wording is slightly altered).

(1) Wherever the properties x and y are combined, either the property z or the property w is present also, but not both of them.

(2) Wherever y and z are combined, x and w are either both present or both absent.

(3) Wherever x and y are both absent, z and w are both absent also, and vice versa.

The problem then is, to determine what may be inferred from the presence of x with respect to the presence or absence of y and z, paying no regard to w; that is, eliminating w.

The symbolic statement of these data stands as follows:—

$$\begin{cases} xy = \tfrac{0}{0}(w\bar{z} + \bar{w}z) \\ yz = \tfrac{0}{0}{'}xw + \bar{x}\bar{w}) \\ \bar{x}\bar{y} = \bar{w}\,\bar{z}. \end{cases}$$

Now it is clearly no good doing anything which will make

the left side of the first two equations vanish ; for this, leaving only indeterminate terms, will lead to nothing. Accordingly we need only ask what factors will make the right side disappear. As regards the first equation, either w or z will destroy the first term, and either w or z will destroy the second. Of the four combinations thus produced two, viz. ww and zz, are of course ineffective since they destroy both sides. This leaves two available factors, viz. wz and wz. Thus the first equation breaks up into $xyzw = 0$, $xyzw = 0$. Similarly for the second there are two available factors, viz. xw and xw, the other two being ineffective as in the last case. Consequently this yields $xyzw = 0$, $xyzw = 0$. In the third case there being no indeterminate factor, the abolition of either term will lead to something. Now either w or z will destroy the right side, and either x or y the left. Consequently, by multiplication, we get four denials here.

The net results of the three premises may be thus written down :—

$$\left. \begin{array}{ll} xywz & x\overline{w}\overline{z} \\ xy\overline{w}z & \overline{y}w\overline{z} \\ xy\overline{w}\overline{z} & x\overline{y}\overline{w} \\ \overline{x}ywz & x\overline{y}\overline{z} \end{array} \right\} = 0 \dots\dots\dots\dots\dots(1).$$

A very little practice and experience would of course avoid even this amount of trouble, for one would soon come to remember that 'All A is either B or C only' was resolvable into 'There is no A which is both B and C, and there is none which is neither'.

Starting again with these eight denials Boole's conclusion may be readily obtained. What we want is an account of x *without* w. Now there is only one of the eight free from w as it stands[1], viz. the 8th; and it is easily seen that there are only

---

[1] For further discussion of this point see the next chapter.

two others which taken together can be freed from w, viz. the 1st and 3rd, for these combined yield $xyz = 0$. Hence what we want is given by the two following:

$$\left.\begin{array}{l} xyz = 0 \\ \overline{x}yz = 0 \end{array}\right\} \dots\dots\dots\dots\dots\dots (2).$$

Add these together and we have

$$x(\overline{y}z - yz) = \overline{y}z$$

$$\text{or } x = \frac{\overline{y}z}{yz - yz}.$$

Develop the right side, and we obtain

$$x = \overline{y}z + \tfrac{0}{0}y\overline{z} + \tfrac{0}{0}\overline{y}\,\overline{z};$$

or, more briefly,

$$x = yz + \tfrac{0}{0}z \dots\dots\dots\dots\dots\dots (3),$$

which is Boole's conclusion, viz. "Wherever x is found there will either y be absent and z present, or z will be absent; and conversely, where y is absent and z present, there will x be present". This may be called, by comparison, the predicative reading of the result. Another reading of it would be "The class x consists of the class which is z but not y, and possibly 'some' of that which is not z".

For the practical purpose of solving problems this plan of looking out for suitable multipliers will generally be found the most expeditious. Though not actually proposed by Boole it is readily suggested by, and indeed is almost contained in, his scheme of solution. The theoretical defect in it, to the eye of a rigid formal thinker, is, that as thus carried out the resultant elementary denials are generally to some extent redundant. They cover the whole ground, and therefore give us the whole available information, but they do a little more; for, trespassing to some extent upon each other's ground, they state the denials with some needless superfluity.

(13) As another instance of an abbreviation in working take the following :—

$$xy = a \atop yz = c \Big\}.$$

It is desired to obtain xz in terms of a and c, y being eliminated. It may be remarked that this is a perfectly general rendering of the syllogism[1], and the solution, involving as it does, five terms, is of almost startling length and complexity if treated in strict accordance with Boole's method. It may be got almost at once as follows :—

$$az = xz(y + \bar{y}) \text{ (developing with respect to } y)$$
$$= xyz + x\bar{y}z$$
$$= xy \cdot yz + x\bar{y} \cdot \bar{y}z$$
$$= ac + x\bar{y} \cdot \bar{y}z \ \dots\dots\dots\dots\dots\dots\dots\dots (1).$$

Now, though $x\bar{y}$ cannot be expressed in terms of xy or a, it can in terms of $1 - xy$ or $\bar{a}$. For $1 - xy - \bar{x}y + \bar{x}\bar{y} + x\bar{y}$, so that $x\bar{y}$ may be described as an uncertain, or $\frac{0}{0}$ part of $1 - xy$ or $\bar{a}$. That is, $x\bar{y} = \frac{0}{0}\bar{a}$. Similarly $\bar{y}z = \frac{0}{0}\bar{c}$, so that $x\bar{y} \cdot \bar{y}z = \frac{0}{0}\bar{a}\bar{c}$.

$$\therefore \text{ Finally } xz = ac + \tfrac{0}{0}\bar{a}\bar{c} \ \dots\dots\dots\dots\dots\dots\dots(2),$$

which is the answer desired.

(14) Develop the expression,

$$w = \frac{1 - xy}{\bar{a}y + xy + z(xy + \bar{x}y)}.$$

The main difficulty of developing this by Boole's rule is the extreme liability to error in substituting 1 and 0 respectively for x, y, z, and their contradictories. Regarding each group as a single class we write it down at once ;

$$w = 1 - xy + \tfrac{0}{0}\{1 - xy - \bar{x}y - z(xy + \bar{x}y)\} ;$$

---

[1] See on, Chapter xv.

or, replacing $1 - xy - xy$ by its equivalent $xy + xy$, this becomes

$$w = 1 - xy + \tfrac{0}{0}z(xy + xy)\dots\dots\dots\dots\dots\dots(1);$$

whilst the condition implied in the form of statement here becomes

$$(1 - \overline{x}\,\overline{y})\,\{1 - x\overline{y} - \overline{x}y - z(xy + \overline{x}\,\overline{y})\} = 0,$$

or, after multiplying out,

$$xyz = 0 \dots\dots\dots\dots\dots\dots\dots (2).$$

This serves to reduce (1) to a still simpler form, viz.

$$w = 1 - \overline{x}\,\overline{y} + \tfrac{0}{0}\overline{x}\,\overline{y}\,z.$$

(15) The following example is, I think, the most intricate of any given by Boole :—(*Laws of Thought*, p. 146.)

1. Wherever x and z are missing, u is found, with one (but not both) of y and w.

2. Wherever x and w are found whilst u is missing, y and z will both be present or both absent.

3. Wherever x is found with either or both of y and u there will z or w (but not both) be found ; and conversely.

They may be written

$$\left\{ \begin{aligned} xz &= \tfrac{0}{0}u(yw + yw) \\ xw\overline{u} &= \tfrac{0}{0}(yz + \overline{y}\,\overline{z}) \\ x(y + \overline{y}u) &= (z\overline{w} + \overline{z}w) \end{aligned} \right. \qquad \begin{aligned} &yw,\ \overline{y}\,\overline{w} \\ &y\overline{z},\ \overline{y}z \\ &zw,\ \overline{z}\,\overline{w}\ ;\ \overline{x},\ \overline{y}u. \end{aligned}$$

The appropriate factors being employed (they are written at the side) these equations resolve into

$$\left.\begin{aligned} &\overline{x}y\overline{z}w,\ \overline{x}\,\overline{y}\,\overline{z}\,\overline{w}, \\ &xyzw\overline{u},\ x\overline{y}zw\overline{u}, \\ &\{xyzw,\ xy\overline{z}\,\overline{w},\ x\overline{y}zwu,\ x\overline{y}\,\overline{z}\,\overline{w}u, \\ &\{\overline{x}z\overline{w},\ \overline{x}\,\overline{z}w,\ \overline{y}z\overline{w}u,\ \overline{y}\,\overline{z}wu. \end{aligned}\right\} = 0.$$

These twelve denials contain all that the equations have to say, with some trivial redundancies. Some of them, as containing fewer terms, that is, as being less subdivided, are more comprehensive in their scope than others.

Now draw the 5-term diagram, and shade out the terms thus marked[1]. (On the pieced diagram board, described in Chap. v., they could be picked out and removed in a few minutes.) We have the following result :—

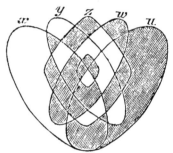

On looking at this diagram, several of the various conclusions which Boole has drawn are almost intuitively obvious. Thus that 'there is no xzw' ($xzw = 0$); that 'all w is either x or z' ($xzw = 0$); that 'all z is either x or w' ($xzw = 0$). These are the sort of conclusions to which diagrams specially lend themselves; for in each case we extinguish a connected group of classes, and each extinction readily catches the eye in a figure.

Similarly it is not difficult to verify the conclusion that 'wherever x is found there will be found either z or w (but not both) or else y, z, and w will all be absent; and conversely' (Boole, p. 148). Symbolically this stands

$$x = z\overline{w} + \overline{z}w + \overline{y}\overline{z}\overline{w}.$$

On looking at the composition of x in the diagram it will readily be seen that it is made up of these three (in their ultimate subdivision, *six*) constituents. This sort of conclusion, though easy to verify by a figure, is probably easier to obtain (apart from the extreme and inevitable tediousness) from the symbolic letters.

[1] We have not troubled to shade the outside of this diagram, viz. $xyzwu$.

The reader will observe that this work of summing up the surviving classes into compendious propositions is that synthetic operation described at the end of the last chapter. What aid can be afforded by appeal to rules and tables, in any cases but those which are mostly too simple to require such aid at all, will be understood by recalling to mind that the total number of possible results is 4,294,967,295 with five terms. Any table which was prepared to supersede the intelligent appeal to graphical or diagrammatic aid would involve the analysis and classification of all these results.

In discussing inverse forms we have naturally taken for consideration, in the first place, those in which the numerator of the fraction is definite, of which $\dfrac{..}{y}$ is the type. But in practice we may often find that they present themselves in what is really equivalent to the form $\frac{0}{0}x \div y$. The logical interpretation here ought not to present the slightest difficulty. All that we were doing in the former case was to enquire for any class the part of which common to it and to y should be *identical with* x; whilst all that we are here doing is to enquire for any class the part of which common to it and to y shall be *included in* x, that is, shall 'be' x in the common predicative sense of the word. Or, stating the questions in the interrogative form, they stand thus ;—

If z which is y is identical with x, find z. $\left(zy - x, \therefore z - \dfrac{..}{y}. \right)$

If z which is y is x, find z. $\left(zy - \frac{0}{0}x, \therefore z - \frac{0}{0}x \div y. \right)$

Whether the latter be stated in the form $zy - \frac{0}{0}x$, or in the form $zy - zyx$, it equally yields $zyx = 0$,

$$\therefore z = \frac{0}{\bar{x}y} = \frac{0}{0}(1 - \bar{x}y),$$
$$= \frac{0}{0}(xy + x\bar{y} + \bar{x}\bar{y}) ;$$
$$\text{or, more briefly,} = \frac{0}{0}x + \frac{0}{0}\bar{x}\bar{y}.$$

That is, in words, z may be 'anything that is x, or that is neither x nor y', under the assigned circumstances.

The reader should carefully observe that there is no con dition implied here in the mere statement of the question, corresponding to the condition $xy = 0$, in the case of $\frac{x}{y}$. That condition arose out of the demand that the restricted or com mon class should be *identical* with x; the mere *reference* of it to x makes no such requirement, provided of course we allow to x as a class term the customary freedom of range from *nothing* to *all* inclusive.

(16) Take a concrete instance. 'When all the books on philosophy are omitted from one of my bookcases there is nothing left but books on mathematics. What did the book case contain originally?' The answer is that it may have contained anything whatever excepting what was neither philosophy nor mathematics; an answer of course which is intuitively obvious, as it could hardly fail to be in such a simple case.

$$\text{Let } z - \text{contents of bookcase,}$$
$$x = \text{philosophy,}$$
$$y - \text{mathematics.}$$
$$\therefore z(1-x) = \tfrac{0}{0}y, \qquad zxy = 0,$$
$$z = \frac{0}{\overline{x}\,\overline{y}} = \tfrac{0}{0}(1 - \overline{x}\overline{y}).$$

(17) The following general formulæ of substitution are worth considering for the sake of their logical interpreta tion :—

(1) $\quad 1 - xyzw\ldots\ldots = x + \overline{x}y + \overline{x}\overline{y}z + \overline{x}\overline{y}\overline{z}w + \ldots\ldots$

(2) $\quad 1 - \overline{x}\overline{y}\overline{z}\overline{w}\ldots\ldots = x + \overline{x}y + \overline{x}\overline{y}z + \overline{x}\overline{y}\overline{z}w + \ldots\ldots$

The former asserts that whatever is not simultaneously x, y, z, w, and so forth, must fail either to be x, or y, or z, or so on; and that conversely, the classes of things which fail to be x, or fail to be y, and so on, together constitute everything which is not at once x, y, z, &c. Common language of course expresses this in words which literally translated would yield the formula $1 - xyzw \ldots = x + y + z + \ldots$, in which it is followed by those symbolists who adopt the non-exclusive no tation for alternatives: to me it seems that rigid symbolic propriety suggests our inserting the letters requisite to make our various classes mutually exclusive.

The latter formula merely differs from the former in a verbal way. It declares that whatever does not simulta neously fail to be x, y, z, w, and so on, must be either x, or, failing that, y, or, failing that, z, and so on.

(18) The continued repetition of the inverse operation will not give rise to any peculiar intricacies in Logic. No doubt such an expression as

$$\tfrac{0}{0}X \div x \div y \div z \div w$$

does not look the kind of thing of which Logic has been accustomed to take cognizance. Put it into words, however, and it is seen to be nothing but a very concise symbolic indication of "the class which on successive restriction by w, z, y, x, shall possess nothing but what is X". Let this class be Y, then we have

$$Yxyzw = \tfrac{0}{0}X,$$
$$YXxyzw = 0,$$
$$Y = \frac{0}{Xxyzw}$$
$$= \tfrac{0}{0}(1 - Xxyzw).$$

The answer therefore is that the only logical condition or determination of the desired class is that it must not contain "anything which is x, y, z, w, and which fails to be X". Whatever fulfils this condition will answer the purpose.

CHAPTER XIII.

ELIMINATION.

ELIMINATION is, both by its etymology and in its ordinary acceptation, the process of getting rid from within the limits of our enquiry of one or more of the symbols with which we are concerned. The reader will of course be more familiar with this term in mathematics than in Logic. That the process is resorted to in the common Logic, however, will be very easy to show; and therefore in accordance with the general object of this work, we will begin with it there. We shall thus be better able to trace the real nature of the process we propose to generalize, as the main characteristics of the Symbolic system rather tend to disguise the substantial identity between the rudimentary and the developed forms which elimination may assume.

Beginning then with immediate inferences, look at the step which might be called "inference by omitted determinants[1]". When this is interpreted in respect of the extension or denotation of the terms involved, it is an exact case in

---

[1] Inference by *added* determinants is already recognized (e.g. Thomson; *Laws of Thought*, p. 158). But the distinction introduced by *omitting* a portion of the predicate might just as well be considered to constitute a new judgment as that introduced by adding on a new portion. Bain (*Deductive Logic*, p. 109) denies that there is any inference here.

point, of a simple kind, of the process of which we have to give an account. 'Men are rational mortals; therefore they are mortals':—Here we have omitted the term 'rational' from our result, that is, we have eliminated it. Or we might have omitted the word 'mortal', by saying that 'men are rational'.

So again the syllogism is a case of the elimination of a middle term. Viewed in its extension, as an arrangement of classes, the mood *Barbara* asserts that a class contained within a second class is contained within the wider class which contains this second one; the reference to this last, or middle term, being omitted from our result, that is, it is eli minated. The *Dictum* of Aristotle may in fact be regarded as a formula of elimination for the simple groups of proposi tions to which it applies. This is obvious enough in the case of the affirmative form of the Dictum, as in Barbara, but may be seen with almost equal ease to be so also in the negative form. For instance, 'No Y is Z; all X is Y; $\therefore$ no X is Z'. Here we say that Y is included in not-Z, i.e. is a part of it; and X is included in Y; therefore X is included *a fortiori* in not-Z. On the view of terms and propositions which is adopted in our system, and which is a rigid class-view, this negative form of the Dictum is therefore the precise equiva lent or formal reproduction of the affirmative forms. Not-X and not-Z are, with us, classes of exactly the same kind and significance as those which we designate by X or Z, and there is no difference of principle in referring sub-classes to one or other of them. In both cases the middle term, or class which at once includes and excludes, is omitted or eliminated.

Now the characteristic of this Elimination to which I wish prominently to direct the reader's attention, as contain-ing the main clue to its significance in Logic, is this:—that we have substituted a *broader or less exact determination* in the place of the one which was first given to us. That is, we have had to let slip a part of the meaning of the data in performing this process.

That this is so in the case of the immediate inference is abundantly clear; for the 'men' who were before identified with 'rational mortals' are now identified with an uncertain part of the larger class 'rational', or 'mortal'. The reason why it is not equally clear in the case of the syllogism is that the premises are given to us separately instead of being combined into one. That is, in the former case we say 'z is xy, therefore (more vaguely) z is y or x'; whilst in the latter we say 'z is x, and x is y, therefore z is y'. Of course the distinction between mediate and immediate inference is on various grounds important, both of speculation and of logical procedure; and nothing here said is meant to gloss over that distinction in its due place. All that is now asserted is that in each case alike, whether there be one premise or two, the full determination of z was xy, and that consequently the statement that it is simply y (in other words, the elimination of x) is so far a vaguer and less exact determination of it than could be given by the retention of that term.

This loss of precision in the process of elimination is the general result, but a certain narrow class of exceptions can be pointed out. When x and y are coextensive the substitution of one for the other leaves the extension unaltered. Thus in the elimination of y from 'all x is all y, all y is all z' the determination of x as z is just as narrow as that given by calling it yz. But of course such a case as this can but rarely occur. It is not generally easy, except when we are dealing with definitions, to find two terms thus coextensive; and the occurrence of three such must be very rare indeed.

It will be understood that this loss of precision is no valid objection to the process of elimination. It is one of the many characteristic distinctions of the class-explanation of propositions to call attention to the fact that there is any such loss at all. On the common explanation we only think of the major term in its capacity of a predicate, and we want to know whether or not it is to be attached to the subject. The middle term is used presumably merely as a means toward deciding this fact, and when it has answered its purpose it is very properly dropped from notice. We only wanted to prove, say, that x is z; to insist upon it that x is yz, though very true, may be a needless trouble. The very words *Discourse* and *Discursive reasoning* seem to point to this. We let the mind run from one thing to another; and we only dwell finally upon, and put into our conclusion, the particular fact or facts which we happen to need. We distinctly want to get rid of the middle terms, and not to carry all our knowledge about in our predicate. It is of the essence, on the other hand, of the Symbolic system, to keep prominently before us every one of the classes represented by all our terms and their contradictories. Accordingly the distinction between yz and z, and the fact that the latter must generally speaking be a broader and looser determination, is much more promi nently set before us here.

The fact is that here, as in various other directions, the associations derived from the mathematical employment of the term are apt to be somewhat misleading. For one thing we are accustomed to believe that there must be some con nexion between the number of equations set before us, and the number of terms involved in them, for the purpose of eli mination; so that one term demands for its elimination two equations, and so forth. In Logic on the other hand we know that the number of statements into which we throw our data is very much of our own choosing, a single logical equation admitting of equally ready statement in the form of a group of several. Accordingly the number of equations at our com-

mand in no way affects the question of the possibility of elim
ination here. Then again, as regards the loss of precision,
in mathematics it is rather the other way. If we have three
equations connecting x, y, z, each of these may be conceived
to represent a surface, which is satisfied by a doubly inde
finite number of values of these variables. But if I eliminate
y and z, I obtain one or more determinate values of x corres
ponding to the particular points where the surfaces intersect.
We have gained, in the process of elimination, an increase of
definiteness which must be estimated as one of kind rather
than of degree.

What we have now to do is to see how the logical process
which has been illustrated in one or two simple instances
can be generalized. As an easy example begin with the
following,—

$$w - xy + xz$$

and suppose we are asked to eliminate y from it. As an
equation its significance is plain enough. It is nothing else
than a definition or description of w in terms of x, y, and z.
Any one therefore who knows the meaning of these terms, or
the limits of the classes for which they stand, will have all
the information which they can furnish him as to the meaning
and limits of w. Assuming that we are confined to the use
of the three terms x, y, z, then w is as precisely determined
as circumstances permit.

This being so, what could be meant by 'eliminating' y
from the equation? If we are not to retain it there, and are
not to introduce some new equivalent for it, the only remain
ing course is to do as well as we can without it. But it
cannot be simply omitted; for this would be inaccurate,
unless we took care to indicate somehow that we had dis
pensed with it. Apparently, therefore, all that is left for us
to do is to take refuge in the vague, and to substitute for y,

wherever it occurs, some such word as 'some'. If we did this we should just write the equation in the form

$$w = \text{`some'}\,x + \overline{x}z$$

$$\text{or } w = \tfrac{0}{0}x + xz \dots\dots\dots\dots\dots \quad (1).$$

This method of elimination has at least the merit of frankness. It points out where we have let go some of the determining elements, and it indicates exactly the nature and amount of the consequent introduction of vagueness. There is another equivalent form to this without the same merit of straightforwardness, which consists in writing the altered equation thus:

$$w = wx + xz.$$

The objections to this form have been already noticed. It disguises the real vagueness under a show of information; and offers us an implicit equation involving w, for the explicit description of w with which we started, and which we wish as far as possible to retain.

Nothing could better show the nature of logical elimina tion than this simple example. The term y was one of the elements employed in the determination of w; hence its abandonment will necessarily entail some loss of precision. If we were dealing with real equations of the mathematical type such loss would generally be fatal to the value of our conclusion. But what we have to do with in Logic is rather the subdivision of classes by other class terms, and the iden tification of a group of individuals under different class designations. Hence the letting slip of one of our class terms will only refer us to a somewhat vaguer and wider class than that with which we started. The relinquishment of y does not destroy all our knowledge of w, but it certainly destroys a part of it.

If the only logical statements with which we were concerned were of this simple type—in which we have a term standing by itself on one side, with a description or definition of it on the other,—no other plan of elimination would be necessary. But, as the reader knows, we have to encounter much more complicated statements than this, viz. those in which every term is implicitly involved. So we must look out for some more general mode of elimination. We should best seek for it in the alternative *negative* interpretation of our propositions. We know that every logical equation can be thrown into the shape of a number of distinct and peremptory denials, without any loss whatever or variation in its significance.

Take then, to begin with, the same statement as before and look at it, for comparison, in the light of what it denies. Adopting the plans described in former chapters, we find that it may be thrown into the form of the five following denials ;—

$$\left.\begin{matrix} wxy \\ wxz \\ wyz \end{matrix}\right\} - 0. \qquad \left.\begin{matrix} wxy \\ w x z \end{matrix}\right\} = 0.$$

(At least this is what we should get by resorting to the plan of looking out for suitable factors, described in the last chapter, and which is generally the simplest plan in practice. As they thus stand they are not in their ultimate form, nor are they perfectly independent ; but of this more presently.)

Now setting before us the same aim as in the preceding example, viz. of determining w as well as we can without making use of y, the course we should naturally adopt would be this ;—we should just omit those amongst the above denials which involve y or y, retaining only the remainder which do not. If we did so the result of the elimination would stand thus ;

$$\left.\begin{matrix} wx\bar{z} = 0 \\ wxz = 0 \end{matrix}\right\} \quad \dots\dots\dots\dots\dots\dots\dots\dots (2).$$

That this form is the precise equivalent of (1) is easily seen. For multiplying both sides of (1) by xz and w, it resolves into these denials and into no other unconditional ones. Similarly on combining and developing (2) we have $w = xz + \frac{0}{0}x$ as in (1).

These two simple methods of elimination are therefore precisely equivalent, at any rate in this instance. The only difference between them is, that, whereas the original deter mination of w was complete and accurate, No. (1) retains as far as possible the same form, marking plainly the position and limits of the lacunæ of information caused by the loss of y, whilst No. (2) contents itself by giving the materials for this latter statement, leaving their solution to be worked out.

Take again such a case as the following :—

$$w = xyz + xyz + xyz$$

in which w is declared to comprise 'those things which possess two, and two only, of the attributes denoted respec tively by x, y, z'. Let it be required to eliminate y, a term (be it observed) which enters into every element of w.

Form No. (1) would express the result off-hand[1] as

$$w = \frac{0}{0}x\bar{z} + \frac{0}{0}xz + \frac{0}{0}\bar{x}z$$
$$\text{or } w = \frac{0}{0}x + \frac{0}{0}\bar{x}z \quad \dots\dots\dots\dots\dots\dots\dots (1)$$

a result in which we have had to depart a good way from the original determination. All that we can substitute for that determination without appeal to y, being, that 'w is contained somewhere within the limits of x and z' :—that is, there is cer tainly no w outside that boundary.

The other form would have led to the denials involved in the equation, and the selection of those amongst them which

[1] In accordance with what has been pointed out more than once we must write $\frac{0}{0}$ for y as well as for y. For the limits of indefiniteness of any term and its contradictory are the same, so that $1-\frac{0}{0}$ is the same as $\frac{0}{0}$ when used as a symbol of indefiniteness. Each is entirely un- certain between 0 and 1.

do not make use of y. There is a very simple way of effect
ing this in practice. Instead of using all the factors which
will disintegrate the given equation, and then selecting only
the elements we want, we had better only make use of those
factors which we see will produce these latter. Thus, here,
x and z would make xyz vanish but not the other two terms;
x and z will make the second vanish, and x and $\bar{z}$ the third.
The only factors therefore that will make all the three
y-terms disappear will be xz. Hence the only elementary
denial which can be found without involving y will be

$$w x z = 0 \quad\dots\dots\dots\dots\dots\dots\dots\dots\dots (2)$$

and this is the required elimination. As in the former case
it may readily be shown that these two results are precisely
equivalent and deductively interchangeable.

Before pointing out the practical or theoretical defects of
these methods it will be worth while to apply them to a group
of statements. As already insisted on, there is no distinction
of principle between the information conveyed by one, and by
a number of statements, but the striking difference in this
respect between the logical and the mathematical calculus
deserves emphatic notice.

Take the following :—

(Every w is either x and y, or z and not x.

(Every w is either x, y, and z, or neither x nor z.

In symbols they stand thus

$$w = \tfrac{0}{0}(xy + \bar{x}z)$$
$$w = \tfrac{0}{0}(xyz + \bar{w}\bar{z})$$

Let it be required to eliminate y from these two statements.

The simplest plan would be to multiply the two together,
when we get $w = \tfrac{0}{0}xyz$. Substitute $\tfrac{0}{0}$ for y, and remember
that $\tfrac{0}{0} \times \tfrac{0}{0} = \tfrac{0}{0}$, (for no such multiplication can alter the range

of indefiniteness of the symbol) and we have w with the desired elimination

$$w = \tfrac{0}{0}xz.$$

If we had begun by eliminating separately from each, we should have had

$$\left\{ \begin{aligned} w &= \tfrac{0}{0}(x + \overline{x}z) \\ w &= \tfrac{0}{0}(xz + x\overline{z}) \end{aligned} \right.$$

the combination of which would lead to the same result as above.

Or had we broken them up into their respective denials, and added these together, we should have been led to the following (omitting those which involve y)

$$wx\overline{z} + w\overline{x}z + wxz = 0$$

which leads again to

$$w = \tfrac{0}{0}xz.$$

If all examples resembled the simple ones discussed above we should need no other methods of elimination than those just described. But the former method is only properly available when we are dealing with equations of an *explicit* kind; so that if our statements were not originally in that shape we should have to reduce them to it. As regards the second there is a cause of possible failure, unless we are on our guard, which will deserve a little closer notice. It is beautifully provided against in Boole's symbolic formula to be explained in the next chapter.

The difficulty arises as follows. We have given directions to break up the equation into its ultimate denials, and then to select those amongst them which do not involve the term to be eliminated. And, in the examples which we took, such terms presented themselves at once. But it is easily seen that none such may be found; in fact, if we have developed every element to the utmost extent, none such *can* be found, for every term will then have been subdivided into its y and not-y parts. Thus in the example on p. 291 we had $w.xz = 0$, $w.xz = 0$, which did not involve y, and we chose them accord ingly. But if these had presented themselves, as they might, in the forms $w.xzy = 0$, $wxzy = 0$, $w.xyz = 0$, $w.xyz = 0$, there would have been apparently no terms free from y.

We have therefore to amend our rule. We must say that the complete results of the elimination of any term from a given equation are obtained by breaking it up into a series of independent denials, and then selecting from amongst these all which either do not involve the term in question, or which *by grouping together can be made not to involve it.* Of course this latter enquiry may sometimes involve a little trouble, when the elements in question are numerous, but generally we can see our way through it easily enough. So understood, the rule for elimination in Logic seems complete. I have preferred to begin by discussing a rule the logical meaning of which is clear at every step, but in the next chapter we shall examine a rule of very remarkable symbolic neatness and ingenuity, invented by Boole.

CHAPTER XIV.

THE expressions $f(1)$ and $f(0)$ are presumably, to the bulk of logicians, the most puzzling and deterrent of all the various mathematical adaptations of which Boole has made use in his system. They play far too prominent a part however in that system to admit of neglect; and indeed on their own account they deserve careful study, as the effort to detect the rational logical significance of such very abstract symbolic generalizations as these seems to me one of the most useful mental exercises which the subject can afford. And that these peculiar expressions are really nothing more than generalizations of very simple logical processes will soon be made manifest.

We will examine these expressions under two heads; firstly as mere class symbols, and secondly as representative of logical equations. That is, we will begin by taking them as derivatives of $f(x)$, and secondly as derivatives of $f(x) = 0$.

[1] The merely logical reader will not find the study of this chapter essential to the comprehension of those which follow.

I.   In order to put an interpretation upon $f(1)$ and $f(0)$ we need only recall what the more general expression $f(x)$,— of which these are merely specialized or altered forms,—stands for.   In Logic, at any rate, we have always insisted upon certain restrictions as to its form and significance.   With us it always stands for a *class*, actual or potential, directly or inversely determined; and we recognize no form of it incon sistent with such interpretation.   Moreover as a class expres sion, we may insist upon its possessing certain characteristics which have often been described.   These amount to the condition that in whatever shape it might originally present itself it must be capable of being arranged as the sum or aggregation of a series of mutually exclusive terms, for thus only will it strictly represent a logical class.   If we had ourselves written down this $f(x)$ as the symbolic translation of a verbal description, then we ought to have taken care so to express it; whilst if it had been got at by logical processes, such as development, from legitimate data, it must certainly retain those characteristics.   Accordingly we shall assume that $f(x)$ is, or may be exhibited as, the sum of a series of mutually exclusive logical class terms.

Take then, as an expression fulfilling these conditions,

$$xz + \overline{x}y + w\overline{y}\,\overline{z}$$

and calling this $f(x)$, examine the significance of $f(1)$ and $f(0)$.

Symbolically, of course, the answer is prompt enough. Write 1 for x all through, and we have $f(1) = z + wyz$; write 0 for x all through, and we have $f(0) = y + wyz$. But what we want is the logical interpretation.   To obtain this it is only necessary to remember that xz means 'z re stricted by x', and xy means 'y restricted by not-x'.   But 1 means "the whole of", so that the substitution of 1 for x is merely the direction to take the *whole* of z instead of merely

the x-part of it[1]. Similarly 0 meaning "none of", the substi
tution of 1 for x, in xy, tells us to take *no y* instead of the
not-x part of it. Hence the exchange of $f(1)$ for $f(x)$ is
only the highly generalized symbolic direction :—Go through
the given class expression ; and of every element of it which
is limited by x take the whole, and of every element limited
by not-x take none, and let the terms which do not involve x
or x remain unaltered.

This indicates the equally simple logical explanation of
$f(0)$. The latter expression is in a way the exact parallel
of $f(1)$; that is, whatever we there did with x we here do
with not-x, and vice versa. Hence what we are directed to
do is to secure that every term that involves x shall just
be dropped out, that every term which involves not-x
shall be taken in its full extent instead of under this
restriction, and that every term independent of x shall be
simply let alone.

In the above explanation we have implied that there may
be terms in our expression which do not involve either x or
not-x. But this need not be so, and if the expression were
fully developed it could not be so, for every term would then
be divided respectively into its x and its not-x part. The
term wyz is so put for simplicity merely, it is really equiva
lent to $wyz(x + x)$. When therefore any logical class expres
sion is completely broken up into its ultimate elements all
these will fall into two ranks, those of x and not-x. The
verbal statements of $f(1)$ and $f(0)$ then become simplified.
The former says, Take the x-members unconditionally, and

[1] The reader will remember the
distinction between this mere *taking
off* the restriction of x, by turning xz
into z, and the true inverse operation
to its imposition. Restrict x by z
and we have simply xz: take off this x-
restriction from xz and we have x:
but the inverse to xz, *i.e.* the class
which will become xz when the condition of x is imposed upon it, is
of course $xz + \frac{0}{0}xz$.

discard those which are not-x: the latter says, Take the $\bar{x}$-members unconditionally, and discard those which are x.

We will now proceed to examine the relation of these expressions, $f(1)$ and $f(0)$, to one another. It might perhaps be hastily inferred that they are complementary to one another, so that they should be mutually exclusive and should together make up $f(x)$;—that is, that

$$f(1) + f(0) = f(x), \text{ and } f(1)\, f(0) = 0.$$

Closer observation however will show that neither of these results need be the case, and that the former certainly will not; but it will be well to discuss these relations in detail, as they have an important bearing upon the problem of Elimination.

Suppose then that $f(x)$ takes the form $Ax + B\bar{x}$, where A and B are combinations involving y, z, and the other class terms which enter into the given expression. We know that $f(x)$ must be representable thus, for when expanded fully it can only yield x and not-x terms, and the factors of these terms can only be composed of various combinations of the other class terms. Then $f(1) = A$, and $f(0) = B$; that is, $f(1)$ is the whole class which we have to restrict by x, and $f(0)$ the whole class which we have to restrict by not-x.

What then are the limits as to class extension of A and B? None necessarily, except that they must conform to the fundamental law of logical classes, viz. that they cannot either of them exceed unity. In the extreme limiting case of A and B being both equal to 1, we should then have taken the whole of x and the whole of not-x, so that our $f(x)$ would have itself to equal 1. That is, when $f(1)$ and $f(0)$ each equal 1, then $f(x) = 1$. (Thus let

$$f(x) = xy + x\bar{y} + \bar{x}y + \bar{x}\bar{y} = 1;$$

then $f(1) = y + y - 1$, $f(0) = y + y = 1$.) An intermediate case is when $A + B = 1$, that is, when the aggregate of the factors of x and x together make up the universe. In this case, since $f(1) + f(0) = 1, f(1)$ and $f(0)$ are the contradictory opposites of one another. (Thus let

$$f(x) = x(yz + yz) + x(yz + yz);$$

then $f(1) = yz + yz$ and $f(0) = yz + yz$, so that

$$f(1) + f(0) = 1.)$$

We gather then, that given $f(x)$ as a correct class group, $f(1)$ and $f(0)$ may, as regards the extent of ground they occupy, just make up between them the whole universe. But they may also in one direction shrink both of them to zero (in which case $f(x) = 0$), or in the other direction extend till both are unity (when $f(x) = 1$). What they do in this way depends entirely upon the aggregate extent of those class groups which were limited respectively by x and x in order to produce $f(x)$.

Similarly as regards the product of these expressions, viz. $f(1)\, f(0)$. Its value depends upon the mutual relation of these aggregate class factors of x and x in the subdivision of $f(x)$. In the intermediate case, when $A + B = 1$, of course $AB = 0$. (Thus when $f(x) = x(yz + yz) + x(yz + yz)$, clearly $f(1)\, f(0) = (yz + yz)(yz + yz) = 0$.) More generally, if A and B are entirely composed of mutually exclusive elements, whether or not these make up the universe between them,— that is, if all those in A are exclusive of all those in B,— then AB, or $f(1)\, f(0)$, must $= 0$; i.e. $f(1)$ and $f(0)$ are classes which are mutually exclusive of one another.

We may sum up therefore by saying that, given $f(x)$ as a true logical expression for a class group, then $f(1)$ and $f(0)$ will also represent class groups. As regards their mutual relations to one another and to the original $f(x)$, we may lay down the following conclusions (omitting various limiting cases which the reader will readily work out with the help of examples):—Each of these expressions, $f(1)$ and $f(0)$, will omit a portion of what was included in $f(x)$, but will also contain a portion of what was not included in it. And as the portions of $f(x)$ which they thus omit will not be the same portion (one being an x and the other a not-x portion) it is certain that between them they must at least cover the whole of $f(x)$, besides including something else. That is, $f(1)$ consists of the whole of A, and $f(0)$ of the whole of B. But $f(x)$, or $Ax + Bx$, comprises only a part (the x-part) of A, and only a part (the not-x-part) of B; so that $f(1)$ and $f(0)$ must between them cover all $f(x)$, and may cover any part of it twice, besides covering once or twice any part of what is not $f(x)$. On the other hand it is equally possible that $f(1)$ and $f(0)$ may be classes entirely exclusive of one another, as in the example in the preceding paragraph.

II. We now turn to the far more important case of logical equations. Nearly all that has been said above, however, will hold good in this case, for, as the reader knows, every logical equation can be expressed in the form of a class group of a peculiar kind. That is, it may be made to say that a certain aggregate of classes is, collectively and individually, non-existent. Of course this needs some modification of form and arrangement, but there is not the slightest change or loss of significance entailed. Take, for instance, the statement $w - xy + xz$. When put in the form

$$w - xy - xz = 0,$$

it is a case of $f(x) = 0$. Now though, as it thus stands, it does not fulfil the conditions assumed above for $f(x)$, for it is not built up entirely of the sum of a number of mutually exclusive elements, we know that it can easily be made to assume that form. Develop and rearrange it, and it stands thus,

$$wxy + wxz + wxy + wxz = 0,$$

this being in every essential respect, as regards assertion and denial, the exact equivalent of $w = xy + xz$. The two are really the same statement differently worded or arranged. Hence it is clear that $f(x) = 0$ is merely a particular case of $f(x)$; and everything that has been said above about the interpretation of $f(1)$ and $f(0)$ and their mutual relations to one another will hold good here also. The form, and the detailed meaning, of a class expression, are entirely unaffected by our having to add that it is known that no such class is in existence, which is the only difference introduced by the equational form.

We are now in a position to understand Boole's rule for Elimination. This rule does not tell its own tale so clearly as the simple plans offered in the last chapter, and in actual performance it is unquestionably apt to prove tedious. Symbolically however nothing can be more beautifully neat and effective, and the penetrative originality which enabled Boole to discover it is quite beyond all praise.

The rule is simply this.—Let $f(x) = 0$ be any logical equation involving the symbol x, then $f(1) f(0) = 0$ is the full expression for the result of the elimination of x from it.

This rule does not, at first sight, appear to have the remotest connection with either of those offered in the last chapter, but a little consideration will show that it is sub stantially identical with the second of them. It only differs in fact by offering a methodical formula for a process which we had partly left to empirical judgment. We shall soon see this by examination of an example. Take the following, and suppose we want to eliminate y from it. We have $f(1) = w - x - xz, f(0) = w - xz$, so that the rule gives us

$$(w - x - xz)(w - xz) = 0.$$

Multiplying out, this reduces to

$$wxz + wxz = 0,$$

or exactly the same result as we should have obtained by breaking up the equation into its separate denials and se lecting those only amongst them which do not involve y. (These separate denials were given on the preceding page.)

But our present object is not so much to show that the two methods agree in their result as to explain the logical meaning underlying this highly abstract symbolic formula. This may readily be done as follows. We have shown that by eliminating y is meant the selection of those elements of denial which do not involve y or y. We were then met by the difficulty that in the complete development *every* term must involve one or other of these. True, but those which are in effect free from y or y are exactly those which involve *both* y and y, for $wxz = wxz(y + y)$. Hence all that we have to do in the complete development is to select those elements only which involve both y and y. Thus if the com plete development of $f(y)$ is $Ay + By$, then the terms really free from y are those, and those only, which occur in both A and B. But the way of finding the elements common to both A and B is simply to multiply A by B. In other words AB, that is, $f(1) f(0)$, is the symbolic expression for those ele ments of denial which the equation can yield free from y or y. And the statement of such denial is as usual given by equation to zero, so that $f(1) f(0) = 0$ is the precise symbolic state ment of that process which we have worked out logically[1].

The same conclusion would follow as a simple corollary from

[1] It is not a little strange to find such a philosophical authority as Ulrici declaring that after careful study of Boole he 'found that at

the results of page 299. Thus the development of $f(y) = 0$ assuming the form $Ay + By = 0$, and these being mutual exclusives, each term must vanish separately. But the meaning of $Ay = 0$ is that none of class A is y, and the meaning of $By = 0$ is that all class B is y. Hence no A is B, or $AB = 0$; that is, as before, $f(1) f(0) = 0$. (It will be remembered that this result was only exceptionally true when $f(1)$ and $f(0)$ were derived from a simple class group instead of from an equation.) This expression being certainly free from y, and moreover all that can be obtained free from it, is a true elimination of y.

The case just hinted at, in which $f(1)$ and $f(0)$ happen to be exclusives, so that $f(1) f(0)$, being formally $= 0$, will lead to no result, deserves a moment's notice. It tells us that the term in question cannot be eliminated. Thus in

$$xyz + \bar{z} = y\bar{z} + x\bar{y}\bar{z},$$

we have, in trying to eliminate x, $f(1) f(0) = yz \times yz - 0$ from which nothing can be deduced. The meaning of this is that every term in the ultimate development involves x or x separately. But where every constituent element is conditioned by the same term it is clear that nothing can be inferred about the data when free from such condition. A more obvious case of this is afforded by the statement $xy = xz$. If we tried to eliminate x we should get nothing better than $\frac{0}{0} y = \frac{0}{0} z$, from which nothing follows. The only known relation here between y and z being given under condition of x, no inference can be drawn as to what relations there may subsist between them in absence of x.

bottom this new Logic offered nothing new, but was essentially nothing else than a translation of the old Formal, that is, Aristotelian Logic, into mathematical formulae'

(*Zeitschrift fur Phil. und phil. Kritik*, 1878). One would like to see the original of the translation in the case of this formula $f(1) f(0) = 0$.

Boole generalizes this formula of elimination to embrace the simultaneous treatment of any number of terms. Thus the formula for eliminating the two terms x and y from $f(x, y) = 0$ is

$$f(1, 1) f(1, 0) f(0, 1) f(0, 0) = 0,$$

and so on, for any number of terms. The reader who has followed the explanation so far will without difficulty see the requisite logical interpretation here. For instance, when the expression $f(x, y)$ is fully developed, the only elements of the series of constituent denials which can be exhibited free from both x and y are those which simultaneously involve xy, xy, xy, and xy (for the sum of these $= 1$). Now the above formula of elimination is nothing but the logical rule for selecting such elements. And so on with three, four, or more simultaneous eliminations.

The employment of the peculiar symbol $\frac{0}{0}$ to express the results of our elimination of a term, affords a convenient opportunity for making a few concluding remarks upon its significance. It is of course a logical factor, standing therefore for a logical term, but its peculiarity is that it stands for any term whatever and is therefore perfectly indefinite. We did not, it will be remembered, borrow it directly from mathematics, but found that it spontaneously presented itself in certain cases of the performance of the inverse operation denoted by the fractional sign. This, I think, suggests a caution or restriction in respect of its use. We ought not to regard it as in any way dividing any ulti mate class subdivision to which it is prefixed. If we had in vented it for ourselves, as a sort of substitute for the 'some' of ordinary logic, it might be asked why we should not prefix it at once to any simple class term, and therefore write down such an expression as $\frac{0}{0} x$. The objection to so doing is, I think, connected with a fundamental characteristic of our whole scheme. Given a class term x, and this only, we have no right to talk of a *part* of x. A class, with us, is only divisible by another class term ; that is, given y also, we can at once contemplate a division of x into xy and $x\bar{y}$, but we need the pressure or suggestion of such another term in order to do this. I call attention to this, because it seems an indication that this Symbolic Logic, so far from being specially mathematical in the sense of having anything special to do with quantity, is in some respects less so than the common system. The class x, say, is given to us as undivided by any other class term. We therefore avoid talking of *some* of its members, because to do so would be to found assertions, not on mere class distinctions given purely by class characteristics, but on some kind of distinction which had been got at by investigating individuals without the help of class characteristics, and which is therefore very much the same thing as proceeding to count them. At least it seems one step towards proceeding so to do.

Herein lies the difficulty,—I should say the impossibi-lity,—of representing the true particular proposition by aid of $\frac{0}{0}$ or any symbolic equivalent. From Boole's $vx = vy$, if v be indefinite, it is clear that nothing whatever can be obtained ; for $\frac{0}{0}x - \frac{0}{0}y$ has not a definite word to say upon any subject. So this expression will not subserve the purposes of ordinary thought. As regards Prof. Jevons' $AB = AC$ the case is rather different. Of course if A were really indefinite (and this it is sometimes called) the two expressions would be exactly equivalent; but as he generally terms his form a 'partial' or 'limited identity', this seems to point to another signification. What we are expressing is the fact that 'the B which is A is the same as the C which is A'. In this expression we must assume that A is unknown, as otherwise we merely have, not a particular, but a convertible universal of the type 'All X is all Y', X and Y being complex terms. Is then $AB - AC$, where A is unknown, a fair type of the particular proposition? I think not, because it postulates that the members common to B and to C have some attribute in common, such attribute being probably connoted by the term A. But what right have we to assume that because there are individuals common to B and to C, that therefore these individuals must possess some attribute in common? *One* such attribute I admit them to possess, viz. that of their common membership in B and C, but this would clearly only yield an identical proposition[1], and we have no warrant for insisting upon any other such attribute. Hence, although $AB = AC$ can be read off, as 'some B is C', it is not true that every 'some B is C' can be formulated as $AB - AC$. I can see no form which will cover all particular propositions, except that which throws them into an assertion of existence, and confines itself to declaring that there are B's which are C, as explained in the seventh chapter.

After what has been already said it hardly needs repeat ing that $\frac{0}{0}$ is not the equivalent of *some*. Probably the best compendious statement of its significance is that it is a con fession of entire ignorance in respect of the term to which it is prefixed[2]. If it be asked why we want such a symbol, the answer has been already given in the results of the Chapter on Development: viz. that the comprehensiveness of our

---

[1] If A stands for the fact of belonging to both B and C, then $AB = AC$ becomes $BCB = BCC$, or $BC = BC$, which is clearly unmean-ing.

[2] Though therefore it is quite true to say that "either 1, 0, or $\frac{0}{0}$, mul-tiplied into itself, equals itself" (*The Logic of Names, an introduction to Boole's Laws of Thought*, by I. P.

Hughlings:—a little book with some fair points in it, but which hardly answers to its designation), this should not be said without a caution. The two former multiplications really do result in known equality; in the third case what is meant is that our ignorance is equally complete before and after the multiplication.

system, in which we frame a perfectly complete subdivision and call for an answer as regards every compartment con tained in it, necessarily demands the equivalent of such a symbol. A confession of perfect ignorance in respect of a single class, taken by itself, has no significance; but the same confession in reference to one or more remaining classes of an exhaustive catalogue, after we have definitely pronounced upon all the preceding classes, has a decided significance.

Thus $\frac{0}{0}x$ intimates nothing; and $xy + \frac{0}{0}x$ intimates no thing in respect of its second term. But make these expres sions members of a logical equation or statement, and the indefinite elements immediately acquire a certain significance. Thus $z = \frac{0}{0}x$ cannot possibly tell us whether z is any actual part of x, but assures us that it is no part of not-x, and this is important. Similarly $z - xy + \frac{0}{0}x$ assures us that z is no part of not-$(xy + x)$, which is by no means the same thing as informing us that it is no part of not-xy. In every case the indeterminate term represents a confession of ignorance over its whole range, but to confine our ignorance within that range is to yield knowledge in reference to what is outside it, and this is done in any of these logical equations.

CHAPTER XV.

WE have now reached the last step of our purely logical analysis. We have shown how to resolve any propositions, and any group of propositions, into all their ultimate denials, that is, into all the unconditional elements which they con tain. This was the first step, and was fully treated in what was said about Equations and the Interpretation of Equations. The next step was to show what could be done with a portion of these elements; that is, how near we could attain towards giving the full force of the propositions in question by the use of a selection only of the total number of terms involved in them. This was treated in the Chapter on Elimination.

What we have now to do is to take a step in the way of Synthesis. We want to investigate some rule for determining the value of new groups of these elements in terms of the given class symbols. The full symbolic statement of the pro posed step would be this;—Given $f_1(x,y,z,...), f_2(x,y,z,...)$, &c, determine[1] $F(x, y, z,...)$ in terms of any assigned selection of

---

[1] This $F(x, y, \&c.)$ may involve any selection, of course, of the terms x, y, &c. It is not only a new function of the class terms, but a new function of a *selection* of them.

the remaining symbols. A special case of this process may be detected in that generalization of the syllogistic process already referred to amongst the examples in Chap. XII., when we determined xz from xy and yz. That is, we have,—

for $f_1(x, y, z, a, c) = 0$, $xy - a = 0$,
for $f_2(x, y, z, a, c) = 0$, $yz - c = 0$.

The problem is, find $F(x, z)$, or xz, in terms of a and c, omitting y from the conclusion; *i.e.* eliminating y.

The general solution of this problem was probably first conceived, and almost certainly first effected, by Boole. As a piece of formal symbolic reasoning there seems nothing to be added to it as he left it, and it is a marvellous example of his penetration and power of generalization. It cannot often be the lot of any one to conceive and so completely to carry out such a generalization in an old and well-studied subject.

We will approach this problem in the same way as we have attacked the previous ones, that is, by first seeing what suggestions our common logical knowledge could offer towards the solution of it. We will then turn to Boole's method of solution; the real logical significance of which is by no means easy to grasp, unless we have thus examined the matter first in a somewhat more empirical way.

Take the simple example offered above: viz.

Given $\begin{array}{l} xy - a \\ yz - c \end{array}\Big\}$, find xz in terms of a and c.

We should naturally begin by breaking up the given equations into all their ultimate denials, so as to obtain the whole materials for whatever they can affirm, deny, or leave in doubt.

These materials are the following:—

$$ax = 0, \qquad cy = 0,$$
$$ay - 0, \qquad cz = 0,$$
$$axy - 0, \qquad cyz = 0.$$

Now develop xz, the quantity to be determined, in terms of the other elements, and we have

$$xz = xz(acy + acy + acy + acy + \bar{a}cy + acy + acy + acy)\ldots(1).$$

This is, the reader will remember, a merely formal result, an expression which must always hold good. We shall, so to say, materialize it, that is, bring it into accordance with the assigned data, by seeing to what it reduces on the introduction of the above denials. Remove then from it all those ele ments which, in virtue of the given equations, can be shown to vanish, and it reduces to

$$xz = xz(acy + \bar{a}cy) \text{ or } xz - \tfrac{0}{0}(acy + acy),$$

or, in the form in which we want it, in which xz is expressed only in terms of a and c, it would stand

$$xz = \tfrac{0}{0}ac + \tfrac{0}{0}ac \ldots\ldots\ldots\ldots\ldots\ldots\ldots(2).$$

It must be observed, here, that the factor $\tfrac{0}{0}$ is introduced by a double right. For one thing we want to eliminate y, and we know that the most direct way of doing this is simply to substitute $\tfrac{0}{0}$ for the term to be eliminated. Then again, anything standing in the form $X - XY$ is known to give an indefinite value of X, since this is one of the alternative forms for $X = \tfrac{0}{0}Y$. Hence even if y had not been eliminated we should have known that we had only got a result of the form

$$xz = \tfrac{0}{0}acy + \tfrac{0}{0}\overline{a}\,\overline{c}\,\overline{y}.$$

When equation (2) is read off into words, it stands,

"All xz is either both a and c, or neither a nor c".

This answer is quite correct so far as it goes, but it must be carefully observed that it does not go so far as it might. One side of the equation is plain enough, but not the other. We know, that is, that xz is confined to ac and ac, but we do not know whether it contains the whole of either or both of these terms. It represents the present state of our knowledge; with further knowledge we might ascertain that one or both of these factors $\frac{0}{0}$ must be converted into 1. In order to decide this point we should, if we continued the same plan, have to examine both the elements ac and ac in terms of xz, in order to determine whether we could thus partially or entirely convert the equation. As it happens, ac is very easily determined. For, multiplying together the two origi nal equations, we have at once $ac = xyz - \frac{0}{0}xz$.

Hence it is clear that the equation can be written

$$xz = ac + \tfrac{0}{0}\overline{a}\,\overline{c},$$

viz. that 'all ac is xz', as well as 'all xz is ac or ac'. Again as regards ac we have

$$\overline{a}\,\overline{c} = (1 - xy)\,(1 - yz).$$

This is not expressible simply in terms of xz. Accordingly we cannot convert the second term in the expression for xz, but must leave the equation as it stands above, viz.

$$xz = ac + \tfrac{0}{0}ac \ \ldots\ldots\ldots\ldots\ldots\ldots\ldots\ (3).$$

(The reader will remember that this result is the same as we obtained in a former chapter by resort to what may be called simple geometrical considerations; that is, by reference to diagrams.)

Let us, for further illustration, vary the example by making it a trifle more complicated. Let it be proposed to determine the expression $xz + xz$ from the same data as before: that is, let $F(x, z) = xz + xz$. Proceeding exactly as before, by developing each of the expressions xz and xz in respect of the remaining three terms, and omitting those elements which the original equations prove to be non-exis tent, we have

$$x\overline{z} = x\overline{z}(a\overline{c}y + \overline{a}\,\overline{c}\,\overline{y}) = \tfrac{0}{0}a\overline{c} + \tfrac{0}{0}\overline{a}\,\overline{c},$$
$$\overline{x}z = \overline{x}z(\overline{a}cy + \overline{a}\,\overline{c}\,\overline{y}) = \tfrac{0}{0}\overline{a}c + \tfrac{0}{0}\overline{a}\,\overline{c}..$$

Gathering the two together, and remembering that the multiplication by 2, or any other factors, of a term affected by the indeterminate factor $\frac{0}{0}$, still leaves it indeterminate, we have

$$F(x,\, z) = x\bar{z} + \bar{x}z = \tfrac{0}{0}a\bar{c} + \tfrac{0}{0}\bar{a}c + \tfrac{0}{0}\bar{a}\bar{c},$$

which is the required answer.

Here, as in the last example, the answer is not quite complete. Of course it is possible that it may yield all that we want, for we may have only wanted to know the constitution of the assigned expression $xz + xz$, in respect of a and c. But if it were also required to know the converse, or con verses, of this equation; that is, to determine whether $xz + xz$ included the *whole* of any one or more of these classes ac, ac, ac, we should have to take each of them in turn, and ascer tain whether either of the three was included in $xz + xz$. We might proceed to do this by the complete method of developing ac, ac, ac, and then striking out the terms which are proved to be non-existent. But as it happens there is a much shorter way, as follows:

We have $a = xy$, $c = yz$,

$$\therefore\ ac = xy(1 - yz)$$
$$- xy - xyz = xy(1 - z) = xyz$$
$$\therefore\ a\bar{c} = \tfrac{0}{0}x\bar{z}.$$

Similarly $ac = \tfrac{0}{0}xz$.

The remaining term ac does not admit of such statement. Hence, finally, we have,

$$x\bar{z} + \bar{x}z = a\bar{c} + \bar{a}c + \tfrac{0}{0}\bar{a}\bar{c},$$

from which it appears that the proposition may be converted as regards the two terms ac and ac. It is fully stated in words by saying, "The classes represented by xz and xz are both certainly contained in the aggregate of the classes com prised by ac, ac, and ac; and conversely, both ac and ac are contained in the aggregate comprised by xz and xz'';—or, in somewhat more familiar language, 'Every xz and every xz is either ac or ac or ac; and conversely, every ac and every ac is either xz or xz'.

The process above illustrated is a perfectly general one, and if nothing more were desired in a logical process than the solution of the assigned problem, it would probably be the best, that is, the most effective and convenient way of setting to work. It may be described as follows, in a series of perfectly intelligible logical steps :—Take the given equa tions and analyze them into all their constituent elements, that is, into all the ultimate denials which they involve and which collectively make up their significance. Then take the given function which we are told to find the value of, and make the requisite synthesis. That is, build up succes sively each part of it, employing for this purpose the above-mentioned denials. This latter stage is really one of rejec tion, for we begin by developing the required function into its full complement of potential classes, and then strike out as many of these as are shown to vanish in consequence of the previous analysis. Having thus gone through the Ana lysis and the Synthesis there remains the third step, namely that of Elimination. It may be required to express the desired function in terms of part only of the terms involved in the equations. If so, the elimination is of that easy kind discussed in the earlier part of Chap. XIII., in which the terms to be eliminated entered on one side only of the explicit equation. Substitute therefore the indefinite symbol $\frac{0}{0}$ for the terms to be eliminated, and the whole problem is solved, so far as the determination of the given function in terms of the assigned class symbols is concerned.

If we want also to go on to determine how many converse statements can be made, that is, to determine not only of what classes the given function is composed, but also in which cases it comprises the *whole* of these classes, then we must go through the same processes in the case of each of these classes. We must take each of them in turn and build it up in the same way as the given function was built up. The same list of elementary denials will serve, of course, in each case, for we are dealing with one and the same set of original equations.

In familiar language the process may be described by saying that we take the given premises, break them up into fragments, and then put these fragments, or a part of them, together in some other arrangement in order to build up the structure we require.

Boole's plan for attaining this end is one which would probably seem the most natural to any mathematician who was disposed to apply to Logic the methods found so success ful in his own science. He takes the assigned function $F(x, y, z)$ and puts it equal to, say, t; where t is of course simply a new symbol, the equivalent for this function. Our equations then stand thus :—

$$f_1(x, y, z) = 0,$$
$$f_2(x, y, z) = 0,$$
$$\dots\dots\dots\dots$$
$$F(x, y, z) - t = 0.$$

Now eliminate from these equations, after reduction by the methods described in a former chapter, every term except t and those terms in which $F(x, y, z)$ was to be determined. Then develop t, by the well-known methods, and what was required is done; for t or $F(x, y, z)$ will be described in terms of those symbols, and those symbols only, which it was desired to make use of in describing it.

If certainty and completeness of symbolic procedure were all we had to look for, there can be no doubt that Boole's method would be the best, as the whole answer is at once and completely given by it; that is, we obtain at one and the same time the converse propositions referred to a page or two back, as well as the direct proposition describing $F(x, y, z)$. But it is a terribly long process; a sort of machine meant to be looked at and explained, rather than to be put in use. Consequently if ever we do feel occasion to solve such a problem there can be little doubt that the comparatively empirical method above offered will answer our purpose best. I call it empirical because it requires us to build up the given function in detail, by exercise so to say of our own observation and sagacity, instead of taking, and trusting to, a precise rule for the purpose of effecting it.

How tedious Boole's method is in practice, in spite of its theoretic perfection, may be seen by taking the very simple example already referred to; viz.

$$\text{Given } \left. \begin{matrix} y \\ yz - v \end{matrix} \right\} \text{ find } xz.$$

We should write them thus:

$$\left. \begin{matrix} xy - a = 0 \\ yz - c = 0 \\ xz - t = 0 \end{matrix} \right\}.$$

Then proceed to eliminate x, y, and z, from these equations and nothing will be left but a, c, and t. This will give therefore an equation for solving t in terms of a and c, which will involve the required answer. I should proceed to do this by first resolving all these three equations into their negative constituents, as follows ;—

$$\left. \begin{matrix} x y \bar{a} \\ a \bar{x} \\ a \bar{y} \end{matrix} \right\} \left. \begin{matrix} y z \bar{c} \\ c \bar{y} \\ c \bar{z} \end{matrix} \right\} \left. \begin{matrix} x z \bar{t} \\ t \bar{x} \\ t \bar{z} \end{matrix} \right\} = 0.$$

The full formula for eliminating x, y, and z from this expression would be rather long : it would be as follows :—

$$(a + c + t)(a + c + t)(a + c + t)(a + c + t)(a + c + t)^4 = 0,$$

this being the result of the requisite substitutions in the formula

$$f(1,1,1)f(1,1,0)f(1,0,1)f(1,0,0)f(0,1,1)f(0,1,0)f(0,0,1)f(0,0,0)=0,$$

the formula for the elimination of three terms from $f(x,y,z) = 0$.

Boole has given various methods of reduction for the simplification of such a formula, but its management will always be tedious. After a page or two of work, which I need not repeat here, the student may find himself brought to the result

$$(c\bar{t} + \bar{a} + \bar{c}t)(a + ct) = 0,$$

$$\text{whence } t = \frac{ac}{ac - ac - ac}.$$

From this, by the ordinary process of development, we have

$$t = ac + \tfrac{0}{0}\bar{a}\bar{c}.$$

That is, $$xz = az + \tfrac{0}{0}\bar{a}\bar{c}.$$

The desired result is therefore obtained, and so far we have an illustration of the power and certainty of the method ; but it can hardly be claimed as showing also its ease and simplicity. (As regards these latter qualifications the reader may contrast the processes in Chapter XII. p. 279). Of course what can be done in this case can be done in any case whatever,— omitting considerations of mere tediousness ;—for, since we have no equations of anything higher than the first degree, every solution is theoretically obtainable with equal certainty, and by the employment of the same method.

We see therefore that this problem, which may be described as the most general problem of Symbolic Logic, is theoretically attainable in every case, and the method for so obtaining it has now been fully exhibited.

THE SYLLOGISM.

The problem just discussed is closely connected with the Syllogism of ordinary Logic, of which indeed it may (as will presently be pointed out) be regarded as a generalized ren dering. We must frankly remark that from our point of view we do not greatly care for this venerable structure, highly useful though it be for purposes of elementary training in thought and expression, and almost perfect as it technically is when regarded from its own standing point. But its ways of thinking are not ours, and it obeys rules to which we own no allegiance. To it the distinction between subject and predicate is essential, to us this is about as important as the difference between the two ends of a ruler which one may hold either way at will. To it the position of the middle term is consequently worth founding a distinction upon, to us this is as significant as is the order in which one adds up the figures in an addition sum.

There are reasons nevertheless for taking some account of the syllogism here; partly because the contrast of treat ment will serve to emphasize this difference in the point of view, partly because the omission of any such reference might possibly be taken as a confession of failure on the part of the Symbolic Logic. Since the Syllogism is a sound process it must admit of some kind of treatment upon any scheme, though we shall take the liberty of freeing it from what we are bound to regard as certain unnecessary restrictions. We cannot consistently recognize the differences upon which the distinctions of Figure are founded, so we look only at the first Figure. Even then we must simplify further. Firstly, we refuse to see any difference of character between x and not-x; whereupon vanishes the distinction between syllogisms with affirmative and with negative major premises. Secondly, our punctilious aversion to anything like enumeration or quantification,—in other words, to the mathematical concessions of the common Logic,—induces us to regard 'some X' in the subject of the major, as a distributed class-term, instead of regarding 'X' as an undistributed term. The justification for doing this is that, when we look only to the first Figure, precisely the same indefinite class 'some X' occurs in the minor premise and in the conclusion, so that its indefinite character has no bearing whatever on the actual process of reasoning[1]. Accordingly our syllogistic type is reduced to the one form,

$$Y\bar{Z} = 0, \qquad\qquad Y = \tfrac{0}{0} Z,$$
$$X Y = 0, \qquad\text{or}\qquad X = \tfrac{0}{0} Y,$$
$$\therefore X\bar{Z} = 0; \qquad\qquad \therefore X = \tfrac{0}{0} Z.$$

When all the three letters here stand for whole terms, these being positive, we have *Barbara*. When X stands for

---

[1] The reader will remember that this was not the form adopted in Chap. VII. for the expression of particular propositions. But the problem before us in the two cases is not the same. What we were there considering was the best way of expressing the real force of such propositions, in symbolic language; taking account, as far as we could, of the attendant difficulties of implication. What is now before us is the best way of similarly expressing a certain process of reasoning. I think that it is not by any means the best rendering of 'Some X is not Z' to say that we thus contemplate the whole class .

'some-X' and refer it to a part of the class 'not-Z'. But it is a perfectly legitimate way of expressing it when, as in the first Figure, this same indefinite class 'some-X' occurs on each occasion as one of three terms. When a Symbolist is forced to syllogize, it is, I consider, a fair rendering of *Ferio* to put it,

> All Y is not-Z,
> Some-X is Y,
> $\therefore$ Some-X is not-Z.

We do not syllogize willingly, nor profess to do it gracefully, but it seems to me that we do not do it inaccurately.

a part-class (*i.e.* for some-*X*), and *Z* is a negative term, we have *Ferio*; and so on with the two remaining forms.   That is, the above symbolic arrangement will, by suitable interpretations of *X*, *Y*, and *Z*, cover all the Moods of the first figure, and consequently all the Moods of the other figures.

The above rendering of the syllogism, it will be seen, is really nothing but a symbolic translation of the *Dictum* of Aristotle; as any single comprehensive rendering of it ought, I suppose, to be.   Or rather it is a slight generalization of that *Dictum*, for, since we recognize no difference of character between x and x, we make but one *dictum* out of *omne* and *nullum*.

Supposing that we feel bound to treat the syllogism at all, the above certainly seems to me the best way of doing so; indeed the only way, in strict consistency with our own principles.   One serious defect, as it seems to me, in the great majority of the attempts to treat Logic symbolically has consisted in the fact that the authors have not sufficiently shaken themselves free from the old trammels.   They have felt bound to adhere as far as possible to all the old distinctions in the form, order, and so forth, of the constituent propositions even of the syllogism.   The majority of the older symbolists (for instance, Maimon) have really done little more than go in detail through the nineteen moods, clothing each in a new symbolic dress.   This is highly unsatisfactory, since most sets of symbols require some violence to force them into recognizing distinctions so utterly alien to their genius and habits.

Boole's plan is very different from the one offered above. He has certainly solved a very general problem, and one which can be made to include, amongst other things, a number of the syllogistic moods.   I cannot however regard it as quite a fair generalization of that process; nor, for that matter, did he seem to regard it so himself. His plan is as follows. He considers the two propositional forms, $vx = v'y$, $wz = w'y$, as containing under them all the possible forms of premise needed for a syllogism. Thus, put $v = 1$ in $vx - v'y$, and we have 'All x is y'; leave $v = 1$, but regard y as negative, and we have 'No x is y'; make v and v indefinite, and we have 'Some x is y'; do the same, regarding y as negative, and we have 'Some x is not y'. Similarly with the interpretation of the other premise. Now eliminate y from these two equations and determine the relation of x to z, and a part[1] of the syllogistic scheme will be completed.

The answer obtained by Boole from these premises, involving seven terms, is somewhat intricate. It is given in the *Laws of Thought* (p. 232). I will not however pursue the subject further for two reasons. In the first place, the whole enquiry seems to me to be carried on upon a wrong line of

---

[1] Only a *part*, on two accounts. Firstly, in the propositions as above expressed, the same middle term y occurs in both. But, in the syllogism, we require that 'all y' and 'no y' shall enter as a middle term; that is, we must take account of the pair of equations $vx = v'y$, $wz = w'y$, or we shall omit some of the recognized pairs of premises. Secondly, syllogistic conclusion demands the determination not only of the relation of x, but also of that of x and vx, to z, or we shall omit some of the recognized conclusions. Consequently the form above worked out is only one of six which demand examination, and which are duly discussed by Boole.

It deserves notice that Lambert attempted much the same problem.

Starting from two perfectly general expressions for the premises, he obtains a similar one for the conclusion, pointing out that by due determination of the arbitrary letters involved we may specialize for any desired figure and mood. His forms (of which some account is given in Chap. xx.) are closely analogous to those of Boole. Thus,

$$\text{``Major} \ \frac{mA}{r} = \frac{nB}{x},$$
$$\text{Minor} \ \frac{nC}{n} = \frac{nB}{p},$$
$$\text{Conclusio} \ \frac{un}{nq}C = \frac{mv}{rp}A.$$

In dieser allgemeinen Formel kann man die Buchstaben nach Belieben bestimmen, wenn man daraus besondere Formeln für die Schlüsse herleiten will" (*Log. Ab.* I. 103).

attack, inasmuch as it involves a concession to a variety of rules and assumptions which from our point of view must be regarded as arbitrary and almost unmeaning. Moreover such a form as $vx = vy$ cannot be regarded as a true representation of a particular proposition unless we reject the value 0 for v and v , a restriction which is not claimed for x and y. .Consequently we are mixing up in the same investigation terms which are subject to different laws of valuation.

If we simply regard v, v , w, w , as ordinary class terms, like x, y, z, the problem in question acquires a very ready interpretation, but one widely remote from anything contemplated in syllogistic Logic. It then becomes, " If every x which is v is a y which is v (and *vice versa*), and every z which is w is a y which is w (and *vice versa*), what is the description of x as given by the other terms, omitting y"? A concrete example of this is given by Boole himself in the words :—" Suppose a number of pieces of cloth striped with different colours were submitted to inspection, and that the two following observations were made upon them ;

(1) That every piece striped with white and green was also striped with black and yellow, and *vice versa*.

(2) That every piece striped with red and orange was also striped with blue and yellow, and *vice versa*.

Suppose it then required to determine how the pieces marked with green stood affected with reference to the colours white, black, red, orange, and blue ".

If we are to take this kind of view of the syllogism at all there seems to me to be a simpler and more symmetrical arrangement. Instead of starting with the premises employed by Boole, let us make use of the following,

By suitable modifications, as explained in Chap. VII., we can make these forms represent a number of the propositions needed for the syllogism, as well as some others besides. We have only to put a and c respectively equal to 1, v, 0. This will furnish one type of pairs of propositions, from which we can then determine xz, $\overline{x}z$ and $x\overline{z}$. For the other type we must take a pair of propositions in which the middle term occurs in the forms y and $\overline{y}$. Thus,

$$\left.\begin{array}{l} xy = a \\ \overline{y}z = c \end{array}\right\},$$

and then again determine xz, $\overline{x}z$ and $x\overline{z}$ from this pair. The problem thus solved is essentially the same as that undertaken by Boole, and can therefore hardly be considered to be a true representation of the syllogism, but it seems to me simpler and more symmetrical than his rendering. Of the results, one or other of which represents every syllogistic mood and which correspond to the six alluded to above, I give two:

From the premises

$$\left.\begin{array}{l} xy = a \\ yz = c \end{array}\right\},$$

we deduce $\qquad xz = ac + \tfrac{0}{0}\,ac\dots\dots\dots\dots(\alpha).$

And from the premises

$$\left.\begin{array}{l} xy = a \\ yz = c \end{array}\right\},$$

we deduce $\qquad xz - \tfrac{0}{0}ac + \tfrac{0}{0}\,ac\dots\dots\dots\dots(\beta).$

It would take too much space to work out all the results, but two may be chosen as samples.

(1) In the premises $xy = a$, $yz = c$, put $z - w$, $a = v$, $c = 0$, and we have

$$\left.\begin{array}{l} xy = v \\ y\overline{w} = 0 \end{array}\right\}.$$

Then, employing formula (α), we have $xw = v + \tfrac{0}{0}$ or $xw = v$.

21—2

Put into words this stands, inverting the order of the premises,

$$\left.\begin{array}{l} \text{All } y \text{ is } w \\ \text{Some } x \text{ is } y \\ \therefore \text{Some } x \text{ is } w \end{array}\right\} Darii$$

(2) In the second pair of premises $xy = a$, $yz = c$, put $a = 0$, $c = 0$, and we have

$$\left.\begin{array}{l} xy = 0 \\ \overline{y}z = 0 \end{array}\right\}.$$

Then, employing formula (β), we have $xz - 0$.

Put into words it stands

$$\left.\begin{array}{l} \text{No } y \text{ is } x \\ \text{All } z \text{ is } y \\ \therefore \text{No } z \text{ is } x \end{array}\right\} Celarent.$$

The syllogistic regulations are however so remote from the ways of the symbolic system that it hardly seems worth the trouble to follow out the enquiry any further. We *can* syllogize, after a fashion, just as one could drive a stage coach from London to Birmingham along the railroad, but to do this would be a needless deference to tradition now that we have engines and carriages specially constructed for the new system.

I take this opportunity of correcting an error, or rather a suggestion of error, in the note on p. 176. It slipped my memory at the time (and indeed till that sheet was printed off) that Boole when discussing the Syllogism in his later work, the *Laws of Thought*, had not confined himself to the four old forms of proposition, but had added on four more, thus adopting a scheme equivalent to that of De Morgan. Thus,

All Y's are X's,
No Y's are X's,
Some Y's are X's,
Some Y's are not-X's,
All not-Y's are X's,
No not-Y's are X's,
Some not-Y's are X's,
Some not-Y's are not-X's.

These forms, as he distinctly says, are not the same as those of Hamilton. They are simply an enlargement of the old scheme by the introduction of negative subjects, and they leave the predicate,— as regards its quantity or distribution, in its customary condition. There is no attempt to distinguish whether we mean 'some only' or 'all' the predi cate to be taken; and this I have always considered to be the whole point of the Quantification doctrine. Moreover his whole treatment of these forms is antagonistic to this doctrine. Thus he here expresses (p. 229) 'All Y's are X's', in his usual way, $y = vx$; but gives at once, as equi valent forms, $yx = 0$, $x = \frac{0}{0} y$. These forms, as I have said in the text of the page referred to, seem to me as directly hostile to all that I have ever understood to be meant by Quan tification of the Predicate, as any forms which I could invent for the purpose of expressing such hostility. If any one will point out to me a passage in which Boole has admitted the distinctive propositions ' All X is some Y', 'Some X is not some Y', I shall admit, not that his system is founded on the Quantification of pre dicates, but that he has there used expressions inconsistent with his system of symbols.

CHAPTER XVI.

HYPOTHETICALS.

In the course of the preceding chapters we have frequently had to touch incidentally upon the treatment of Hypotheti cal propositions, both in the symbolic expression of our data and in the interpretation of our results. The subject how ever is too large and intricate for merely incidental treatment, so a separate chapter is here devoted to a more detailed discussion of it.

The reader will have had repeated opportunities of in ferring that the only tenable symbolic view is that there is no real distinction between the hypothetical and categorical forms of statement, these distinct renderings being regarded as a matter of private option, so that it is open to any one to read off the symbols in whichever way he pleases. In the sym bolic statements themselves there is nothing to intimate in which way the premises were worded when they were handed over to us, nor is there anything to force us to translate them back again into one form rather than the other.

Here, as at every other point, we have to consider the de mands of our own scheme and not those of other schemes. Doubtless there are systems of Logic to which the distinction in question is by no means insignificant. For instance, those who adopt a more subjective view of the nature of the reason ing processes might fairly insist upon the distinction between categorical and hypothetical judgments. On the other hand there are ways of treating Logic objectively,—for example by the discussion of Induction,—in which the distinctive charac teristic of the Hypothetical brings it (as will presently be pointed out) into such close proximity with the estimation of Probability as to entitle it to distinct consideration.

As just remarked, all that here directly concerns us is the most appropriate symbolic account of the matter. In this we must have regard not merely to the fact that we make very large employment of symbols, but also to the character of the propositions to which this employment introduces us. Now the sort of proposition with which we constantly have to deal, and which we class with others of a more simple and familiar description, is one wherein the subject or predicate, or both, are complex. Take, as a type of this character, the statement $AB = ABCD$. This may be read off in a variety of ways:—All AB is CD;—If any A is B then it is CD;—If any B is A then it is CD;—Every A which is B is a C which is D;—Whenever A concurs with B then will C concur with D; and so forth. That these different renderings of the same original statement involve somewhat different *judgments* may be freely conceded; and therefore, as already remarked, on a more subjective system of Logic we might have to distinguish between them. But it has been abundantly illustrated in the course of this work that what we look to are the class re lations involved, and therefore we are prepared to allow con siderable latitude in respect of the way of reading off our statements, provided the relations themselves be left un disturbed.

It is quite true that logical equations which involve complex terms are more naturally interpreted in a hypothetical form than are those of a simpler kind. Indeed, in a recent treatise on Symbolic Logic[1], the form $xy - c$ is chosen as the type of the Hypothetical, as $x = c$ is of the Categorical. It will be instructive to enquire into the ground of this choice. There is no doubt that each of these forms can, if we please, be interpreted in either way. Thus $xy = c$ may be read off either 'All xy is c', or 'If any x is y then it is c'; whilst $x - c$ may be read off either 'All x is c or 'If anything is x then it is c'. Why then is the former regarded as more appropriately hypothetical? Mainly, I apprehend, for the following reason. It was shown in a previous chapter (Chap. VI.) that every universal affirmative proposition must be in terpreted as involving something of a hypothesis; 'All x is c' having to be understood, if we wish to work with it success fully, as meaning 'All x, if there be any, is c'. But this hypothetical element is generally so faint as scarcely to be perceptible in common discourse, where indeed it is often entirely rejected. Names are seldom employed except to denote what we suppose to exist. so that we come to feel much reluctance to assert that 'All x is c' unless we are con vinced of the existence of x. Hence any doubt on this score commonly drops out of sight, and the categorical is safely assumed in most cases to carry with it an assurance of the existence of the subject and predicate. But though such an assurance may be justified in the case of x and y separately,

[1] Macfarlane's *Algebra of Logic*, p. 81. Lambert, so far as I know, was the first to explicitly assign this notation for the expression of a hypothetical: — "Die allgemeinste Formel der hypothetischen Satze ist diese: Wenn *A* ein *B* ist, so ist es *C*. Diese Formel kann allezeit mit der folgenden verwechselt werden; Alles *A* so *B* ist, ist *C*. Nun ist, Alles *A* so *B* ist $= AB$; folglich, Alles *AB* ist *C*. Daher die Zeichnung: $AB > C$, $AB = mC$" (*Log. Abhandlungen*, I. 128). Some explanation of the sym bols thus employed will be found in the final chapter.

it is quite another thing to justify it in the case of the com
pound xy. These symbols, when occurring separately, stand
presumably for common terms which are familiar to every
one, but their combination into one may be something en
tirely novel. Hence the enquiry whether there be any such
thing as the subject of the proposition, which would seem al
most impertinent in the case of the simple propositions typified
by $x = c$, becomes quite pertinent in the case of the complex
ones typified by $xy = c$. The doubt thus suggested naturally
expresses itself by our adopting, as the verbal equivalent of
the latter form, such a conditional statement as, 'If x is y then
it is c', the rest of the complete statement, indicated by the
symbols, taking the form 'c is xy, if there be such'. Proposi
tions therefore with complex subjects almost force upon us
that hypothetical interpretation which we have found it
advisable to extend to all propositions without exception.

There are, it must be admitted, certain grammatical diffi
culties in this way of framing our hypothetical propositions,
but these seem really common to all systems of Logic. Take
as an example, 'If the harvest is bad in England, then corn
dealers in America will gain', which seems a fair concrete
example of 'If A is B then C is D'. We have said (Chap.
XII) that we should frame this in the symbolic expression
$(1 - AB)\, CD = 0$, or $CD = CDAB$. This identifies 'C that
is not D' with some uncertain part of 'A that is not B'; that
is, literally interpreted, we seem to be declaring that 'Ameri
can corn dealers who do not gain' *are* 'harvests which are
not bad in England'.

Such a difficulty as this ought hardly to trouble any
logician. It surely arises only out of the impossibility of in
flecting our literal symbols, which compels us to make con
siderable modifications in the structure of our sentences
before submitting them to symbolic treatment. If, in accord-

ance with a hint from De Morgan, we were at liberty to inflect our logical letter symbols (*Camb. Phil. Tr.* x. 207), if we might talk of the A-ness of B, or of X-ing and Y-ing Z, and so forth, we should need less freedom of interpretation. As it is, the great license of interpretation which we are obliged to claim, is nothing but a set off for the absence of power to inflect. Every logician claims this license. Just as we do not hesitate to transform 'A killed B unjustly', into 'A is the-unjust-killer-of-B', and thus to express it in the form 'X is Y', so we claim a like liberty as regards the above hypothetical. We transform the sentence into some such shape as 'Bad English harvests are followed by gain to American corn dealers', and put it symbolically $(1 - AB)CD = 0$. This intimates correctly enough that when the English harvest is bad ($AB = 0$, or A is B) then gain accrues to American corn dealers ($CD = 0$, or C is D). We must of course insist that no alteration be made in the signification of the symbols during the process of reasoning, but we fairly claim a large license in the statement of our data and the interpretation of our results, so as to mould our verbal statements in such a way that our symbolic expressions shall be able to grapple with them. All that is necessary to secure is, not merely that the substance of the given sentence shall be preserved intact, but also that the four component elements in it (corresponding here to A, B, C, D) shall also be retained distinctly. Provided that he does this, the logician has performed all that can be expected of him.

Having thus explained the view as to the nature of Hypotheticals which seems most appropriate to the Symbolic Logic, some remarks ought to be added in the way of criticism and explanation of the popular account of them[1]. It is

---

[1] I must again remind the reader of the three very distinct topics involved in such an enquiry: viz. the explanation most suitable to the

all very well for our purposes to say that we shall insist upon treating them exactly as we treat Categoricals, but we cannot disguise the fact that this is not the popular view. And since popular phraseology is not used at random, the wide prevalence through so many languages of a distinct hypothetical form, indicates beyond question the existence of some tolerably distinct class of facts for which that form is considered the most appropriate. It is important on two grounds to determine what these facts may be; partly, in order to ascertain that our system does not overlook any really essential distinction, and partly as a preparative to noticing certain interesting extreme cases which symbolic consistency forces into prominence.

Briefly put, my own view as to the true significance of the hypothetical form is best expressed by saying that it (1) implies a connection, of the kind called a uniformity, between two or more phenomena; and (2) implies, along with this, some doubt on our part as to the actual occurrence, in a given instance, of the pair or more of events which compose this uniformity. In other words, when we feel tolerably sure that we have got hold of a true connection between certain events, but are distinctly doubtful whether the case before us is one in point, then we naturally express ourselves in the language of hypothesis. As the latter of these two elements is perhaps the most distinctively characteristic, I will begin with it, and the reasons why the symbolic system is entitled to pass it by.

In what sense then, it may be asked, can this characteris-

Symbolic Logic; that explicitly adopted by the common Logic; and that which underlies the speech of common life. As regards the first of these it is an imperative duty to be precise, but as regards the others we are really far less concerned with the second than with the third. I mention this in justification of what would otherwise be too superficial a discussion of so intricate a matter as the treatment of Hypotheticals in the common Logic.

tic of doubt be considered by us as extra-logical? Why are
we to regard it as giving rise to no more than an optional
difference of formal statement? Simply because no attempt
is made to quantify or measure our degree of doubt. Some
times we are able to say how much doubt we entertain about
our propositions; that is, we are able to give some statistical
details as to the proportion of cases in which our statement
would be right. When this is so the proposition is at once
rightfully claimed by the Theory of Probability, and the
reader must be referred to that subject for the proper methods
of treating it[1]. But often the case is otherwise. We may
merely entertain a vague degree of doubt which we could
never venture to estimate, or, having means of estimating it
if we chose, we may not at the moment wish to do so. Pro
positions thus entertained are what the Theory of Chances
would not care to accept, and it seems to me that they form
the bulk of what are commonly put into the guise of Hypo
theticals. In this respect popular language seems to have
rather happily seized upon a characteristic form for a distinc
tion which, though not capable of accurate definition, and
though not leading to any logical distinctions worth mention,
is of very considerable practical importance in the communi
cation of our thought.

As regards the limits of this characteristic doubt, it should
be observed that it refers only to the actual occurrence, under
some given circumstances, of the elements which compose
this connection or uniformity: it does not affect their mutual
relation of invariable or general sequence or coexistence.
We ought to feel tolerably sure of the connection, but feel
some doubt about its individual occurrence then and there.
I know, say, that a fall of the barometer will be followed by

[1] I have explained my own view *Chance*, Ed. ii. 1876.
fully on this point in the *Logic of*

rain ; this is the general regularity. But I do not know whether it will fall tomorrow ; this lets in the specific doubt. If I did know that it would fall for certain tomorrow, I should only require categorical propositions. I should say, The glass will fall and it will rain ; not finding place for any hypothesis. Or again, if I knew how likely it was that the barometer would fall, I might say ; 'The chances are so and so that it will fall, and that consequently (so far as this is concerned) it will rain'. Here again there seems no natu ral opening for anything in the way of a Hypothesis. But it is when I entertain a vague degree of doubt as to what the barometer will do, that I naturally take to using an 'if' to indicate my state of mind. I express myself by saying ' If the glass falls it will rain'. Here at any rate, whatever may be found in other examples, a categorical proposition, suffused with doubt as to its present application, would seem to ex press all that we have to say : 'All falling barometers are followed by rain, but I don't know that the barometer will fall tomorrow'.

The two elements :—connection between the phenomena, and a degree of doubt on our part :—appear to be present in the case of every hypothetical, at any rate when it is most appropriately used ; though sometimes one or other of the two may seem to be missing. The distinction therefore which is sometimes drawn between the 'if' of inference and the 'if' of doubt, does not seem to me quite accurate. There ought always to be a uniformity, giving ground to the inference, and there ought always to be a doubt whether the case before us is one in which that inference applies. But sometimes one, and sometimes the other of these two elements may seem to drop out of sight.

Sometimes, for instance, we may affect a degree of doubt which we do not really entertain, and the inferential part becomes unduly prominent. This is a perfectly legitimate rhetorical device, and will serve to bring most categorical propositions into the hypothetical form; as when I say, 'If so and so is a man he must have the feelings of a man'. Often however such a transformation as this can hardly be classed amongst rhetorical devices but represents the true functions of the hypothetical. Thus when we put 'All x is y' into the form 'If anything is x then it must be y' we distinctly pro mulgate the doubt whether everything which professes to be an x is really one. That is, we are in a state of doubt as to the application of some general rule in such and such a case.

It is to this latter class of cases on the whole that the hypotheticals of mathematics and the more rigid of the Physical Sciences should apparently be referred. They are plentiful enough in most treatises on these subjects, but where is the accompanying doubt to be detected? In one or two points. For one thing it is not certain that the problem or the experiment will be gone through. 'If two chords inter sect within a circle the products of their respective segments will be equal'. Perfectly certain as it is that the chords will intersect one another thus if they be drawn, *will* they be drawn? it is optional with the performer to do it or not as he pleases. A general statement of the problem may fairly inti mate some doubt to this effect. Moreover it must be remem bered that however certain any individual may be about the circles and lines he means to draw, he is standing here in the midst of certainties of a far higher order. The glare of such formal assurance may well make any moral or physical con fidence seem pale and doubtful in contrast. Moreover there is another point which seems worth notice in reference to geometrical constructions. When I do draw my figure, what sort of a circle and chord do I obtain? one so defective in comparison with its ideal that we may well throw a doubt over the actual execution of that which was intended to be done. The depression of the one element throws into relief the height of the other. The greater the stress we lay upon the doubt, the more prominent do we render that rigid connection into which no shadow of a doubt can enter.

So again the other constituent element,—that of the connection or uniformity,—may sometimes not be perceptible, though we shall always come upon signs of it if we look closely. It may often be suggested only by some implication rather than be actually stated. The Spartans answered ' If ', implying that however certain the consequences of the advance of the enemy might be, the advance itself was not certain. Again 'What if we be detected'?—the sort of reply that might often be given, ' Well, what then'? shows that we are contemplating not a doubtful isolated fact, but a connection of some kind whose actual occurrence is considered doubtful.

This connection or uniformity, as we need scarcely observe, may be exhibited in any order as to time, for the so-called 'consequent' clause in the hypothetical sentence may in reality either succeed the 'antecedent', or be coexistent with it, or be succeeded by it. All that is requisite is a reasonable degree of regularity of occurrence as between the two factors which constitute the connection. For example, starting with the doubtful fact intimated in the antecedent 'if I have a headache tomorrow', I may attach to this doubtful fact a certain 'consequent' in any order of time past, present, or future. I may go on to say, 'then I must have eaten something unwholesome today'; or, 'I shall keep to my bed so long as it lasts'; or, 'I shall be more careful as to my diet in future'.

It may fairly be enquired, why the case of these doubtful *connections* should be thus singled out? Doubtful *facts* obtain no special treatment; why should groups of facts which have a doubt about them be distinguished, both grammatically, by the appropriation of distinct linguistic forms, and also logically, by being commonly discussed in a section apart? The answer must be, because of their great importance. A doubtful isolated fact, if such a thing were found, would be of very little service to any one, unless as a hint towards further and more careful observation. But generalized connections of any kind may be of the utmost importance to us, for these constitute the basis, and indicate the limits, of all knowledge and of all sure and safe practice. It seems to me that the Hypothetical proposition, as above interpreted, precisely indicates the mental attitude of the most thoughtful and best informed persons at almost every moment of their lives, but especially at critical conjunctures. They are familiar with abundance of suitable uniformities, under the name of laws; as to which they feel, or should feel, no manner of doubt. But what they must feel doubtful about is the individual application, the occurrence of the antecedent. Doubt here is in many cases just as desirable and scientific as is certainty there. This double element seems happily indicated by the form of the hypothetical sentence and it seems to me to be only where both of these are present that this form can be used with rigid propriety. Common language is therefore abundantly justified in making a separate class of propositions of this description, but it does not follow that Logic in general,—still less Symbolic Logic,—should follow the ex ample, and regard them as falling under any distinct rules of treatment. On the contrary, it seems to me that such characteristics as these are, so to say, strained out and left behind in passing through the framework of what is formal; they are too material and psychological to effect an entrance.

It may be remarked that the word 'if', though very commonly employed to introduce a hypothesis, is by no means the only word used for the purpose. There are various other suitable grammatical forms, a reference to some of which may serve to confirm the fact of the essential identity, for purely logical purposes, of such propositions with those which are categorical. 'Whenever A is B then C is D', 'A's that happen to be B are always C's that are D', and so forth. Amongst these various forms a slight trace of distinction of conventional meaning may be noticed. The two just mentioned do not emphasize our doubt as to the occurrence of an A nearly so strongly as the employment of an 'if' commonly does; they seem to occupy here a sort of midway position between the more characteristic hypothetical and the categorical. They certainly seem however to suggest a doubt, for it would be considered very appropriate to enquire 'Yes, but are we sure that A is B in this case?' They seem to lay the stress upon the *generality* of the connexion between the events, whereas when we make use of an 'if' we call attention to the fact that we feel a doubt as to some individual occurrence of this general connexion. We can therefore suitably employ an 'if' when we are referring to an apparently isolated pair of events, whereas the word 'whenever' definitely implies a plurality of cases. But there seems to me nothing in all this of which Logic need take account.

There is another important point which awaits discussion before we quit this part of the subject. It concerns a certain extension of the Hypothetical which has to be taken into account when we study Symbolic Logic, and arises as follows. It is universally understood in logical treatises that we are at liberty to convert negatively, or, as it is termed, 'destructively', any hypothetical judgment or reasoning. Given 'If A is B then C is D' we never hesitate to convert it into the form 'If C is not D then A is not B'. This amounts to putting the second clause of the Hypothetical upon exactly the same kind of footing as the first, and calls for a similar explanation. We are still expressing a uniform connexion, though it is now one of absence and not of presence; and we are also intimating, by our form of speech, a measure of doubt about the actual occurrence in question; for doubt in negation is equivalent to doubt in affirmation. Now arises the question whether we are at liberty to extend our application of the term 'hypothetical', and consequently our rules of inference, to the case in which the second element of the connexion is certainly true? Suppose we know that C *must* be D, which are we to do :—to insist upon retaining the right of conversion, to forego that right, or to reject such an instance as not a suitable example of the hypothetical?

The Common Logic is rather shy of touching such ques tions, but there can be no doubt whatever as to our own course. We must cling to the formal right of conversion, that is, to contemplating and discussing it, and trust that a way of reconciliation will be found open to us. On the view here adopted, viz. that hypotheticals differ in no symbolic respect from categoricals, this is the only course which we could consistently choose, for the same question has been in reality raised and decided in a former chapter[1]. It deserves however some further discussion in the present context, since however identical our treatment of the categorical and hypo thetical may be at bottom, the language in which they have to be explained and illustrated is different.

As was remarked, when the corresponding case was dis cussed in a former chapter, we are here in face of one of those

---

[1] The corresponding question in the categorical case, framed in common logical language, is of course this :—May we contraposit 'All X is Y', by saying 'No not-Y is X', when Y is known to be '*all*', that is, when there is no not-Y? The prevalent doctrine as to the infinitude of negative terms naturally stood in the way of such a question being raised.

interesting 'limiting cases' with which every one who has studied mathematics is familiar. We know well what it is there to take a formula which works smoothly enough within familiar limits, and to be called upon to apply it to some extreme case. If it be a sound formula it must stand such a test, but it will often save its integrity by some device which calls for a little ingenuity in interpretation. It may insist upon demanding that some element shall be absent which we had tacitly assumed would be present as usual, or *vice versa;* or it may call for some extreme and almost grotesque interpretation of a term, which we cannot deny to be valid, but which is outside the bounds of all ordinary usage[1].

So it is here. We must be prepared to admit as one of these limiting cases such a hypothetical as 'If I have a head ache then the sea is salt'. Admitting it, we dare not object to its destructive converse, 'If the sea is not salt then I have not a headache'; either of these apparent inferences holding good whatever may be the case as regards the state of my head. The nature of the limiting case here is obvious. That degree of doubt which the hypothetical form contemplates, and which invariable usage demands shall have some positive value, is here exactly at the bottom of the scale, for it is $= 0$. That is, the truth of the consequent in the constructive form, and the falsity of the antecedent in the destructive, are enter-

---

[1] I once had some strawberry plants furnished me which the vendor admitted would not bear many berries. But he assured me that this did not matter, since they made up in their size what they lost in their number. (He gave me in fact the hyperbolic formula, $xy = c^2$, to connect the number and magnitude.) When summer came *no* fruit whatever appeared. I saw that it would be no use to complain, because the man would urge that the size of the non-existent berry was infinite, which I could not see my way to disprove. I had forgotten to bar zero values of either variable.

tained without any doubt at all; and accordingly we know for certain in each case whether the instance before us falls under the general rule. But we may go further than this. The sea being known to be salt, we may with equal reason posit the hypothetical 'If I have not a headache the sea is salt', with the corresponding destructive. Now put it that the sea is not salt, then we conclude that I both have and have not a headache. The paradox here is not worth considering except as an illustration of what is meant by limiting cases in our formulæ, and of the lessons they can teach. There is no insurmountable contradiction in the result. The two hypotheses postulated that the sea is always salt : what we infer is that when this is not the case,—in other words *never*,—we are able to draw two contradictory conclusions[1].

Though such propositions as those just mentioned cannot, on technical or symbolic grounds, be refused a place amongst hypotheticals, it must be admitted that the proposal to admit them is really something of an abuse[2]. In any physical sense of the term, a connexion or uniformity between A and B surely implies that both A and B may sometimes individually fail. How indeed could we ascertain that the uniformity exists, except by taking note of such failures?—as witness the employment of the familiar Four Methods of Herschel and Mill. So with the doubt which should exist as to the applicability of the general uniformity to the case before us. When the consequent is rendered certain all such doubt dis-

---

[1] The reader who remembers the discussion in Chap. vi. may possibly enquire whether we are here showing the courage of our convictions in shrinking from such a catastrophe as this. The answer will be given almost immediately, when it will appear that the contradiction here 'is of a kind which rightfully deters us.

[2] They have in fact no better claim to be considered to involve a 'connexion', than (to apply an apt saying by Whately) has a clock which does not go to be called 'right' every twelve hours.

appears. But these considerations support the whole drift and purport of this chapter. My contention is that the really characteristic elements of the hypothetical of common life and of Inductive Logic are of a non-formal nature. Those characteristics are partly material and partly psycholo gical, and therefore the determination to force these proposi tions through the forms of our system will naturally, so to say, crush all the life out of them[1].

Such a loss as this is inevitable. Whenever we substitute anything resembling machine work for hand or head work, we find that though the former possesses vast superiority of power there are always some delicacies of performance in which it exhibits comparative failure. So it is here. We gain a prodigious increase of power in the manipulation of propositions, as we choose to treat them, but it would be vain to pretend that our treatment elicits all the delicate im plications which common thought detects in them. These remarks are not directed solely against the Symbolic System: as was shown in a former chapter, when discussing the import of Propositions, the Common Logic also has to disregard many of the finer suggestions and implications which popular thought and speech never fail to recognize. People who lay down a railroad gain in speed and certainty, but they must consent to forego the innumerable hints which are open to those who wander at will amongst the customary devious foot-tracks.

---

[1] Several logicians,—for instance, Mr Maccoll and Dr Frege (*Begriffs- schrift*, p. 3)—have recognized the symbolic necessity, when dealing with hypotheticals, of divesting the pro- position 'If A then B' of any sug- gestion of *connexion* between A and B. That is, we must extend it so as to cover the case of B being always true, or known to be true inde- pendently of A; which, as above re- marked, is quite hostile to the no- tion of any true physical connec- tion as commonly understood. A paper also by Mr C. S. Peirce (already referred to; see p. 146) may well be consulted upon these limiting cases of hypothetical statements.

As regards the application of these remarks to the case in point, a few paragraphs of explanation will make my meaning plain. We know that 'All x is y' is represented by $xy = 0$. This form really does no more than deny that there can be any x without y; all else it leaves open, and in so doing we frankly admit that it somewhat departs from customary im plications. The hypothetical form, as we undertake to repre sent it, shows of course a like insensibility to convention. As we have said, 'If A is B then C is D' is symbolically indicated by $(1 - AB)\, CD = 0$. We regard it as a correct formula because, when AB is put $= 0$ (significant of 'A is B') we have at once $CD = 0$ (significant of 'C is D') ; and also because, when CD is not $= 0$, AB cannot $= 0$ either. The latter con clusion is easily seen thus ;— CD is identical with $AB \cdot CD$, and therefore, when it does not vanish, its equivalent $AB.CD$ cannot vanish either : that is, a part of AB must be retained intact.

Now turn to certain of those limiting cases previously suggested. Put $CD - 1$ and we have at once $AB = 1$: what does this mean ? It means not merely that CD cannot $= 0$, or in other words that C cannot be D, but that this *im*possibility is the only possibility. It asserts that the collective denial of CD, CD, and $\overline{C}D$ leads to the collective denial of AB, AB, and $\overline{A}B$; or, more briefly, that the assertion that CD is *all* proves that AB is *all*. This case of 'destructive' inference has no counterpart in the common procedure, and for the following reason, as I apprehend. According to the popular interpretation of 'If A is B then C is D', it is unquestionably assumed that A and C are existent or present[1] (this is in ac-

[1] Hence I should say that if we wished to keep close to the popular meaning of the Hypothetical here we must regard A and C as certain, when there becomes no need to intro- duce them as symbols at all. That is, write $B\overline{D} = 0$, where we are to interpret B as 'B following on A', and D as 'D following on C'. We thus get the desired two alternatives requisite to keep us in harmony with the popu- lar interpretation of the proposition.

cordance with the common implication as to the existence of
the subject of a proposition). Hence, on this view, the two
alternatives 'A is B', 'A is not B', represent the only ones
that are possible; and similarly with regard to C and D.
But, with us, 'A is B' appears as $AB = 0$, and is consequently
but one out of *four* alternatives, every one of which must be
reckoned with. Therefore to establish the existence of CD it
is requisite to make a clean sweep of all the three remaining
alternatives. This of course is only another reminder of the
important fact, which I hope has been sufficiently admitted,
that our symbolic representation of propositions is not the
most natural representation of their conventional meaning,
but merely the best substitute in accordance with the conditions at our disposal. In fact the very consideration now
before us had to be faced and accounted for in Chap. VII.
when we were discussing categorical propositions.

The reader who has fully entered into the spirit of these
methods will perhaps here discover a new difficulty which has
been stirred up by our solution of the last one. We say that
'If A is B then C is D' is represented by $(1 - AB) CD = 0$.
Accordingly, if we had been asked to represent 'If A is not B
then C is D' we should have naturally formulated it $(1 - AB)$
$CD = 0$. Now if we work out the aggregate denials involved in
these two expressions, we find that between them they destroy
all CD; that is, they necessarily force us to the conclusion
$CD = 0$, or 'C is D'. Were it not therefore for the explanation
offered in the last paragraph we should seem to be nicely in
accord with current assumptions, for the two hypotheses in their
common verbal form equally force us to the conclusion that
C must be D. But we have just cut this support from under
our feet, by maintaining that AB and AB are but two out of
four symbolic alternatives, and cannot therefore by themselves
exhaust the possibilities. Here again, in order to see our

way clearly, we must look back a little and determine what our symbols actually say, and not merely what conventional significations we could find it possible to attach to their words. We see then that the simple expression $xy = 0$ (or its equivalents $x = xy$, $x = \frac{0}{0}y$) by making y a necessary conse quence of x excludes the possibility of any not-y being also a consequence :—that is, to combine ' If x then y' with 'If x then not y' abolishes x entirely. Now 'If A is B then C is D', and 'If A is not B then C is D', are represented respectively in forms equivalent to $CD = CDAB$ and $C\bar{D} = CDAB$. Hence this is to refer CD to the two contradictory determina tions AB and AB, and a reference to two contradictory determinations entails as effectual a destruction as a reference to all four.

A concrete instance will serve to show where we should thus have gone astray in interpreting our symbols. There are four bells in the house, and if I ring some one of them the servant will come. Clearly therefore to ring *two* only of them is not sufficient to insure his appearance, and yet it appears as if this were what we had just assumed must be the case. The reason is connected with the old question as to the expression of alternatives. The ringing of one bell does not interfere with the ringing of another, whereas AB is of course incompatible with AB. Hence to make CD dependent upon both AB and AB is to abolish it effectually, because these cannot concur, which is not the case as to the occurrence of most physical alternatives[1].

[1] Not, let it be understood, that we imply that alternatives must *be* exclusive, but merely that whether they are so or not we throw our symbolic form into one of mutual exclusion. (It will be fully shown in Chap. xix. that the question at issue is not at all as to how alternatives present themselves in nature, nor how popular speech or Common Logic express them, but merely how they may best be expressed symbolically.)

It may be added here, to the re

Another view of the Hypothetical should be noticed here : it will serve both as a conclusion to this chapter and an introduction to the next but one, in which a closely allied topic will present itself from a somewhat different side. On this view the characteristic of the Hypothetical is regarded as consisting in the fact that it is a proposition about propositions, as contrasted with one about facts.

Mill, for instance, has laid down something to this effect ; though in his case, considering the analysis he has given of the nature of a proposition, and the general scheme of Material Logic which he entertains, such a view does not appear to be very appropriate. He says, "Though he [Hamilton] takes much pains to determine what is the real import of an Hypothetical Judgment, the thought never occurs to him that it is a judgment concerning judgments. If A is B, C is D, means, The judgment C is D follows as a consequence from the judgment A is B" (*Examination*, p. 455).

But far the most systematic enunciation of the doctrine in question that I have seen, is that by Boole. He drew a rather elaborate distinction between the two kinds of proposition, terming them respectively primary and secondary propositions, or propositions referring to facts and to assertions about facts. In the case of the latter kind he adopted what seems to me a somewhat fanciful interpretation, viz. that they are to be regarded as having a reference to *time* :—" Let us take, as an instance for examination, the conditional proposition, ' If the proposition X is true the proposition Y is true'. An undoubted meaning of this proposition is that the *time* in

marks in the text above, that the alternatives 'If A is P then C is D', and 'If A is Q then C is D', would by no means necessitate the fact of C being D, because AP and AQ are not contradictory of one another. Accordingly such a case as this would be a fairer symbolic representation of the above example as to the ringing of the bells.

which the proposition X is true is *time* in which the proposi
tion Y is true " (*Laws of Thought*, p. 163).   And he applied
the same explanation to every proposition which asserted
truths instead of facts.   One must dissent from such a man
as Boole with deference, especially on a point which he him
self regarded as being of decided importance to his scheme,
but I must express my own opinion that such a distinction is
not only untenable in itself, but also quite unessential to his
system.   The latter point will recur for notice in another
chapter.

Is there then any logical distinction (to slightly vary the
question) between asserting a proposition, and asserting that
the same proposition is true ?   Grammatically considered,
there can be no doubt that there is a difference, for in the
verbal statement in the two cases the subject and predicate
are not the same.   Conventionally, also, it would probably be
admitted that there is some appreciable distinction.   To most
minds the mere utterance of a proposition does not carry
quite so much assurance as an explicit statement that that
same proposition is true ; the latter form having more of an
objective reference than the other.   There are so many pro
positions in circulation which are correct as regards predica
tion, but which can hardly be called true,—definitions, obsolete
or decaying opinions, and so forth,—that there is a tendency
for the general standard of mere assertion to become depre
ciated.   Hence, when we want it to be understood that our
statement is in actual accordance with fact, we should feel
that we had a better chance of insuring this by saying that
such and such a proposition is true, than by its simple
enunciation.

It does not seem however that there is any distinction
here of which Logic can take account.   A rude conventional
difference between statements which the speaker believes to

be founded in fact, and those which he does not intend to mark as such, may of course be tolerated; but any attempt to carry this out systematically would demand logical omni science. And failing this, can any difference whatever be detected between 'X is Y', and 'It is true that X is Y'? If we answer that there is, we shall be drawn a good deal further than we meant to go. For if the truth of a proposi tion is thus distinct from its mere enunciation, ought we not also to distinguish between the necessity of its truth and the mere probability of it, and between various degrees of the latter? I think we should be bound thus to follow up the enquiry,—in other words to treat of the Theory of Proba bility,—and the very largeness of the discussion into which we should be drawn is a strong reason for relegating it to a separate branch of Logic. Again if the assertion of the truth of X is different from its bare assertion, and is yet a proposi tion, does not *its* truth give rise to a new proposition, and so on? If so, we are like a man trying to determine the last image of a light between two parallel mirrors.

It must be admitted that the *denial* of the truth of a given proposition does not stand in quite so simple a relation to its mere utterance as does the *assertion* of its truth. This is owing however not to our being introduced into any different order of facts in the two cases, but because the denial gene rally opens out a choice of ambiguities. To deny the truth of a proposition is to assert that of its contradictory, and this in turn is to simply assert that contradictory. But Common Logic has only provided a contradictory in the case of its four selected forms, and even in these there is an ambiguity ex cept when we are dealing with individuals. To deny the truth of the statement that Milton was born in London is simply to say that he was not born there, as to deny the truth of the statement that he was not born there is simply to assert that he was. But when we deny the truth of 'All X is Y' we do not quite know how to choose between 'Some X is not Y', and 'No X is Y'. The Common Logic meets this by prescribing that the particular negative here shall do duty for both, in other words by translating 'some' as 'some it may be all'. Similarly the denial of the truth that 'No X is Y' would be commonly understood as the assertion of the truth of the contradictory 'Some X is Y', which is merely equivalent to its simple assertion. When we come to more complicated propositions, or rather to any except the esta blished four, we find no rules laid down as to the formation of contradictories. There does not seem any simple unambigu ous form for denying that 'All X is all Y', or 'All X is either Y or Z', or any other more complicated form that might be invented. We may readily enough find instances of *a* contra dictory, that is, we may find propositions incompatible with the one in question; but for a proposition to be considered *the* contradictory it is surely essential that the relation should be mutual, so that the contradictory of the latter should lead us back necessarily to the former. This has only been pro vided for in the case of the old-fashioned four.

In these last remarks we have purposely discussed the question from the point of view of the Common Logic. As regards our Symbolic scheme it was shown in a former chapter that the conception of what constitutes 'contradic tion' between propositions had to be differently interpreted, and that it was indeed quite a question whether we could well make room at all for such a word. We saw that every proposition, whether originally presented as an affirma tive or a negative, could be thrown into an unconditional negation or aggregate of negations; that this in fact was its import. To say that such a proposition is true, is here, as elsewhere, equivalent to its simple repetition; it is merely to say that these negations are correct negations. No change whatever is made in the nature of the assertion. On the other hand to *deny* the truth of the proposition is simply to upset these negations. But how many of them? If there were but one (as in our expression of an ordinary negative proposition) the answer would be easy:—that the compartment which that proposition had emptied out was to be occupied again; that the ejected tenant was simply to be re instated. This, as we showed, would lead on our system also to a particular affirmative. But if there was a group of negations implied, as is mostly the case, there is no legislation provided as to the use of the term 'contradictory', and it seems hardly worth the trouble of endeavouring to determine what arrangement should be made.

CHAPTER XVII.

GENERALIZATIONS OF THE COMMON LOGIC.

THROUGHOUT this work we have been occupied at almost every step in considering the extensions which can be effected in the processes and results of ordinary Logic ; but it will be convenient at this point, having now finished the sys tematic exposition of the subject, to gather together these various generalizations so as to see what sort of an ap pearance they present in the aggregate. This is the more necessary since their importance consists not merely in the fact of their being generalizations, but also in the great change of view which the admission of them would demand in matters like the Import of Propositions, and so forth. Those points which have been adequately discussed in the foregoing chapters will only demand a very brief notice here.

To begin then : In place of the old dichotomy we have substituted a system of polytomy; that is, we divide the universe of things into all the ultimate subdivisions attain able by taking every term and its contradictory into account. We start at once with all these subdivisions as our normal requirement, instead of regarding them as merely a possible attainment[1].

The point here which seems most characteristic of our system is the following :—That we put every one of the classes thus obtained, whether positive or negative, upon exactly the same footing. With us, xy and $x\bar{y}$ are classes of precisely the same kind. We do not indeed strictly speak of positive or negative terms at all, regarding these words as grammatical or conventional expressions founded upon the popular necessities of classification. Any compound term, such as xyz, will commonly contain both positive and negative elements, and therefore the words cease to apply to the compound. We have no reason indeed to assume that x, rather than $\bar{x}$, should represent what popular language would regard as a positive term; this being a matter for our own choice. We regard x and $\bar{x}$, of course, as contradictories, but we almost decline to call either of them positive or negative[2].

---

[1] The writer (before Boole) who has most strongly insisted on this enumeration of all the possible combinations produced by all the class terms, is Semler (*Versuch über die combinatorische Methode*, 1811). The empirical method which he proposes, viz. that of writing down all the combinations, and then scratching out or removing, individually or in groups, all those elements which are contradicted by the data, closely resembles that of Prof. Jevons. "Setzen wir zum Beispiel man hatte die 56 Conternationen, die sich aus den Begriffen a, b, c, d, e, f, g, h, bilden lassen, wohlgeordnet aufgeschrieben, und man bemerkte die Begriffe a und b, desgleichen b und d konnten ohne Widerspruch nicht zusammengedacht werden, so kostete es auch nur ein Paar Federstriche, um die Columnen der 10 Conternationen wo die Zeichen dieser Begriffe beisammen stünden, wegzuschaffen " (p. 48).

[2] This view of the primary indifference of application of x and $\bar{x}$, as such, is very alien to popular ways of thinking. To most persons the interpretation of concrete problems which turn upon the employment of negative classes is not a little perplexing. To borrow one or two of those apt and ingenious examples with which all De Morgan's logical writings abound, how many persons would be able to say confidently and off-hand whether either, and if so

When this view is taken it is seen at once that we must insist upon an entire reconsideration, for our special purposes, of the old logical account of contrariety and contradiction, both as regards classes and propositions.

First as regards *Classes.* The 'contradictory' of any class is best interpreted in its ordinary sense, viz., as com prising all which does not belong to that class. The points characteristic of our Logic are mainly these, that we apply the same notation to contradict any class however com plicated, and that we keep prominently in view all those elements of the full development into which the contradiction of any such class can be broken up. As regards the notation, what we require is either some symbol for the universe of discourse from which the given class has to be excepted, or some convenient symbol which can be applied to any class as a whole. The notation we have adopted meets both these requirements. Thus, if we want to contradict $xyz + xyz$ all we have to do is to write it $1 - (xyz + xyz)$; or, more briefly, draw a single line over the whole expression, just as we write x for $1 - x$. Other methods of performing the same process will be found described in the concluding chapter, but it seems to me a serious drawback[1] in any symbolic sys tem if it does not meet these requirements.

The extended signification of the word *contrary* does not however seem by any means so clear and simple. In

which, of these two statements is true? (1) The English who do not take snuff are included in the Europeans who do not take tobacco. (2) The English who do not take tobacco are included in the Europeans who do not take snuff. (Snuff-takers of course being included in tobacco-takers.)—Or, again, Who are the non-ancestors of all the non-descend-ants of $A . B$? (*Cam. Phil. Tr.* x. 334).

[1] This is the case with Prof. Jevons' system, in which neither of these requirements is met. In his lately published *Studies in Deductive Logic*, he borrows Mr Maccoll's nota-tion for the purpose.

fact the word is so bound up with the traditional restrictions of the ordinary Logic that we shall have to make a con siderable departure from customary usage if we want to assign a signification to it upon sound principles. Perhaps the best account we could give (founded as far as possible on the customary usage) would be the following:—that as the contradictory of a given class is the sum total of what is exclusive of it, so the contrary of the given class is that class within all this contradictory region which is farthest removed from it. At least I presume that this is most in accordance with common usage. If we adopt this account we should say that such a class as xyz, involving three terms, has a con tradictory of seven classes; and out of these seven we should select as the 'contrary' to it that one which contradicts it in every detail, in other words the class in which every con stituent element is a contradictory of the corresponding element of the aforesaid class. Thus xyz would be the contrary of xyz, xyz of xyz, and so on.

A much better plan however than this might be proposed if we had often occasion to speak of relations of this kind. It would be better to abandon the term 'contrary' altogether and to use instead some such expression as that of two class terms being contradictory in one, two, three degrees, &c., and congruent in respect of the remaining, according to the number of constituent elements. We do not really find much occasion to employ technical expressions of this kind, but if we did, the best way of describing the relations in this respect of two such classes as $abcde$ and $abcde$ would be by saying that they are contradictory in the third degree and congruent in the second degree. But in saying this it must be remembered that the two classes in question are just as exclusive of one another as if the contradiction were more complete, for the state of exclusion of one class by another is absolute and does not admit of degrees. When we thus came to deal with classes not fully subdivided, as for example xy and xz, we should have to analyse them fully and then describe the degree of contradiction of their constituent elements separately. Thus xy and xz resolve respectively into $xyz + xyz$, and $xyz + xyz$. Of these the coincident, or doubly repeated element xyz, furnishes no contradiction; the remaining elements xyz and xyz would have a two-fold contradiction[1].

Propositions. As regards the application of the terms contrary and contradictory to propositions, a moment's consideration will show us how far we have here wandered from the customary view. So much is this the case that it really seems impossible to assign any rational signification to the terms which shall remain in harmony with their customary meaning. Thus for instance the two propositions, $xy = 0$, $xy = 0$, represent respectively 'no x is y', and 'all x is y'; and on the predicative view of propositions they certainly involve between them a contradiction, indeed a contrariety. But on the compartment or occupation view they simply clear out between them the whole of x, one accounting for the y-part of it and the other for the not-y part of it. On this view therefore they would much more truly be described as supplementary than as contradictory.

If we were determined to find a use of the term which should be in harmony with our system we should best seek it in the following way:—We know that $xy = 0$ denies that there is such a class as xy, that $xy = v$ (on the special

---

[1] The late Prof. Clifford has proposed a scheme of nomenclature for propositions as grouped from this point of view, but it is too intimately connected with the particular discussion with which he is there occupied to be easily reproduced here. That discussion was alluded to in Chap. XI. p. 256. It is published in his Essays, and also an abstract of it in Jevons' *Principles of Science* (p. 143).

interpretation of v adopted in Ch. VII. p. 165) asserts that there is such a class, and that $xy - 1$ asserts the existence of that class to the exclusion of all else. We might therefore lay it down, with a reasonable conformity to common usage, that any one of these forms is contradictory of the others, and that the two extreme ones, $xy = 0$ and $xy = 1$, form a pair of contraries.

Such an interpretation as that last suggested is of course rather a shifting of the meaning of the terms in question than a generalization of them. Hardly any better instance could be found of the difficulty, in fact impossibility, of fitting in the details of the old system into the fabric of the new, or of the consequent necessity of reconsidering from the foundation all the technical terms which we have occasion to employ. The value of these particular technical terms seems to me considerable in the old Logic, since they compel the student to realize the precise force and scope of such propositions as he is every day in the habit of using. But on our system there is no opening of this kind for them. There would have been no use in discussing them here but for the fact that every effort to generalize the signification of well-known terms is a good mental exercise, and still more the attempt to realize so thoroughly the spirit and methods of different systems as to determine whether the technical terms of one system can be transferred at all, even in an extended sense, to another.

So much for the Opposition of Propositions: we will now turn to their Conversion. Here again we are soon reminded how far we have wandered from the customary mode of treating this question. The predicative explanation of propositions, founded as of course it is upon a real distinction between the subject and the predicate, naturally leads to a demand for rules for this process of converting subjects into predicates and vice versa; whilst on the compartment view of proposi tions we really have to stop and think what interpretation should be applied to the rules for such a process. For instance, the conversion of a Universal Negative, $xy - 0$, can imply nothing more with us than an optional difference in the reading off of the proposition; we may utter it as we please, 'No x is y' or 'No y is x'. And since we do not recognize any real distinction between positive and negative terms the same may be said of any other form. Given $xy = 0$ we may utter it indifferently, 'All x is y' 'No x is not-y', or 'No not-y is x'. With us these are rather conversational than logical distinctions.

It seems therefore that in this direction we should not be led to any distinction of value. But there is another way of regarding the process which is by no means synonymous with reading off one and the same statement with the other end foremost, as in common Conversion. From the statement 'all x is y' we have obtained 'some y is x'. When we look at this in the light of our symbolic system we see that it may be regarded as a very special case of this general problem[1]: —Given x as a function of y, find y as a function of x.

If we take this view of the process to be performed:—it would be almost absurd to continue to use the old term 'conversion' in reference to it:—we should describe it as follows. Let x be a logical expression, involving y amongst other terms, so that we may exhibit it in the form $x = f(y)$. It is desired to 'convert' this relation into one which shall exhibit y in terms of x. We indicate the desired expression,

---

[1] It should be noticed that we must not speak of *the* generalization of a process, as if there could be but one. A process carried out (as must always be the case) under a variety of restrictions, will necessarily lead to a variety of generalizations, according to the number of such restrictions removed, and the extent to which we remove them.

in accordance with familiar mathematical usage, in the form $y = f^{-1}(x)$. The reader must not for a moment suppose that this solves the problem; or even implies that it admits of solution, whether determinately or indeterminately. It is rather a definition of what we want, $f^{-1}(x)$ being definable as anything which when acted upon by the process f will yield x; in other words, $f\{f^{-1}(x)\} = x$. This, of course, is only a generalization of a procedure with which the reader became familiar in the third chapter. Just as $\dfrac{x}{y}$ indicated any class which when logically restricted by y will yield x, so does $f^{-1}(x)$ indicate any class which when operated on by the general logical procedure represented by f, will yield x.

As it happens, the desired result can not merely be symbolically indicated, but admits of actual performance; though here, as in most other cases of inverse procedure, the result is usually indefinite within certain limits. For, beginning with $f(y)$, this must be either a directly or an inversely assignable logical class, these being the only logical functions which we recognize as data or can deduce as results. In other words $f(y)$ must be one of our integral or fractional forms, and, if a fractional one, is reducible by development to an integral form. Hence x, or $f(y)$, can be exhibited as the sum of a number of logical class elements, these being of course in the first degree. Accordingly, conversely, y can be exhibited (by logical processes corresponding to the solution of a simple equation of the first degree) as either an integral or a fractional function of x, and consequently, by development, as an integral function. That is, given $x = f(y)$, $y = f^{-1}(x)$ can always be solved and the result exhibited in a strictly intelligible logical shape. And we may call this a generalization of the ordinary process of Conversion.

I need not remind the reader that this is a process which we have perpetually had to perform in the course of this work. Suppose, for example, that we had the relation $x = 1 - yz$, and were told to determine y in terms of x. We have

$$y = \frac{1-x}{z} = \overline{x}z + \tfrac{0}{0}\, x\overline{z},$$

which is the requisite result, viz. y in terms of x.

Most of the remaining generalizations which the Symbolic Logic introduces have been already fully expounded in the preceding chapters, but for the sake of aiding the total impression the more important of them may be briefly represented here.

The Schedule of Propositional Forms. The change here is more in respect of the import and significance than in that of mere generalization, great as the latter is. Thus we entirely discard the common distinction between affirmative and negative, whilst we attach quite a new kind of importance to that between universal and particular. Thus for the old four propositional forms we substituted, as a beginning, the following twelve[1]:

$$xy = 0,\ v,\ 1,$$
$$x\overline{y} = 0,\ v,\ 1,$$
$$\overline{x}y = 0,\ v,\ 1,$$
$$\overline{x}\,\overline{y} = 0,\ v,\ 1.$$

[1] Lambert proposed a three-fold quantitative arrangement of propositions: "Auf diese Art dehnt sich die logische Arithmetic nur auf das *alle, etliche, kein* aus. *Alle* ist = 1, *kein* is = 0, *etliche* ist ein Bruch der zwischen 1 und 0 fallt, den man aber unbestimmt lasst" (*Architectonic*, I. 202).—This note should have been inserted in Ch. VII., but at the time when that chapter was written I had not seen this work. I may here repeat a remark already made, viz., that though this tabular arrangement of propositions answers well for most empirical purposes, it does not seem to fit in with those higher generalizations in which we deal with the logical expression $f(x)$ as such. In these cases 1 and 0 seem the only working values of x.

To these we might continue to add other forms, by com bining two or more of the four kinds of class compartments. How rapidly the number of possible forms mounts up when we thus group the possibilities furnished by the introduction of more than two class terms was indicated in Chapter XI. It was seen there that the mere declarations that such and such compartments were empty furnished no less than 4,294,967,295 cases, when there were four class terms con cerned in their production. If we wished to retain some plan of grouping and arranging, which should be in accor dance as far as possible with the old lines of arrangement, probably the best mode of doing so would be to proceed in the way proposed by Prof. Jevons and already referred to in the chapter in question.

In reference to the above scheme of propositions some remarks may here be inserted to account for the extremely little use, in fact the almost entire absence of use, that has been made throughout this work of any propositions which can strictly be called 'particular'. In thus insisting upon strictness of designation I mean of course to exclude those pseudo-particulars which are represented in the form $AB = AC$. No doubt a proposition which tells us that 'the B which are A are the same as the C which are A', may be re garded as telling us that 'some B are C', but as it determines the 'some' by an ordinary class term its pretensions to particularity are spurious and misleading. The true par ticular is that which offers us, within the terms in question, no clue whatever by which we can determine what the 'some' may be.

As regards then these true particulars, I think that the scheme given above is a sound and appropriate one for all empirical purposes. By this I mean that it will not only serve to tabulate and distinguish all ordinary propositions,

with due insistance on their essential characteristics ; but
will also enable us to do everything with them in the way of
inference, short of attaining to those widest generalizations
by which we develop $f(x, y)$, say, and eliminate x or y from
it.   For instance in the immediate inference, 'Some x is
not y', as following from 'No x is y ; we must understand the
latter to imply that there *is* certainly some x, but inasmuch
as in the same breath we say that there is not xy, it is
implied that there is $x\bar{y}$.   Hence 'No x is y', when we elicit
its popular implications, amounts to the two, $xy - 0$, $x\bar{y} = v$.
Of these the latter, when taken separately, yields the desired
immediate inference 'Some x is not y'.   Or again, look at the
syllogism *Bokardo*.   I place it, and its symbolic expression,
side by side;—

Some Y is not Z $yz = v,$

All Y is X $y\bar{x} = 0,$

Some X is not Z $xz = v.$

Expand $yz = v$ into $xyz + \bar{x}yz = v$; we are therefore assured
that both these terms cannot vanish.   But the term $\bar{x}yz$ does
vanish (by the minor premise); accordingly xyz must survive,
which justifies the conclusion.

On this plan, by regarding any equation of the type
$X = v$ as a simple assurance that one or more of the con
stituent terms in X must be saved, we can I think work out
most logical examples in an empirical way.   Under the name
of empirical I include not only the ground covered by the
syllogism, but also all such methods as those which form the
bulk of several recent treatises on Symbolic Logic.   So long
as we only subdivide or develop our logical classes by treating
each term separately, instead of resorting to such formulæ as
$f(x) = f(1)x + f(0)\bar{x}$; so long as we work out inverse problems
indirectly merely, by seeing which of all the various possibili
ties can subsist as actualities, instead of proceeding directly

from $x = f(y)$ to $y = f^{-1}(x)$; so long as we eliminate tentative
ly by substitutions instead of resorting to such a formula
as $f(1)f(0) = 0$; so long a scheme of propositions such as
that above will succeed well enough.

For the purposes of the higher generalizations it does
not seem to me as if any theory were yet proposed, which
would answer except for a dichotomous scheme, represented
symbolically by 1 and 0, and logically by the contradictories
'is' and 'is not'. Into such a dichotomous scheme truly
particular propositions will not apparently fit, and they have
accordingly to be rejected from all the higher generalizations.
If such propositions were of real scientific importance, or
forced themselves into many of our familiar problems, this
inability to grapple effectually with them would certainly be
a blemish in the Symbolic Logic. As it is, we can afford to
part with them without much sense of loss.

Elimination. What we undertake under this name is a
real generalization of familiar processes. The scope however
of these processes, in the traditional treatment, is so slight
that probably many logicians would have to pause and think,
if asked whether, and under what conditions, rules could be
laid down for the process of elimination of terms from a
group of propositions. They do, of course, recognize such
rules, but only to the trifling extent of eliminating one term
out of three; the three being given two and two, in a pair of
propositions of a specified kind, and the term to be eliminated
being the one which occurs in both premises. What the
Symbolic Logic proposes is the problem:—Given any number
of terms, contained in any number of propositions, assign
a formula for the result of eliminating any number of those
terms.

Reasonings. Here again we have a true process of gene
ralization. A mode of stating the ordinary process would be

the following: Given two propositions involving three terms, two and two, so that one term occurs in both; these proposi tions, remember, being selected from an assigned schedule containing four admissible types; find in what cases a third proposition distinct from those two, but drawn from the same schedule, can be inferred from them. The problem of the Symbolic Logic is: Given any number of non-quantitative propositions, of any type whatever, and involving any number of terms, assign a general formula indicating what class combinations can be established (conditionally) from them, what combinations can be negatived absolutely, and what combinations can receive no such solution either way. It will be seen therefore that whereas the problems of elimina tion and inference are almost exactly the same thing when regarded from the common or restricted point of view, they develop in very different directions when generalized.

CHAPTER XVIII.

CLASS SYMBOLS AS DENOTING PROPOSITIONS.

IN a preceding chapter we had to say something about the existence of a certain 'universe of discourse', within which our symbols must always be considered to have their applica tion, for the time being, confined. As to the *nature* of this universe we said nothing ; or rather we gave it to be under stood that this depended entirely upon the data, and the intention of those who employ the data. It was merely insisted on that the various ultimate compartments or sub divisions were to be considered as being, within the limits assigned to the universe, mutually exclusive and collectively exhaustive. Our only assumption as to the mutual relations of x and x was, that, whatever x stood for,—and it might stand for almost anything we pleased,—x should stand for the rest which constituted the 'all' of which we took account.

Current logical prepossessions, fortified by the suggestions furnished in many of the examples which we have had occasion to employ, will have disposed most readers to put a special interpretation upon the nature of this logical universe, the insufficiency of which must now be pointed out. For one thing it will probably be assumed that x and x, &c. stand for classes of things as opposed to individuals; that is, that they are in their actual usage, what we have indeed commonly called them, *class terms.* And again, it will, I think, be tacitly assumed that the whole group of things referred to in the universe will generally be possessors in common of some substratum of attributes, however they may be differentiated from one another by the presence and absence of other attri butes.

The removal of the first of these restrictions will not give much trouble, since very familiar admissions on the part of the Common Logic have already prepared the way. It is fully recognized everywhere that the 'class' represented by a term in our propositions may be an individual: what is not so commonly recognized is the fact that the contradictory of that class may also be nothing more than another individual; that is, that we may reject the old doctrine as to the infini tude of a negative term, which still survives in so many quarters. Of course, if our universe were very wide, the selection out of it of one individual would leave a miscellane ous host behind, but there is no necessity that the universe should be thus wide. Look, for instance, at the expression $xy + xy$. There is nothing to hinder us from restricting our universe here to Mr Gladstone and Lord Beaconsfield, and to the fact of their being in or out of office. Whichever then of the two statesmen we mark by x, the other will be marked by x; and if we indicate the fact of being in office by y, then that of being out of office will be indicated by y. Hence the formula $1 = xy + xy$ simply asserts the fact that one of them must be in office and the other out of it. When this statement is combined with our standard formal condition, $1 = xy + xy + xy + xy$, we have $xy = 0, xy = 0$, indicating that both cannot be in office together, nor both out of office

together.   All this is simply a matter of application or inter
pretation of our rules, it in no way touches their formal
validity.

The other restriction which has to be laid aside may
perhaps demand a little more explanation.   When dealing
with classes of things, especially in common conversation, it
is so usual to group things together only when they are some
what homogeneous, that we come to assume almost as a
matter of course that the objects composing these classes
have, so to say, a deep bottom in common, with only a super
ficial diversity.   For instance, the kind of concrete example
which people would naturally fit in to the formal framework
$xy + xy$ would be, say, 'French who are not Catholics and
Catholics who are not French'.   If so, it is clear that the
great bulk of the attributes involved are common to these
two mutually exclusive classes, those which differentiate
them being by comparison few.   And this will mostly be the
case, except when we designedly stretch our universe beyond
the habitual reference of common thought, and make it
approximate towards the logician's limits of what is con
ceivable.

The grounds of the belief that these represent the most
appropriate kind of logical example lie far down in the neces
sities of language, and the physical and mental causes which
have produced them.   They seem to me connected with the
general practice of making the subject and the predicate in
most cases nearly correspond respectively to substance and
attribute.   In affirmation at any rate, if not in negation, we
commonly regard the subject as a *thing* endowed with miscel
laneous and indefinitely numerous attributes, the function of
the predicate being to modify the subject by adding on one
or more fresh attributes.   The leading conception is through
out that of a substratum of permanent qualities with a

relatively small number of differentiating ones. The ordinary logician has done something to liberalize our usage in this respect, but not with very great success, the grammarian being rather too powerful for him. We encounter the difficulty, for instance, in conversion[1], for when we want to make the subject and predicate change places the proprieties of language greatly thwart our logical rules. 'Some men are passionate', has to be changed into 'Some passionate (persons, things, or what not) are men'. We feel it necessary, so to say, to *weight* the subject, since it sounds awkward to have a slight subject with a heavy predicate attached to it[2]. Propriety of language suggests that the subject should contain the bulk of the attributes; should, in fact, be by comparison a substance of some kind modified by attributes.

Recur for a minute to the example about the French Catholics. This might be written in the form: 'Men (whether French and not-Catholic, or Catholic and not-French)': in which the bulk of the attributes, namely those conveyed by 'men', are common to both the distinct classes. So customary is it thus to group homogeneous things, that the forms of language tend to keep up the illusion of it even when there is no reality underlying them. They succeed in doing this in one or two different ways. Let, for instance, our terms and their contradictories stand for the presence and the absence of two men A and B; what constant common element is there throughout the expression $xy + xy$? Its two elements stand respectively for 'the presence of A and the absence of B', and 'the absence of A and the presence of B'; and these have really nothing in common. But when we

---

[1] Mr Macfarlane has called attention to this in his *Algebra of Logic*, p. 14.

[2] De Morgan has humorously enquired why we should not speak of "the horseness of the speed" as well as of "the speed of the horse." (*Camb. Phil. Trans.* x. 340.)

group these together we should very commonly talk of 'the case of' A being present and B absent, just as we talked about 'the men' whether Catholics or not. But the one phrase does, and the other does not, imply a real substratum of attributes, that is, of relevant attributes, in common.

In other instances this device of language is less thinly veiled. Thus if $xy + xy$ stand for 'wind without rain' and 'rain without wind', we should very probably apply the common word 'weather' to both cases, by speaking of the weather being windy and not rainy or rainy and not windy. But the wind and the rain together *are* the weather, or at most some additional phenomena of the same kind must be called for in order to constitute all that is signified by the word. The constituent elements therefore in the logical expression have really little or nothing in common, and the common word prefixed to them all alike is scarcely more than a device of language.

Whether or not this interpretation of the above examples be accepted, they will equally serve to call attention to an extremely important generalization upon which we now have to insist. It is indeed difficult to exaggerate the importance of the step before us, since its due realization is, to my think ing, quite the most valuable speculative advantage to be gained by the study of a generalized Logic. It has come under our notice incidentally more than once already, but must now be deliberately insisted on.

Our present position then is this. Starting with the familiar conception of classes composed of an indefinite num ber of individuals, we found that we could conveniently express the desired logical relations of these classes by aid of a set of symbols, borrowed, as it happens, from mathematics. But those who call in the aid of symbols generally find that they have got possession of a machine which is capable of doing a great deal more work, and even very different kinds of work, besides what they originally expected from it. To the mathematician, of course, this is perfectly familiar. Indeed the history of the formal part of his science is in great part an account of the successive extensions opened out by new interpretations and applications of the same set of formal rules[1]. Sometimes the machine needs a slight structural alteration to enable it to perform its new work :—thus, in mathematics, in order to make our algebraic symbols do Quaternion work we have to suspend the commutative law. But, as a rule, we retain the old laws unchanged, merely looking out for new work which they are fitted to perform.

This then is the step now before us in Logic. Look again at our fundamental formula, $1 = xy + x\bar{y} + \bar{x}y + \bar{x}\bar{y}$. It may be quite true that when we first appealed to it we only had in view such classes of things as those denoted by general names. But a little reflection soon convinces us that the symbols have wider capabilities. All that they imperatively demand is that the various elements xy, $\bar{x}y$, and so forth, shall be mutually exclusive and collectively exhaustive, and that they shall obey those few simple laws of operation described in the second chapter. Our formal framework may have been originally devised to cover a system of classes each composed of a plurality of individuals, but now that we have acquired it we find that it is best regarded as simply a scheme of contradictories of a certain kind, subject to certain laws, and that it will therefore cover any set of contradictories which fulfil the same requirements.

As we do not at present propose to admit anything that can be called a structural change in our symbolic machine, by

---

[1] In accordance with what is sometimes called the Principle of the Permanence of Equivalent Forms.

modifying the laws of operation[1], all that we have to do is to see how many of the tacit or customary restrictions upon the nature of a 'class' can be laid aside without affecting the validity of our symbolic operations. Now a moment's consi deration will show that such restrictions as those noticed towards the commencement of this chapter are of no signifi cance whatever. Whether xy and xy have any attributes in common; whether they stand for indefinitely numerous groups, for definite groups, or for individuals; is indifferent. Accordingly we may generalize without hesitation up to this extent.

But a good deal more than this can be done by our dis carding any obligation on the part of the symbols to represent material objects at all. Let x, for instance, denote the truth of a given proposition and x its falsity. This assumption (as will presently be shown in more detail) will fit in excellently with all our requirements. We should then have to interpret the expression $xy + xy$ as representing the alternative of the truth of one, and one only, of the two propositions referred to by x and y. Again, we might understand by x something abstract, but still more complex, by regarding it as represent ing the validity of some whole train of argument. In this case x stands for the invalidity of the same argument, that is, for its failure to establish its conclusion, whether that conclu sion in itself be true or false. Combine these symbols with others of a like significance, and we have at once expressions for the combination of arguments sound and unsound. Thus xyz might stand for the validity of the two arguments indi cated by x and z, and the invalidity of that indicated by y.

Again, we may set the symbols to stand for the trust worthiness of assigned witnesses. Thus if x stand for some man's trustworthiness, x will stand for the contradiction of

[1] This question will have to be discussed in the next chapter.

this, viz. for his untrustworthiness, and therefore indicates that we have so far no grounds of opinion either for or against the fact testified. A distinct case from this last is produced by letting x stand for the *truthfulness* of the witness, that is, for the fact that his statement is actually true. This leads to some difference of interpretation throughout our use of the pair of contradictories x and x. The antithesis now is not merely between the fact of a thing being established and not being established, but between its having actually happened and not having happened. Hence combinations admissible under the former interpretation may become inadmissible under the latter. To say that the witness is untrue implies that his statement is false ; to say that he is untrustworthy leaves a way open to either the truth or falsehood of his statement. Problems belonging to these latter classes play a large part, under numerical treatment, in the Theory of Probability[1], but do not deserve any special notice in a purely logical treatise.

It must not be assumed that the interpretations above indicated represent the only ones available for us, or even the only suitable kinds. It would be the height of temerity to maintain that a symbolic apparatus will only do those kinds of work for which we may have happened at present to find it capable. But the reader will readily trace the same formal antithesis between ' is ' and ' is not ', and the perma nency of the same laws of operation, throughout the whole field of available application, whatever its extent may be. It must be clearly understood that none of these various interpretations can be regarded as giving rise to anything deserving the name of a distinct scheme or system. Symbo lically, the scheme is absolutely one and the same through-

---

[1] A very good account of the meaning and consequences of the distinction in question is to be found in De Morgan's *Formal Logic* (p. 191).

out. Indeed, if we abstract sufficiently, we can also say that there is only one and the same *interpretation* throughout, for in every case we deal with the various combinations in which 'presences' and 'absences' may be arranged. To the one formal framework built up out of x and x and the like, corresponds the verbal framework which may be built up out of *Yes* and *No* variously combined and applied. Symbolically and verbally, alike, there is in each case a primary and necessary scheme of possibilities, which is limited by the accidental and material conditions afforded by the data.

Amongst all the various interpretations which are thus opened out to us in the use of our symbols, there is one which deserves particular notice, both from the generality of its possible application and the special nomenclature to which it leads. It is that in which the symbols stand for propositions, i.e. for their truth or falsehood. That this interpretation could be imposed upon the symbolic processes did not escape the penetration of Boole[1]. He seems to have regarded it however as yielding a perfectly distinct set of meanings which, so to say, happened to fit in with his method, by being subject to the same set of laws. He devotes a large part of his volume to their consideration, under the head of 'secondary

---

[1] In a certain sense the employment of single letters to denote whole propositions has often been adopted in Logic. Some writers have carried this out very systematically, with a special notation to denote the contradictory of any proposition. For instance, Maass (*Grundriss der Logik*, 1793) has used Arabic letters to stand for ordinary subjects and predicates and Greek letters to stand for whole judgments or propositions. Thus, if we wished to represent the whole judgment 'all a is b' as a single element, we should put the letter a, say, to stand for it, and na to stand for its contradictory. Some of the deductions on this mode of notation will be familiar to readers of De Morgan and other modern symbolists: e.g. 'when β follows from a, and is false, then a must be false too; when β follows from a, γ, δ... together, and is false, then a, γ, δ... cannot all be true, and so on' (p. 126).

propositions', and discusses the definitions and deduces the laws of operation independently for them, as he did at the outset for the more familiar application to classes of things. This mode of treatment, combined with his rather far-fetched and unnecessary doctrine (as it seems to me) that propositions of this secondary kind were somehow interpretable in terms of *time,* has probably contributed to make some writers forget how completely Boole had grasped the possibility of this interpretation of his symbolic methods[1]. There is much in

[1] This seems to me to be the case as regards the scheme of Mr H. Maccoll, as described in the *Proc. of the London Math. Society* (Vols. IX., X.), and in *Mind*, No. XVI. After a careful study of it, aided by a long correspondence with the author, I am unable to find much more in it than the introduction of one more scheme of notation to express certain modifications and simplifications of a part of Boole's system:—to which however one exception should be made in respect of a real improvement in notation to be presently noticed. That he should have worked it out, as he assures us is the case, in comparative ignorance of what had been already done in this way, is, no doubt, proof of considerable sagacity and originality. (The general view which he adopts as to the nature of propositions in their symbolic treatment is that which may be called the implication view as contrasted with the equation view. Some account of this distinction is given in the concluding chapter.)

On this particular point the case seems to me to be as follows. Boole gave two distinct interpretations to his symbols; in one of these x is regarded as a class of things, and in the other as a proposition. Those who have followed in his steps have, broadly speaking, confined themselves to one only of these interpretations (or rather to a part only of one, for they have not admitted any special signs for *inverse* operations). Thus Mr Maccoll makes it a "cardinal point" of distinction in his scheme that "every single letter, as well as every combination of letters, always denotes a *statement*", and this he somehow conceives to "necessitate an essentially different treatment of the whole subject". Prof. Jevons, on the other hand, though not expressly defining his position here, invariably confines his interpretation, unless I am mistaken, to what may be called the material class view of the symbols.

My only complaint against Boole on this point is that even he did not generalize sufficiently. Doubtless he directed attention to what are far

his treatment of this part of the subject which invites criticism, but as we are here concerned with Symbolic Logic itself rather than with the particular opinions held by its main originator, I pass these by wherever it is possible.

It may be well to go a little more into the details of this interpretation, starting with the most general symbolic statement where two terms are combined, viz. $xy + x\bar{y} + \bar{x}y + \bar{x}\bar{y} = 1$. As there are supposed to be two propositions involved we may at once, for the sake of distinction and brevity, call them the propositions x and y. We might have described the propositions as A and B, or as I and II, respectively, so as to employ different symbols for the proposition itself and for the fact of its being true ; but the two-fold application of the same symbol cannot possibly lead to confusion in the processes of working. We say then that the symbol x standing for the truth of the one proposition, and y standing for that of the other, the left side of the symbolic equation represents the only four possibilities. Its four component elements stand for the truth of both propositions (xy), the truth of x and falsity of y $(x\bar{y})$, the truth of y and falsity of x $(\bar{x}y)$, and the falsity of both $(\bar{x}\bar{y})$.

What then is here the signification of *unity*, or 1? In the general formulæ as hitherto interpreted, unity stands for the sum-total of all the individuals composing all the possible classes, in other words for our universe. The best verbal account perhaps, in the present application, is given by saying that it stands for the sum-total of possibilities or possible cases. The formula asserts that the four cases above enumerated, as to the truth and falsity of x and y, exhaust the whole field of possibilities. Of course the actual limits of

the most important interpretations, but I prefer to regard even these as constituting only a portion of what is potentially an indefinitely wide field of application.

this field, that is, of this universe, have to be assigned on the same principles as in the more familiar case. It may be that the propositions are necessarily true or false, in which case the universe is altogether unlimited. It may be that they are true only under certain conditions,—conditions of time, of place, of circumstance, or what not,—the universe of possi bilities is then limited by these considerations. The deter mination of this question really ranks as part of our data; it is one of the elements of information which we must assume to be contributed to the solution of the problem; for clearly the general symbolic laws can no more throw light upon the material limits within which they are to be held to apply, than they can upon the special signification which it is pro posed to assign to the terms.

So with the sign for *nothing*, or 0. Just as it is elsewhere interpreted 'no individual', so here it means 'no possibility'. At least this seems the best verbal translation; though, as the symbolist has to reckon with the grammarian, he is often somewhat put to it in trying to express himself unambiguous ly and yet without reproach. We may say then that $x = 0$ indicates that within our determinate field, that is, subject to our determinate conditions, there is no possibility for the pro position x; that that proposition is false. So $x - 1$ indicates that there is nothing but such possibility, that that proposi tion is true. It will be seen therefore that the question whether the proposition is, in common parlance, 'necessarily' true is of very little importance. If we like to interpret the symbol 1, in $x = 1$, as meaning 'everywhere and always', then x may be regarded presumably as a necessary proposition; if we interpret it as meaning 'at some specified or definite time or place,' then x is merely empirically true.

The reader will be able without much difficulty to work out this view into all its details. He must bear in mind that this is not a process of original legislation, but simply one of interpretation. We are not recurring to the business of settling the general employment of our terms and operations; —this was done once for all at the outset ;—but merely con sidering now what is the most suitable phraseology for trans lating and describing our results in one well-marked and distinctive group of cases. We see at once, for instance, that $x + x = 1$ should be interpreted as saying that either a propo sition or its contradictory must certainly be true, and that $xx = 0$ asserts that a proposition and its contradictory cannot both be true. Again $xy - 1$ (implying, as it does, $x = 1, y - 1$) necessarily leads to the truth of both propositions. But $xy = 0$ only insures the denial of the particular compound xy ; that is, it tells us that both propositions cannot be true, so that it leaves three possibilities open ; viz. that either of the two, or both together, may be false. We see this more plainly by looking at the alternative or disjunctive side. From $1 = xy + xy + xy + xy$ blot out xy, and we have as remainder $1 = xy + xy + xy$. That is, if we deny that both the proposi tions are true, we are reduced to the three alternatives, that one at least, or both, must be false. Blot out xy and xy and we have $1 = xy + xy$. That is, if we can deny that 'x and y are both true', and also that 'x is true and y false', we are led to the conclusion that either x is false and y true, or else that x is false and y false. In other words x must be false, and y doubtful, so far as this information goes.

In proposing 'All x is y' and 'If x is true y is true', respectively, as the most natural pair of interpretations of the formula $xy = 0$ (or its equivalents $x = xy, x = \frac{0}{0} y$) according as we submit it to the class explanation or the proposition explanation, we know that we have to face a good deal of ad verse association. The two interpretations meet the shock at somewhat different points ; the former when it maintains that 'All x is y' covers the case of there being no x or no y, and the latter in maintaining that 'If x is true y is true' covers the case of y having no connexion whatever with x provided only y is known to be true. That is, the former has a difficulty in carrying the extreme values $x - 0$, $y = 0$, and the latter in carrying the extreme value $y = 1$.

The general propriety of admitting, or rather the necessity of insisting upon the admission of, both these extreme values, has been fully discussed already (see chh. VI., XVI.) and needs no further justification. But the language in which they are sometimes expressed, upon the special propositional interpre tation now under review, needs notice, since it seems to me to involve a needless violence to popular association. We have seen that we can stretch the language of hypothesis in the phrase 'If x then y' to reach the case of y being certain : I think it will just reach this. But is it not going even further to try to do the same with the word *implication ?* The phrase 'x implies y' surely 'implies' that the facts con cerned are known to be connected, or that the one proposition is formally inferrible from the other.

It is of course solely to the *word* 'implication' that I am objecting, the results themselves being a matter of symbolic necessity. As regards the particular notation employed by Mr Maccoll (the writer here principally referred to) one ad vantage must be admitted, though I think that it is far out weighed by the general advantages of the system mainly introduced by Boole. He expresses 'x implies y' by $x : y$, and employs an accent to mark negation, so that $x : y$ means 'x implies the contradiction of y'. Under the peculiar interpre tation of 'implication' just adverted to, the formula $x : y$ be comes the precise equivalent of $xy = 0$ (and its substitutes $x = xy$, $x = \frac{0}{0} y$); for the meaning of any one of these formulæ is exhausted when we have said that it excludes x not-y, and consequently admits the three remaining alternatives. The one merit of Mr Maccoll's notation is, I think, in the symmetry with which it expresses compound implications; thus $(x:y):(z:w)$ would be read off 'the fact that x implies y implies the fact that z implies w', with of course the same peculiar interpretation of 'implication' all through[1]. It would be a mistake to suppose that the expression of compound implications of this kind is in any way restricted to this style of notation :—as has been already shown, our expression of the same relation between the symbols in question is $(1 - xy)\, zw - 0$. In this case the implicational mode of expression certainly tells its tale more simply and obviously ; but this is not always the case. For instance, the condition $(x:y)(y:z):(x:z)$ is read off 'the combination of the implication of y by x, and z by y, leads to the implication of z by x'. On our plan of expression this would stand $xz = xy\,.\,z + x\,.\,yz$. This expression is intuitively obvious (remembering that $y + y = 1$) and shows the dependence of $xz = 0$ upon $xy = 0$ and $yz = 0$ better, to my thinking, than the other rendering does.

It was intimated at the outset of this chapter that every statement could be thrown into the form of the truth of some corresponding proposition. Whether it will be convenient or not to adopt this plan depends upon circumstances. Sometimes it seems to be a matter of pure indifference, amounting

---

[1] The earliest attempt at the expression of compound hypothetical propositions, in this kind of way, that I have seen, is by Maimon: "Hypothetische Sätze können durch das algebraische Verhältnisszeichen (:) angedeutet werden." Thus, with his employment of + to mark affirmation, the proposition 'If a is b then c is d' is represented by $a + b : c + d$ (*Versuch einer neuen Logik*, p. 69), but he does not work this out any further. The first to attempt it systematically was probably R. Grassmann (*Begriffslehre*), but there are decided defects in his procedure. The neat and effective rendering of a number of compound implications of this description is the best feature in Mr Maccoll's papers.

at most to a trifling verbal change, sometimes such a render
ing represents a distinct economy of language and labour,
sometimes the reverse.   As an instance of the class of cases
in which either mode of interpretation does equally well, we
might take the following:—

It will either blow a gale to-morrow or the mail will start.

He will go if the mail starts.

∴ If he does not go it will blow a gale.

This may be written out symbolically, thus,

$$\begin{cases} x + \bar{x}y = 1, \\ \qquad yz = 0, \end{cases}$$
$$\therefore xz = 0 \text{ or } \bar{z} = \tfrac{0}{0}\, x.$$

(This may be worked out as follows:—substitute the
value of y, viz. $y - \tfrac{0}{0} z$, obtained by the second equation, in
the first, and we have $x + \tfrac{0}{0} xz = 1$, or $x = \tfrac{0}{0} xz$, ∴ $xz = 0$.)

Here it surely represents such a trifling difference as
hardly to be worth notice in a system of Logic, whether we
say, Let x represent the blowing of a gale, and y the starting of
the mail; or say, Let x represent the proposition that it will
blow a gale and y the corresponding proposition about the
starting of the mail.

Now consider a case in which the proposition explanation
seems decidedly less appropriate.   Take the familiar syllo
gism;—

No B is C,

All A is B,

∴ No A is C.

The most natural course here, upon the propositional ex
planation now under discussion, would be to put a single
symbol for each of these propositions.   Let them be repre
sented respectively by x, y, z; so that $x = 1$ is to assert the
truth of 'No B is C', $y = 1$ that of 'All A is B', and $z = 1$
that of 'No A is C'.   It is clear that we are at once brought
to a complete standstill symbolically, for nothing having been

assigned by way of connexion between x, y, and z, no conclu
sion about one of them can be elicited from the other two.
If from $x = 0$ and $y - 0$ we could infer directly that $z = 0$, we
should have produced a great simplification; but clearly the
only way of deducing this is to go through the syllogistic pro
cess.   If we did this we should be found to be taking a rather
roundabout course by introducing any special symbols for the
entire propositions.   The simplest plan would of course be to
write our propositions down fully in the ordinary way, putting
x, y, and z, for A, B, C themselves directly instead of for pro
positions about them, thus;—

$$yz = 0,$$
$$\begin{cases} x\bar{y} = 0, & \therefore xz = {}^{0}_{0}\, yz = 0. \end{cases}$$

For these represent the real relations between the proposi
tions, and they must therefore be introduced somehow if any
conclusion has to be drawn.

Accordingly those who adhere to the uniform propositional
rendering of our symbols have to state the syllogism some
what as follows;—Let x stand for the statement, made in
reference to any object, 'it is A', y for 'it is B', z for 'it is C'.
The premise 'No B is C' then takes the form $yz = 0$ or one
of its equivalents; 'All A is B' becomes $xy = 0$, and so on.
In fact this rendering simply gives us the ordinary symbolic
statement over again, with a slightly different and, as it seems
to me, more cumbrous interpretation attached to it.

The cases in which this particular interpretation of our
symbols is distinctly the most appropriate, seem to me to be
almost confined to questions of Probability, and therefore I
pass them by without special illustration.   In the works of
De Morgan and Boole a variety of examples will be found
which afford convenient exemplifications of the modes of
combining statements, arguments, and reports of witnesses.
It was indeed for the purpose of improving the Calculus of
Probabilities that Boole mainly worked out his system.

CHAPTER XIX.

VARIATIONS IN SYMBOLIC PROCEDURE.

In the system of Symbolic Logic, as we have throughout expounded it, nothing amounting to what may be called *structural* variation has been admitted into our laws of procedure. Two chapters indeed have been largely devoted to explaining certain extensions of the interpretation of our terms, but the laws which govern the combination and arrangement of the terms have been preserved unchanged. But having done this it will be well now to direct attention to some other ways of regarding and expounding the subject, in which changes of the latter kind are introduced. These grow out of three different causes which will have to be dis cussed separately : (1) the plan of writing alternatives in the non-exclusive fashion, (2) the attempt to interpret our terms intensively instead of extensively, and (3) the attempt to extend our rules so as to embrace what is called the Logic of Relatives; that is, of relative terms as distinguished from mere class terms.

I. As regards the first of these departures from our sys tem something was said in the second chapter. So to clear the ground from confusion I will merely remind the reader briefly that we have nothing whatever now to do with questions of usage in popular language, or of logical tradition. What we have to discuss is purely a question of symbolic procedure. There are two classes, x and y, before us, which, for aught we know, may overlap one another; and it is taken for granted by all parties that we do not intend to reckon the common part twice over. Is it better to express the whole class, formed by the aggregation of the two, in the form of $x + y$ or in that of $x + xy$? In other words, shall we leave it to be understood that the common part xy is not reckoned twice over, or shall we explicitly and formally reject any such double reckoning by putting our symbolic alternatives into a mutually exclusive shape?

There is no doubt that a logical system can be developed, to a certain extent, upon either plan, so that our choice turns upon a balance of comparative advantages. A simple example will serve to illustrate this. It is of course universally agreed, in all such cases, that $xx = x$; that is, that the repetition of a class-name twice or oftener leaves the class unaltered. And this must hold equally when the class is an aggregate, built up of alternatives connected by *and, or*, and such other particles. That is, we must secure that

$$(x \text{ or } y)\,(x \text{ or } y) = (x \text{ or } y).$$

Suppose it were laid down that all politicians are knaves or fools, and that all in office are so too; then the politicians in office are expressed by (knaves or fools) (knaves or fools), and this must be the same as simply (knaves or fools), whatever may be the symbolic procedure by which we equate these expressions, and whether a knave can be a fool or not. This is what popular thought distinctly contemplates, and the symbols must follow suit, so far at least as their final result is concerned.

But although the final result is not affected by the way in which we connect x and y, yet there is a decided difference in the process of reaching that result, according as we adopt one plan or the other. On Boole's plan, of course, when we know that the classes x and y are not exclusive, or do not know that they are so, we write $(x + xy)(x + xy)$. The ordinary processes of algebraic multiplication being then employed (subject to the one bye-law, $xx = x$) we have at once the simple result $(x + xy)$. On the other plan we start with $(x + y)(x + y)$, which if multiplied out by the same rules would yield $x + 2xy + y$. To reduce this to $x + y$ as required, we invoke a second bye-law, or special logical restriction, expressible in the words,—'A and A are the same as A'. Since xy is a part of x, and of y, the logical addition of it to either of these does not actually add anything; the apparent addendum being absorbed without enlarging the result. This being known to be the case we naturally do not go through the form of fully multiplying out, but recognize at once that the addition of any term or part of any term already included in a given aggregate class, is altogether inoperative.

It must be admitted that the verdict, so far as regards the number of writers is concerned, is against Boole. The first proposer of the 'x or y', as contrasted with the 'x or xy' form, was probably Leibnitz[1]; for here, as on so many other logical

---

[1] "$A + B \infty L$ significat A inesse ipsi L, vel contineri a L...Etsi A et B habeant aliquid commune, ita ut ambo simul sumta sint majora ipso L, nihilominus locum habebunt quæ hoc loco diximus aut dicemus" (*Specimen demonstrandi*, Erdmann, p. 94).

Ploucquet again says much the same. Having obtained the result $nA + nA = m + b$, he goes on; "da aber $nA + nA$ nur eine Zeichenwiederholung, nicht aber eine Sachwiederholung ist [a clear and terse way of putting it] so kommt $nA = m + b$". (*Sammlung*, p. 254;—but the context involves several misconceptions.)

To those who looked upon A and B as standing for *notions* or *attributes*, rather than for classes, it seems to me that such a view as this was most natural, and indeed almost

points, we find that he had already proffered some suggestive
hints. Prof. Jevons was the first to call attention promi
nently to this view, in his *Pure Logic* (1864), where he
pointed out the duality of logical formulæ which resulted;
i.e. $A + A = A$, and $AA = A$. A much fuller exposition of
this dual characteristic was given by R. Grassmann, who in
his *Begriffslehre* (1872) has worked out a number of formulæ
in illustration of the parallelism between logical multipli
cation and logical addition. Mr C. S. Peirce has adopted the
same non-exclusive mode of connecting the symbols in his
various papers. So has Mr Maccoll. And Prof. Schroder has
recently given an extensive and elegant development of
Grassmann's results, proceeding on the same general plan,
and exhibiting the parallel formulæ in double columns, so as
to bring them under the eye at a glance (*Operationskreis des
Logikkalkuls*, 1877). To these may be added Prof. Wundt, in
the short account which he has given (*Logik*, 1880) of the
principles of Symbolic Logic. I proceed to give a brief
statement of my reasons for preferring the Boolian form
adopted in this work.

(1) In the first place then we thus bring our logical
usage into better harmony with that of mathematics generally.
In every employment of symbols it seems desirable that they
should be employed as far as possible with mechanical facility.
Their *sense* may be varied or extended from time to time
without harm, but their *laws* ought if possible to be retained
unaltered. It may be urged indeed that since we have
already introduced one innovation we ought not to complain
of a second; that, in fact, $x + x - x$ is no more of a license

obligatory; the non-repetition of the
attribute is only a case of "the one
in the many". Lambert, however,
so far as he is explicit here, rather
takes the opposite view:—"man

drücke die eigenen Merkmale des a
durch $a \mid b$ aus, und die eigenen Merkmale des b durch $b \mid a$; so hat man
$a \mid b + b \mid a + ab + ab = a + b$" (*Log. Abhandlungen*, I. 11).

than $xx = x$. The cases however do not seem to me to be at all the same, the former being far the more serious departure of the two. Amid all the various significations of the sign $+$ in mathematics, it is always assumed that it connects ex clusive symbols; that is, whether A and B be magnitudes or operations or anything else, in $A + B$, it is taken for granted that B begins, so to say, at the point where A leaves off, or that otherwise the common part is doubly reckoned. To depart from this usage seems therefore a more serious step than to confine ourselves to what is after all merely a limiting or special case of a general formula.

(2) But again there is a special anomaly, in respect of one detail, which follows from this usage. If $x + x = x$ gene rally, it must also hold in the limiting case of x standing for the universe of discourse. Accordingly we must either forego the use of *unity* for this universe (which offers certain decided advantages for this purpose, and which there is a very preva lent consent in adopting)[1], or we must face the direct conflict with all arithmetical association implied in the acceptance of $1 + 1 = 1$.

(3) Again, the arrangement in mutual exclusives is much more convenient, if it is not absolutely necessary, in many applications of our Logic. I have said more than once already that Logic itself is concerned only with the relations of classes to one another, or with their existence and non-

---

[1] I have already pointed out that *unity* is not invariably used as the symbol of the universe (ch. VIII. p. 189). But, even when it is not, some of the results that have to be faced on this system are, to say the least of it, rather startling. Thus R. Grass-mann has $a + T = T$, and $aT = a$; and Mr C. S. Pierce has $a + \infty = \infty$, and $a \times \infty = a$. Professor Jevons, in his later works, avoids this particular awkwardness, but at the cost of introducing a new symbol ($\cdot |\cdot$) instead of ($+$). He reads $A \cdot|\cdot A = A$; but does not, I think, employ any special symbol for the logical uni-verse.

existence, and not at all with any valuation or enumeration
of their contents.   But nevertheless when we come to *apply*
our formulæ questions of number or quantity may have to be
taken into account, and then it appears absolutely necessary
that each sub-class be made exclusive of all the rest.   Take,
for instance, such problems as those of which Prof. Jevons has
discussed a sample under the name of Numerical Logic
(*Pr. of Science*, p. 169), as any of those which play so large
a part in Mr Macfarlane's volume, or, still more, as those
problems in Probability which Boole justly regarded as the
crowning triumph of his system.   I have avoided discussing
these applications myself, because they seem to lie outside
the bounds of strictly Formal Logic, yet they certainly are
important applications.   But whenever we take into account
the number of individuals included in x or y, or the relative
magnitude in extension of these classes to one another, or the
numerical probability of x and y as propositions, in such an
expression as $x + y$, we run the risk of counting the common
part twice over.   Indeed we cannot well avoid this double
reckoning except by writing the aggregate in the form $x + xy$.
But if many applications of our formulæ demand this caution,
it would appear that this, as being the more general method,
is the safest and best to adopt throughout.

(4)   But there is another reason still, which seems to me
the strongest of all.   I have urged throughout that the prin
cipal merit of the Symbolic System consists in the speculative
questions to which it introduces us ; the nature and object of
symbolic language, as such, being one of the most important
of these questions.   Now none of those beautiful generaliza
tions introduced by Boole,—such as the formula for Develop
ment and that for Elimination,—can (so far as has yet been
shown) be admitted, unless we adopt his principles of notation
in this respect.

In saying this, I do not mean that these formulæ cannot be employed up to a certain point on either system of notation. Indeed we have shown, in a former chapter, how the formula for Development is a convenient means of determining whether or not a class expression is duly stated. Thus expand $x + y$ and we obtain the element $2xy$, showing that this element was doubly reckoned; if therefore we omit the factor 2 from it the result will be in accordance with the other scheme. That is, when *we* write $x + y$ it denotes what both parties would express in detail by $xy + xy + 2xy$; when *they* write $x + y$ it denotes what both parties would express in detail by $xy + xy + xy$. A correction therefore has to be inserted in order to make the same symbolic rule yield these two different results. But this being the case it is hardly correct to speak of applying the same formula except when the original elements were actually exclusive, whether formally or materially. Thus Boole's rule would apply, on either system, to such an expression as $x + xy$; or to $x + y$ in case we happened to know that 'No x is y', but not otherwise[1].

Where we should most feel our loss is in the treatment of

[1] As a further illustration of the different interpretation which results, when the same expression is dealt with on these two plans, take the following;—$x + y = z + w$. Both plans agree up to a certain point, in regarding it as a statement that the class comprised by x and y together is the same as that comprised by z and w together. But *our* rules demand a further condition, viz.; that the doubly reckoned part must also be the same, that is (as the reader will see) that $xy = zw$, as we should otherwise be equating disparate things in case they do not both vanish.

(Of course if both xy and wz vanish, then x and y, as also z and w, are exclusives.) Leibnitz had clearly realized the fact that we cannot subtract in Logic except when we are dealing with mutual exclusives ("incommunicantia"). Thus, "Si $A + B \infty C + D$, et $A \infty C$, erit $B \infty D$, modo A et B itemque C et D sint incommunicantia" (Erdmann, p. 96. The sign ∞ corresponds to our $=$). Again on the same principle he solves the problem, "Sit $A \infty A$, dico reperiri posse duo B et N sic ut B non sit ∞N et tamen $A + B$ sit $\infty A + N$" (*ib.* 97).

inverse determinations. Thus the power of subtraction or exception is lost, at least as a general procedure. For in stance, if we have $x + y = z$ we cannot conclude that $x = z - y$ unless we know that x and y are entirely clear of one another. We should have to substitute $x = z - xy$; in other words we must reintroduce the exclusive mode of notation, or abandon the right of transposing a term from one side to the other with its sign changed. Prof. Schroder meets the diffi culty by the insertion of a correcting element in the perform ance of the subtraction. Thus "$(a + b) - b = a - ab$ or $a - b$; correcting element, $- ab$ or $- b$" (*Operationskreis*, p. 34); but by others the right of subtraction is resigned.

So again, we lose in respect of the analogue of division. Even here indeed something more might be done than actually is done by the advocates of the other scheme. There is no reason whatever why the explanation, offered in the third chapter, should not be retained for such an expression as $\dfrac{x}{y}$, so as to develop it into $xy + \frac{0}{0}xy$, if the aversion to the employment of $\frac{0}{0}$ can be surmounted. We might adopt the same treatment with more complex expressions, for instance $\dfrac{x + y}{x + z}$, if we first retranslate the meaning into one which is consistent with the non-exclusive interpretation; though here, as in a paragraph above, we cannot be said to employ one and the same really general symbolic formula in the two cases respectively. So again, with $\dfrac{x}{y}$, we might say that what $x - y$ *means* is 'x which is not y', or xy, and therefore resolve the fraction into the correct result $xy + \frac{0}{0}xy$. But in all such cases the necessity of the retranslation invalidates the true generality of the formula $f(x) = f(1) x + f(0) x$.

Probably more than this could be done to introduce the

employment of inverse expressions, and to make partial appli
cation of Boole's general rules to their treatment, on the par
ticular scheme now under notice. But naturally those who
feel independent objections to that scheme will hardly find
themselves called upon to work it out in detail. The general
formula for Elimination, $f(1)f(0) = 0$, does not seem to be
thus capable of introduction except under restrictions which
almost amount to doing without it altogether.

What then are the advantages of the non-exclusive plan
to set against these disadvantages? Sound and thoughtful
advocates of the former plead as follows in its favour.

(1) For one thing there is its superior brevity. It is
decidedly shorter to write $x + y$ than to write $x + xy$, and
when we throw the latter into the symmetrical form
$(xy + xy + xy)$ the contrast is greater still. And this dif
ference would be increased if we were to compare such
abbreviations as those recently introduced by R. Grassmann,
Prof. Schroder, and Mr Maccoll, some of which were noticed
in the last chapter, with the processes by which Boole did as
a matter of fact work out his conclusions :—though clearly
such a comparison would not be a fair test of the rival plans
of notation. I quite appreciate the value of such brevity ;
and have already said that if the mere attainment of results
were the main object in Logic, as is more nearly the case in
mathematics, such considerations would greatly gain in weight.
They would indeed probably turn the scale. But as things
are in Logic, with speculative considerations overwhelmingly
preponderant, I attach very little importance to mere brevity
of procedure ; though, as the reader will have often noticed in
the course of this work, there are plenty of legitimate re
sources for avoiding the excessive prolixity of Boole's actual
procedure.

(2) There is also a certain speculative attraction in

working out the dualistic symmetry which results from the two rules $A + A = A$, and $AA = A$. The reader will find these given in some detail in the short treatises of Grassmann and Schroder[1]. For instance the formulæ

If $ab = a$ If $a + b = b$
then $a + b = b$,   then $ab = a$,

are thus correspondent to one another. So again

$$(a + u)^- = au, \qquad (au)^- = a + u.$$

Such problems as these are worth working through, and are arranged with much skill in the treatises in question[2]. To myself, I confess, this multiplicity of interchangeable and correspondent formulæ is somewhat confusing in actual calculation. The best summary advocacy of this scheme is by Prof. Schroder: "The rejection of such formulæ as $a + a$, as against the acceptance of aa, is altogether unjustified, in that the former is no more absurd than the latter. Moreover, the introduction of these formulæ is of indisputable service in the abbreviation of our expressions; and they are universally employed in the language of common life. Finally they yield the advantages of this dualism" (*Operationskreis*, p. 37).

Having thus stated my own reasons on the one side, and indicated the nature of those on the other side, I must here leave the question to the judgment of the reader.

[1] Probably De Morgan was the first actually to point out this duality (*Camb. Phil. Trans.* 1858). "Thus (A, B) and AB have ab and (a, b) for contraries (p. 208)". It deserves notice however that when he translates these expressions into mathematical symbols he adopts the exclusive notation, "And (A, B) is not $A + B$, but $A + B - AB$; as pointed out by Mr Boole" *ib.* (p. 185).

[2] Schroder's results are summed up thus (p. 3):—"From every valid general formula in Logic another such formula must be derivable, if we exchange throughout the signs of *plus* and *minus* for those of multiplication and division, and also the symbols 0 and 1".

II. The next question for consideration is, what changes of treatment are demanded by the resolve to interpret our terms in respect of their intension, instead of regarding them (as we have done throughout) extensively, viz. as merely representing classes. I must say at once, however, that the question here is not so much what treatment *is* adopted as what ought to be adopted, since it is very doubtful if there has ever been a systematic attempt to work out this view in detail. That there have been claims to do this, and a number of partial attempts in this direction, the reader will have gathered from various notes and references which have been given from time to time[1]. My main object for going into so much detail here is to explain the schemes of the authors referred to, and the plans of notation they have adopted, but I confess that the attempt to carry out their scheme seems to me a hopeless one.

In order to come to a clear understanding of the treatment thus demanded in Symbolic Logic, we shall find it best to try back a little so as to ascertain how the corresponding questions have been decided in common Logic. Here we are at once involved in some perplexity owing to variety of usage. The views entertained amongst logicians as to what is the meaning, connotation, or intension of a term, range from considering it to be any attributes, even a single one, by

[1] As regards the treatment of symbolic logic, I should say that most recent writers have inclined decidedly towards the extensive, and most of the older writers (less decidedly) towards the intensive interpretation. But there has been almost no critical discussion of the distinction between the two views. Professor Schroder stands probably alone in perfectly explicit statement on the one side;—"In diesem ganzlichen Absehen vom Inhalte [intent] der Begriffe liegt nun allerdings eine Einseitigkeit" (Review of Frege in the *Zeits. f. Math. u. Phys.* xxv. 3), and Professor Jevons on the other;— "I do not wish to express any opinion here as to the nature of a system of logic in extent" (*Pure Logic*, p. 2).

which the things denoted by the term can be distinguished from others, up to considering it to embrace every attribute possessed by that class in common. Fortunately however for our present purpose almost any of these views (except the extreme ones) will answer equally well; that is, will call for a precisely similar mode of treatment. We shall have indeed to make a postulate, and one which does not altogether coincide with facts, but without which no such thing as a Science of Logic could possibly exist. This postulate is that there is a common agreement as to what attributes form the intension of a term. Whether this intension comprise few attributes or many, and whatever the principle in accordance with which they are selected, we postulate that all the people whom we take into account are agreed as to what these attributes shall be. We have to insist, in fact, upon what may be called a sort of universe of reasoners, just as we insist upon a universe of discourse within which we reason. Of course this is not strictly justified in fact, for hardly any two people agree exactly as to what a name really 'means', but some such postulate seems forced upon us, if we want to rise out of a mere description and comparison of beliefs entertained, into a Formal Science of Logic. Otherwise we could have no general definitions, and any distinction between the essential and the accidental would be lost.

By the intension, connotation, or logical meaning of a term I understand then a group of attributes; and we postulate that people are agreed as to the constituent members of every such group. What we now want to do is to compare the meaning, arrangements, expression, and so forth, of propositions when looked at from this point of view, with those yielded by looking at them from the point of view of extension. But we have already examined, in the first chapter, the outcome of a rigid class interpretation

of propositions; all that is now wanted for the purpose
of comparison is therefore an equally rigid intensive inter
pretation.

Recalling the results of the first chapter, we there saw
that if we take two classes or extensions, A and B, and
examine the possible relations in which they may stand
to one another, we find that there are five, and only five such
relations. For the relation may be that of the inclusion
of A by B, of B by A, their partial inclusion of each other,
their mutual exclusion, and their coincidence. When how
ever we regard A and B as groups of attributes we can see
our way to only four of these relations, but the parallel
in their case seems at first sight tolerably close.

One group of attributes may include or exclude another,
partially or wholly, just as a class of concrete objects may do:
which appears to afford four relations of the kind we seek:
but can one such group *coincide* with another and yet
be recognized as a distinct entity from it? I think not, and
therefore the frequency with which such a relation is verbally
admitted[1] by those who speak a pure Conceptualist speech
seems to me a sign with what little consistency this view
is adopted. There is the widest possible distinction between
the extension and the intension in this respect. As regards

---

[1] For instance, many German
logicians refer to this relation under
the name of "Wechselbegriffe", the
Begriff being composed of *Merkmale*
and therefore by rights abstract.
But what they actually understand
by them are generally two concepts
whose extension happens to be the
same, whatever their marks may be.
Beneke, *e.g.* plainly says so, "In
Hinsicht auf den Umfang nennt man
die Begriffe Wechselbegriffe wenn sie
den gleichen Umfang haben" (*Logik*,
p. 28). Some again more consistently, as I should say, deny the possibility of equivalent, as distinguished
from identical concepts. Thus Bachmann, "Wer in B nicht mehr und
nicht weniger denkt als *A*, der denkt
eben *A*; und *B*, der genau dieselben
Merkmale hat wie *A*, ist eben *A*,
weil es von diesem durch nichts
unterschieden werden kann" (*Logik*,
p. 111).

the former we saw that the case of coincidence might fairly be recognized as a distinct one; for, though the individuals included were identical, we could conceive their being called up under different names and by reference to different attri butes. Hence 'All A is all B' is not necessarily an identical proposition. But when A and B are groups of attributes their coincidence merges into absolute identity; for these being results of Abstraction, every distinguishing character istic has been stripped off them. So we do not obtain what we can represent as an 'All A is all B' proposition, but rather an 'All A is all A' proposition.

When however we come to work out the scheme of pro positions demanded by this way of interpreting our terms,—or rather our 'concepts', as we will call them, in order to use an appropriate conceptualist expression,—we find that the ap parent parallel is very far from holding throughout. The two cases indeed of entire inclusion seem to repeat themselves on either interpretation; for, if the concept A is a part of B, we have the proposition 'All B is A', and conversely if B be a part of A. But the remaining two cases exhibit a wide divergence. For instance, if the concepts A and B are partially the same, we shall most likely find that this gives rise, not to a 'Some A is B', but to a 'No A is B' proposition, for the presence of a single really differentiating attribute on each side is sufficient to separate entirely the classes A and B. On the other hand, even though the concepts A and B have not a single element in common we shall not neces sarily obtain an ordinary universal negative, for attributes may be quite distinct and yet compatible with each other. In fact we might even have an 'All A is all B' in such a case. Thus 'existent marsupial' and 'large quadruped indigenous to Australasia' comprise very distinct groups of attributes but denote approximately coincident groups of things; whilst 'men under thirty' and 'men over thirty' have every essential point in common with only one divergence, and yet denote entirely distinct groups.

It is clear then that the arrangement of propositions in accordance with this scheme is of a somewhat peculiar kind. It will be most easily carried out by the aid of a little symbolic notation. Suppose then two concepts A and AB, where the extra intension indicated by B is of course not contradictory of A. Give these concepts the names P and Q and we have the ordinary universal affirmative, All Q is P. Had the names P and Q been inverted we should have had the similar proposition All P is Q. Now suppose that the concepts had been AB and AC, we see at once that we cannot with certainty conclude any ordinary proposition from this, in the absence of information as to the mutual relations of B and C. If B and C are really contradictory, so that they might be written pq and pq, then we conclude that No P is Q. If B includes C, so that these might be written p and pq, then we know that All Q is P, and similarly if C includes B. If however B and C are really distinct in their meaning, so that one cannot be shown, in the present state of our know ledge, to be a part of the other, then no proposition whatever can with certainty be elicited out of these concepts AB and AC. As regards concepts which are entirely distinct from each other, say A and B, the remark just made may be repeated verbatim. Without further analysis of A and B, and discovery of identities or contradictions in the constituent elements, no proposition of the ordinary kind can with confi dence be enunciated.

One or two remarks may be added in explanation of the above analysis. It will be seen that the only universal pro positions which can thus effect an entrance are those called verbal, necessary, analytic, or essential. Given A and AB as concepts, it is inevitable that we should conclude that 'All AB is A'. So in the case of universal negatives. If A and B can be analysed into say pq and pq, it is equally inevitable that 'No A is B'. From the former by conversion, a particular proposition can be inferred, provided of course that we understand '*some*' in its ordinary sense of 'some at least', for we can infer that 'Some A is AB'. As regards those universal propositions which are accidental, I cannot see that they have any·right to admission on such a scheme as this, where we start from concepts and their intension. For example, 'All American citizens know the name of their President': how can we fairly interpret this with strictness from the side of its intension? Surely on no admissible sense of the term can this incident be regarded as a part of the intension of 'American'; nor have we any thought of making it such for the future, and so agreeing to enlarge the intension. If the fact were new to us the most we should do would be to take a note of it, so as to regard this mark as an accidental one of all individual Americans.

I am aware that some logicians would explain that what is meant in such a case as the above is that we are to 'attach' (or something equivalent to this) the new attribute to the old group, without however regarding it as any part of the essence or intension. I really do not know exactly what this can mean. The sole bond of coherence in the attributes consists in the fact of our keeping the members of it together in our minds, so that if a new-comer takes up its permanent abode amongst them, it obtains thenceforth every right of occupancy which they possess. An attribute attached to a group of attributes *is* one of the group. At least I can see no ground for disputing this unless we admit Kant's doctrine as to the existence of *à priori* synthetic judgments.

The general position adopted here will not, I hope, be

misunderstood. I hold very decidedly that all names (with certain trifling exceptions which need not be specified) possess both intension and extension, and that we may conceivably examine the mutual relations of terms, and through these develop a system of propositions and of reasonings, from either of these two sides. Popular speech appears to adopt an inter mediate course, not adhering strictly to either of these sides. In this it has been followed, and very rightly so, by the tra ditional Logic, which appears to me (broadly speaking) to prefer regarding the subject in respect of extension and the predicate in respect of the attributes which it conveys. This is certainly the view which I should endeavour to work out if I were composing a systematic work upon the ordinary lines.

When however we develop a system of Symbolic Logic we are forced to be more consistent in our adherence to one side or the other, for symbols do not readily tolerate an uncertain and hesitating attitude. The question therefore is, which view we had best adopt. In this choice I cannot hesitate for a moment, and it must be left to the reader to judge by the whole drift of this work how far the decision is justified. In fact as regards the alternative view, we cannot so much say that it has broken down on trial, as that it never has been fairly tried at all.

We shall see this best by examining the most appropriate usage, on this plan, of some of the now familiar signs of our logical operations. Begin with the sign (+). If A and B are attributes or partial concepts, we should I presume agree in saying that $A + B$ will signify those attributes 'taken to gether'. But when we go on to enquire what is meant by taking attributes together we perceive that this is a very different thing from taking classes together. The only con sistent meaning surely is that we do this when we construct a new concept which contains them both. But this is clearly the analogue not of addition but of multiplication. Thus let 'man' be 'rational animal'; it would naturally be said that the concept *humanity* is made up of the attributes *rationality* and *animality* taken together. This clearly results in a process of restriction in extension such as we have throughout indicated by $A \times B$ and not by $A + B$. In fact 'extensive multiplication' corresponds to 'intensive addition[1]'.

So again with the subtractive sign. There can be little doubt that the most natural and appropriate employment of it here would be to indicate *abstraction* rather than *exception*. Reverting to the same example, the subduction of 'rationality' from 'humanity' would leave 'animality', and this process is precisely that which logicians mean by abstraction: does not indeed the very etymology of the word suggest the taking of one attribute from others just as we remove one material object from a group? Now logical abstraction, when modified so as to bring it into accordance with our class interpretation, was seen to correspond to the process which we mark by $A \div B$ rather than $A - B$. This is, in fact, exactly what Leibnitz does, in a passage referred to in the Introduction, when he makes (man) − (rational) = (brute).

---

[1] It deserves notice that the sign of addition has actually been employed for this purpose. Thus Hamilton (whose usage however of mathematical terms and symbols is almost always an indication of something not to be done) has said, "The concept as a unity, is equal to the characters taken together, $Z = a + b + c$" (*Logic* I. 80). And he has had predecessors here, for instance Twesten (*Logik* p. 211), who has also used the *minus* sign for Abstraction; but neither of these is more than a slight suggestion. This was apparently the only employment of these signs which had come under Trendelenburg's notice, and forms the ground of his objections to their introduction into Logic (*Logische Untersuchungen* I. 20).

It may interest the mathematician to remark that 'addition' of attributes is like that of powers or logarithms; it performs 'multiplication' of extension and therefore does not leave any convenient opening for the mere addition of the same.

On the whole then it seems that a consistent intensive interpretation would find an opening for the symbols + and −, but that it would use them for the purpose of expressing, (approximately only, in the case of the latter), operations which we have indicated by × and ÷. And those operations which *we* denote by + and − it would not find any place for, nor therefore for symbols to represent them.

It need hardly be remarked that this is not the course which has been actually adopted. Nearly all logicians, so far as I know, have consulted convenience at the expense of rigid consistency, and, whenever they have employed these four simple arithmetical signs, have done so in a way more in harmony with that adopted in this work. Their words have been the words of the conceptualist, but their deeds have been mostly those of the nominalist. Hence their language is often tinged, and their usage modified,—especially in the case of the older symbolists,—in a way which it would be very difficult to understand unless we keep in mind the characteristics of the system which they nominally professed[1]. The reader will find plenty of illustrations in support of this remark in the historical references in the next chapter. My main object in fact in making the present remarks is to aid in the intelligent study of some of those anticipations of modern results.

Whatever such writers may have said, what they have actually done has been briefly this. They have taken the sign +, say, and employed it, not to connect real attributes,

---

[1] One example may be given here from Lambert: "Die Redensart, '*A* so nicht m ist,' wird so gezeichnet $\frac{A}{m}$, weil nun *m* von *A* als eine Modification von ihrer Substanz kann abstrahirt werden." This is a purely intensive interpretation; whereas *we* should proceed to represent '*A* which is not *m*' extensively in some such way as $A - Am$ or $A - m$. Elsewhere Lambert himself has used this subtractive sign very nearly as we do.

but rather the extensions referred to by those attributes. They may have defined in a way which would have led to the expression 'rationality + animality', but what they have really intended to do was, not to combine these two attributes or concepts into a more determinate concept, but to obtain a concept whose extent should be equal to that of the other two together. And a similar explanation would apply to their usage of the other three signs. This I cannot but regard as an awkward way of expressing ourselves, as compared with saying at once that A and B and our other terms stand directly for classes of things. Moreover this want of harmony between theory and practice, produces, as it seems to me, a perpetually recurring confusion and inaccuracy in matters of detail [1].

III. The third of the symbolic variations to be here noticed stands upon a very different footing, and, if admitted, would involve far more serious changes than any which we have yet contemplated. The best way of introducing the question will be by referring to a simple example of a kind familiar to every student of Logic. For instance, every beginner has learnt to avoid the pitfall of attempting to syllogize from two such premises as 'A is equal to B', 'B is equal to C'. He sees that however certain and obvious the step may be, we cannot avoid resorting to four terms, instead of three, in stating these premises according to strict rule. If we adhere to the correct logical copula, 'is', we have in one premise the term B, and in the other premise 'an equal to B'. Accor-

---

[1] The nearest approach, perhaps, to a consistent intensive interpretation is to be found in Hamilton's attempt to translate judgments and reasonings in this way as well as extensively. But I cannot find there any serious recognition of what appear to be the insurmountable difficulties of carrying out this interpretation in the case of universal propositions when accidental, or of any ordinary particular propositions.

dingly, on the common system, we have either to reject such examples, or else to admit them under what is little better than a subterfuge. We have to abandon any analysis of the process by which every mind does as a matter of fact proceed, (viz. from B to its equal,) and to throw the real process of reasoning into the major premise, by assuming that all things which are equal to the same thing are equal to one another.

What the so called Logic of Relatives seems to aim at is to frame a set of rules which shall deal directly with reason ings of this kind; or, in other words, shall take account of relations generally, instead of those merely which are indicated by the ordinary logical copula 'is'. It would be quite im possible to treat this question in a portion of a single chapter; so the reader must understand that I am here only making a few remarks upon a subject which cannot well be passed entirely by, but which would need a separate work for its adequate discussion.

Suppose then that we have the relation assigned of A to B, and of B to C, and that we wish to determine the relation of A to C, how should we proceed? Symbolically we find no difficulty in starting. Express the relations in the form $A = L_1 B$, $B = L_2 C$, and the conclusion will be repre sented by $A = L_1 (L_2 C)$ if we want A in terms of C, or $C = L^{-1} (L^{-1} A)$ if we want C in terms of A. But, as the reader knows by this time, symbolic representation of a desired result is by no means a performance of the desired process, nor is it even an assurance that that process admits of performance. Accordingly what we have to do, if we are to take any steps whatever towards our aim, is to ascertain the rules according to which the L_1 and L_2 of the above formulae can be analysed and compounded. As soon as we proceed to do this we find that instead of one simple and uniform set of rules, as in the system hitherto expounded, we are introduced to a most perplexing variety of them.

Begin with the simplest case, by supposing that the two relations in the premises are the same, may we conclude that $L(LA) = LA$, in accordance with the familiar rule of our logic, that $xx = x$? Certainly not, as a general rule; for though, as is abundantly obvious, 'equal of (equal of A)' is equivalent to 'equal of A', and 'brother of (brother of A)' is equivalent to 'brother of A', (provided we assume that a man may be his own brother), yet this is a very exceptional state of things, and accordingly one great resource in our logical procedure has to be given up. If we attempted to make any set of rules here at all, we should be forced to subdivide, by assigning to a separate class all those cases in which $LL = L$, (these are what De Morgan has termed *transitive* relations). Having done this, we should find further subdivisions awaiting us. For instance there is one kind of relation, and for logical purposes one of extreme importance, in which all *odd* powers of L are equivalent, and also all *even* powers, but these are distinct from each other. Let L represent 'contradiction of', and it is plain that $L^2 = L^4 = etc. = 1$. That is, if A be a statement, then $LLA = A$, and so on. But after having thus distinguished these, and possibly other similar special cases, we should be left with a bulk of relations on our hands which admitted of no simplification of this kind, and which had to be left in the merely symbolic form LLA, or its equivalent L^2A, when twice repeated.

Again, we know what perpetual recourse has to be made to the *commutative* law, $xy = yx$. Does this hold of relations? Certainly not, as a general rule, though presumably 'father of grandfather' is equivalent to 'grandfather of father'. But 'father of a brother' is very different from 'brother of a father'; in fact it would not be easy to hit upon relations which could thus be commuted at will without altering the result. Accordingly we must be careful to distinguish[1] be tween $L_1 L_2 A$ and $L_2 L_1 A$.

Once more; some relations when inverted yield a definite result, others yield an indefinite result, and thus are in more agreement with our ordinary logical formulæ. That is, $L^{-1}LA$ may $= A$ simply, or it may have A as one only out of a possibly infinite number of solutions. Thus if A be the husband of B, (in a monogamous country) B must be *the* person of whom A is the husband; elsewhere she may only be one of a number of women who will all equally answer the description.

It is this immensely extensive signification of the word *relation,* and the consequent variety of symbolic procedure which is called for if we attempt to treat it symbolically, which seem to me to render it hopeless to establish any thing in the least deserving the name of a Logic of Relatives. The attempt however to introduce relative terms into Logic was made by some of the first who employed symbolic notation. Lambert indeed has treated these questions more fully perhaps than any one since his time:—I cannot but think that his attempt to introduce them into his system was one of the principal causes of his failure to work it out more completely and successfully than he did. He expressly dis cusses the question whether *powers* are to be admitted in

---

[1] The earliest definite notice that I have seen of the fact that, in certain cases, the commutative law must be rejected, is in Semler (*Versuch uber die combinatorische Methode,* 1811), but it is scarcely more than a passing statement. Thus, putting B for *bequem,* D for *dauerhaft,* W for *wohlfeil,* S for *schon,* he remarks that $WBDS$ is by no means the same as $WDBS$, on the ground that the position of a term is often an index of the relative importance to be attached to the attributes referred to. Semler, it may be remarked, was acquainted with the works of Lambert and Ploucquet.

symbolic notation, and decides that they are ; as indeed was unavoidable in such a wide extent of signification as must then be accepted. Thus in his *Architectonic* (1, 82) where he has discussed this question more fully than elsewhere, he expressly includes such various relations as 'cause and effect, means, intention, ground, species and genus'. Thus γ representing a genus of A we have the result $\alpha\gamma$; a higher genus of this will be indicated by $\alpha\gamma^2$, and so on. Similarly with the relation of species.

As I have already intimated, the attempt to construct a Logic of Relatives seems to me altogether hopeless owing to the extreme vagueness and generality of this conception of a Relation. Almost anything may be regarded as a relation, and when we attempt to group them into manageable portions we find that several distinct codes of laws are required. Even in one of the simplest possible kinds of relation we find that the inverse processes may be quite insoluble. Given the relation of A to C, and of B to C, it might be assumed that that of A to B was determinable. But a moment's consideration shows that this is not so. If the distance (to take one of the simplest and most definite of all relations) of A and of B from C is exactly a mile, that of A from B, (the relation desired), may be anything not exceeding two miles : a similar result holds if that distance be anything under one mile. But if the 'relation' were that the distance is not less than a mile in each case, the resultant distance of A from B might be absolutely anything whatever.

What therefore a Logic of Relatives has to do is to make a selection out of an altogether infinite field, confining itself to those relations only which obey certain definite symbolic laws. Mr Murphy, for instance, following some suggestions by De Morgan (*Camb. Phil. Trans.* x, 336), has proposed a scheme of the following kind :—"Relations (indicated by the symbol L) may be divided into those which are 'transitive' and those which are 'intransitive', *i.e.* according as L^2 is or is not equal to L. They are also invertible or uninvertible, that is to say, L^{-1} is or is not equal to L. There are thus four classes, *i.e.*

1. Transitive and invertible.
2. Transitive but uninvertible.
3. Intransitive but invertible.
4. Intransitive and uninvertible.

To the first belong equality, brotherhood, and various other relations. To the second inclusion, causation, sequence, greater magnitude, &c. To the third exclusion, difference, &c. To the fourth the great majority of relations.

I certainly think that this scheme is sound as a classifica tion. But for the purposes of a logical system it does not seem to me that it would add any large domain to our pro vince. The two last classes indeed are surely unworkable in anything which can be called a logical system; for, involving powers, they would in all but the simplest cases lead to quadratic or higher equations.

(The reader who wishes to study the little that has yet been done on this subject may consult the following notices and papers:—

Ellis L. *Mathematical and other writings,* p. 391. (Also published by Mr Harley in the *Report of the Brit. Ass.,* 1870.)

De Morgan. *Syllabus of Logic.*

———— *Trans. of Camb. Phil. Soc.* Vol. x. (In my opinion one of the fullest and best papers yet produced on the subject.) ·

Peirce C. S. *American Acad. of Arts and Sciences.* Vol. ix.

Macfarlane A. *Proc. of R. Soc. Edinburgh,* 1879.

Murphy J. J. *Belfast Nat. Hist. and Phil. Soc.,* 1875.

———— *Manchester Lit. and Phil. Soc.,* Vol. vii. (1880); *do.* Feb. 1881.)

CHAPTER XX.

HISTORIC NOTES.

I. *On the various notations adopted for expressing the common propositions of Logic.*

Attention has been already called to the general fact of the perplexing variety of symbolic forms which have been proposed from time to time by various writers, but probably few persons have any adequate conception of the extent to which this license of invention has been carried. I have therefore thought it well to put together into one list the principal forms, so far as I have observed them, in which one and the same proposition has thus been expressed[1]. For this purpose the Universal Negative has been selected, as being about the simplest and least ambiguous of all forms of statement. This arrangement has not been drawn up with a mere wish to make a collection. Most of these forms, it

---

[1] The reader will, of course, understand that I am not attempting to give an account of the schemes of the various authors referred to, but merely indicating the principal different points of view that have been adopted. It is not to be supposed that each author has only made use of the notation here assigned to him.

must be remembered, have been made the instruments of a more or less systematic exposition of the subject. In so far, therefore, as the notation is not entirely arbitrary—which it is in very few instances—we shall find it instructive to compare the different aspects of the same operation to which they respectively direct attention. For convenience of re ference and comparison they are expressed in the same letters in each case, S and P standing respectively for the subject and predicate of the original proposition; viz. no S is P.

The analysis by which I should reach these various forms would be somewhat of the following kind:

I.   In the first place we may regard the proposition as an *existential* one. In this case what it does is to deny the existence of the class of things which are both S and P.

II.   We may cast the proposition into the form of an *identity*. What we then do is to make the terms of the propo sition respectively S and not-P, and to identify the former with an undetermined part of the latter. The appropriate copula is then of course $(=)$.

III.   Another plan is to regard the proposition as ex pressing a *consequence* or *implication*: 'If S then not-P', or, 'the presence of S implies the absence of P'. This relation, of course, is not convertible, for it does not follow that the absence of P implies the presence of S. Accordingly, some kind of unsymmetrical symbol becomes appropriate to repre sent the copula in this case.

IV.   Again, keeping more closely to the common ex pression of the proposition, we may regard it as expressing a relation not, as above, between S and not-P, but between S and P. This relation is convertible, and we should therefore naturally seek in this case for some symmetrical symbol.

V. Again, we may couch the proposition in conceptualist or notional phraseology, regarding S and P not as classes of things but as attributes or groups of attributes.

VI. Lastly, we may meet with nondescript attempts which aim at little more than translating the proposition as it stands, or adopting some arbitrary notation for it.

Grouping them thus, we may arrange our species as follows :—

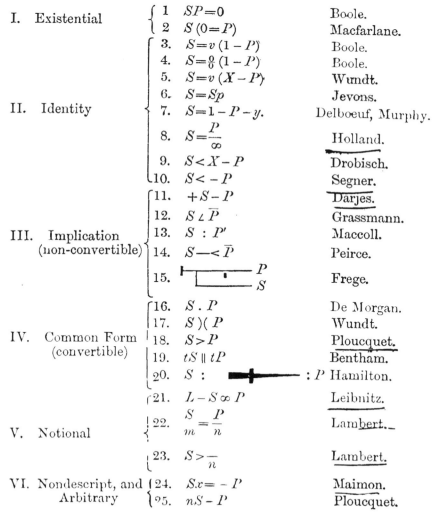

I.　Existential	$\begin{cases}1 & SP=0 \\ 2 & S\,(0=P)\end{cases}$	Boole. / Macfarlane.
II.　Identity	3.　$S=v\,(1-P)$	Boole.
	4.　$S=\tfrac{0}{0}(1-P)$	Boole.
	5.　$S=v\,(X-P)$	Wundt.
	6.　$S=Sp$	Jevons.
	7.　$S=1-P-y.$	Delbœuf, Murphy.
	8.　$S=\dfrac{P}{\infty}$	Holland.
	9.　$S<X-P$	Drobisch.
	10.　$S<-P$	Segner.
III.　Implication (non-convertible)	11.　$+S-P$	Darjes.
	12.　$S\angle\overline{P}$	Grassmann.
	13.　$S\,:\,P'$	Maccoll.
	14.　$S—<\overline{P}$	Peirce.
	15.	Frege.
IV.　Common Form (convertible)	16.　$S\,.\,P$	De Morgan.
	17.　$S\,)(\,P$	Wundt.
	18.　$S>P$	Ploucquet.
	19.　$tS\parallel tP$	Bentham.
	20.　$S:$ ▬▬▬ $:P$	Hamilton.
V.　Notional	21.　$L-S\infty P$	Leibnitz.
	22.　$\dfrac{S}{m}=\dfrac{P}{n}$	Lambert.
	23.　$S>\dfrac{}{n}$	Lambert.
VI.　Nondescript, and Arbitrary	24.　$Sx=-P$	Maimon.
	25.　$nS-P$	Ploucquet.

As most of these forms are marked off from each other
by more or less distinct specific differences, it will be well to
go a little into detail in describing them.

1.   This will be perfectly familiar to the reader. It
simply indicates the destruction of the class SP, or the empti
ness of the corresponding compartment. I prefer it myself as
a primary statement of such a proposition.

2.   The characteristic of Mr Macfarlane's notation here
lies in the attempt to mark the limits of the 'universe'. He
considers that the subject of the proposition marks the limits
of the implied universe. "Every general proposition refers to
a definite universe; which is the subject of the judgment, and,
it may be, of a series of judgments. For example, 'all men
are mortal' refers to the universe 'men'. 'No men are
perfect' refers to the same universe" (*Algebra of Logic*, p.
29). Hence his symbolic form is read off, Within the uni
verse of S there is no such thing as a P. I have already
(Chap. VIII. p. 185) given my reasons for dissenting from such
an assumption as to the nature of this universe. In any
case it seems to me arbitrary to seek its limits in the subject
of the negative proposition.

3—6.   These four forms are to all intents and purposes
identical. The only distinction between them is that (3)
introduces an arbitrary sign (v) to express the indeterminateness of the selection to be made from not-P; that (4) employs
a well-known mathematical symbol to express the same idea;
whilst (6) disguises this indeterminateness by describing S
as the S-part of what is not P instead of directly reminding
us that it is an unknown part. It also abbreviates by sub
stituting a single letter p for the fuller equivalent $1 - P$.
No. (5) is employed by Wundt (*Logik*, 1880) in his account
of symbolic procedure. It only differs from the third and
fourth by making use of X as the universe-symbol, instead of

unity. As regards the representation of the class not-P by p, in (6), there is one serious defect. We cannot thus represent the negation of a composite class. The other schemes meet the difficulty. "What is not both B and C" can be readily represented by $1 - BC$, and "what is neither B nor C" by $(1 - B)(1 - C)$; and the similar devices of a bar over two or more letters, or an accent put outside a bracket which contains them (as in specimens 12 and 13) will subserve the same purpose. But on the plan of employing small letters to mark negations, ab would stand for "What is neither A nor B", and there seems no ready mode of simply expressing the negation of AB *as a whole.* We have to break it up into detail and write it $a + Ab$, or in some equivalent form. This is a serious symbolic blemish.

7.   This form is employed by Prof. Delboeuf (*Logique Algorithmique*, 1877), and seems to me identical with one proposed by Mr J. J. Murphy (*Relation of Logic to Language*, 1875; *Mind*, v. 52). It only differs from the preceding forms by adopting the subtractive instead of the multiplicative symbol. Whereas those four say, Make an indeterminate *selection* from not-P and we obtain S; this says, Make an indeterminate *rejection* by omission, and we obtain S. It is not incorrect, but seems to me to suffer from the drawback of demanding a tacit condition, viz. that y shall be included in $1 - P$. When this condition is clearly expressed, it coincides with Boole's form (If B is included in A, so that $B = vA$, then $A - B = (1 - v)A$: but, $1 - v$ having the same limits of uncertainty as v, this may be written vA), and becomes exactly equivalent to $S = v(1 - P)$. It should be remarked that Delboeuf divides this general form into several distinct cases according to the extent of the whole universe covered by S and not-P, and so forth (*Log. Alg.* p. 58).

8.   This was a scheme proposed by Holland, a friend and

correspondent of J. H. Lambert. Though not sound in this particular application it deserves notice, both for its ingenuity, and historically as an anticipation of some more modern results. (It is given in Lambert's *Deutscher gelehrter Briefwechsel*, I. 17.) The general propositional form which he proposed was $\frac{S}{r} = \frac{P}{..}$, which is really nothing else than Boole's $vS = v'P$, with the difference that the arbitrary factor is put into the denominator instead of the numerator (i.e. the factor *multiplies* by $\frac{1}{r}$ and $\frac{1}{..}$, it does not *divide* by p and π; there is no notion here of an inverse logical operation, though Holland had realized it elsewhere). The consequent condition as to the range of value of p and π is of course that they must lie between 1 and ∞, just as in Boole's form v and v' lie between 1 and 0. What we express symbolically therefore is 'some S is some P', where 'some' may range from *none* to *all*. So far good. Where he goes astray, as already noticed in Ch. VII., is by interpreting the limiting case $S = 0P$ (viz. when $p = 1$, $\pi = \infty$) as meaning "all S is no P", instead of "all S is *nothing*". The fact is that his form is extensible enough to cover particular and universal affirmatives, with distributed and undistributed predicates ; but in order to make it stretch so as to cover negative propositions we must either use a negative predicate, not-P, or else join S and P together into one complex subject and equate this to 0 as in (1).

All of these six concur in employing the equation symbol (=), and rightly so, for what they represent is the identity of the subject S with a portion of not-P. The two following must really be considered to belong to the same general class, though actually employing a different, and decidedly less suitable symbol, viz. (<).

9.　This was employed by Drobisch in the first edition of

his *Neue Darstellung der Logik* (1836), but is omitted in later editions. Two points deserve notice about it. First as regards the connecting symbol itself. We are familiar with it in mathematics as meaning 'less than'; and it is here trans ferred to the signification 'is included in', or 'is identical with a part of'. It is therefore exactly equivalent to the equation symbol when, as in the last examples, this is affixed to a predicate affected by some indeterminate factor. This transfer of the sign < does not seem to me a very convenient or accurate one, though its signification is quite clear[1]; it need hardly be remarked that it here refers to the *extent* not the *intent* of the terms S and P. Secondly, as regards the predicate, the notation is curious as shewing the great diffi culty which logicians brought up in the old traditions had in realizing the conception of a 'universe' which could be repre sented by a single symbol. The letter X does not here stand for really "all", for this would be to introduce an "unend- licher Begriff", or "infinite term", quite alien to old tradition. Drobisch only ventures symbolically to embrace a finite but uncertain portion of this infinite universe. Let us then take a class term X of uncertain extent, only demanding that its extent shall be greater than those of S and P together, and we may regard this as finite, and therefore suitable to logical treatment. When our negative predicate, not-P, is

---

[1] Lambert, who was perhaps the first to employ this sign for this purpose in Logic, (as presently point- ed out, he employed it *intensively*) takes its propriety for granted: "Die Zeichnung A > B scheint ganz natür- lich zu bedeuten der Begriff A ent- halte ausser den Merkmalen des B noch mehrere" (*Briefwechsel* I. 10).

There is a much earlier *sugges-* *tion* of this notation (if indeed it may not be called something more than a suggestion) in a short logical paper, consisting of heads of theses, by James Bernoulli, in 1685 (*Opera* I. 214). My attention was called to this paper by a reference in De Morgan's articles in the *Camb. Phil. Transactions*. Hoffbauer (*Analytik der Urtheile*) has used the same sign.

thus brought down to finite extent in the form of $X - P$, we can venture to refer S to it. We imply, in fact, that S is a portion of not-P; and we write it not by an express equation formula, but by an inclusion formula, as $S < X - P$.

10. This is of considerable interest historically, since Segner's *Specimen Logicæ* (1740), is the first systematic attempt, so far as I have seen, to construct a symbolic Logic. (He had nothing before him of this kind to appeal to beyond a few ingenious suggestions by Leibnitz.) The sign $<$ is used in the same sense as by Drobisch, $A < B$ marking that the extent of B is inclusive of that of A. But in one respect he seems to me distinctly in advance of Drobisch, and very much in advance of his time. This is in his free use of negative terms in their full extent (he preserves the old name of 'infinite' for them), for the representation of which he uses the negative sign. Thus if A stands for man, $- A$ stands for not-man. It may be added that he had fully realized the fact that it is symbolically indifferent whether we apply A to a positive or to its contradictory, provided we preserve the antithesis between $+$ and $-$. Thus if A stands for *non-triangulum*, $- A$ will stand for *triangulum*, and so forth. Hence his expression $S < - P$ marks quite correctly that S is extensively a portion of not-P.

This notation of course is very crude, being not of much value even within the limits of the syllogism. The various syllogistic moods are however worked through with its aid, but with certain departures from the common view which need not here be described. It may interest the historical student of this part of the subject to say that Segner not only describes the symbolic procedure by which from two such premises as $A < B$, $C < D$, we can infer $AC < BD$; but also expressly calls attention to the "law of duality" as it is sometimes termed, viz. that $AA = A$; that is, he points out that when A and C are the same no change is produced :— "subjecti enim idea, cum se ipsa composita, novam ideam producere nequit". There are many other interesting points about the work which must be passed over here.

We now come to a group of forms which I have thrown together as adopting somewhat of an *implication* arrange ment : some of them indeed expressly describe themselves as indicating an implication. Thus,

11. The scheme of Darjes will be found in his *Weg zur Wahrheit* (1776). His expression for the proposition in question is best put into words as, "posit S, and we sublate P". It turns entirely upon the representation of contradictories by $+$ and $-$, a representation which, as in the closely analogous case just discussed, will do fairly well up to a certain point. If we only want to deal with pairs of con tradictories, whether terms or propositions, and only want, as above remarked, to posit and sublate them, the signs $+$ and $-$ are convenient. But then we lose the use of these signs for far more appropriate purposes, viz. for logical aggregation and exception. Moreover the antithesis thus suggested of a contradictory, rather than a supplementary relation between S and not-S, soon leads to difficulties. How are we to represent not-S.not-P? By $(-S-P)$ or by $(-S)\times(-P)$? There is no convenient opening here for compounding terms or premises.

The only brief and convenient rule for working this nota tion seems to apply to the process of *conversion*. From 'Posit S and sublate P', we deduce of course 'Posit P and sublate S'. Generalizing this to cover the four possible cases we see that it may be summed up in the words 'change the order of the terms and both the signs': i.e. from $(+S+P)$ we infer $(-P-S)$, and so on.

Though therefore the scheme of employing $+$ and $-$ in

Logic, for this purpose, repeatedly presents itself, it does not seem to me to merit any more detailed investigation.

12—14.   These are, to my thinking, precisely equivalent to one another.   It is true that Mr Maccoll insists upon it that his interpretation of his class symbols as standing for *statements*, marks a 'cardinal point' of distinction; but I regard this as an arbitrary restriction of the full generality of our symbolic language. Phrase it how we will,—the presence of S implies that of P, the existence of S implies that of P, the truth of S implies that of P, and so forth ;—the antithesis at bottom is always the same, or rather it comes under one generalized signification.

It may be added, in explanation of the differences of detail, that the line over a letter, and the accent, respectively mark contradiction; and the three copula-symbols may in each case alike be read 'implies'.   We may read them there-fore, 'S marks, or implies, the absence of P or the contradic-tion of P, as the case may be'.   The converse of course does not hold; that is, not-P does not imply S.   If this additional information were given to us we should in each case employ the copula $(=)$, and write them $S = P'$, $S = P$. The sign of equality marks in fact the double implication, just as 'All S is all P' contains the two propositions, 'All S is P', and 'All P is S'.

Of course, in saying this, it must not for a moment be supposed that the various systems which make use of these notations are themselves coincident.   On the contrary, there are various differences, both in the detailed treatment and in the rest of the notation, even between (12) and (13); whilst Prof. Peirce has made his symbols a means of attacking various problems (such as the Logic of Relatives) which have not seemed to me to lie across the path we have had to take.

(For Grassmann's scheme, see his *Begriffslehre*, 1872 ; for that of Mr Maccoll, the *Proc. Lond. Math. Soc.*, 1877; and for that of Prof. Peirce, the *American Journal of Math.*, Vol. III.)

15.   Frege's scheme (*Begriffsschrift*, 1879) deserves almost as much to be called diagrammatic as symbolic.   It is one of those instances of an ingenious man working out a scheme,—in this case a very cumbrous one,—in entire ignorance that anything of the kind had ever been achieved before.   A word or two only of explanation can be devoted to it here.   A hori zontal dash with a short vertical stroke at the end signifies a proposition.   The line S running into P means that P is dependent upon S;—this is in fact his sign of dependence or implication.   The little stroke under the P-line marks negation.   So that the whole arrangement stands for 'If S then not P'.   We can proceed in this way to build up more complicated dependencies.   For instance, by joining this whole arrangement on to another such line, we can represent the compound dependency 'The fact that S implies the absence of P, implies Q', and so on.   One obvious defect in this scheme is the inordinate amount of space demanded by it; nearly half a page is sometimes demanded for an implica tion which any reasonable scheme would compress into half a line.

The members of the group now before us, expressing a relation between S and not-P, are essentially non-convertible, and therefore appropriately employ non-symmetrical symbols for the copula[1].   In this respect they depart somewhat from tradition and each is the scheme of a logical innovator.   The next group keeps closer to old custom, in respect that its members express directly a relation between S and P, and therefore call for a symmetrical copula-symbol.

[1] No. (13) is of course non-symmetrical in regard to the recog-nized signification of the sign (:) in mathematics, as also here in Logic, though this symbol is symmetrical in actual form.

16—18. These three of course employ purely arbitrary symbols, and are meant to do so, the symbols being mere substitutes for the copula of ordinary Logic. Wundt's symbol is one of a group (*Logik*, p. 244) some of which mark recip rocal relations between the terms, and some non-reciprocal, and its symmetrical form is meant to shew that it belongs to the former class. Thus $S = P$ marks identity; $S > P$ super-ordination of S to P; $S \angle P$ subordination of S to P, and $S \mathbb{X} P$ the intersection of S and P. These, with $S)(P$, make up the five possible distinct forms of class relations. To these however Wundt adds some others which are not so much class relations as dependencies or implications. De Morgan, I suspect, had not this distinction between symmetrical and unsymmetrical forms clearly in view. His notation here is that which he adopted in his *Formal Logic;* he changed it subsequently in his papers in the *Camb. Phil. Transactions.*

As regards Ploucquet's expression, this is mainly employed in the more symbolical parts of his logical treatises (e.g. his *Methodus Calculandi*, 1763). He there uses only two signs; one, an arbitrary and somewhat misleading sign for negation, $(>)$; and one for affirmation (juxtaposition of the letters). The predicate is always distributed, the whole and part of it being indicated by large and small letters respectively. Thus 'All A is B' stands, Ab, viz. 'All A is some B'. 'No A is C' stands $A > C$, viz. 'No A is any C'. The processes of reason ing are then resolved into substitution of identities and recog nition of non-identities. It may be remarked that had Ploucquet broken sufficiently with the past to make a free use of negative, or infinite predicates, he might have adopted another form for these negative propositions. It is true that he does occasionally employ such predicates, but not suffi ciently often to have devoted a special symbol to them. Had he written, for instance, P for 'all not-P', and p for 'some ιot-P', his expression for 'No S is P' might have been Sp, viz. 'All S is some not-P', in better accordance with the familiar symbolic view at the present time, and as illustrated in group (II.).

19, 20. These two must be regarded as precisely equi valent, with one exception to be presently noticed. They are both founded upon the doctrine of the Quantification of the Predicate, and are meant to call attention to that character istic. They may be translated as saying 'the whole of S is distinct from the whole of P'. Mr Bentham's t means total ity, like Hamilton's (:), and the parallel lines of the one bear the same signification as the crossed wedge of the other, viz. 'distinct from', or as Hamilton sometimes puts it, not 'con gruent' with. The differential characteristic of Hamilton's symbol lies in the distinction between the thick and thin ends of the wedge, which is meant to mark whether the pro position is read in extension or in intension. This attempt to compress both these interpretations into one form is now, I presume, generally regarded as a mistake. (See Hamilton's *Logic*, II. p. 473; Bentham's *Logic*, p. 134.)

We now turn to a group the interpretation of which is necessarily one of intension, that is, in which the letters stand for notions or attributes and not for classes.

21. Leibnitz's formula is given in his *Specimen demon- strandi* (Erdmann, p. 96). It is not definitely assigned as a symbolic expression of the proposition; and like some other of the logical speculations in his shorter works seems indeed to have been thrown out as little more than a hint. His view is this. The sign $(-)$ is the sign of 'detraction', i.e. abstrac- tion, or the withdrawal of an attribute from a notion; and (∞) is the sign of identity. Now let L and P be two notions which have something in common, but that when S is thrown out of the former the remainder is P. This is expressed by

$L - S \infty P$, and implies that S and P are distinct notions, or that No S is P. His own account of the matter (I have changed some of the letters) is this. "Sit $L - S \infty P$. Dico S et P nihil habere commune. Nam ex definitione detracti et residui omnia quæ sunt in L manent in P præter ea quæ sunt in S, quorum nihil manet in P": so that no S is P.

This particular suggestion is very brief, and seems to me decidedly obscure, but it deserves mention, both historically and as having possibly given occasion to the similar but much more complete suggestions of Lambert. I proceed to their discussion.

22. This scheme proposed by Lambert might at first sight be considered identical with that of Holland (No. 8), or rather with the general propositional form of which that is a particular case ; for the two expressions are formally the same. In reality, however, they are in striking contrast with each other. With Holland, the letters p and π, in the denominators, really stood for numerical factors. What he meant to signify was that 'some portion of the extent (estimated by $1 \div p$) of S, is identical with some portion (similarly estimated by $1 \div \pi$) of that of P'; though he blundered when he came to interpret this into a negative proposition. But with Lambert, m and n have a better right to stand in the denominator. They mark *attributes*, and division by them stands for *abstraction*, so that the proposition is interpreted here not in respect of extent but of intent. His idea is this. Though S and P are distinct as classes they must have some attributes in common ; that is, they must both belong to some higher genus. Abstract then certain attributes from each, as indicated in the division respectively by m and n, and the remaining groups of attributes will coincide.

This is quite true, and highly ingenious, but what one

does not see is how this symbolic expression becomes a fitting representative of the universal negative proposition rather than of any other. Whatever the relations of extent of two notions, S and P, it will always hold good that some of the attributes in one are different from some of those in the other. This points, I think, to an essential defect in the attempt to interpret propositions in respect of the intent of both their subjects and predicates; it gives us, for instance, no means of distinguishing between 'some X is Y', and 'some X is not Y', or indeed for adequately characterising any 'particular' pro position whatever.

It is rather curious that Segner, whose work (see above) Lambert had read, could have set him right here. He has expressly discussed almost exactly the same question, and realized its logical bearings clearly, though he did not reach the very important symbolic step of introducing the inverse or division sign to mark it. He stated this theorem : Given that two classes indicated by composite terms, AB and CD, have something in common, and we abstract an attribute from each, say A and C, then the resultant classes, B and D, must also have something in common. But such community may be of any one of four kinds which he marks respectively by $B = D$, $B < D$, $B > D$, $B \times D$; that is, coextension, inclusion of B in D, inclusion of D in B, and intersection.

23. The above expression will be found described in Lambert's *Deutscher gelehrter Briefwechsel*, I. 37; and in the *Nova Act. Erudit.* 1765. The present one is a slight modifi cation of it given in his *Log. Abhandlungen*, I. 98. The general idea is exactly the same. Abstract sufficient attri butes from P until only those are left which are common to it and to S. This does not yield an *identity* as before, for S is now more determinate than P, but it makes the remaining attributes of P *included in* those of S. Interpreted therefore

in intension, we have 'All $\frac{D}{m v}$ is S', and this we express, by use of the sign $>$, in the form $S > \frac{D}{m v}$. Another equivalent form given by Lambert, and which the reader will readily interpret for himself, is $\frac{C}{m v} < P$. It is obvious that in order to get an identity of subject and predicate, instead of a mere inclusion of one by the other, we must abstract from *both* of them, as in (22).

24. This is a form employed by S. Maimon (*Versuch einer neuen Logik*, 1794). The negative sign here indicates, as in several other schemes, the contradictory of a class, so that $(-P)$ means not-P. The term x is intended to repre sent an arbitrary logical factor or determination. Hence the interpretation is, "S, howsoever determined, is not-P"; i. e. by no kind of qualification can we reduce it to any part of P. Of course the qualification here can only be in the way of logical *determination*: not *abstraction*, as in the two preceding. There are a variety of serious defects in this notation, and it represents altogether a great falling off from some of its pre decessors, though Maimon has contrived with more or less success to carry it through all the syllogistic moods. One obvious inaccuracy is to be seen in the use of the sign $(=)$. We have no right to adopt the equational form unless the subject and predicate are identified, which they are not in this case, the former being a part only of the latter.

25. Ploucquet frequently uses this form in some of his logical writings (e.g. *Fundamenta Philosophiæ speculativæ*, 1764). It must be observed that the sign $(-)$ here stands for affirmation, or rather for that and negation indifferently, the negation being put into the subject, where N stands for *nullum*. It is therefore merely a rendering of the common

form 'No S is P', whereas $S - P$ would have stood for 'S is P'.

(The reader will understand that a variety of other notations might have been added to the above had there been any object in making a longer list.)

II. *On the employment of geometrical diagrams for the sensible representation of logical propositions.*

A few preliminary words will be desirable in order to point out the limits of this notice. It is intended here to take account of those schemes only which deal directly with propositions, and which *analyse* them ; that is, which in some way or other exhibit the relation of the subject to the predicate. Hence two kinds of diagram of great antiquity in Logic, will have to be entirely rejected. The first of these is the so-called *Porphyrian tree.* This only represents the mutual relation of classes to one another in the way of genus and species, by continued subdivision ; and though of course giving rise to propositions it cannot be said in any way to portray them. The other is the *triangle* of which the three extremities are used to represent the three terms of the syllogism. The same outline of a diagram here serves for any kind of proposition, and all that is meant to be illustrated by the figure, is, that we may by means of reasoning connect the extremes A and C (so to say, along one side) instead of connecting A with B, and then B with C (along the two sides). In this sort of diagrams no kind of analysis of propositions is attempted, and it can hardly be claimed for them that they are any real aid to the mind in complicated trains of reasoning. A historic sketch of their origin will be found in Hamilton's *Discussions,* Ed. III. p. 666.

As regards then the employment of what I term analytical diagrams,—viz. those meant to distinguish between subject and predicate, and also between the different kinds of proposition,—there can be little doubt that their practical employment dates from Euler. That is to say, he first familiarized logicians to their use, and the particular kind of circular diagram which he employed has consequently very commonly been named after him. But their actual origin is very much earlier than this. The earliest instance that I have seen is in the *De Censura Veri* of Ludovicus Vives[1], where the mutual relations of the three terms in *Barbara,* as given by the two premises, are represented very much as on the Eulerian plan. He speaks of repre senting them by means of containing *triangles,* but the actual figures drawn are those of the letter V, as thus,

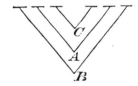

This is the only diagram to be found, I believe, in the work.

Priority in this direction has also been claimed by Hamilton for Alsted, who, as he maintains, had in his *Systema logicæ* (1614) anticipated the linear kind of diagram proposed by Lambert and which will presently be explained. I cannot however perceive that Alsted had the slightest idea of representing what Euler and the others aimed at repre-

[1] His words are: "Si aliqua pars *a* capit totum *b,* et aliqua pars *b* capit totum *c, c* totum capietur ab *a* : ut, si tres trianguli pingantur, quorum unus *B* sit maximus, et capiet alterum *A,* tertius sit minimus intra *A,* qui sit *C,* ita dicimus, si omne *b* est *a,* et omne *c* est *b,* omne *c* est *a* : adhibeatur regula quam diximus esse canonem artium et vitæ totius". *De Censura Veri,* Lib. II. (My attention was directed to this by F. A. Lange's *Logische Studien,* p. 10.) I do not understand how the capital and small letters here agree with each other.

senting. All that he says (speaking of the first figure), is that the middle term is 'below' the major term and 'above' the minor, and he just draws three lines of equal length, one under the other, to illustrate what he means. " Etenim omne medium, quod est inter duo extrema secundum altitudinem, id est, inter extremum superius et inferius, illud inquam medium debet habere aliquod extremum supra se, et aliquod infra se. Atqui medius terminus in prima figura est talis: habet enim terminum supra se, nempe praedicatum conclusionis in majore propositione positum, et habet terminum infra se positum, nempe subjectum conclusionis in minore propositione positum....Diagramma est tale :—

$$a \quad \frac{\text{Animal}}{\substack{\text{sentit} \\ \text{homo}}} \begin{matrix} - \ b \\ d \\ -f. \end{matrix}"$$

There is nothing in this,—the only diagram of the sort which he gives,—even to suggest the distinction between affirmative and negative, universal and particular, propositions, which is the least we can look for in these sensible illustrations.

The first logician apparently to make free use of diagrams was Chr. Weise, Rector of Zittau, who died in 1708. He seems to have published some works on logic himself, and his system is said to be given in the *Nucleus Logicae Weisianae* of J. C. Lange, (1712). I have not succeeded in seeing this work, but judging by what Lambert says of it (*Architectonic*, I. 128), I gather that he makes free use of circles and squares for the purpose of representing propositions. Hamilton (*Logic*, I. 256) confirms this statement.

In the only work by Lange to which I have been able to obtain access, viz. his *Inventum novum Quadratilogici*, there is nothing which strikes me as of any great merit.

There are a number of geometrical figures represented, both plane and solid, but the author does not seem to have grasped the essential conception of illustrating in this way the *mutual intersection*, or otherwise, of two or more classes by means of his figures. All that he represents is *continued sub-division*: e.g. that of A into B and C, of B into D and E, and C into F and G, and so forth. This he sets forth by a parallelogram for A; under it is put a similar one divided into two equal parts to denote B and C, the next in order having four divisions, and so on. All that this properly represents is the doctrine of Division or continued Dichotomy; i.e. the entire exclusion of B by C, and the entire inclusion of D and E in B, and so forth. There is no attempt to represent the various relations of two terms, B and C, to one another, as set forth in the various forms of proposition which have B and C for their subject and predicate.

We now come to Euler's well-known circles which were first described in his *Lettres a une Princesse d'Allemagne* (Letters 102—105). The weak point about these consists in the fact that they only illustrate in strictness the actual relations of classes to one another, rather than the imperfect knowledge of these relations which we may possess, or wish to convey, by means of the proposition. Accordingly they will not fit in with the propositions of common logic, but demand the constitution of a new group of appropriate elementary propositions[1]. This defect must have been noticed from the first in the case of the particular affirmative and negative, for the same diagram is commonly employed to stand for them both, which it does indifferently well:

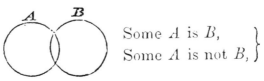

Some A is B,
Some A is not B,

[1] See the discussion on this point in ch. I, p. 5.

for the real relation thus exhibited by the figure is of course "some (only) A is some (only) B", and this quantified proposition has no place in the ordinary scheme.

Euler himself indicated the distinction (at least so I judge by his diagram) by the position in which he put the letter A ; if this stood in the 'A not-B' compartment it meant 'some A is not B', if in the AB compartment it meant 'some A is B'. But the common way of meeting the difficulty where it is at all recognized, is by the use of dotted lines to indicate our uncertainty as to where the boundary should lie. So far as I have been able to find, this plan (as applied to closed figures) was first employed by Dr Thomson in his *Laws of Thought*, but was doubtless suggested by the device of Lambert, to be presently explained. It has been praised for its ingenuity and success by De Morgan, and adopted by Prof. Jevons and a number of others. Ueberweg has employed a somewhat more complicated scheme of a similar kind.

Any modifications of this sort seem to me (as already explained in Chap. I.) wholly mis-aimed and ineffectual. If we want to represent our uncertainty about the correct employment of a diagram, the only consistent way is to draw *all* the figures which are covered by the assigned propositions and say frankly that we do not know which is the appropriate one. Of course this plan would be troublesome when several propositions have to be combined, as the consequent number of diagrams would be considerable. Thus in *Bokardo*, two diagrams would be needed for the major premise and two for the minor, making four in all.

The traditional logic has been so entirely confined to the simultaneous treatment of three terms only (this being the number demanded for the syllogism) that hardly any attempts have been made to represent diagrammatically the combinations of four terms and upwards. The only serious attempt that I have seen in this way is by Bolzano[1]. He was evidently trying under the right conception, viz. to construct diagrams which should illustrate *all* the combinations producible by the class terms employed, but he adopted an impracticable method in using modified Eulerian diagrams. The consequence is that he has effected no general solution, though exhibiting a number of more or less ingenious figures to illustrate special cases. Thus a collection of small circles included in a large one represents a number of species (mutually exclusive) comprehended under one genus, though, since the small circles cannot fill up all the contents of the large one we cannot thus conveniently represent the exhaustion of the genus by the aggregate of the species; a row of such circles, each of them interlinked with the next, represents the case of a succession of species each of which has something in common with the next, and so forth.

The most ingenious of his figures for four terms is the following. I give it here in order to show the necessary shortcomings of this method :—

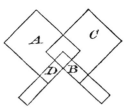

It is offered in representation of the proposition "*A* which is *B* is the same as *C* which is *D*". It must have taken some trouble to arrange it, so that as regards economy of time any such resort would be decidedly the reverse of an

[1] This statement should be corrected here by reference to Scheffler's *Naturgesetze*, as referred to in the Introductory chapter.

aid. Moreover, as the reader will readily perceive, it is not quite correct. One possible subdivision, viz. *ABCD*, has been omitted, for there is nothing in the statement to forbid the occurrence of *BD* which is neither *A* nor *C*. Hence the correct state of things would be better exhibited thus, on the scheme of notation adopted in this work:

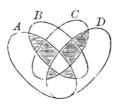

With the exception of that of Bolzano, I have seen no attempt to extend diagrammatic notation to the results of four terms, and it is only quite recently that really adequate figures have been proposed for those of three terms:—for instance both Drobisch and Schroder have used what we may call the three-circle diagram[1]. In saying this, I do not of course mean to imply that the problem was one of any particular difficulty, but merely state the fact that general satisfaction being felt with the Eulerian plan no serious attempts were made to modify it. Indeed, except on the part of those who wrote and thought under the influence of Boole, directly or indirectly, it was scarcely likely that need should be felt for any more generalized scheme.

The essential characteristic of the Eulerian plan being that of representing directly and immediately the inclusion and exclusion of classes, it is clear that the employment of circles as distinguished from any other closed figures is a mere accident. Nor have circles in fact always been

[1] These writers merely represent in this way the class combinations or subdivisions as such: they do not adopt the subsequent step of using them as a basis for representing propositions.

employed. Thus Ploucquet,—whose system however, as he himself pointed out, in contrast with that of Lambert, is essentially symbolic and not diagrammatic,—has made use of squares. Kant (*Logik*, I. § 21) and De Morgan (*Formal Logic*, p. 9) have introduced or suggested both a square and a circle into the same diagram, one standing for subject and the other for predicate; with the view of distinguishing between these. Mr R. G. Latham (*Logic*, p. 88) and Mr Leechman (*Logic*, p. 66) have a square, circle, and triangle all in one figure for the same purpose, presumably, of distinguishing between the three terms in the syllogism. Bolzano again, in one of the examples above adduced, has had resort to parallelograms: to which indeed, or to ellipses or to some such figure, it is evident he must have appealed if he wished to set before us the outcome of four class terms. But to regard these as constituting distinct schemes of notation would be idle. They all do exactly the same thing, viz. they aim at so arranging two (or more) closed figures that these shall represent the mutual relation of inclusion and exclusion of the various classes denoted by the terms we employ.

There is one modification of this plan which deserves passing notice both on its own account and because it has been so misjudged by Hamilton. It is that of Maass. In order to understand it we must recall one essential defect of the customary plan.—Representing as this does the final outcome of the class relation, it is clear that every fresh proposition may demand a diagram new from the beginning. If we have drawn a scheme for "All *A* is *B*", we must abandon it and draw another for "All *B* is *A*". Seeing this, apparently, Maass took two fixed lines enclosing an angle, and regarded the third line which combined with them to form the necessary closed figure, as movable. Hence only one line had to be altered in order to meet the new information contained in such a second proposition. (*Logik*, p. 294.)

Thus let AB and AC be the fixed lines; and the triangle ADE represent the class X, and AFG represent the class Y. If FG remain where it is we have "All X is Y", whilst in order to represent "All X is all Y" we have only to conceive FG transferred so as to coincide with DE. This

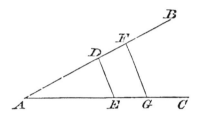

seems to me to constitute the essential characteristic of his scheme, which is worked out in a variety of figures of a more or less complicated kind. It is decidedly cumbrous, and not entirely effective as regards this its main aim, but it deserves recognition as an attempt to remedy a real defect in the ordinary scheme.

Hamilton who, as we know, never could succeed in grasping the nature of a triangle, entirely misconceived all this; and seeing that Maass began by talking of an angle, he concluded that angles were being employed as the representative of class relations. Hence his judgment, hurled in a blast of wrathful and contemptuous epithets, that this is "the only attempt made to illustrate Logic, not by the relations of geometrical quantities, but by the relations of geometrical relations,—angles" (*Logic*, II. 463).

The above schemes aim at representing the relative extent of class terms by the really analogous case of the relative extent of closed figures, which therefore tell their tale somewhat directly. A departure from this plan was made, very shortly after the date of Euler's letters, by Lambert, who introduced a more indirect scheme of diagrammatic notation. He indicates the extent of a class term by a straight line; the inclusion of one term in another being represented by drawing a shorter line under the other, the exclusion of two by each other by drawing them side by side, whilst the corresponding case to the intersecting circles is presented by drawing one line partially under the other, thus ‾ ‾‾ ‗

Hence Celarent might be represented:

$$B \text{ _____ } A \qquad \text{No } B \text{ is } A,$$
$$C \text{ - - } \qquad\qquad \text{All } C \text{ is } B,$$
$$\therefore \text{No } C \text{ is } A.$$

So far the scheme is of essentially the same kind as that of Euler[1], the only important difference being that the common part of the extent of the two terms is not here indicative of *identity*; for the line C is thus only drawn under B and not made coincident with it. This was noticed at once by Ploucquet, whose theory of propositions turned entirely on the identity of subject and predicate and consequent quantification of the predicate. He maintains that Lambert would do better to draw the second line, in an affirmative proposition, wholly or partially *coincident* with the first, and so secure this identity (*Sammlung*, p. 182). Since however

---

[1] The analogy which Lambert actually had in view seems however to have been different. He evidently was influenced, like Alsted, by the technical expression, "thinking objects as *under* such and such a concept", which to modern ears would sound as little more than a play on words. Thus he draws a line to represent the general concept and puts a row of dots underneath to represent the individuals which stand under that concept. And again, "Ferner fordert der Ausdruck, dass alle *A* unter *B* gehoren, von Wort zu Wort genommen, dass man die Linie *A* unter *B* setzen müsse". (*Dian.* § 181.) The impropriety of this analogy was pointed out at the time by Holland (Lambert's *Briefwechsel*, I. 17).

the help to the eye would then be nearly lost, such an alteration would simply result in a poor and faulty imitation of the Eulerian scheme.

Lambert however did not stop here. Like most other clear thinkers he recognized the flaw in all these methods, viz. that we cannot represent the uncertain distribution of the predicate whilst we employ one and the same diagram for "All *A* is *B*", whether the predicate be 'all' or only 'some' *B*. He endeavoured to remedy this defect by the employment of dotted lines, thus:

B............   . . . .
A   _   _

This means that *A* certainly covers a part of *B*, viz. the continuous part; and may cover the rest, viz. the dotted part, the dots representing our uncertainty. In this case the scheme answers fairly well, such use of dots not being open to the objection maintainable against it when circles are employed. But when he comes to extend this to particular propositions his use of dotted lines ceases to be consistent or even, to me, intelligible. One would have expected him to write 'some *A* is *B*' thus,

B   ....
A   ....

for by different filling in of the lines we could cover the case of there being '*B* which is not *A*', and so forth. But he does draw it

B   -
A ....

which might consistently be interpreted to cover the case of 'no *A* is *B*', as well as suggesting the possibility of there being no *A* at all.

Lambert's use however of this modification of his scheme

is so obscure, and, when he comes to work out the syllogistic figures in detail, is so partially adhered to, that it does not seem worth the expenditure of further time and thought. As a whole, it seems to me distinctly inferior to the scheme of Euler, and has in consequence been very little employed by other logicians. Indeed I cannot recall any who have made use of it except Ulrich (*Institutiones log. et met.* p. 171). Hamilton also (Logic, I. p. 189) has a plan something of the same sort, but no use is elsewhere made of it by him.

Hamilton's own system of notation is pretty well known. It is given in his *Logic* (end of Vol. II.) with a table, and is described in his *Discussions*. Some account of it will also be found in Dr Thomson's *Laws of Thought*. It has been described (by himself) as "easy, simple, compendious, all-sufficient, consistent, manifest, precise, complete"; the corresponding antithetic adjectives being freely expended in the description of the schemes of those who had gone before him. To my thinking it does not deserve to rank as a diagrammatic scheme at all, though he does class it with the others as "geometric": but is purely symbolical. What was aimed at in the methods above described was something that should explain itself at once, as in the circles of Euler, or need but a hint of explanation, as in the lines of Lambert. But there is clearly nothing in the two ends of a wedge to suggest subjects and predicates, or in a colon and comma to suggest distribution and non-distribution.

So far we have considered merely the case of categorical propositions; it still remains to say a few words as to the attempts made thus to represent other kinds of proposition. The Hypothetical may be dismissed at once, probably no logician having supposed that these should be exhibited in diagrams so as to come out in any way distinct from categoricals. Of course when we consider the hypothetical form as an optional rendering which only differs verbally from the categorical, we may regard our diagrams as representing either form indifferently.   But this course, which I regard as the sound one, belongs essentially to the modern or class view of the import of propositions.   Those who adopt the judgment interpretation can hardly in consistency come to any other conclusion than that hypotheticals are distinct from categoricals, and do not as such admit of diagrammatic representation.

The Disjunctive stands on a rather different footing, and some attention has been directed to its representation from the very first.   Lambert, for instance, has represented what we must regard as a particular case of disjunction, viz. the subordination of a plurality of species to a genus, after this fashion :—

$$A \: - \qquad \qquad - \quad -$$
$$X \qquad Y \qquad Z$$

This of course indicates the fact that the three classes, X, Y, Z, together make up the extent of A.

It will be seen that we thus treat the species as mutually exclusive, and very appropriately so, such mutual exclusiveness being the natural characteristic of all true species. When however we attempt to adapt this linear scheme to the more comprehensive case of alternatives which are not mutually exclusive, we soon find it fail us.   *Two* non-exclusive alternatives indeed can be thus displayed, for such a scheme as the following will adequately mark the three cases

$$A \: \cdot \quad - \qquad \qquad -$$
$$X$$
$$1 \: — \: \cdot \: \cdot \: —$$

covered by "All A is either X or Y"; viz. that of any particular A being X only, Y only, and both X and Y.   But make the same attempt with three classes, X, Y, Z; and we readily see that it breaks down. We cannot possibly represent, by lines, the seven cases covered by "All A is either X or Y or Z": (If the reader will try he will find that no arrangement will yield more than six of the needed com binations unless we make one of the lines discontinuous, by breaking it into portions,) and accordingly we should be forced to appeal to closed figures which possess slightly greater capabilities in this respect.

Having just stated that Lambert has fairly represented a case of exclusive alternatives in disjunction, I must call at tention to the fact that he expressly says that disjunctives do *not* admit of diagrammatic representation[1]. And his reason for so thinking deserves notice, as indicative of that deep distinction between the different accounts of the nature of propositions to which I have already had to allude. Starting with the assumption that B and C must be exclusive, he says that to represent 'A is either B or C' we may begin by drawing the lines for B and C beside one another, but then comes in the uncertainty that we do not know under which of the two we are to set the A line. We have grounded on a mere hypothetical and can get no further. What we are here doing is to regard A as a *Begriff* or concept, in which case it becomes a unity, and we are then naturally in uncertainty as to whether to refer it to B or C. The case is much the same as if we had to exhibit the individual dis junctive 'Socrates is either awake or asleep'. But interpret A in its class extent, and the disjunctive 'A is either B or C' becomes 'the classes B and C together make up A', which is essentially the same state of things as is readily represented by the subordination of species to a genus.

---

[1] "Die disjunctiven Satze lassen sich gar nicht zeichnen, und zwar wiederum, weil sie nichts positives setzen." (*Neues Organon*, *Dian.* § 190.)

For the general representation of disjunctives, on this plan, Euler's circles do not answer much better than Lambert's lines. In fact we cannot even represent 'All *A* is *B* or *C* (only)' by circles, but are confined to 'All *A* is *B* or *C* (or both)', as thus :—

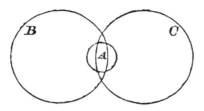

for if the *B* and *C* circles are not caused to intersect one another, the *A* circle will of course have to include something which lies outside them, and accordingly the point aimed at in the disjunction fails to be represented.

Kant (*Logik*, I. § 29) may be also noticed here as one of the very few logicians who have given a diagram to illustrate disjunctives. Like Lambert,—in fact like so many logicians,—he makes all disjunctives mutually exclusive. All he does indeed is to take a square and divide it up into four smaller squares; these four dividing members therefore just make up between them the whole sphere of the divided concept. So few however have been the attempts to represent Disjunctives in Logic that it seems hardly worth while to pursue the subject any further.

Before quitting these historical points I may briefly notice an application to which diagrammatic notation very readily lends itself, but which seems to me none the less an abusive employment of it. I refer to the attempt to represent quantitatively the relative extent of the terms. When, for instance, we have drawn, either by lines or circles, a figure to represent 'All *A* is *B*' it strikes us at once that we have got another element at our service; or, as a mathematician would say, there is still a disposable constant. We may draw the *B* circle, or line, of any size or length we please; why not then so draw it as to represent the relative ex tension of the *B* class as compared with the *A* class ?

This idea seems to have occurred to logicians almost from the first, as was indeed natural, considering that the use of diagrams was of course borrowed from mathematics, and that a clear boundary line was not always drawn between the two sciences. Thus Lambert certainly seems to maintain that in strictness we must suppose each line to bear to any other the due proportionate length assigned by the extension of the terms. He even recognizes the difficulty in the case of a single line, viz. as to what length it should be drawn, resolving this however by the consideration that the unit of length being at our choice, any length will do if the unit be chosen accordingly. In the latter part of the *Neues Organon,*—where he is dealing with questions of Probability, and the numerically, or rather proportionately, definite syllo gism,—the length of the lines which represent the extent of the concepts becomes very important. So little was he prepared to regard the diagram as referring solely to the purely logical considerations of presence and absence of class characteristics, of inclusion and exclusion of classes by one another.

Of course if considerations of this kind were to be taken into account it would follow almost necessarily that circles should be abandoned in the formation of our diagrams; since their relative magnitude, or rather the relative magnitude of the figures produced by their intersection, is not at all an easy matter of intuitive observation. We should be reduced to the choice of lines or parallelograms, so that the almost exclusive employment of Eulerian circles has caused this quantitative application to be much less adopted than would otherwise probably have been the case. This application, however, has been made quite recently by F. A. Lange (*Logische Studien*), who in one of his Essays has made considerable use of diagrammatic methods in illustration of the Logic of Probability[1]. But I cannot regard the success of such a plan as encouraging. For the alternative forced upon us is this:—If we adhere to geometrical figures that are continuous, then the shapes of the various subdivisions soon become complicated; for, by the time we have reached four or even three terms, their combinations would result in yielding awkward compartments, whose relative areas could not be estimated intuitively. If, on the other hand, we take our stand on having ultimate compartments whose relative magnitudes admit of ready computation we are driven to abandon continuous figures. Our ABC compartment, say, instead of being enclosed in a ring fence is scattered about the field like an ill-arranged German principality of olden times, and its component portions require to be brought together in order to collect the whole before the eye. We draw a parallelogram to stand for A, and divide it into its B and not-B parts. If we divide each of these again into their C and not-C parts, we shall find that the B and not-B, the C and not-C compartments will not lie in juxtaposition with each other, and therefore the eye cannot conveniently gather them up into single groups. In fact such a plan almost necessarily leads to that primitive arrangement proposed by J. C. Lange, and mentioned at the outset of this discussion. Whatever elegance logical diagrams can possess,

---

[1] Every student of Probability is of course familiar enough with the converse case, viz. that of reducing spatial relations to symbolic statement. Whenever we compute the chance that a ball dropped at random upon a frame-work will strike such and such a partition we are employing the same analogy as when we resort to diagrammatic representation of one of these quantitative logical propositions.

and whatever aid they can give to the mind through the sense of sight, seem thus to be forfeited.

My own conviction is very decided that all introduction of considerations such as these should be avoided as tending to confound the domains of Logic and Mathematics; of that which is, broadly speaking, qualitative, and that which is quantitative. The compartments yielded by our diagrams must be regarded solely in the light of being bounded by such and such contours, as lying inside or outside such and such lines. We must abstract entirely from all considera tion of their relative magnitude, as we do of their actual shape, and trace no more connection between these facts and the logical extension of the terms which they represent than we do between this logical extension and the size and shape of the letter symbols, A and B and C.

INDEX OF BIBLIOGRAPHICAL REFERENCES.

[The reader will understand that this Index does not aim at being in any way exhaustive. It is merely a list of publications referred to as bearing on the topics specially characteristic of this work. It is confined also, with one exception, to such as I have consulted myself; and which seemed to me to be worth referring to. The asterisk marks those which are specially symbolic in a logical sense, in the whole or some part of their treatment. For conve nience of reference I indicate the date of the work, or of the particular edition consulted.]

Alsted, J. H.   Logicæ systema harmonicum (1614), 422.

Bachmann, C. F.   System der Logik (1828), 94, 392.

* Bain, A.   Logic; Deduction, pp. 190—207 (1870), xxxix, 285.

* Bardili, E. G.   Grundriss der ersten Logik (1800), 81.

Baynes, T. S.   Essay on the New Analytic of Logical Forms (1850), 9, 88, 174.

Beneke, F. E.   Lehrbuch der Logik (1832), 134, 392.

Bentham, G.   Outline of a New System of Logic (1827), 8, 417.

Bernoulli, James.   Parallelismus ratiocinii logici et algebraici (1685; *Opera* I. 214), xi, 411.

Bolzano, B.   Logik (1837), 426.

* Boole, G.   The mathematical Analysis of Logic (1847), 165, 174.

*   —— *Camb. Math. Journal.* Vol. III. (1848), xxxvii.

    —— The claims of Science (Lecture at Cork, 1851), xviii.

*   —— The Laws of Thought (1854). *Passim.*

    —— Differential Equations (1865), 68, 70.

*   —— *Camb. Phil. Tr.* No. xi, "On propositions numerically definite," **xxxvii.**

Bowen, F.   Treatise on Logic (1872), 139.

Brentano, F.   Psychologie vom empirischen Standpunkte (1874), 165.

* Cayley, A.   Note on the Calculus of Logic. (*Quart. Journ. of pure and app. Math.* 1871.)

Chase, D. P.   First Logic Book (1875), 94.

* Clifford, W. K.   Lectures and Essays (1879), 258, 354.

Contemporary Review (1873), 9.

Dalgarno, G.   Ars signorum (ed. 1834), 99.

* Darjes. J. G.   Weg zur Wahrheit (1776), 52, 54, 94, 138, 413.´

* Delbœuf, J.   Logique algorithmique (1877), 95, 98, 163, 409.

* De Morgan, A.   Formal Logic (1847), 9, 18, 95, 370, 416, 428.

*   ——   *Camb. Phil. Trans.* (vii, viii, ix, x), 14, 182, 330, 352, 366, 389, 404.

——   Trigonometry and Double Algebra (1849), xiii, 68.

*   ——   Syllabus of a proposed System of Logic (1860), xxiii, 134, 225, 404.

——   *English Cyclopædia. Article 'Logic'.* 134.

* Drobisch, M. W.   Neue Darstellung der Logik (1875), 94, 411.

* Ellis, A. J.   Algebraical Analogies of Logical relations, (*Proc. of R. Society, Vol.* 21), 144.

Ellis, R. L.   Edition of Bacon's Works (1858), xxxi.

*   ——   Mathematical and other writings (1863), 404.

Erdmann, J. E.   Geschichte der neuern Philosophie (1834—53), 81.

Euler, L.   Letters to a German Princess (*Ed.* Brewster, 1823), 15, 104, 424.

* Frege, G.   Begriffsschrift, eine der arithmetischen nachgebildete Formelsprache des reinen Denkens (1879), 341, 415.

Gergonne, J. D.   Essai de Dialectique rationnelle (*Annales de Mathématiques,* Vol. III.), 6, 95.

Grassmann, H.   Die lineale Ausdehnungslehre (1844), xxxv, 97, 204.

* Grassmann, R.   Die Begriffslehre oder Logik (1872), 95, 189, 377, 384, 414.

* Günther, S.   *Vierteljahrsschrift für wiss. Phil.* (1879 :—The name and date are erroneously given in the text), 78.

* Halsted, G. B.   *Journal of Spec. Phil.* (XII. 1, 4; XIII. 1), 78, 214.

*   ——   Algebras, Spaces, Logics (*Pop. Sc. Monthly,* Aug. 1880).

Hamilton, W.   Lectures on Logic (1860), 8, 10, 17, 52, 94, 397, 417.

——   Discussions on Philosophy (1866), xxx, 14, 421.

Hamilton, W. R.   Elements of Quaternions (1866), 55.

Hankel, H.   Vorlesungen über die complexen Zahlen (1867), xiii, 55, 68.

* Harley, R.   *British Quarterly Review,* (July, 1866), xxxviii.

*   ——   *Reports of Brit. Assoc.* (1866, 1870), xvii, xxxi.

Hauber, F. C.   Scholæ logico-mathematicæ (1829), 275.

Herbart, J. F.   Einleitung in die Philosophie (Ed. iv. 1850), 134, 168.

Hoffbauer, J. C.   Analytik der Urtheile und Schlüsse (1792), 411.

* Holland, G. J.   Abhandlung über die Mathematik, die allgemeine Zeichenkunst, und die Verschiedenheit der Rechnungsarten (1764), xxxvi, 78, 157, 409.

Venn, J. Logic of Chance, (Ed. ii. 1876), 332.

ϵ —— *Mind (Oct.* 1876 ; *July*, 1880), viii.

ϵ —— *Philosophical Magazine (July*, 1880), viii.'

ϵ —— *Princeton Review (Sep.* 1880), viii.

ϵ —— *Camb. Phil. Trans. (Dec.* 1880), viii.

Vives, L. De censura veri (1555), 422.

Weise, Ch. Nucleus logicæ Weisianæ, 423.

Wilkins, J. Essay towards a real character and philosophical language (1668), 99.

Wolf Ch. Psychologia empirica (1779), 98.

* Wundt, W. Logik (1880), 7 9, 91, 95, 184, 189, 383, 408.

To the above list the following works may be added. I have found references to them of a kind which make me suppose that they must be of interest on this subject; but every effort to discover their existence in this country, or to obtain them from abroad, has proved fruitless.

Busch, M. Anfangsgründe der logikalischen Algebra (Tubingen, 1768).

Castillon, G. F. Sur un nouvel algorithme logique (Berlin, 1803).

Schlosser, F. P. Disputatio de sororio Logices et Matheseos nexu, et applicatione præceptorum logicorum in disciplinis mathematicis (1727).

Tonnies. De Logicæ scientiæ ad exemplum arithmeticæ instituenda ratione (1752).

INDEX OF SUBJECT MATTER.

CAMBRIDGE : PRINTED BY C. J. CLAY, M.A. AT THE UNIVERSITY PRESS.

BY THE SAME AUTHOR.

On some Characteristics of Belief, Scientific and Religious. Hulsean Lectures for 1869. 8vo. 7s. 6d.

The Logic of Chance: an Essay on the Foundations and Province of the Theory of Probability, with Special Reference to its Logical Bearings, and its Application to Moral and Social Science. Second Edition, re-written and greatly enlarged. Crown 8vo. 10s. 6d.

"One of the most thoughtful and philosophical treatises on any subject connected with Logic and Evidence which has been produced in this or any other country for many years."—MILL's *Logic*, Vol. II. p. 77. Seventh Edition.

WORKS BY W. STANLEY JEVONS, LL.D., M.A., F.R.S.

The Principles of Science. A Treatise on Logic and Scientific Method. New and Cheaper Edition, revised. Crown 8vo. 12s. 6d.

The Substitution of Similars the True Principle of Reasoning. Derived from a Modification of Aristotle's Dictum. Fcap. 8vo. 2s. 6d.

Elementary Lessons in Logic: Deductive and Inductive. With copious Questions and Examples, and a Vocabulary of Logical Terms. Sixth Edition. 18mo. 3s. 6d.

Primer of Logic. 18mo. 1s.

The Theory of Political Economy. Second Edition, Revised and Enlarged, with New Preface, &c. 8vo. 10s. 6d.

Primer of Political Economy. 18mo. 1s.

Studies in Deductive Logic. A Manual for Students. Crown 8vo. 6s.

Manual of Political Economy. Fifth Edition, Revised and Enlarged, with New Chapters on the Depreciation of Silver. By the Right Hon. Henry Fawcett, M.P. Crown 8vo. 12s.

Guide to the Study of Political Economy. From the Italian of Dr Luigi Cossa, Professor in the University of Pavia. With a Preface by W. Stanley Jevons, F.R.S. Crown 8vo. 4s. 6d.

Made in the USA
Lexington, KY
02 July 2013